MACMILLAN ANTHOLOGIES
OF ENGLISH LITERATURE

THE
NINETEENTH
CENTURY
(1798–1900)

Edited by
Brian Martin

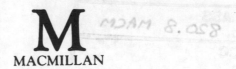

M
MACMILLAN

First published 1989

Published by
MACMILLAN EDUCATION LTD
Houndmills, Basingstoke, Hampshire RG21 2XS
and London
Companies and representatives
throughout the world

Typeset by Wessex Typesetters
(Division of The Eastern Press Ltd)
Frome, Somerset

Printed in Hong Kong

British Library Cataloguing in Publication Data
The Nineteenth century (1798–1900).—(Macmillan
anthologies of English literature; V4)
1. English literature, 1798–1900 — Anthologies
I. Martin, Brian
820.8'007
ISBN 0–333–39272–8
ISBN 0–333–46479–6 Pbk

119 735

OF ENGLISH LITERATURE

General Editors:
A. Norman Jeffares, formerly Professor of English,
University of Stirling
Michael Alexander, Berry Professor of English Literature,
University of St Andrews

£9.9

MACMILLAN ANTHOLOGIES
OF ENGLISH LITERATURE

Contents

Acknowledgements

This volume of the anthology would have taken more years than it did to complete, had it not been for the help and indulgence of a number of individuals and institutions. I must thank my wife and children for putting up with my retiral from the domestic scene for long stretches at a time. My thanks go, too, to the Bodleian Library and the Oxford University English Faculty Library, and to their staffs, who helped me with their resources; and to Magdalen College School, the Principal and Fellows of Hertford College, Oxford, and the President and Fellows of Magdalen College, for providing me with time and facilities.

BWM

General Introduction

There can often be a gulf between the restricted reading required by a school, college or university syllabus and the great expanse of English literature which is there to be explored and enjoyed. There are two effective ways of bridging that gulf. One is to be aware of how authors relate or have related to their contemporary situations and their contemporaries, how they accept, develop or react against what has been written by their predecessors or older contemporaries, how, in short, they fit into the long history of English literature. Good histories of literature – and there is a welcome increase of interest in them – serve to place authors in their context, as well as giving a panoptic view of their careers.

The second way is to sample their work, to discover the kind or kinds of writing they have produced. Here is where the anthology contributes to an enjoyment of reading. It conveys the flavour of an author as nothing but reading that author can. And when an author is compared to his or her fellow writers – a thing a good anthology facilitates – the reader gains several extra dimensions, not least an insight into what thoughts, what fears, what delights have occupied writers at different times. To gain such insights is to see, among other things, the relevance of past authors to the present, to the reader. Reading an anthology shows something of the vast range of our literature, its variety of form and outlook, of mood and expression, from black despair to ecstatic happiness; it is an expansive experience widening our horizons, enhancing specialised study, but also conveying its own particular pleasures, the joy of finding familiar pieces among unfamiliar, of reacting to fresh stimuli, of reaching new conclusions about authors, in short, of making literature a part of oneself.

Anthologies also play a part in the life of a literature. If we are the beneficiaries of our literary inheritance, we are also trustees for it, and the maintenance of the inheritance for future generations requires new selections of properly edited texts. The Macmillan Literary Anthologies, which have followed on from the Macmillan Histories of Literature, are designed to present these texts with the essential pertinent information. The selection made of poetry, prose and plays has been wide and inclusive, authors appear in the order of their dates

of birth, texts – with the exception of the Middle English section –
are largely modernised and footnotes are kept to a minimum. A
broadly representative policy has been the aim of the general editors,
who have maintained a similar format and proportion in each volume,
though the medieval volume has required more annotation.

ANJ
MJA

Introduction: The Nineteenth Century

It is generally accepted that the neo-classical, or Augustan, age in English literature came to an end in 1798 with the publication of *Lyrical Ballads*, a collection of poems by Wordsworth and Coleridge which was revolutionary in style and content. Their poetry was part of a literature which, like art or politics, was the product of society at that particular time; and, of course, as society slowly altered, so, too, did the things which arose from it or depended on it.

The French Revolution of 1789 had seriously affected political and social outlooks: so had the Agrarian Revolution, which forced a shift of the labouring class in England away from the countryside to the towns and cities, and the Industrial Revolution, which caused changes in living conditions in urban areas. The nation's literature was bound to be coloured by such changes. Nevertheless, it was a gradual process. The order, harmony, objectivity, restraint and logicality of the neo-classical approach to literature gave way gently to the variety, contrast, immediacy and imaginative freedom of the romantic frame of mind which characterised writing of the first half of the nineteenth century.

The American philosopher Arthur O. Lovejoy has argued that the word 'romantic' has come to mean so many things, that by itself, it means nothing. Yet the phenomenon of romanticism has still to be investigated and some sort of definition sought. The creative influences which arise from society itself have first to be understood, in order to understand the nature of the literature which they themselves have produced. The English critic F. W. Bateson considered the key to romanticism a tenor of mind, a subjectivity which is perhaps best expressed by Wordsworth's claim for his lyrical ballads 'that the feeling therein developed gives importance to the action and the situation, and not the action and situation to the feeling'. The Romantic Movement, which dominated art and literature particularly in Germany, France and England, involved a heightened consciousness of 'individualism', itself connected in various ways with the radical French Revolution and the Industrial Revolution, and also with nationalism.

On one level, social and political factors influenced the minds of authors; there is evidence for this in the work of, for example, Byron, Hazlitt or Cobbett. On another level, aesthetic and intellectual forces were at work: great stress was given to inspiration and the working of the imagination, particularly by Coleridge in his famous chapter IX of *Biographia Literaria*, and to a personal response to the natural world, especially by Wordsworth. In short, what was of paramount importance for most early-nineteenth-century writers had not been so for eighteenth-century writers. Times, and concerns, had changed: literature changed with them.

Naturally, the process was gradual. The poetry of Collins, Shenstone, Churchill, Akenside, Crabbe, Cowper, gave a hint of a change in tone from the strictly classical, while Blake and Burns (who died in 1796) wrote poetry in complete contrast to that of, for example, Alexander Pope or Samuel Johnson. Most of Burns's poems are unrestrained, direct and intensely personal, couched in colloquial dialect: the penultimate stanza of 'To a Mouse' is a good example:

> But Mousie, thou art no thy lane, [not alone]
> In proving foresight may be vain:
> The best-laid schemes o' mice an' men
>   Gang aft a-gley,   [go often awry]
> An' lea'e us nought but grief an' pain,
>   For promised joy.

John Keble, on the other hand, an eminent nineteenth-century cleric and man-of-letters, published in 1827 a Victorian best-seller, *The Christian Year*, his collection of poems written in the archaic, out-of-date diction of the eighteenth century. Much of his diction was precisely what Wordsworth had in mind when he condemned neo-classical style in his *Preface* to *Lyrical Ballads*. Readers should not draw clear lines of distinction between periods conveniently labelled by critics and teachers: they should see literature as a development, as a body of writing which changes gradually in style and attitude as much as the language in which it is written constantly changes. Jane Austen, the last writer of the Augustan tradition, was a younger contemporary of Wordsworth, the greatest of the English romantics.

The shift to Romanticism is most clearly seen in poetry. The first half of the nineteenth century provided some of England's greatest poets. Wordsworth wrote some of the most memorable poems of the period. 'Tintern Abbey', and the 'Immortality Ode' which Keble regarded as 'The finest poem of the greatest poet in our times'.

Coleridge produced 'Kubla Khan', now regarded without dispute as the most romantic of Romantic poems, and *The Rime of the Ancient Mariner*, a revival of the ballad form which tells in a flight of imaginative fancy the damnation and salvation of an old sailor. John Keats, Shelley and Byron followed in the new Romantic vein. Keats clearly recognised the difference between himself and his predecessors, and expressed it in the romantic couplets of 'Sleep and Poetry':

> The blue
> Bared its eternal bosom, and the dew
> Of summer night collected still to make
> The morning precious: Beauty was awake.
> Why were ye not awake? But ye were dead
> To things ye knew not of, – were close wed
> To musty laws lived out with wretched rule
> And compass vile; so that ye taught a
> school
> Of dolts to smooth, inlay, and clip, and fit,
> Till, like the certain wands of Jacob's wit,
> Their verses tallied. Easy was the task:
> A thousand handicraftsmen wore the mask
> Of Poesy.

In addition to his great odes, of which 'Ode to a Nightingale' is the most celebrated, Keats wrote some of the finest poems of the romantic imagination, for example, the narrative poem 'The Eve of St Agnes', and the short, haunting poem, 'La Belle Dame Sans Merci'. His poetry has a sensuous beauty which is unparalleled by any of his contemporaries: a stanza from 'The Eve of St Agnes' shows this:

> A casement high and triple-arch'd there was,
> All garlanded with carven imag'ries
> Of fruits, and flowers, and bunches of knot-grass,
> And diamonded with panes of quaint device,
> Innumerable of stains and splendid dyes,
> As are the tiger-moth's deep-damask'd wings;
> And in the midst, 'mong thousand heraldries,
> And twilight saints, and dim emblazonings,
> A shielded scutcheon blush'd with blood of queens
> and kings.

Byron's poetry is as dashing and romantic as the poet was himself. Today many hotels in Greece are named after him because he was a hero in the struggle for Greek independence. Ostracised by polite

English society, he sought refuge abroad, and finally, ill from a chill caught after riding his horse through dank marshlands, he died far from home, bled to death by his doctors. This was the man who had swum the Hellespont to prove it was possible, and who swam for a wager, in trousers, from the island of the Lido up the Grand Canal of Venice to the spot where the lagoon opens to Fusina. His long, unfinished epic satire in *ottava rima*, 'Don Juan', survives as his most popular poem.

At first glance, Shelley seems to have little in common with his friend, Byron. Yet both were aristocratic, both opposed to the social and literary establishments in England, both made the continent their home, and both looked to Greece as the land of liberty. They wrote quickly and gave little time to correction of their work. Byron was a wordly man, a materialist: Shelley, by contrast, an idealist, whose vigorous poem 'Ode to the West Wind' best illustrates the point. Shelley contributed, in his time, spiritual freedom and audacity to English literature, and the conviction that the intellect was subordinate to the imagination. He was possessed by a vision of neo-Platonic intellectual beauty, demonstrated in his 'To A Skylark':

> What thou art we know not;
>   What is most like thee?
> From rainbow clouds there flow not
>   Drops so bright to see
> As from thy presence showers a rain of melody.
>
> Like a Poet hidden
>   In the light of thought,
> Singing hymns unbidden,
>   Till the world is wrought
> To sympathy with hopes and fears it heeded not:
>
> Like a high-born maiden
>   In a palace-tower
> Soothing her love-laden
>   Soul in secret hour
> With music sweet as love, which overflows her bower:

The creative, literary spirit was at work in more than poetry. The novel had already made a diversion into the Gothic in romances such as Mrs Radcliffe's *The Mysteries of Udolpho*; Mary Shelley's *Frankenstein* took it to its purest extreme and the novel again advanced in the hands of Sir Walter Scott who found a stimulus for his own imagination and that of his readers in tales of medieval romance. Jane Austen explored that level of society in which she was brought up, and exposed its manners and foibles. The familiar essay, as practised by Hazlitt and Lamb, became popular; and many famous literary reviews were founded, the *Edinburgh Review* in 1802, the *Quarterly Review* in 1809, and *Blackwood's Magazine* in 1817. Criticism, and Shakespearean criticism in particular, found voice in Coleridge, Lamb and Hazlitt. Coleridge was one of the century's most influential critics. His originality revealed itself in the huge, uneven range of *Biographia Literaria*, and was the means of disseminating ideas from the continent, especially from Germany. Many of his ideas on Shakespeare, as the American critic Norman Fruman has shown, were the result of plagiarising the views of A. W. Schlegel.

A change in style and tone of thought, reflected in literature, began to take place in the 1830s. In 1830 Tennyson published his *Poems*; in 1832 the Reform Bill was passed in Parliament. Queen Victoria succeeded to the throne in 1837. Romantic tales, imaginative fantasies, still gripped readers' minds, but increasingly as an escape from the ordinary, and rather philistine preoccupations of urban, industrial and commercial life. Tennyson composed long narrative poems based on the Arthurian legend: the Pre-Raphaelites looked back to the Middle Ages for sources of inspiration and diversion. Their paintings, too, reflected this interest; and D. G. Rossetti painted pictures to illustrate some of Tennyson's poems, for example, 'Sir Galahad' in the Moxon edition of his *Poems* (1857). Architects modelled designs on medieval Gothic buildings, a fashion which drew to a close with William Butterfield's extravagantly decorated, polychromatic Keble College, Oxford, the high point of that style.

The nation's chief concern was with the creation of wealth, and to that end, the extension and consolidation of empire after the accession of Queen Victoria. Literature, itself a product of society, became occupied with industrial, materialist themes. It was forced to assert its ideals in the face of a hostile world of money and economic theory. The latter had its exponents in the Utilitarians and political economists: J. S. Mill and Jeremy Bentham are representative. Conversely, writers such as Carlyle, Kingsley, Tennyson (in poems such as 'Maud' and 'Locksley Hall') and Dickens (in *Hard Times*) showed the world of economic materialism, the nation's grovelling to Mammon, for what it really was. Pursuit of material gain more often than not stifled the interests of the soul, aesthetic sensibility, and faculties of artistic creation and appreciation. The accumulation of wealth could become all-consuming. It was necessary, in such an age, for polemicists to emphasise the virtues of art and literature: Ruskin was an agitator in this cause. Those who made great wealth had to be persuaded that art and literature needed time and attention, and, equally, finance and patronage. The vigorous ferment in Victorian society produced other significant thinkers, spiritual masters such as Cardinal Newman, and aestheticians such as Walter Pater.

Of all Victorian writers, Tennyson and Browning were foremost among the poets, and Dickens and George Eliot among the novelists. Tennyson was Poet Laureate from 1850 until his death in 1892. His *Poems* (1842), of which many were revisions of those in his 1832 volume, firmly established his reputation. He retreated from the intellectual romanticism of Wordsworth or Shelley which preceded him, and paid greater attention to craftsmanship and technique. In *Morte D'Arthur* his verse reflects exactly the difficulty of Sir Bedivere's progress through rugged terrain:

> Dry clashed his harness in the icy caves
> And barren chasms, and all to left and right
> The bare black cliff clanged round him, as he based
> His feet on juts of slippery crag that rang
> Sharp-smitten with the dint of armed heels –
> And on a sudden, lo! the level lake,
> And the long glories of the winter moon.

The long monosyllables and the labials of the last two lines reinforce the relief of reaching the shoreline of the lake. He was the master of narrative, descriptive verse, which was wanting only in profound or witty thought: Carlyle remarked of the 'Idylls of the King' that they were the 'inward perfection of vacancy' but that 'the lollipops were so superlative'.

At the same time, Tennyson showed himself a child of the Industrial Revolution who did not quite understand its technicalities. In 'Locksley Hall' he used a train image: 'Let the great world spin for ever down the ringing grooves of time.' Subsequently he confessed, 'When I went by the first train from Liverpool to Manchester [1830], I thought the wheels ran in grooves'.

Some of his poems are remarkable for their declaration of Victorian values hardly acceptable now. In 'Locksley Hall' the narrator's arrogance, and extreme self-confidence, are expressed in his view of

the superiority of European civilisation: 'Better fifty years of Europe
than a cycle of Cathay'. What he really meant, of course, was England
rather than Europe. Typical of the people and the age, though, and
admirable in tone, is the sentiment which rings clearly out from the
closing lines of *Ulysses*. The Victorian spirit of action and adventure,
the expression of the Protestant work ethic which took root-hold in
society, show themselves with force and conviction in lines with which
the nation closely identified:

> that which we are, we are;
> One equal temper of heroic hearts,
> Made weak by time and fate, but strong in will
> To strive, to seek, to find, and not to yield.

Towards the end of the century Robert Browning's reputation
rivalled Tennyson's. Browning was quite a different poet. His two
series of *Dramatic Lyrics*, included in *Bells and Pomegranates*
(1841–6), established his greatness as a lyric poet, and indicated the
way in which his dramatic genius could develop. The lyrics possess a
variety of form, and are noted for their vividness and sense of
immediate reality: many of them give promise, too, of the dramatic
monologues which were to appear in *Men and Women* (1855). Some
of the monologues combine lyric form with a sense of the full emotional
significance of a glance or chance remark, of a landscape or of an
ambition. 'The Last Ride Together' is an example:

> My mistress bent that brow of hers,
> Those deep dark eyes where pride demurs
> When pity would be softening through,
> Fixed me a breathing-while or two
>   With life or death in the balance: Right!
>
> The blood replenished me again;
> My last thought was at least not vain.
> I and my mistress, side by side
> Shall be together, breathe and ride,
> So, one day more am I deified.
> Who knows but the world may end to-night?

Others are more complex, sustained intellectual exercises such as
'Bishop Blougram's Apology' which shows Browning's profound,
subtle, jesuitical turn of mind. On an intellectual level, Browning was

thought the equal of Henry James, and London literary society courted them both to attend salons, soirées and dinner-parties; James presents an enigmatic portrait of Browning as the poet Clare Vawdrey in his short story, 'The Private Life'.

The practitioners of prose fiction had nothing to fear from comparison with the achievements of Tennyson and Browning in poetry. The novel had many exponents, and in Charles Dickens and George Eliot, two of the most outstanding novelists in the history of English literature. Dickens was remarkable for his incessant industry and extraordinary craftsmanship: he allowed little to interfere with the act of composition. He would continue writing at his fireside table, simultaneously conversing with friends who had dropped in to see him. Such were the demands of deadlines for instalment writers. A busy magazine editor himself, he could not fail to keep them. He is distinguished for his highly developed social conscience. It has become fashionable to regard him as a mere reflector of public opinion on social issues, but *Hard Times* and *Our Mutual Friend* give the lie to that impression. The postscript to *Our Mutual Friend* in particular, makes it quite clear that one of his main intentions in the novel was to persuade his readers that the operation of the Poor Law was iniquitous: he brought a reformer's zeal to his writing, and was unequivocal in his condemnation of the law:

I believe there has been in England, since the days of the STUARTS, no law so often violated, no law habitually so ill-supervised. In the majority of shameful cases of disease and death from destitution, that shock the Public and disgrace the country, the illegality is quite equal to the inhumanity – and known language could say no more of their lawlessness.

He revealed here, too, that he was a victim of the Industrial Revolution. He was involved in one of the first recorded train derailments and nearly lost part of the manuscript of *Our Mutual Friend*. After a 'terribly destructive accident' on the South-Eastern Railway, he climbed back into his carriage which had nearly fallen into a viaduct and rescued 'Mr and Mrs Boffin (in their manuscript dress of receiving Mr and Mrs Lammle at breakfast)'.

George Eliot is an example of the strong tradition of women novelists in the nineteenth century which includes Jane Austen, the Brontës and Elizabeth Gaskell. Her novels are distinguished for her faculty of close observation, which enabled her to reproduce authentically the mannerisms of rustic habit and speech. She understood the countryside, villages and small towns, their interrelations, their social hierarchies and different standards of value: she composed a comprehensive picture of life. Occasionally her intellect dominated her novelist's gift, and her interest in scientific progress and her philosophical digressions stand out awkwardly in her writing.

In the early part of the century the most influential critical thinker had been Coleridge. In the later part it was Matthew Arnold. Dismayed by the huge, ill-educated mass of working people which had resulted from the rapid advance of a successful, prosperous, industrial and commercial society, he elaborated his ideas for the cultural enlightenment of the middle class. He envisaged a clerisy which would dispense 'sweetness and light' to an under-privileged, ignorant multitude. Arnold indeed paved the way for twentieth-century criticism, which has been much concerned with the relation of literature to society, particularly in the work of T. S. Eliot, F. R. Leavis and Raymond Williams.

Drama, of all the literary genres, suffered an eclipse during the century: there was a dearth of playwrights. It had partly to do with the Theatre Licensing Act, not repealed until 1843, which restricted 'legitimate theatre' productions to two London theatres, Drury Lane and Covent Garden. It is true that some of the poets tried their hands at verse plays, Shelley with his *Cenci* and Browning with *Stafford*, but they did not appeal to the theatregoing public; and then, as now, the test of a successful production lay in box-office receipts. It was not until the end of the century, with the arrival of Oscar Wilde and his plays, revivals of the comedy of manners, that drama gained momentum again.

Readers will discover that the nineteenth century is one of the richest periods in literature: it produced a great number of different sorts of writers, many of whom found time, or enjoyed leisure, to write copiously. There were brilliant story-tellers, inspired poets, provocative, stimulating and often abrasive thinkers, polemicists and controversialists. Subjects were aired that are of lasting concern and are still discussed today – liberty, conscience, human rights, the nature of God. The literature of the century remains the most lasting monument to the spirit, aspirations and achievements of the age.

BWM

Note on Annotation and Glossing

An asterisk * at the end of a word indicates that such words are glossed in the margin.

A dagger † at the end of a word or phrase indicates that the word or phrase is annotated, or given a longer gloss, at the foot of the page.

Note on Dates

Where dates appear at the end of extracts, that on the left denotes the date of composition, that on the right, the date of publication.

William Blake

1757–1827

Blake was a mystic and a visionary. He was born and brought up in
London, apprenticed to an engraver to the Society of Antiquaries, and
later became a student at the Royal Academy. In 1779 he was
employed as an engraver by J. Johnson, bookseller, and through his
work met both Fuseli and Flaxman. He embraced the mysticism of
Swedenborg. In 1782 he married Catherine Boucher. It was a long
and mostly happy marriage, though childless. 1783 saw the publication
of his first volume of poetry, *Poetical Sketches*. There followed, in the
following year, the satirical *An Island of the Moon*.

Blake's most famous poems are contained in *Songs of Innocence*,
1789, and the complementary *Songs of Experience* which were added
in 1794: they contain such popular lyrics as 'The Lamb' and 'The
Tiger'. *The Book of Thel*, which revealed his mystic vision and began
the evolution of his personal mythology, was also published in 1789.
Tiriel was written in that year, although not published until 1874,
and so was *The Marriage of Heaven and Hell*, his major prose work,
largely a collection of paradoxical aphorisms.

In 1790 he moved to Lambeth and there followed numerous
publications which developed his visionary and prophetic beliefs:
America: A Prophecy (1793); *Visions of the Daughters of Albion*
(1793); *The Book of Urizen* and *Europe: a Prophecy*, both 1794; *The
Book of Los* (1795); *The Four Zoas* (1797–1800); *Milton* (1804–8);
and *Jerusalem: the Emanation of the Giant Albion* (1804–20). His
work was marked for its objection to, and outcry against, restrictions
on personal liberty and natural behaviour, for its attacks on the fetters
of organised and traditional institutions, and for its condemnation of
social injustices, the slave trade in particular.

He spent only three years away from London, 1800–3, when he
lived at Felpham, Sussex. His work failed to find a sympathetic
audience, and his last years were lived in obscurity. He failed to get
on with former friends and, at his death, he was generally considered
to have been gifted but mad. His poems became, however, an influence
on, and inspiration for, many later poets, particularly W. B. Yeats
who, in 1893, together with the American E. J. Ellis, published a
three-volume edition of his work.

TO AUTUMN

O Autumn! laden with fruit, and stained
With the blood of the grape, pass not, but sit
Beneath my shady roof; there thou may'st rest,
And tune thy jolly voice to my fresh pipe,
5   And all the daughters of the year shall dance!
Sing now the lusty song of fruits and flowers.

'The narrow bud opens her beauties to
The sun, and love runs in her thrilling veins;
Blossoms hang round the brows of morning, and
10   Flourish down the bright cheek of modest eve,
Till clustering summer breaks forth into singing,
And feathered clouds strew flowers round her head.

'The spirits of the air live on the smells
Of fruit; and joy, with pinions* light, roves round   wings
15   The gardens, or sits singing in the trees.'
Thus sang the jolly Autumn as he sat;
Then rose, girded himself, and o'er the bleak
Hills fled from our sight: but left his golden load.

c. 1777   1783

SONG†

My silks and fine array,
My smiles and languished air,
By love are driven away;
And mournful lean Despair
5   Brings me yew† to deck my grave;
Such end true lovers have.

His face is fair as heaven
When springing buds unfold;
O! why to him was't given

Song this poem shows the strong influence of
Shakespeare, cf. the songs in *Twelfth Night*
and *Cymbeline*, particularly 'Come away,

come away, death', and 'Fear no more the
heat of the sun'
yew traditional emblem of mourning

10 Whose heart is wintry cold?
His breast is love's all-worshipped tomb,
Where all love's pilgrims come.

Bring me an axe and spade,
Bring me a winding-sheet;†
15 When I my grave have made
Let winds and tempests beat:
Then down I'll lie as cold as clay.
True love doth pass away!

c. 1777   1783

From SONGS OF INNOCENCE (1789)†

Introduction

Piping down the valleys wild,
Piping songs of pleasant glee,
On a cloud I saw a child,
And he laughing said to me,

5 'Pipe a song about a Lamb!'
So I piped with merry cheer.
'Piper, pipe that song again!'
So I piped. He wept to hear.†

'Drop thy pipe, thy happy pipe;
10 Sing thy songs of happy cheer.'
So I sung the same again
While he wept with joy to hear.

'Piper, sit thee down and write
In a book that all may read.'
15 So he vanished from my sight
And I plucked a hollow reed,

---

winding-sheet cloth used to wrap corpses
Songs of Innocence a collection of poems,
originally meant for children, which Blake

wrote and etched
He wept to hear an indication that tears and
joy are closely related

And I made a rural pen,
And I stained the water clear,†
And I wrote my happy songs
20 Every child may joy to hear.

_c_. 1788–9   1789

The Lamb†

Little lamb, who made thee?
Dost thou know who made thee?
Gave thee life and bid thee feed
By the stream and o'er the mead;*   meadow
5 Gave thee clothing of delight,
Softest clothing, woolly, bright;
Gave thee such a tender voice,
Making all the vales rejoice?
Little lamb, who made thee?
10 Dost thou know who made thee?

Little lamb, I'll tell thee,
Little lamb, I'll tell thee:
He is called by thy name,
For he calls himself a Lamb.
15 He is meek, and he is mild,
He became a little child.
I a child and thou a lamb,
We are called by his name.
Little lamb, God bless thee!
20 Little lamb, God bless thee!

_c_. 1788–9   1789

The Little Black Boy†

My mother bore me in the southern wild,
And I am black, but O! my soul is white;
White as an angel is the English child,
But I am black as if bereaved of light.

And I stained . . . clear   either for ink or water-
colour
The Lamb   symbol of Jesus Christ, the
Redeemer: John 1. 29, 'Behold the Lamb of

God, which taketh away the sins of the world'
The Little Black Boy   in the age of slavery, this
poem shows Blake's concern for negroes'
spiritual welfare

5   My mother taught me underneath a tree,
And sitting down before the heat of day,
She took me on her lap and kissed me,
And pointing to the east, began to say,

'Look on the rising sun: there God does live,
10 And gives his light, and gives his heat away,
And flowers and trees and beasts and men receive
Comfort in morning, joy in the noonday.

'And we are put on earth a little space,
That we may learn to bear the beams of love,
15 And these black bodies and this sunburnt face
Is but a cloud, and like a shady grove.

'For when our souls have learned the heat to bear,
The cloud will vanish; we shall hear his voice
Saying, "Come out from the grove, my love and care,
20 And round my golden tent like lambs rejoice."'

Thus did my mother say, and kissèd me;
And thus I say to little English boy:
When I from black and he from white cloud free,
And round the tent of God like lambs we joy,

25 I'll shade him from the heat, till he can bear
To lean in joy upon our father's knee;
And then I'll stand and stroke his silver hair,
And be like him, and he will then love me.

c. 1788–9   1789

The Chimney Sweeper

When my mother died I was very young,
And my father sold me while yet my tongue
Could scarcely cry ''weep! 'weep! 'weep! 'weep!'†
So your chimneys I sweep,† and in soot I sleep.

'weep! i.e. 'sweep!', tradesman's cry: a play on 'weep'
So your . . . sweep chimneys were swept by young boys who climbed inside the chimneys and worked their way to the top

5   There's little Tom Dacre who cried when his head,
    That curled like a lamb's back, was shaved. So I said
    'Hush, Tom! never mind it, for when your head's bare
    You know that the soot cannot spoil your white hair.'

    And so he was quiet, and that very night
10 As Tom was a-sleeping, he had such a sight!
    That thousands of sweepers, Dick, Joe, Ned and Jack,
    Were all of them locked up in coffins of black.†

    And by came an angel who had a bright key,
    And he opened the coffins and set them all free;
15 Then down a green plain leaping, laughing, they run
    And wash in a river, and shine in the sun.

    Then naked and white, all their bags left behind,
    They rise upon clouds and sport in the wind;
    And the angel told Tom, if he'd be a good boy,
20 He'd have God for his father, and never want joy.

    And so Tom awoke, and we rose in the dark,†
    And got with our bags and our brushes to work.
    Though the morning was cold, Tom was happy and warm;
    So if all do their duty they need not fear harm.

    c. 1788–9   1789

THE BOOK OF THEL†

Thel's Motto

Does the eagle know what is in the pit?
Or wilt thou go ask the mole?
Can wisdom be put in a silver rod?
Or love in a golden bowl?

Were . . . *black*   many young sweeps died from
 suffocation or from being trapped
rose . . . dark   sweeping began usually at
 5 a.m. in summer, and 7 a.m. in winter
Thel   of all Blake's mythological creatures,
 Thel is the most easy to understand. She is
'the virgin of the skies' who laments
transience and mutability by the banks of the
river Adona. There are strong Biblical echoes
throughout the poem, from the Prophets and
the Book of Genesis

i

The daughters of the Seraphim† led round their sunny flocks,
All but the youngest; she in paleness sought the secret air,
To fade away like morning beauty from her mortal day.
Down by the river of Adona† her soft voice is heard,
5   And thus her gentle lamentation falls like morning dew:

'O life of this our spring! why fades the lotus of the water,
Why fade these children of the spring, born but to smile and fall?
Ah! Thel is like a watery bow, and like a parting cloud;
Like a reflection in a glass, like shadows in the water;
10   Like dreams of Infants, like a smile upon an infant's face;
Like the dove's voice, like transient day, like music in the air.
Ah! gentle may I lay me down, and gentle rest my head,
And gentle sleep the sleep of death, and gentle hear the voice
Of him that walketh in the garden in the evening time.'

15   The Lily of the Valley, breathing in the humble grass,
Answered the lovely maid and said, 'I am a watery weed,
And I am very small and love to dwell in lowly vales;
So weak, the gilded butterfly scarce perches on my head.
Yet I am visited from heaven, and he that smiles on all
20   Walks in the valley and each morn over me spreads his hand,
Saying, "Rejoice, thou humble grass, thou new-born lily flower,
Thou gentle maid of silent valleys and of modest brooks,
For thou shalt be clothed in light and fed with morning manna,
Till summer's heat melts thee beside the fountains and the springs
25   To flourish in eternal vales." Then why should Thel complain?
Why should the mistress of the vales of Har utter a sigh?'

She ceased and smiled in tears, then sat down in her silver shrine.

Thel answered, 'O thou little virgin of the peaceful valley,
Giving to those that cannot crave, the voiceless, the o'ertired;
30   Thy breath doth nourish the innocent lamb, he smells thy milky
    garments,
He crops thy flowers while thou sittest smiling in his face,
Wiping his mild and meekin* mouth from all contagious taints.   meek
Thy wine doth purify the golden honey; thy perfume
Which thou dost scatter on every little blade of grass that springs,
35   Revives the milked cow and tames the fire-breathing steed.
But Thel is like a faint cloud kindled at the rising sun:

Seraphim   the highest of the nine choirs of   *Adona*   names (of places and people) belong to
angels   Blake's personal mythology

I vanish from my pearly throne, and who shall find my place?'

'Queen of the vales,' the Lily answered, 'ask the tender Cloud
And it shall tell thee why it glitters in the morning sky,
40   And why it scatters its bright beauty through the humid air.
Descend, O little Cloud, and hover before the eyes of Thel.'

The Cloud descended and the Lily bowed her modest head
And went to mind her numerous charge among the verdant grass.

ii

'O little Cloud,' the virgin said, 'I charge thee tell to me
45   Why thou complainest not when in one hour thou fade away:
Then we shall seek thee, but not find. Ah! Thel is like to thee.
I pass away, yet I complain and no one hears my voice.'
The Cloud then shewed his golden head and his bright form emerged
Hovering and glittering on the air before the face of Thel.

50   'O virgin, knowest thou not our steeds drink of the golden springs
Where Luvah† doth renew his horses? Look'st thou on my youth,
And fearest thou, because I vanish and am seen no more,
Nothing remains? O maid, I tell thee, when I pass away
It is to tenfold life, to love, to peace and raptures holy:
55   Unseen descending, weigh my light wings upon balmy flowers,
And court the fair-eyed dew to take me to her shining tent.
The weeping virgin, trembling kneels before the risen sun,
Till we arise linked in a golden band and never part,
But walk united, bearing food to all our tender flowers.'

60   'Dost thou, O little Cloud? I fear that I am not like thee,
For I walk through the vales of Har and smell the sweetest flowers,
But I feed not the little flowers; I hear the warbling birds,
But I feed not the warbling birds; they fly and seek their food.
But Thel delights in these no more, because I fade away;
65   And all shall say, "Without a use this shining woman lived,
Or did she only live to be at death the food of worms?"'

The Cloud reclined upon his airy throne and answered thus:

'Then if thou art the food of worms, O virgin of the skies,
How great thy use, how great thy blessing! Everything that lives
70   Lives not alone nor for itself. Fear not, and I will call

Luvah   one of Blake's mythological male figures representing love, fertility, the life- force, who is often associated with the sun and sunrise

The weak worm from its lowly bed and thou shalt hear its voice.
Come forth, worm of the silent valley, to thy pensive queen.'

The helpless Worm arose and sat upon the Lily's leaf,
And the bright Cloud sailed on to find his partner in the vale.

iii

75 Then Thel astonished viewed the Worm upon its dewy bed.

'Art thou a Worm? Image of weakness, art thou but a Worm?
I see thee like an infant wrapped in the Lily's leaf.
Ah! weep not, little voice, thou canst not speak, but thou canst weep.
Is this a Worm? I see thee lay helpless and naked, weeping,
80 And none to answer, none to cherish thee with mother's smiles.'

The Clod of Clay heard the worm's voice and raised her pitying head.
She bowed over the weeping infant, and her life exhaled
In milky fondness. Then on Thel she fixed her humble eyes.

'O beauty of the vales of Har! we live not for ourselves.
85 Thou seest me the meanest thing, and so I am indeed.
My bosom of itself is cold and of itself is dark;
But he that loves the lowly pours his oil upon my head,
And kisses me, and binds his nuptial bands around my breast,
And says, "Thou mother of my children, I have loved thee
90 "And I have given thee a crown that none can take away."
But how this is, sweet maid, I know not and I cannot know;
I ponder and I cannot ponder; yet I live and love.'

The daughter of beauty wiped her pitying tears with her white veil,
And said, 'Alas! I knew not this, and therefore did I weep.
95 That God would love a Worm I knew and punish the evil foot
That wilful bruised its helpless form; but that he cherished it
With milk and oil I never knew, and therefore did I weep;
And I complained in the mild air, because I fade away,
And lay me down in thy cold bed and leave my shining lot.'
100 'Queen of the vales,' the matron Clay answered, 'I heard thy sighs,
And all thy moans flew o'er my roof, but I have called them down.
Wilt thou, O Queen, enter my house? 'Tis given thee to enter
And to return. Fear nothing, enter with thy virgin feet.'

iv

The eternal gates' terrific† porter lifted the northern bar.

terrific causing terror, terrible

105 Thel entered in and saw the secrets of the land unknown.
She saw the couches of the dead, and where the fibrous roots
Of every heart on earth infixes deep its restless twists:
A land of sorrows and of tears where never smile was seen.

She wandered in the land of clouds through valleys dark, listening
110 Dolours* and lamentations. Waiting oft beside a dewy grave   sorrows
She stood in silence, listening to the voices of the ground
Till to her own grave plot she came, and there she sat down,
And heard this voice of sorrow breathed from the hollow pit.

'Why cannot the ear be closed to its own destruction?
115 Or the glistening eye to the poison of a smile?
Why are eyelids stored with arrows ready drawn
Where a thousand fighting men in ambush lie?
Or an eye of gifts and graces showering fruits and coined gold?
Why a tongue impressed with honey from every wind?
120 Why an ear, a whirlpool fierce to draw creations* in?   falsehoods
Why a nostril wide inhaling terror, trembling, and affright?
Why a tender curb upon the youthful burning boy?
Why a little curtain of flesh on the bed or our desire?'

The virgin started from her seat, and with a shriek
125 Fled back unhindered till she came into the vales of Har.

1789–91   1789–91

VISIONS OF THE DAUGHTERS OF ALBION†

The Argument

       I loved Theotormon,†
       And I was not ashamed;
       I trembled in my virgin fears,
       And I hid in Leutha's† vale!

Visions of the Daughters of Albion a poem of revolt against authority of all kinds. It has underlying personal, spiritual, moral, political, economic and social themes. The Daughters represent both the women and the commerce of England. The poem possesses a visionary ecstasy

Theotormon names belong to Blake's personal mythology. Theotormon is the lover of Oothoon, sick with fear of life, who wishes to act but cannot

Leutha a potent, erotic spirit, associated with the temptations of the Garden of Eden

5   I plucked Leutha's flower,
       And I rose up from the vale;
       But the terrible thunders tore
       My virgin mantle in twain.

Visions

Enslaved, the Daughters of Albion weep; a trembling lamentation
10   Upon their mountains; in their valleys, sighs toward America.

For the soft soul of America, Oothoon,[†] wandered in woe
Along the vales of Leutha, seeking flowers to comfort her;
And thus she spoke to the bright Marigold of Leutha's vale.

'Art thou a flower? art thou a nymph? I see thee now a flower,
15   Now a nymph! I dare not pluck thee from thy dewy bed!'

The golden nymph replied: 'Pluck thou my flower, Oothoon the mild!
Another flower shall spring, because the soul of sweet delight
Can never pass away.' She ceased, and closed her golden shrine.

Then Oothoon plucked the flower, saying: 'I pluck thee from thy bed,
20   Sweet flower, and put thee here to glow between my breasts;
And thus I turn my face to where my whole soul seeks.'

Over the waves she went in winged exulting swift delight,
And over Theotormon's reign took her impetuous course.

Bromion[†] rent her with his thunders; on his stormy bed
25   Lay the faint maid, and soon her woes appalled his thunders hoarse.

Bromion spoke: 'Behold this harlot here on Bromion's bed,
And let the jealous dolphins sport around the lovely maid!
Thy soft American plains are mine, and mine thy north and south.
Stamped with my signet are the swarthy children of the sun;
30   They are obedient, they resist not, they obey the scourge;
Their daughters worship terrors and obey the violent.
Now thou mayest marry Bromion's harlot, and protect the child
Of Bromion's rage, that Oothoon shall put forth in nine moons' time.'

Then storms rent Theotormon's limbs. He rolled his waves around,
35   And folded his black jealous waters round the adulterate pair.

Oothoon   spirit of freedom from the New
       World
Bromion   a representative figure of repression,

inhibition and exploitation, all established in
the Old World

Bound back to back in Bromion's caves, terror and meekness dwell.
At entrance Theotormon sits, wearing the threshold hard
With secret tears; beneath him sound like waves on a desert shore
The voice of slaves beneath the sun, and children bought with money,
40   That shiver in religious caves beneath the burning fires
Of lust, that belch incessant from the summits of the earth.

Oothoon weeps not. She cannot weep, her tears are locked up;
But she can howl incessant, writhing her soft snowy limbs,
And calling Theotormon's eagles to prey upon her flesh.
45   'I call with holy voice! King's of the sounding air,
Rend away this defiled bosom that I may reflect
The image of Theotormon on my pure transparent breast.'

The eagles at her call descend and rend their bleeding prey.
Theotormon severely smiles; her soul reflects the smile,
50   As the clear spring, mudded with feet of beasts, grows pure and smiles.

The Daughters of Albion hear her woes, and echo back her sighs.

'Why does my Theotormon sit weeping upon the threshold,
And Oothoon hovers by his side, persuading him in vain?
I cry: Arise, O Theotormon! for the village dog
55   Barks at the breaking day; the nightingale has done lamenting;
The lark does rustle in the ripe corn, and the eagle returns
From nightly prey, and lifts his golden beak to the pure east,
Shaking the dust from his immortal pinions to awake
The sun that sleeps too long. Arise, my Theotormon! I am pure,
60   Because the night is gone that closed me in its deadly black.
They told me that the night and day were all that I could see;
They told me that I had five senses to enclose me up;
And they enclosed my infinite brain into a narrow circle,
And sunk my heart into the abyss, a red, round globe, hot burning,
65   Till all from life I was obliterated and erased.
Instead of morn arises a bright shadow, like an eye
In the eastern cloud; instead of night a sickly charnel-house,[†]
That Theotormon hears me not. To him the night and morn
Are both alike – a night of sighs, a morning of fresh tears.
70   And none but Bromion can hear my lamentations.

'With what sense is it that the chicken shuns the ravenous hawk?
With what sense does the tame pigeon measure out the expanse?

---

charnel-house   a building where corpses or bones are piled

With what sense does the bee form cells? Have not the mouse and frog
Eyes and ears and sense of touch? Yet are their habitations
75 And their pursuits as different as their forms and as their joys.
Ask the wild ass why he refuses burdens, and the meek camel
Why he loves man. Is it because of eye, ear, mouth, or skin,
Or breathing nostrils? No! for these the wolf and tiger have.
Ask the blind worm the secrets of the grave, and why her spires*   coils
80 Love to curl round the bones of death; and ask the ravenous snake
Where she gets poison, and the winged eagle why he loves the sun;
And then tell me the thoughts of man, that have been hid of old.

'Silent I hover all the night, and all day could be silent,
If Theotormon once would turn his loved eyes upon me.
85 How can I be defiled when I reflect thy image pure?
Sweetest the fruit that the worm feeds on, and the soul preyed on by
   woe,
The new-washed lamb tinged with the village smoke, and the bright
   swan
By the red earth of our immortal river. I bathe my wings,
And I am white and pure to hover round Theotormon's breast.'

90 Then Theotormon broke his silence, and he answered:

'Tell me what is the night or day to one o'erflowed with woe?
Tell me what is a thought, and of what substance is it made?
Tell me what is a joy, and in what gardens do joys grow?
And in what rivers swim the sorrows? And upon what mountains
95 Wave shadows of discontent? And in what houses dwell the wretched,
Drunken with woe forgotten, and shut up from cold despair?

'Tell me where dwell the thoughts, forgotten till thou call them forth?
Tell me where dwell the joys of old, and where the ancient loves,
And when will they renew again, and the night of oblivion past,
100 That I might traverse times and spaces far remote, and bring
Comforts into a present sorrow and a night of pain?
Where goest thou, O thought? To what remote land is thy flight?
If thou returnest to the present moment of affliction,
Wilt thou bring comforts on thy wings, and dews and honey and balm,
105 Or poison from the desert wilds, from the eyes of the envier?'

Then Bromion said, and shook the cavern with his lamentation:

'Thou knowest that the ancient trees seen by thine eyes have fruit,
But knowest thou that trees and fruits flourish upon the earth
To gratify senses unknown – trees, beast, and birds unknown;

110   Unknown, not unperceived, spread in the infinite microscope,
      In places yet unvisited by the voyager, and in worlds
      Over another kind of seas, and in atmospheres unknown?
      Ah! are there other wars beside the wars of sword and fire?
      And are there other sorrows beside the sorrows of poverty?
115   And are there other joys beside the joys of riches and ease?
      And is there not one law for both the lion and the ox?
      And is there not eternal fire and eternal chains
      To bind the phantoms of existence from eternal life?'

      Then Oothoon waited silent all the day and all the night;
120   But when the morn arose her lamentation renewed.
      The Daughters of Albion hear her woes and echo back her sighs.

      'O Urizen!† Creator of men! mistaken demon of heaven!
      Thy joys are tears, thy labour vain to form men to thine image.
      How can one joy absorb another? Are not different joys
125   Holy, eternal, infinite? and each joy is a Love.
      Does not the great mouth laugh at a gift, and the narrow eyelids mock
      At the labour that is above payment? And wilt thou take the ape
      For thy counsellor, or the dog for a schoolmaster to thy children?
      Does he who contemns poverty, and he who turns with abhorrence
130   From usury† feel the same passion, or are they moved alike?
      How can the giver of gifts experience the delights of the merchant?
      How the industrious citizen the pains of the husbandman?
      How different far that fat fed hireling with hollow drum,
      Who buys whole corn-fields into wastes,† and sings upon the heath!
135   How different their eye and ear! How different the world to them!
      With what sense does the parson claim the labour of the farmer?
      What are his nets and gins† and traps; and how does he surround him
      With cold floods of abstraction and with forests of solitude,
      To build him castles and high spires, where kings and priests may
        dwell,
140   Till she who burns with youth, and knows no fixed lot, is bound
      In spells of law to one she loathes? And must she drag the chain
      Of life in weary lust? Must chilling, murderous thoughts obscure
      The clear heaven of her eternal spring, to bear the wintry rage
      Of a harsh terror, driven to madness, bound to hold a rod
145   Over her shrinking shoulders all the day, and all the night
      To turn the wheel of false desire, and longings that wake her womb
      To the abhorred birth of cherubs† in the human form,

Urizen deviser of moral codes
usury money-lending
buys . . . wastes by purchase turns cultivated
  land into waste land

gins snares or traps
cherubs the second order of the ninefold
  heavenly hierarchy, gifted with knowledge

That live a pestilence and die a meteor,† and are no more;
Till the child dwell with one he hates, and do the deed he loathes,
150 And the impure scourge force his seed into its unripe birth,
Ere yet his eyelids can behold the arrows of the day?

'Does the whale worship at thy footsteps as the hungry dog,
Or does he scent the mountain prey because his nostrils wide
Draw in the ocean? Does his eye discern the flying cloud
155 As the raven's eye; or does he measure the expanse like the vulture?
Does the still spider view the cliffs where eagles hide their young;
Or does the fly rejoice because the harvest is brought in?
Does not the eagle scorn the earth, and despise the treasures beneath?
But the mole knoweth what is there, and the worm shall tell it thee.
160 Does not the worm erect a pillar in the mouldering churchyard
And a place of eternity in the jaws of the hungry grave?
Over his porch these words are written: "Take thy bliss, O Man!
And sweet shall be thy taste, and sweet thy infant joys renew!"

'Infancy! fearless, lustful,† happy, nestling for delight
165 In laps of pleasure: Innocence! honest, open, seeking
The vigorous joys of morning light, open to virgin bliss!
Who taught thee modesty, subtle modesty, child of night and sleep?
When thou awakest wilt thou dissemble all thy secret joys,
Or wert thou not awake when all this mystery was disclosed?
170 Then comest thou forth a modest virgin knowing to dissemble,
With nets found under thy night pillow, to catch virgin joy
And brand it with the name of whore, and sell it in the night
In silence, even without a whisper, and in seeming sleep.
Religious dreams and holy vespers light thy smoky fires.
175 Once were thy fires lighted by the eyes of honest morn.
And does my Theotormon seek this hypocrite modesty,
This knowing, artful, secret, fearful, cautious, trembling hypocrite?
Then is Oothoon a whore indeed! And all the virgin joys
Of life are harlots; and Theotormon is a sick man's dream;
180 And Oothoon is the crafty slave of selfish holiness.

'But Oothoon is not so, a virgin filled with virgin fancies,
Open to joy and to delight wherever beauty appears.
If in the morning sun I find it, there my eyes are fixed
In happy copulation; if in evening mild, wearied with work,
185 Sit on a bank and draw the pleasures of this free-born joy.

'The moment of desire! the moment of desire! The virgin

---

meteor a thing of short duration   *lustful* seeking pleasure in general sense

That pines for man shall awaken her womb to enormous joys
In the secret shadows of her chamber. The youth shut up from
The lustful joy shall forget to generate, and create an amorous image
190   In the shadows of his curtains and in the folds of his silent pillow.
Are not these the places of religion, the rewards of continence,
The self-enjoyings of self-denial? Why dost thou seek religion?
Is it because acts are not lovely that thou seekest solitude,
Where the horrible darkness is impressed with reflections of desire?

195   'Father of Jealousy, be thou accursed from the earth!
Why hast thou taught my Theotormon this accursed thing,
Till beauty fades from off my shoulders, darkened and cast out,
A solitary shadow wailing on the margin of non-entity?

'I cry: Love! Love! Love! happy happy Love! free as the mountain
      wind!
200   Can that be Love, that drinks another as a sponge drinks water,
That clouds with jealousy his nights, with weepings all the day,
To spin a web of age around him, grey and hoary, dark;
Till his eyes sicken at the fruit that hangs before his sight?
Such is self-love that envies all, a creeping skeleton,
205   With lamplike eyes watching around the frozen marriage bed!

'But silken nets and traps of adamant† will Oothoon spread,
And catch for thee girls of mild silver, or of furious gold.
I'll lie beside thee on a bank, and view their wanton play
In lovely copulation, bliss on bliss, with Theotormon.
210   Red as the rosy morning, lustful as the first-born beam,
Oothoon shall view his dear delight; nor e'er with jealous cloud
Come in the heaven of generous love, nor selfish blightings bring.

'Does the sun walk, in glorious raiment, on the secret floor
Where the cold miser spreads his gold; or does the bright cloud drop
215   On his stone threshold? Does his eye behold the beam that brings
Expansion to the eye of pity; or will he bind himself
Beside the ox to thy hard furrow? Does not that mild beam blot
The bat, the owl, the glowing tiger, and the king of night?
The sea-fowl takes the wintry blast for a covering to her limbs,
220   And the wild snake the pestilence to adorn him with gems and gold;
And trees and birds and beasts and men behold their eternal joy.
Arise, you little glancing wings, and sing your infant joy!
Arise, and drink your bliss, for everything that lives is holy!'

---

adamant   impenetrably hard stone

225 Thus every morning wails Oothoon; but Theotormon sits
Upon the margined ocean coversing with shadows dire.

The Daughters of Albion hear her woes, and echo back her sighs.

1793   1793

From SONGS OF EXPERIENCE†

Introduction

Hear the voice of the Bard!
Who present, past and future sees;
Whose ears have heard
The Holy Word
5 That walked among the ancient trees,

Calling the lapsed soul,
And weeping in the evening dew;
That might control
The starry pole,
10 And fallen, fallen light renew!

'O Earth, O Earth, return!
Arise from out the dewy grass;
Night is worn,
And the morn
15 Rises from the slumberous mass.

'Turn away no more;
Why wilt thou turn away?
The starry floor,
The watery shore,
20 Is given thee till the break of day.'

c. 1790–4   1794

Songs of Experience   in 1795, Blake added to
the original Songs of Innocence and
published Songs of Innocence and
Experience: Shewing the Two Contrary
States of the Human Soul. The Songs of
Experience, many bearing the same titles as
poems in the Innocence collection, elaborate
them in tone and content in the light of adult
experience and offset their simplicity. Many
are attacks on unnatural restraint and
condemn the frustration of natural energy
and desire

Earth's Answer

Earth raised up her head
From the darkness dread and drear.
Her light fled,
Stony dread!
5   And her locks covered with grey despair.

'Prisoned on watery shore,
Starry Jealousy does keep my den:
Cold and hoar,
Weeping o'er
10   I hear the father of the ancient men.

'Selfish father of men!
Cruel, jealous, selfish fear!
Can delight,
Chained in night,
15   The virgins of youth and morning bear?

'Does spring hide its joy
When buds and blossoms grow?
Does the sower
Sow by night,
20   Or the ploughman in darkness plough?

'Break this heavy chain
That does freeze my bones around.
Selfish! vain!
Eternal bane!†
25   That free love with bondage bound.'

c. 1790–4   1794

The Sick Rose

O rose, thou art sick!
The invisible worm
That flies in the night,
In the howling storm,

---

bane poison, cause of ruin

5 Has found out thy bed
   Of crimson joy,
   And his dark secret love
   Does thy life destroy.

   c. 1790–4   1794

The Chimney Sweeper

A little black thing among the snow,
Crying "weep! 'weep!' in notes of woe!
'Where are thy father and mother? say?'
'They are both gone up to the church to pray

5 'Because I was happy upon the heath,
   And smiled among the winter's snow,
   They clothed me in the clothes of death,
   And taught me to sing the notes of woe.

   And because I am happy and dance and sing
10 They think they have done me no injury,
   And are gone to praise God and his Priest and King,
   Who make up a heaven of our misery.'

   c. 1790–2   1794

The Garden of Love

I went to the Garden of Love,
And saw what I never had seen:
A chapel was built in the midst
Where I used to play on the green.

5 And the gates of this chapel were shut,
   And *Thou shalt not* writ over the door;
   So I turned to the Garden of Love
   That so many sweet flowers bore;

   And I saw it was filled with graves,
10 And tomb-stones where flowers should be;
   And priests in black gowns were walking their rounds,
   And binding with briars my joys and desires.

   c. 1790–2   1794

London

I wander through each chartered[†] street,
Near where the chartered Thames does flow,
And mark in every face I meet
Marks of weakness, marks of woe.

5   In every cry of every man,
In every infant's cry of fear,
In every voice, in every ban,*   curse
The mind-forged manacles[†] I hear.

How the chimney sweeper's cry
10 Every blackening[†] church appalls;
And the hapless soldier's sigh
Runs in blood down palace walls.

But most through midnight streets I hear
How the youthful harlot's curse
15 Blasts the new born infant's tear,
And blights with plagues[†] the marriage hearse.

1790–2   1794

The Tiger

Tiger! Tiger! burning bright
In the forests of the night,
What immortal hand or eye
Could frame thy fearful symmetry?

5   In what distant deeps or skies
Burnt the fire of thine eyes?
On what wings dare he aspire?
What the hand dare seize the fire?

And what shoulder, and what art,
10 Could twist the sinews of thy heart?

---

chartered charters and corporations, Blake
  thought, restricted the rights of the majority
  of citizens
mind-forged manacles manacles (restraints)
  forged for the mind

blackening churches built in stone or stucco
  quickly turned black from pollution of smoke
  from domestic fires and factory chimneys
plagues veneral diseases

And when thy heart began to beat,
What dread hand, and what dread feet?

What the hammer? what the chain?
In what furnace was thy brain?
15   What the anvil? what dread grasp
Dare its deadly terrors clasp?

When the stars threw down their spears,
And watered heaven with their tears,
Did he smile his work to see?
20   Did he who made the Lamb make thee?

Tiger! Tiger! burning bright
In the forests of the night,
What immortal hand or eye,
Dare frame thy fearful symmetry?

1790–2   1794

AND DID THOSE FEET IN ANCIENT TIME†

And did those feet† in ancient time
   Walk upon England's mountains green?
And was the holy Lamb of God
   On England's pleasant pastures seen?

5   And did the Countenance Divine
   Shine forth upon our clouded hills?
And was Jerusalem† builded here
   Among these dark Satanic Mills?†

'And did those feet in ancient time' from the Preface to Milton, 1804. The poem follows a prose commentary which attacks the 'stolen and perverted' writings of Greece and Rome: 'We do not want either Greek or Roman models if we are but just and true to our own imaginations, those worlds of eternity in which we shall live for ever in Jesus our Lord'

those feet Albion's. The giant Albion represents mankind as well as England
Jerusalem Albion's holy city
Satanic Mills recurrent symbols in Blake's prophetic writings of mechanical and analytical rationalism. Sometimes they are water-mills, occasionally windmills, usually handmills

Bring me my bow of burning gold!†
10 Bring me my arrows of desire!
Bring me my spear! O clouds, unfold!
Bring me my chariot of fire!

I will not cease from mental fight,
Nor shall my sword sleep in my hand,
15 Till we have built Jerusalem
In England's green and pleasant land.

c. 1804   1804

Bring me . . . gold the last two stanzas are
made up of energy symbols which have
primarily a sexual force

William Cobbett
1763–1835

Cobbett's life was a long record of adherence to principle. Born at 'the greatest corn-market in England', Farnham, Hampshire, where his father was publican of 'The Jolly Farmer', he consistently nurtured the interests of working men. He started out a Tory by inclination, believing in ancient, established, good ways, but was convinced by experience of bribery, jobbery, corruption and the iniquities of Pitt's 'system' by which even the reviewers of books were paid by the authors of books, that radical policies had to be followed. His *Political Register* (1802–35) began as a conservative journal and finished as a popular paper aimed at farmworkers and day-labourers. He spent two periods in America as a semi-exile, the first time upholding the values of old England chiefly in *The Life and Adventures of Peter Porcupine*, and after the second stay expounding the advantages of America's way of life to the English.

He was a man of many parts – soldier, farmer, politician, editor, forerunner of Hansard, and body-snatcher: opposed to Tom Paine's corpse being buried in unconsecrated ground, he robbed the grave and removed the bones to England. He built successfully a barrack for four hundred men, 'without aid of draughtsman, architect or bricklayer'. He was an 'old lag' too, imprisoned for two years for seditious libel, although for payment of a substantial fee he secured comfortable lodgings at Newgate, even if they did overlook the execution yard. The Court of King's Bench became yet another target of his brilliant and savage pen.

His admirable ambition was to make England a better place for everyone to live in. Corrupt government had to be exposed: 'The cause of the people has been betrayed by hundreds of men.' When Pitt was dying in 1806, Cobbett declared that the old corrupt politicians, 'the Hawkesburies, the Cannings and the old Roses' had to be kept out of office.

He was not afraid to change his mind. 'The doctrine of consistency, as now in vogue, is the most absurd that ever was broached.' He said to William Huskisson, 'I do not blame you for changing your opinions: I blame you for changing from good to bad'. A man of decided and determined views, he advocated a principle that politicians should be people of personal integrity.

His most important publications were *Parliamentary Debates*, taken over by, and now known as, Hansard, and *State Trials*. Amongst many other writings, he composed a popular English grammar, and published *American Gardener* (1821), *English Gardener* (1828), *Cobbett's Corn* (1828) and *The Woodlands* (1828). He is best remembered for *Rural Rides* (1830), a record of his tour round the English countryside in the 1820s, embellished with political asides and humorous insights: he wrote an entertaining, graceful prose, which lent interest to the most ordinary scene or event.

From RURAL RIDES

THROUGH THE SOUTH-EAST OF HAMPSHIRE, BACK THROUGH THE SOUTH-WEST OF SURREY, ALONG THE WEALD OF SURREY, AND THEN OVER THE SURREY HILLS DOWN TO THE WEN.

Botley (Hampshire), 5th August, 1823.

I got to Fareham on Saturday night, after having got a soaking on the South Downs, on the morning of that day. On the Sunday morning, intending to go and spend the day at Titchfield (about two miles and a half from Fareham), and perceiving, upon looking out of the window,
5   about 5 o'clock in the morning, that it was likely to rain, I got up, struck a bustle,† got up the ostler;† set off and got to my destined point before 7 o'clock in the morning. And here I experienced the benefits of early rising; for I had scarcely got well and safely under cover, when St Swithin† began to pour down again, and he continued to pour during
10   the whole of the day. From Fareham to Titchfield village a large part of the ground is a common enclosed some years ago. It is therefore amongst the worst of the land in the country. Yet, I did not see a bad field of corn along here, and the Swedish turnips were, I think, full as fine as any that I saw upon the South Downs. But it is to be observed
15   that this land is in the hands of dead-weight† people, and is conveniently situated for the receiving of manure from Portsmouth. Before I got to my friend's house, I passed by a farm where I expected to find a wheat-rick standing. I did not, however; and this is the strongest possible proof, that the stock of corn is gone out of the hands of the farmers. I

struck a bustle hurried
ostler stableman at an inn
St Swithin the saint associated with rainy weather. He was Bishop of Winchester, died in 862, and desired to be buried in the minster

churchyard so that the 'sweet rain of heaven' might fall on his grave
dead-weight people who are of little use or assistance

20 set out from Titchfield at 7 o'clock in the evening, and had seven miles
to go to reach Botley. It rained, but I got myself well furnished forth as
a defence against the rain. I had not gone two hundred yards before
the rain ceased; so that I was singularly fortunate as to rain this day;
and I had now to congratulate myself on the success of the remedy for
25 the whooping-cough which I used the day before on the South Downs;
for really, though I had a spell or two of coughing on Saturday morning,
when I set out from Petworth, I have not had, up to this hour, any spell
at all since I got wet upon the South Downs. I got to Botley about nine
o'clock, having stopped two or three times to look about me as I went
30 along; for, I had, in the first place, to ride, for about three miles of my
road, upon a turnpike-road† of which I was the projector, and, indeed,
the maker. In the next place I had to ride, for something better than
half a mile of my way, along between fields and coppices that were
mine, until they came into the hands of the mortgagee, and by the side
35 of cottages of my own building. The only matter of much interest with
me was the state of the inhabitants of those cottages. I stopped at two
or three places, and made some little inquiries; I rode up to two or
three houses in the village of Botley, which I had to pass through, and,
just before it was dark I got to a farm-house close by the Church, and
40 what was more, not a great many yards from the dwelling of that
delectable creature, the Botley Parson, whom, however, I have not seen
during my stay at this place.

Botley lies in a valley, the soil of which is a deep and stiff clay. Oak
trees grow well; and this year the wheat grows well, as it does upon all
45 the clays that I have seen. I have never seen the wheat better in general,
in this part of the country, than it is now. I have, I think, seen it heavier;
but never clearer from blight. It is backward compared to the wheat in
many other parts; some of it is quite green; but none of it has any
appearance of blight. This is not much of a barley country. The oats
50 are good. The beans that I have seen, very indifferent.

The best news that I have learnt here is, that the Botley Parson is
become quite a gentle creature, compared to what he used to be. The
people in the village have told me some most ridiculous stories, about
his having been hoaxed in London! It seems that somebody danced him
55 up from Botley to London, by telling him that a legacy had been left
him, or some such story. Up went the parson on horseback, being in
too great a hurry to run the risk of coach. The hoaxers, it appears, got
him to some hotel, and there set upon him a whole tribe of applicants,
wet-nurses, dry-nurses, lawyers with deeds of conveyance for borrowed
60 money, curates in want of churches, coffin-makers, travelling companions, ladies' maids, dealers in Yorkshire hams, Newcastle coals, and

---

turnpike-road a road gated to ensure that a toll is paid

dealers in dried night-soil at Islington. In short, if I am rightly informed,
they kept the parson in town for several days, bothered him three parts
out of his senses, compelled him to escape, as it were, from a fire; and
65   then, when he got home he found the village posted all over with
handbills giving an account of his adventure, under the pretence of
offering £500 reward, for a discovery of the hoaxers! The good of it
was, the parson ascribed his disgrace *to me*, and they say that he
perseveres to this hour in accusing me of it. Upon my word, I had
70   nothing to do with the matter, and this affair only shows that I am not
the only friend[†] that the Parson has in the world. Though this may
have had a tendency to produce in the Parson that amelioration[†] of
deportment which is said to become him so well, there is something
else that has taken place, which has, in all probability, had a more
75   powerful influence in this way; namely, a great reduction in the value
of the Parson's living, which was at one time little short of five hundred
pounds a year, and which, I believe, is now not the half of that sum!
This, to be sure, is not only a natural but a necessary consequence of
the change in the value of money. The parsons are neither more nor
80   less, than another sort of landlords. They must fall, of course, in their
demands, or their demands will not be paid. They may take in kind,
but that will answer them no purpose at all. They will be less people
than they have been, and will continue to grow less and less, until the
day when the whole of the tithes[†] and other Church property, as it is
85   called, shall be applied to public purposes.

1823   1830

I am . . . friend the statement is ironical   *tithes* church tax of one-tenth, usually payable
amelioration improvement   in kind

Maria Edgeworth
1768–1849

The chief influence on Maria Edgeworth's development derived from her father, an eccentric and radical landlord of a large and wealthy Irish estate. He was interested in scientific discovery and education and, while directing Maria's career and editing most of her writings, he passed on to her many of his enthusiasms.

She was noted in her own time particularly for *Letters to Literary Ladies* (1795), a progressive plea for women's education, and for popular stories and lessons for children, *The Parent's Assistant* (1796–1800), *Moral Tales* (1801), *Popular Tales* (1804), *Harry and Lucy Concluded* (1825). She met a number of famous literati, including Byron and Sydney Smith; she even visited Sir Walter Scott, an admirer of *Castle Rackrent* (1800), at Abbotsford.

Her father did not know she had written *Castle Rackrent*, and therefore was unable to edit it. It stands as the first important regional and historical novel, and survives as her best known work.

From CASTLE RACKRENT†

[Sir Condy's Generosity]

Things in a twelve-month or so came to such a pass, there was no making a shift to go on any longer, though we were all of us well enough used to live from hand to mouth at Castle Rackrent. One day, I remember, when there was a power of company, all sitting after dinner in the dusk, not to say dark, in the drawing-room, my lady having rung five times for candles and none to go up, the housekeeper sent up the footman, who went to my mistress and whispered behind her chair how it was. – 'My lady, (says he) there are no candles in the house.' – 'Bless me, (says she) then take a horse, and gallop off as fast as you can to Carrick O'Fungus and get some.' – 'And in the mean time tell them

---

Castle Rackrent The narrator's voice is that of Thady Quirk, steward to three generations of Rackrents on their Irish estate. The present owner of the Rackrent estate in this extract is Sir Condy who is lavish in his hospitality, exhausts the resources of Castle Rackrent, and wastes his inheritance

to step into the play-house, and try if there are not some bits left,' added Sir Condy, who happened to be within hearing. The man was sent up again to my lady, to let her know there was no horse to go but one that wanted a shoe. – 'Go to Sir Condy, then, I know nothing at all
15 about the horses, (said my lady) why do you plague me with these things?' – How it was settled I really forget, but to the best of my remembrance, the boy was sent down to my son Jason's to borrow candles for the night. Another time in the winter, and on a desperate cold day, there was no turf† in for the parlour and above stairs, and
20 scarce enough for the cook in the kitchen, the little *gossoon*† was sent off to the neighbours to see and beg or borrow some, but none could he bring back with him for love or money; so as needs must we were forced to trouble Sir Condy – 'Well, and if there's no turf to be had in the town or country, why what signifies talking any more about it,
25 can't ye go and cut down a tree?' – 'Which tree, please your honor?' I made bold to say. – 'Any tree at all that's good to burn, (said Sir Condy); send off smart, and get one down and the fires lighted before my lady gets up to breakfast, or the house will be too hot to hold us.' – He was always very considerate in all things about my lady, and she
30 wanted for nothing whilst he had it to give.

1800   1800

---

turf   fuel for fires

gossoon   from the French *garçon*. A servant-boy who mainly helped the cook and butler, and ran errands

James Hogg
1770–1835

James Hogg was a minor literary figure, a friend of Sir Walter Scott, who first came to prominence as a poet. He was born at Ettrick Forest and became known as the 'Ettrick Shepherd'. His first volume of ballads, *The Mountain Bard*, was published in 1807. He was attracted to Edinburgh in 1810, and the publication of his second volume of poetry, *The Queen's Wake* (1813), established his reputation as a poet.

He became a friend of Wordsworth, Byron and John Murray, and joined the editorial board of *Blackwood's Edinburgh Magazine*, in which the notorious *Chaldee MS* of 1817 was published. Written in biblical style, the manuscript records the conflict between publishers Blackwood and Constable: the latter owned the rival *Edinburgh Review*. The idea of the *Chaldee Manuscript* was Hogg's, but as he said, the 'devilry' in it was provided by two young literary blades, John Wilson and John Lockhart. Although *Blackwood's Magazine* was sued and had to pay damages, the resulting publicity increased the magazine's circulation and profits.

In 1816 Hogg removed from Edinburgh to a farm in Yarrow, where he divided his time between farming and writing. His most famous and important work is the novel *The Private Memoirs and Confessions of a Justified Sinner* (1824) a disturbing, macabre, psychological novel. In 1834 he published *The Domestic Manners and Private Life of Sir Walter Scott*. On his death, Wordsworth remembered him and paid tribute to him, in the poem 'Upon the death of James Hogg'.

From THE CONFESSIONS OF A JUSTIFIED SINNER†

[Colwan's Predicament]

Immediately after this I was seized with a strange distemper,† which
neither my friends nor physicians could comprehend, and it confined
me to my chamber for many days; but I knew, myself, that I was
bewitched, and suspected my father's reputed concubine† of the deed. I
5   told my fears to my reverend protector,† who hestitated concerning
them, but I knew by his words and looks that he was conscious I was
right. I generally conceived myself to be two people. When I lay in bed,
I deemed there were two of us in it; when I sat up I always beheld
another person, and always in the same position from the place where
10   I sat or stood, which was about three paces off me towards my left
side. It mattered not how many or how few were present: this my
second self was sure to be present in his place, and this occasioned a
confusion in all my words and ideas that utterly astounded my friends,
who all declared that, instead of being deranged in my intellect, they
15   had never heard my conversation manifest so much energy or sublimity
of conception; but, for all that, over the singular delusion that I was
two persons my reasoning faculties had no power. The most perverse
part of it was that I rarely conceived *myself* to be any of the two
persons. I thought for the most part that my companion was one of
20   them, and my brother the other; and I found that, to be obliged to
speak and answer in the character of another man, was a most awkward
business at the long run.

Who can doubt, from this statement, that I was bewitched, and that
my relatives were at the ground of it? The constant and unnatural
25   persuasion that I was my brother proved it to my own satisfaction, and
must, I think, do so to every unprejudiced person. This victory of the
Wicked One over me kept me confined in my chamber at Mr Millar's
house for nearly a month, until the prayers of the faithful prevailed,
and I was restored. I knew it was a chastisement for my pride, because
30   my heart was lifted up at my superiority over the enemies of the Church;
nevertheless I determined to make short work with the aggressor, that
the righteous might not be subjected to the effect of his diabolical arts
again.

Justified Sinner an extract from the memoir
of Colwan who believes himself to be 'saved'
according to the Calvinist doctrine of
predestination. He has fallen under the spell
of an evil stranger and is in process of
committing a series of horrific crimes

distemper an illness of body or mind
concubine a woman who co-habits with a man
  but who is not his wife
reverend protector his pastor, a 'faithful
  minister of the gospel', who had been his
  mother's early instructor

I say I was confined a month. I beg he that readeth to take note of
35 this, that he may estimate how much the word, or even the oath, of a
wicked man is to depend on. For a month I saw no one but such as
came into my room, and, for all that, it will be seen that there were
plenty of the same set to attest upon oath that I saw my brother every
day during this period; that I persecuted him with my presence day and
40 night, while all the time I never saw his face save in a delusive dream. I
cannot comprehend what manoeuvres my illustrious friend† was playing
off with them about this time; for he, having the art of personating
whom he chose, had peradventure deceived them, else many of them
had never all attested the same thing. I never saw any man so steady in
45 his friendships and attentions as he; but as he made a rule of never
calling at private houses, for fear of some discovery being made of his
person, so I never saw him while my malady lasted; but, as soon as I
grew better, I knew I had nothing ado but to attend at some of our
places of meeting to see him again. He was punctual, as usual, and I
50 had not to wait.

My reception was precisely as I apprehended. There was no flaring,
no flummery,† nor bombastical pretensions, but a dignified return to
my obeisance,† and an immediate recurrence, in converse, to the
important duties incumbent on us, in our stations, as reformers and
55 purifiers of the Church.

'I have marked out a number of most dangerous characters in this
city,' said he, 'all of whom must be cut off from cumbering the true
vineyard before we leave this land. And, if you bestir not yourself in
the work to which you are called, I must raise up others who shall have
60 the honour of it.'

'I am, most illustrious prince, wholly at your service,' said I. 'Show
but what ought to be done, and here is the heart to dare, and the hand
to execute. You pointed out my relations, according to the flesh, as
brands fitted to be thrown into the burning. I approve peremptorily of
65 the award; nay, I thirst to accomplish it; for I myself have suffered
severely from their diabolical arts. When once that trial of my devotion
to the faith is accomplished, then be your future operations disclosed.'

'You are free of your words and promises,' said he.

'So will I be of my deeds in the service of my master, and that shalt
70 thou see,' said I. 'I lack not the spirit, nor the will, but I lack experience
woefully; and, because of that shortcoming, must bow to your sugges-
tions.'

'Meet me here tomorrow betimes,' said he, 'and perhaps you may

---

illustrious friend   a malign stranger who
    becomes his friend: an 'alter ego' figure
    whom he grows to believe is the devil

flummery   insincere compliments
obeisance   bow, or salutation

hear of some opportunity of displaying your zeal in the cause of
75 righteousness.'
     I met him as he desired me; and he addressed me with a hurried and
joyful expression, telling me that my brother was astir, and that a few
minutes ago he had seen him pass on his way to the mountain. 'The
hill is wrapped in a cloud,' added he, 'and never was there such an
80 opportunity of executing divine justice on a guilty sinner. You may
trace him in the dew, and shall infallibly find him on the top of some
precipice; for it is only in secret that he dares show his debased head
to the sun.'
     'I have no arms, else assuredly I would pursue him and discomfit
85 him,' said I.
     'Here is a small dagger,' said he; 'I have nothing of weapon-kind
about me save that, but it is a potent one; and, should you require it,
there is nothing more ready or sure.'
     'Will not you accompany me?' said I. 'Sure you will?'
90   'I will be with you, or near you,' said he. 'Go you on before.'
     I hurried away as he directed me, and imprudently asked some of
Queensberry's guards if such and such a young man passed by them
going out from the city. I was answered in the affirmative, and till then
had doubted of my friend's intelligence, it was so inconsistent with a
95 profligate's life to be so early astir. When I got the certain intelligence
that my brother was before me, I fell a-running, scarcely knowing what
I did; and, looking several times behind me, I perceived nothing of my
zealous and arbitrary friend. The consequence of which was that, by
the time I reached St Anthony's well, my resolution began to give way.
100 It was not my courage, for, now that I had once shed blood in the cause
of the true faith, I was exceedingly bold and ardent, but, whenever I
was left to myself, I was subject to sinful doubtings. These always
hankered[†] on one point. I doubted if the elect were infallible, and if the
Scripture promises to them were binding in all situations and relations.
105 I confess this, and that it was a sinful and shameful weakness in me,
but my nature was subject to it, and I could not eschew[†] it. I never
doubted that I was one of the elect myself; for, beside the strong inward
and spiritual conviction that I possessed, I had my kind father's
assurance; and these had been revealed to him in that way and measure
110 that they could not be doubted.
     In this desponding state, I sat myself down on a stone, and bethought
me of the rashness of my undertaking. I tried to ascertain, to my own
satisfaction, whether or not I really had been commissioned of God to
perpetrate these crimes in His behalf, for, in the eyes and by the laws

hankered on   inclined towards with a sense of   *eschew*   avoid
          longing

115   of men, they were great and crying transgressions. While I sat pondering
on these things, I was involved in a veil of white misty vapour, and,
looking up to heaven, I was just about to ask direction from above,
when I heard as it were a still small voice close by me, which uttered
some words of derision and chiding. I looked intensely in the direction
120   whence it seemed to come, and perceived a lady robed in white, who
hastened towards me. She regarded me with a severity of look and
gesture that appalled me so much I could not address her; but she
waited not for that, but coming close to my side said, without stopping:
'Preposterous wretch! How dare you lift your eyes to Heaven with such
125   purposes in your heart? Escape homewards, and save your soul, or
farewell for ever!'

These were all the words that she uttered, as far as I could ever
recollect, but my spirits were kept in such a tumult that morning that
something might have escaped me. I followed her eagerly with my eyes,
130   but in a moment she glided over the rocks above the holy well, and
vanished. I persuaded myself that I had seen a vision, and that the
radiant being that had addressed me was one of the good angels, or
guardian spirits, commissioned by the Almighty to watch over the steps
of the just. My first impulse was to follow her advice, and make my
135   escape home; for I thought to myself: 'How is this interested and
mysterious foreigner a proper judge of the actions of a free Christian?'

1824   1824

William Wordsworth
1770–1850

Wordsworth is one of the greatest poets in the history of English literature, particularly noted for his long autobiographical poem, *The Prelude*, and famous as a sonneteer. Although the greatest poet of the first half of the nineteenth century he was Poet Laureate for only seven years, 1843–50, when he succeeded Southey who had held the position for thirty years.

Wordsworth was born at Cockermouth in Cumbria, and attended Hawkshead Grammar School and St John's College, Cambridge. A walking tour in France, and a year's residence there, 1791–2, gave him a passionate sympathy for the ideal of the French Revolution. He had an affair with Annette Vallon of Blois, who bore him a daughter.

In 1793 he published two poems in heroic couplets, *An Evening Walk* and *Descriptive Sketches*. The same year saw in him a gradual disillusionment with the ideals of the French Revolution as a direct result of the period of Terror.

In 1795, he received a legacy of £900 a year from his friend Raisley Calvert which enabled him to pursue his vocation as poet and he was able to reunite, and live, with his sister Dorothy. He moved firstly to Racedown in Dorset, and then to Alfoxden in Somerset, to be near Samuel Taylor Coleridge whom he had met and admired earlier, and who was living at Nether Stowey. Together they wrote poems for the *Lyrical Ballads* (1798). The volume is a cornerstone of English Romanticism, and its preface, composed by Wordsworth, is the movement's manifesto.

After a period spent in Germany, he moved to Home Cottage, Grasmere, in 1799, where he composed 'The Recluse', 'The Brothers' and 'Michael' which were included in the 1800 edition of *Lyrical Ballads*.

He returned to France in 1802, visited Annette Vallon and later that year married an old schoolfriend, Mary Hutchinson. He wrote 'Resolution and Independence' and 'Ode on Intimations of Immortality from Recollections of Early Childhood', which were published in *Poems in Two Volumes* (1807). These were years of estrangement from Coleridge, and although there was reconciliation, it was never complete. The years up to 1819 saw a succession of publications: *The*

Excursion (1814), *The White Doe of Rylestone* and two volumes of *Miscellaneous Poems* (1815), and *Peter Bell* and *The Waggoner* (1819). In 1808 he moved to Allan Bank, and finally in 1813 to Rydal Mount, Grasmere. He lived until 1850, and during the last thirty-five years of his life the writer who had been a political radical became a pillar of the establishment, orthodox, conservative, patriotic: it was fitting that he should end his life as Poet Laureate. His greatest achievement, *The Prelude*, was published posthumously in 1850.

From LYRICAL BALLADS, 1798

Lines†

COMPOSED A FEW MILES ABOVE TINTERN ABBEY, ON REVISITING THE BANKS
OF THE WYE DURING A TOUR. JULY 13, 1798

    Five years† have past; five summers, with the length
Of five long winters! and again I hear
These waters, rolling from their mountain-springs
With a soft inland murmur. – Once again
5 Do I behold these steep and lofty cliffs,
That on a wild secluded scene impress
Thoughts of more deep seclusion; and connect
The landscape with the quiet of the sky.
The day is come when I again repose
10 Here, under this dark sycamore, and view
These plots of cottage-ground, these orchard-tufts,
Which at this season, with their unripe fruits,
Are clad in one green hue, and lose themselves
'Mid groves and copses. Once again I see
15 These hedge-rows, hardly hedge-rows, little lines
Of sportive wood run wild: these pastoral farms,
Green to the very door; and wreaths of smoke
Sent up, in silence, from among the trees!
With some uncertain notice, as might seem

Lines Wordsworth wrote to Isabella Fenwick, 'I began it upon leaving Tintern after crossing the Wye, and concluded it just as I was entering Bristol in the evening, after a ramble of 4 or 5 days, with my sister. Not a line of it was altered, and not any part of it written down till I reached Bristol. It was published almost immediately after.' Tintern has a ruined abbey where the Cistercian monks had sought seclusion
Five years the five years since his previous visit had been years of political disillusion for Wordsworth

20   Of vagrant dwellers in the houseless woods,
      Or of some Hermit's cave, where by his fire
      The Hermit sits alone.
                    These beauteous forms,
      Through a long absence, have not been to me
      As is a landscape to a blind man's eye:
25   But oft, in lonely rooms, and 'mid the din
      Of towns and cities, I have owed to them
      In hours of weariness, sensations sweet,
      Felt in the blood, and felt along the heart;
      And passing even into my purer mind,
30   With tranquil restoration: – feelings too
      Of unremembered pleasure: such, perhaps,
      As have no slight or trivial influence
      On that best portion of a good man's life,
      His little, nameless, unremembered, acts
35   Of kindness and of love. Nor less, I trust,
      To them I may have owed another gift,
      Of aspect more sublime; that blessed mood
      In which the burden of the mystery,
      In which the heavy and the weary weight
40   Of all this unintelligible world,
      Is lightened: – that serene and blessed mood,
      In which the affections gently lead us on, –
      Until, the breath of this corporeal frame†
      And even the motion of our human blood
45   Almost suspended, we are laid asleep
      In body, and become a living soul:
      While with an eye made quiet by the power
      Of harmony, and the deep power of joy,
      We see into the life of things.
                        If this
50   Be but a vain belief, yet, oh! how oft –
      In darkness and amid the many shapes
      Of joyless daylight; when the fretful stir
      Unprofitable, and the fever of the world,
      Have hung upon the beatings of my heart –
55   How oft, in spirit, have I turned to thee,
      O sylvan Wye! thou wanderer thro' the woods,
      How often has my spirit turned to thee!

      And now, with gleams of half-extinguished thought,

---

corporeal frame human body

With many recognitions dim and faint,
60   And somewhat of a sad perplexity,
The picture of the mind revives again:
While here I stand, not only with the sense
Of present pleasure, but with pleasing thoughts
That in this moment there is life and food
65   For future years. And so I dare to hope,
Though changed, no doubt, from what I was when first
I came among these hills; when like a roe
I bounded o'er the mountains, by the sides
Of the deep rivers, and the lonely streams,
70   Wherever nature led: more like a man
Flying from something that he dreads than one
Who sought the thing he loved. For nature then
(The coarser pleasures of my boyish days,
And their glad animal movements all gone by)
75   To me was all in all. – I cannot paint
What then I was. The sounding cataract
Haunted me like a passion: the tall rock,
The mountain, and the deep and gloomy wood,
Their colours and their forms, were then to me
80   An appetite; a feeling and a love,
That had no need of a remoter charm,
By thought supplied nor any interest
Unborrowed from the eye. – That time is past,
And all its aching joys are now no more,
85   And all its dizzy raptures. Not for this
Faint I, nor mourn nor murmur; other gifts
Have followed; for such loss, I would believe,
Abundant recompense. For I have learned
To look on nature, not as in the hour
90   Of thoughtless youth; but hearing oftentimes
The still, sad music of humanity,
Nor harsh nor grating, though of ample power
To chasten and subdue. And I have felt
A presence that disturbs me with the joy
95   Of elevated thoughts; a sense sublime
Of something far more deeply interfused*   mixed
Whose dwelling is the light of setting suns,
And the round ocean and the living air,
And the blue sky, and in the mind of man:
100   A motion and a spirit, that impels
All thinking things, all objects of all thought,
And rolls through all things. Therefore am I still

A lover of the meadows and the woods,
And mountains; and of all that we behold
105   From this green earth; of all the mighty world
Of eye, and ear, – both what they half create,
And what perceive; well pleased to recognise
In nature and the language of the sense
The anchor of my purest thoughts, the nurse,
110   The guide, the guardian of my heart, and soul
Of all my moral being.
                                    Nor perchance,
If I were not thus taught, should I the more
Suffer my genial† spirits to decay:
For thou art with me here upon the banks
115   Of this fair river; thou my dearest Friend,†
My dear, dear Friend; and in thy voice I catch
The language of my former heart, and read
My former pleasures in the shooting lights
Of thy wild eyes. Oh! yet a little while
120   May I behold in thee what I was once,
My dear, dear Sister! and this prayer I make,
Knowing that Nature never did betray
The heart that loved her; 'tis her privilege,
Through all the years of this our life, to lead
125   From joy to joy: for she can so inform
The mind that is within us, so impress
With quietness and beauty, and so feed
With lofty thoughts, that neither evil tongues,
Rash judgments, nor the sneers of selfish men,
130   Nor greetings where no kindness is, nor all
The dreary intercourse† of daily life,
Shall e'er prevail against us, or disturb
Our cheerful faith, that all which we behold
Is full of blessings. Therefore let the moon
135   Shine on thee in thy solitary walk;
And let the misty mountain-winds be free
To blow against thee: and, in after years,
When these wild ecstasies shall be matured
Into a sober pleasure; when thy mind
140   Shall be a mansion for all lovely forms,
Thy memory be as a dwelling-place
For all sweet sounds and harmonies; oh! then,

---

genial   enlivening, kindly   *intercourse*   social communication or business
Friend   his sister, Dorothy

If solitude, or fear, or pain, or grief,
Should be thy portion, with what healing thoughts
145 Of tender joy wilt thou remember me
And these my exhortations! Nor, perchance –
If I should be where I no more can hear
Thy voice, nor catch from thy wild eyes these gleams
Of past existence – wilt thou then forget
150 That on the banks of this delightful stream
We stood together; and that I, so long
A worshipper of Nature, hither came
Unwearied in that service: rather say
With warmer love – oh! with far deeper zeal
155 Of holier love. Nor wilt thou then forget,
That after many wanderings, many years
Of absence, these steep woods and lofty cliffs,
And this green pastoral landscape, were to me
More dear, both for themselves and for thy sake!

1798   1798

From LYRICAL BALLADS, Volume II, 1800

She dwelt among the untrodden ways
   Beside the springs of Dove,†
A Maid whom there were none to praise
   And very few to love:

5 A violet by a mossy stone
   Half hidden from the eye!
– Fair as a star, when only one
   Is shining in the sky.

She lived unknown, and few could know
10   When Lucy† ceased to be;
But she is in her grave, and, oh,
   The difference to me!

1799   1800

Dove a river in Cumbria
Lucy there has been much speculation about

her identity, but to no effect. It is a common
name in eighteenth-century pastoral ballads

A slumber did my spirit seal;
   I had no human fears:
She seemed a thing that could not feel
   The touch of earthly years.

5   No motion has she now, no force;
   She neither hears nor sees;
Rolled round in earth's diurnal* course,   daily
   With rocks, and stones, and trees.

1799   1800

COMPOSED UPON WESTMINSTER BRIDGE, SEPTEMBER 3, 1802

Earth has not anything to show more fair:
Dull would he be of soul who could pass by
A sight so touching in its majesty:
This City now doth, like a garment, wear
5   The beauty of the morning; silent, bare,
Ships, towers, domes, theatres, and temples lie
Open unto the fields, and to the sky;
All bright and glittering in the smokeless air.
Never did sun more beautifully steep
10   In his first splendour, valley, rock, or hill;
Ne'er saw I, never felt, a calm so deep!
The river glideth at his own sweet will:
Dear God! the very houses seem asleep;
And all that mighty heart is lying still!

1802   1807

I WANDERED LONELY AS A CLOUD

I wandered lonely as a cloud†
That floats on high o'er vales and hills,
When all at once I saw a crowd,
A host, of golden daffodils;

I wandered lonely as a cloud   this poem might   extract from Dorothy Wordsworth's *Journal*
be read in association with the following

5   Beside the lake, beneath the trees,
      Fluttering and dancing in the breeze.

      Continuous as the stars that shine
      And twinkle on the milky way,
      They stretched in never-ending line
10   Along the margin of a bay:
      Ten thousand saw I at a glance,
      Tossing their heads in sprightly dance.

      The waves beside them danced; but they
      Out-did the sparkling waves in glee:
15   A poet could not but be gay,
      In such a jocund[†] company:
      I gazed – and gazed – but little thought
      What wealth the show to me had brought:

      For oft, when on my couch I lie
20   In vacant or in pensive mood,
      They flash upon that inward eye
      Which is the bliss of solitude;
      And then my heart with pleasure fills,
      And dances with the daffodils.

1802   1807

From DOROTHY WORDSWORTH'S JOURNAL

[Daffodils]

[April] 15th. *Thursday* [1802]. It was a threatening, misty morning, but mild. We set off after dinner from Eusemere. Mrs. Clarkson went a short way with us, but turned back. The wind was furious, and we thought we must have returned. We first rested in the large Boat-house,
5   then under a furze[†] bush opposite Mr. Clarkson's. Saw the plough going in the field. The wind seized our breath. The Lake was rough. There was a Boat by itself floating in the middle of the Bay below Water

---

jocund happy, merry
furze gorse: spiny yellow-flowered, evergreen bush

Millock. We rested again in the Water Millock Lane. The hawthorns
are black and green, the birches here and there greenish, but there is
10 yet more of purple to be seen on the twigs. We got over into a field to
avoid some cows – people working. A few primroses by the roadside –
woodsorrel flower, the anemone, scentless violets, strawberries, and
that starry, yellow flower which Mrs C. calls pile wort. When we were
in the woods beyond Gowbarrow park we saw a few daffodils close to
15 the water-side. We fancied that the lake had floated the seeds ashore,
and that the little colony had so sprung up. But as we went along there
were more and yet more; and at last, under the boughs of the trees, we
saw that there was a long belt of them along the shore, about the
breadth of a country turnpike road. I never saw daffodils so beautiful.
20 They grew among the mossy stones about and about them; some rested
their heads upon these stones as on a pillow for weariness; and the rest
tossed and reeled and danced, and seemed as if they verily laughed with
the wind, that blew upon them over the lake; they looked so gay, ever
glancing, ever changing. This wind blew directly over the lake to them.
25 There was here and there a little knot, and a few stragglers a few yards
higher up; but they were so few as not to disturb the simplicity, unity,
and life of that one busy highway. We rested again and again. The bays
were stormy, and we heard the waves at different distances, and in the
middle of the water, like the sea. Rain came in – we were wet when we
30 reached Luff's, but we called in. Luckily all was cheerless and gloomy,
so we faced the storm – we *must* have been wet if we had waited – put
on dry clothes at Dobson's. I was very kindly treated by a young
woman, the Landlady looked sour, but it is her way. She gave us a
goodish supper, excellent ham and potatoes. We paid 7/-† when we
35 came away. William was sitting by a bright fire when I came downstairs.
He soon made his way to the library, piled up in a corner of the
window. He brought out a volume of Enfield's *Speaker*, another
miscellany, and an odd volume of Congreve's plays. We had a glass of
warm rum and water. We enjoyed ourselves, and wished for Mary.† It
40 rained and blew when we went to bed. N.B. Deer in Gowbarrow park
like skeletons.

From POEMS 1807

My heart leaps up when I behold
    A rainbow in the sky:

7/-   seven shillings (old currency)   *Mary*   Mary (Hutchinson), Wordsworth's wife

So was it when my life began;
So is it now I am a man;
5 So be it when I shall grow old,
    Or let me die!
The Child is father of the Man;
And I could wish my days to be
Bound each to each by natural piety.

1802   1807

ODE: INTIMATIONS OF IMMORTALITY FROM RECOLLECTIONS OF EARLY CHILDHOOD

The Child is father of the Man;
And I could wish my days to be
Bound each to each by natural piety.

I

There was a time when meadow, grove, and stream,
The earth, and every common sight,
    To me did seem
    Apparelled in celestial light,
5 The glory and the freshness of a dream.
It is not now as it hath been of yore; –
    Turn wheresoe'er I may,
    By night or day,
The things which I have seen I now can see no more.

II

10   The Rainbow comes and goes,
    And lovely is the Rose,
    The Moon doth with delight
Look round her when the heavens are bare;
    Waters on a starry night
15   Are beautiful and fair;
    The sunshine is a glorious birth;
    But yet I know, where'er I go,
That there hath past away a glory from the earth.

III

Now, while the birds thus sing a joyous song,
20   And while the young lambs bound
            As to the tabor's† sound,
To me alone there came a thought of grief:
A timely utterance† gave that thought relief,
            And I again am strong:
25   The cataracts* blow their trumpets from the steep;   waterfalls
No more shall grief of mine the season wrong;
I hear the Echoes through the mountains throng,
The Winds come to me from the fields of sleep,
            And all the earth is gay;
30   Land and sea
            Give themselves up to jollity,
            And with the heart of May
            Doth every Beast keep holiday; –
            Thou Child of Joy,
35   Shout round me, let me hear thy shouts, thou happy Shepherd-boy!

IV

Ye blessèd Creatures, I have heard the call
      Ye to each other make; I see
The heavens laugh with you in your jubilee;
      My heart is at your festival,
40   My head hath its coronal,†
The fulness of your bliss, I feel – I feel it all.
            Oh evil day! if I were sullen
            While Earth herself is adorning,
            This sweet May-morning,
45   And the Children are culling*   picking
                  On every side,
            In a thousand valleys far and wide,
            Fresh flowers; while the sun shines warm,
And the Babe leaps up on his Mother's arm: –
50   I hear, I hear, with joy I hear!
            – But there's a Tree, of many, one,
A single Field which I have looked upon,
Both of them speak of something that is gone:
            The Pansy at my feet
55   Doth the same tale repeat:
Whither is fled the visionary gleam?
Where is it now, the glory and the dream?

---

tabor a small drum, especially one that
   accompanies the pipe

A timely utterance possibly the preceding
      poem, 'My heart leaps up'
   coronal wreath, garland

V

Our birth is but a sleep and forgetting:
The Soul that rises with us, our life's Star,
60   Hath had elsewhere its setting,
               And cometh from afar:
          Not in entire forgetfulness,
          And not in utter nakedness,
But trailing clouds of glory do we come
65   From God, who is our home:

Heaven lies about us in our infancy!
Shades of the prison-house† begin to close
               Upon the growing Boy,
                    But He
70   Beholds the light, and whence it flows,
               He sees it in his joy;
The Youth, who daily farther from the east
          Must travel, still is Nature's Priest,
          And by the vision splendid
75   Is on his way attended;
At length the Man perceives it die away,
And fade into the light of common day.

VI

Earth fills her lap with pleasures of her own;
Yearnings she hath in her own natural kind,
80   And, even with something of a Mother's mind,
               And no unworthy aim,
          The homely Nurse doth all she can
To make her Foster-child, her Inmate Man,
          Forget the glories he hath known,
85   And that imperial palace* whence he came.   heaven

VII

Behold the Child among his new-born blisses,
A six years' Darling† of a pigmy size!
See, where 'mid work of his own hand he lies,
Fretted by sallies† of his mother's kisses,
90   With light upon him from his father's eyes!

Shades . . . prison-house as the boy grows up,
   experience encroaches upon innocence

A six years' Darling Wordsworth's thought is
      of Coleridge's son, Hartley
   sallies outbursts, attacks

See, at his feet, some little plan or chart,
Some fragment from his dream of human life,
Shaped by himself with newly-learned art;
    A wedding or a festival,
95   A mourning or a funeral;
    And this hath now his heart,
And unto this he frames his song:
    Then will be fit his tongue
To dialogues of business, love, or strife;
100   But it will not be long
    Ere this be thrown aside,
    And with new joy and pride
The little Actor cons† another part;
Filling from time to time his 'humorous stage'†
105   With all the Persons, down to palsied Age,
That Life brings with her in her equipage;†
    As if his whole vocation
    Were endless imitation.

VIII

Thou, whose exterior semblance doth belie
110   Thy Soul's immensity;
Thou best Philosopher, who yet dost keep
Thy heritage, thou Eye among the blind,
That, deaf and silent, read'st the eternal deep,
Haunted for ever by the eternal mind, –
115   Mighty Prophet! Seer* blest!   prophet
    On whom those truths do rest,
Which we are toiling all our lives to find,
In darkness lost, the darkness of the grave;
Thou, over whom thy Immortality
120   Broods like the Day, a Master o'er a Slave,
A Presence which is not to be put by;
Thou little Child, yet glorious in the might
Of heaven-born freedom on thy being's height.
Why with such earnest pains dost thou provoke
125   The years to bring the inevitable yoke,
Thus blindly with thy blessedness at strife?
Full soon thy Soul shall have her earthly freight,
And custom lie upon thee with a weight,
Heavy as frost, and deep almost as life!

---

cons learns by heart   *As You Like It*, II. 7; Jaques' speech
'humorous stage' reference to Shakespeare's   *equipage* requisites for a journey

IX

130 O joy! that is our embers
  Is something that doth live,
  That nature yet remembers
  What was so fugitive!
The thought of our past years in me doth breed
135 Perpetual benediction:[†] not indeed
For that which is most worthy to be blest;
Delight and liberty, the simple creed
Of Childhood, whether busy or at rest,
With new-fledged hope still fluttering in his breast: –
140   Not for these I raise
    The song of thanks and praise;
  But for those obstinate questionings
  Of sense and outward things,
  Fallings from us, vanishings;
145 Blank misgivings of a Creature
Moving about in worlds not realised,
High instincts before which our mortal Nature
Did tremble like a guilty Thing surprised:
   But for those first affections,
150   Those shadowy recollections,
   Which, be they what they may,
Are yet the fountain light of all our day,
Are yet a master light of all our seeing;
  Uphold us, cherish, and have power to make
155 Our noisy years seem moments in the being
Of the eternal Silence: truths that wake,
    To perish never;
Which neither listlessness, nor mad endeavour,
    Nor Man nor Boy,
160 Nor all that is at enmity with joy,
Can utterly abolish or destroy!
    Hence in a season of calm weather
    Though inland far we be,
Our Souls have sight of that immortal sea
165   Which brought us hither,
   Can in a moment travel thither,
And see the Children sport upon the shore,
And hear the mighty waters rolling evermore.

---

benediction utterance of a blessing

X

Then sing, ye Birds, sing, sing a joyous song!
170   And let the young Lambs bound
     As to the tabor's sound!
We in thought will join your throng,
     Ye that pipe and ye that play,
     Ye that through your hearts to-day
175   Feel the gladness of the May!
What though the radiance which was once so bright
Be now for ever taken from my sight,
     Though nothing can bring back the hour
Of splendour in the grass, of glory in the flower;
180   We will grieve not, rather find
     Strength in what remains behind;
     In the primal sympathy†
     Which having been must ever be;
     In the soothing thoughts that spring
185   Out of human suffering;
     In the faith that looks through death,
In years that bring the philosophic mind.

XI

And O, ye Fountains, Meadows, Hills, and Groves,
Forebode not any severing of our loves!
190 Yet in my heart of hearts I feel your might;
I only have relinquished one delight
To live beneath your more habitual sway.
I love the Brooks which down their channels fret,
Even more than when I tripped lightly as they;
195 The innocent brightness of a new-born Day
     Is lovely yet;
The Clouds that gather round the setting sun
Do take a sober colouring from an eye
That hath kept watch o'er man's mortality;
200 Another race hath been, and other palms are won.
Thanks to the human heart by which we live,
Thanks to its tenderness, its joys, and fears,
To me the meanest flower that blows can give
Thoughts that do often lie too deep for tears.

1802–4   1807

primal sympathy   first, early state of sharing
experience with nature

NUNS FRET NOT

Nuns fret not at their convent's narrow room;
And hermits are contented with their cells;
And students with their pensive citadels;
Maids at the wheel, the weaver at his loom,
5   Sit blithe* and happy; bees that soar for bloom,   joyful
High as the highest Peak of Furness-fells,
Will murmur by the hour in foxglove bells:
In truth the prison, unto which we doom
Ourselves, no prison is: and hence for me,
10   In sundry moods, 'twas pastime to be bound
Within the Sonnet's scanty plot of ground;
Pleased if some Souls (for such there needs must be)
Who have felt the weight of too much liberty,
Should find brief solace there, as I have found.

1806   1807

SHE WAS A PHANTOM OF DELIGHT

She was a Phantom of delight†
When first she gleamed upon my sight;
A lovely Apparition, sent
To be a moment's ornament;
5   Her eyes as stars of Twilight fair;
Like Twilight's too, her dusky hair;
But all things else about her drawn
From May-time and the cheerful Dawn;
A dancing Shape, an Image gay,
10   To haunt, to startle, and way-lay.

I saw her upon nearer view,
A Spirit, yet a Woman too!
Her household motions light and free,
And steps of virgin-liberty;
15   A countenance in which did meet
Sweet records, promises as sweet;
A Creature not too bright or good
For human nature's daily food;
For transient† sorrows, simple wiles,
20   Praise, blame, love, kisses, tears, and smiles.

She was a Phantom of delight   written as a
tribute to his wife, Mary

transient   impermanent, passing

And now I see with eye serene
The very pulse of the machine;
A Being breathing thoughtful breath,
A Traveller between life and death;
25   The reason firm, the temperate will,
Endurance, foresight, strength, and skill;
A perfect Woman, nobly planned,
To warn, to comfort, and command;
And yet a Spirit still, and bright
30   With something of angelic light.

1804   1807

From THE PRELUDE, Book I

Fair seed-time had my soul, and I grew up
Fostered alike by beauty and by fear:
Much favoured in my birth-place, and no less
In that beloved Vale to which erelong
305   We were transplanted† – there were we let loose
For sports of wider range. Ere I had told†
Ten birth-days, when among the mountain slopes
Frost, and the breath of frosty wind, had snapped
The last autumnal crocus, 'twas my joy
310   With store of springes† o'er my shoulder hung
To range the open heights where woodcocks ran
Along the smooth green turf. Through half the night,
Scudding away from snare to snare, I plied
That anxious visitation, – moon and stars
315   Were shining o'er my head. I was alone,
And seemed to be a trouble to the peace
That dwelt among them. Sometimes it befel
In these night wanderings, that a strong desire
O'erpowered my better reason, and the bird
320   Which was the captive of another's toil†
Became my prey; and when the deed was done
I heard among the solitary hills

---

transplanted   the experiences that follow relate
to the time when Wordsworth was
'transplanted' to board at Hawkshead
Grammar School

told   counted
springes   snares
toil   snare or labour

Low breathing coming after me, and sounds
Of undistinguishable motion, steps
325   Almost as silent as the turf they trod.

    Nor less when spring had warmed the cultured Vale,[†]
Roved we as plunderers where the mother-bird
Had in high places built her lodge; though mean
Our object and inglorious, yet the end
330   Was not ignoble. Oh! when I have hung
Above the raven's nest, by knots of grass
And half-inch fissures in the slippery rock
But ill-sustained, and almost (so it seemed)
Suspended by the blast that blew amain,
335   Shouldering the naked crag, oh, at that time
While on the perilous ridge I hung alone,
With what strange utterance did the loud dry wind
Blow through my ear! the sky seemed not a sky
Of earth – and with what motion moved the clouds!

340   Dust as we are, the immortal spirit grows
Like harmony in music; there is a dark
Inscrutable* workmanship that reconciles   mysterious
Discordant elements, makes them cling together
In one society. How strange that all
345   The terrors, pains, and early miseries,
Regrets, vexations, lassitudes* interfused   weariness
Within my mind, should e'er have borne a part,
And that a needful part, in making up
The calm existence that is mine when I
350   Am worthy of myself! Praise to the end![†]
Thanks to the means which Nature deigned[†] to employ;
Whether her fearless visitings, or those
That came with soft alarm, like hurtless light
Opening the peaceful clouds; or she may use
355   Severer interventions, ministry
More palpable[†] as best might suit her aim.

    One summer evening (led by her*) I found   Nature
A little boat tied to a willow tree
Within a rocky cave, its usual home.
360   Straight I unloosed her chain, and stepping in
Pushed from the shore. It was an act of stealth

---

cultured Vale   that part of the valley which
  had been cultivated
Praise to the end   'Let us give praise to the

purpose of life'
deigned   thought fit, condescended
palpable   readily felt

And troubled pleasure, nor without the voice
Of mountain-echoes did my boat move on;
Leaving behind her still, on either side,
365   Small circles glittering idly in the moon,
Until they melted all into one track
Of sparkling light. But now, like one who rows,
Proud of his skill, to reach a chosen point
With an unswerving line, I fixed my view
370   Upon the summit of a craggy ridge,
The horizon's utmost boundary; for above
Was nothing but the stars and the grey sky.
She was an elfin pinnace;[†] lustily
I dipped my oars into the silent lake,
375   And, as I rose upon the stroke, my boat
Went heaving through the water like a swan;
When, from behind that craggy steep till then
The horizon's bound, a huge peak,[†] black and huge,
As if with voluntary power instinct
380   Upreared its head. I struck and struck again,
And growing still in stature the grim shape
Towered up between me and the stars, and still,
For so it seemed, with purpose of its own
And measured motion like a living thing,
385   Strode after me. With trembling oars I turned,
And through the silent water stole my way
Back to the covert* of the willow tree;   shelter
There in her mooring-place I left my bark,* –   boat
And through the meadows homeward went, in grave
390   And serious mood; but after I had seen
That spectacle, for many days, my brain
Worked with a dim and undetermined sense
Of unknown modes of being; o'er my thoughts
There hung a darkness, call it solitude
395   Or blank desertion. No familiar shapes
Remained, no pleasant images of trees,
Of sea or sky, no colours of green fields;
But huge and mighty forms, that do not live
Like living men, moved slowly through the mind
400   By day, and were a trouble to my dreams.

Wisdom and Spirit of the universe!
Thou Soul that art the eternity of thought,
That givest to forms and images a breath

---

pinnace small rowing-boat   *peak* probably Black Crag, west of Ullswater

And everlasting motion, not in vain
405 By day or star-light thus from my first dawn
Of childhood didst thou intwine for me
The passions that build up our human soul;
Not with the mean and vulgar* works of man,   ordinary
But with high objects, with enduring things –
410 With life and nature, purifying thus
The elements of feeling and of thought,
And sanctifying, by such discipline,
Both pain and fear, until we recognise
A grandeur in the beatings of the heart.
415 Nor was this fellowship vouchsafed to me
With stinted kindness. In November days,
When vapours rolling down the valley made
A lonely scene more lonesome, among woods
At noon, and 'mid the calm of summer nights,
420 When, by the margin of the trembling lake,
Beneath the gloomy hills homeward I went
In solitude, such intercourse* was mine;   communion
Mine was it in the fields both day and night,
And by the waters, all the summer long.

425   And in the frosty season, when the sun
Was set, and visible for many a mile
The cottage windows blazed through twilight gloom,
I heeded not their summons: happy time
It was indeed for all of us – for me
430 It was a time of rapture! Clear and loud
The village clock tolled six, – I wheeled about,
Proud and exulting like an untired horse
That cares not for his home. All shod with steel,
We hissed along the polished ice in games
435 Confederate,† imitative of the chase
And woodland pleasures, – the resounding horn,
The pack loud chiming, and the hunted hare.
So through the darkness and the cold we flew,
And not a voice was idle; with the din
440 Smitten, the precipices rang aloud;
The leafless trees and every icy crag
Tinkled like iron; while far distant hills
Into the tumult sent an alien sound
Of melancholy not unnoticed, while the stars

confederate agreed upon

445   Eastward were sparkling clear, and in the west
    The orange sky of evening died away.
    Not seldom from the uproar I retired
    Into a silent bay, or sportively
    Glanced sideway, leaving the tumultuous throng,
450   To cut across the reflex* of a star   reflection
    That fled, and, flying still before me, gleamed
    Upon the glassy plain; and oftentimes,
    When we had given our bodies to the wind,
    And all the shadowy banks on either side
455   Came sweeping through the darkness, spinning still
    The rapid line of motion, then at once
    Have I, reclining back upon my heels,
    Stopped short; yet still the solitary cliffs
    Wheeled by me – even as if the earth had rolled
460   With visible motion her diurnal* round!   daily
    Behind me did they stretch in solemn train,*   sequence
    Feebler and feebler, and I stood and watched
    Till all was tranquil as a dreamless sleep.

      Ye Presences of Nature in the sky
465   And on the earth! Ye Visions of the hills!
    And Souls of lonely places! can I think
    A vulgar* hope was yours when ye employed   common
    Such ministry, when ye through many a year
    Haunting me thus among my boyish sports,
470   On caves and trees, upon the woods and hills,
    Impressed upon all forms the characters†
    Of danger or desire; and thus did make
    The surface of the universal earth
    With triumph and delight, with hope and fear,
475   Work† like a sea?
             Not uselessly employed,
    Might I pursue this theme through every change
    Of exercise and play, to which the year
    Did summon us in his delightful round.

      We were a noisy crew; the sun in heaven
480   Beheld not vales more beautiful than ours;
    Nor saw a band in happiness and joy
    Richer, or worthier of the ground they trod.
    I could record with no reluctant voice

---

characters marks, signs   *work* move restlessly

The woods of autumn, and their hazel bowers
485   With milk-white clusters hung; the rod and line,
True symbol of hope's foolishness, whose strong
And unreproved enchantment led us on
By rocks and pools shut out from every star,
All the green summer, to forlorn cascades
490   Among the windings hid of mountain brooks
– Unfading recollections! at this hour
The heart is almost mine with which I felt,
From some hill-top of sunny afternoons,
The paper kite high among fleecy clouds
495   Pull at her rein like an impetuous courser;
Or, from the meadows sent on gusty days,
Beheld her breast the wind, then suddenly
Dashed headlong, and rejected by the storm.

From THE PRELUDE, Book II

Our daily meals were frugal† Sabine fare!†
More than we wished we knew the blessing then
80   Of vigorous hunger – hence corporeal* strength   bodily
Unsapped by delicate viands† for, exclude
A little weekly stipend,* and we lived   pocket-money
Through three divisions of the quartered year
In penniless poverty. But now to school
85   From the half-yearly holidays returned,
We came with weightier purses, that sufficed
To furnish treats more costly than the Dame†
Of the old grey stone, from her scant board, supplied.
Hence rustic dinners on the cool green ground,
90   Or in the woods, or by a river side
Or shady fountains,† while among the leaves
Soft airs were stirring, and the mid-day sun
Unfelt shone brightly round us in our joy.
Nor is my aim neglected if I tell
95   How sometimes, in the length of those half-years,
We from our funds drew largely; – proud to curb,

---

frugal sparing, economical
Sabine fare the Roman poet, Horace, led a
   frugal existence on his Sabine farm

viands articles of food
Dame the school Dame, or Matron
fountains springs or streams

And eager to spur on, the galloping steed;
And with the cautious inn-keeper, whose stud[†]
Supplied our want, we haply might employ
100   Sly subterfuges,[†] if the adventure's bound*   limit
Were distant: some framed temple[†] where of yore
The Druids worshipped, or the antique walls
Of that large abbey[†] where within the Vale
Of Nightshade, to St Mary's honour built,
105   Stands yet a mouldering pile with fractured arch,
Belfry, and images, and living trees,
A holy scene! Along the smooth green turf
Our horses grazed. To more than inland peace
Left by the west wind sweeping overhead
110   From a tumultuous ocean, trees and towers
In that sequestered valley may be seen,
Both silent and both motionless alike;
Such the deep shelter that is there, and such
The safeguard for repose and quietness.

115   Our steeds remounted and the summons given,
With a whip and spur we through the chauntry[†] flew
In uncouth[†] race, and left the cross-legged knight,
And the stone-abbot, and that single wren
Which one day sang so sweetly in the nave
120   Of the old church, that – though from recent showers
The earth was comfortless, and touched by faint
Internal breezes, sobbings of the place
And respirations from the roofless walls
The shuddering ivy dripped large drops – yet still
125   So sweetly 'mid the gloom the invisible bird
Sang to herself, that there I could have made
My dwelling-place, and lived for ever there
To hear such music. Through the walls we flew
And down the valley, and, a circuit made
130   In wantonness of heart, through rough and smooth
We scampered homewards. Oh, ye rocks and streams,
And that still spirit shed from evening air!
Even in this joyous time I sometimes felt
Your presence, when with slackened step we breathed[†]

---

stud   number of horses kept for breeding,
coaching, hunting etc.
subterfuges   misleading arguments
temple   stone temple at Swinside, west of
Duddon Bridge, mistakenly associated with
the Druids

abbey   Furness Abbey
chauntry   a chapel endowed for priests to sing
masses for the founder's soul
uncouth   uncivilised, clumsy
breathed   allowed our horses to get their breath
back

135   Along the sides of the steep hills, or when
       Lighted by gleams of moonlight from the sea
       We beat with thundering hoofs the level sand.[†]

       Midway on long Winander's[†] eastern shore,
       Within the crescent of a pleasant bay,
140   A tavern[†] stood; no homely-featured house,
       Primeval* like its neighbouring cottages,   ancient
       But 'twas a splendid place, the door beset
       With chaises,[†] grooms, and liveries, and within
       Decanters, glasses, and the blood-red wine.
145   In ancient times, or ere the Hall[†] was built
       On the large island, had this dwelling been
       More worthy of a poet's love, a hut
       Proud of its one bright fire and sycamore shade.
       But – though the rhymes were gone that once inscribed
150   The threshold, and large golden characters,*   letters
       Spread o'er the spangled sign-board, had dislodged
       The old Lion and usurped his place, in slight
       And mockery of the rustic painter's hand –
       Yet, to this hour, the spot to me is dear
155   With all its foolish pomp. The garden lay
       Upon a slope surmounted by the plain
       Of a small bowling-green; beneath us stood
       A grove, with gleams of water through the trees
       And over the tree-tops; nor did we want
160   Refreshment, strawberries and mellow cream.
       There, while through half an afternoon we played
       On the smooth platform, whether skill prevailed
       Or happy blunder triumphed, bursts of glee
       Made all the mountains ring. But, ere night-fall,
165   When in our pinnace[†] we returned at leisure
       Over the shadowy lake, and to the beach
       Of some small island steered our course with one,
       The Minstrel[†] of the Troop, and left him there,
       And rowed off gently, while he blew his flute
170   Alone upon the rock – oh, then, the calm
       And dead still water lay upon my mind
       Even with a weight of pleasure, and the sky,
       Never before so beautiful, sank down

---

level sand Levens Sands
Winander one of the Cumbrian lakes
tavern the White Lion at Bowness
chaises light, four-wheeled horse-carriages

Hall the hall of Belle Isle on Windermere
pinnace small rowing-boat
The Minstrel Robert Greenwood, later Senior
    Fellow of Trinity College, Cambridge

Into my heart, and held me like a dream!
175   Thus were my sympathies enlarged, and thus
Daily the common range of visible things
Grew dear to me: already I began
To love the sun; a boy I loved the sun,
Not as I since have loved him, as a pledge
180   And surety of our earthly life, a light
Which we behold and feel we are alive;
Nor for his bounty to so many worlds –
But for this cause, that I had seen him lay
His beauty on the morning hills, and seen
185   The western mountains touch his setting orb,
In many a thoughtless hour, when, from excess
Of happiness, my blood appeared to flow
For its own pleasure, and I breathed with joy.
And, from like feelings, humble though intense,
190   To patriotic and domestic love
Analogous, the moon to me was dear;
For I would dream away my purposes,
Standing to gaze upon her while she hung
Midway between the hills, as if she knew
195   No other region, but belonged to thee,
Yea, appertained by a peculiar right
To thee and my grey huts,† thou one dear Vale!

Those incidental charms which first attached
My heart to rural objects, day by day
200   Grew weaker, and I hasten on to tell
How Nature, intervenient† till this time
And secondary, now at length was sought
For her own sake. But who shall parcel out
His intellect by geometric rules,
205   Split like a province into round and square?
Who knows the individual hour in which
His habits were first sown, even as a seed?
Who that shall point as with a wand and say
'This portion of the river of my mind
210   Came from yon fountain?' Thou, my Friend!† art one
More deeply read in thy own thoughts; to thee
Science appears but what in truth she is,
Not as our glory and our absolute boast,

---

grey huts   cottages built of local gray stone   *Friend*   S. T. Coleridge
intervenient   coming between

But as a succedaneum,* and a prop   remedy
215 To our infirmity. No officious slave
Art thou of that false secondary power
By which we multiply distinctions, then
Deem that our puny boundaries are things
That we perceive, and not that we have made.
220 To thee, unblinded by these formal arts,
The unity of all hath been revealed,
And thou wilt doubt with me, less aptly skilled
Than many are to range the faculties
In scale and order, class the cabinet†
225 Of their sensations,† and in voluble phrase†
Run through the history and birth of each
As of a single independent thing.
Hard task, vain hope, to analyse the mind,
If each most obvious and particular thought,
230 Not in a mystical and idle sense,
But in the words of Reason deeply weighed,
Hath no beginning.

From THE PRELUDE, Book XII

There are in our existence spots of time,
That with distinct pre-eminence retain
210 A renovating virtue, whence, depressed
By false opinion and contentious* thought,   quarrelsome
Or aught of heavier or more deadly weight,
In trivial occupations, and the round
Of ordinary intercourse, our minds
215 Are nourished and invisibly repaired;
A virtue, by which pleasure is enhanced,
That penetrates, enables us to mount,
When high, more high, and lifts us up when fallen.
This efficacious† spirit chiefly lurks
220 Among those passages of life that give
Profoundest knowledge to what point, and how,
The mind is lord and master — outward sense

---

class the cabinet/Of their sensations classify
feelings as if they were exhibits in a display
case

voluble phrase fluent, glib style
efficacious producing desired effect

The obedient servant of her will. Such moments
Are scattered everywhere, taking their date
225   From our first childhood. I remember well,
That once, while yet my inexperienced hand
Could scarcely hold a bridle, with proud hopes
I mounted, and we journeyed towards the hills:
An ancient servant of my father's house
230   Was with me, my encourager and guide:
We had not travelled long, ere some mischance
Disjoined* me from my comrade; and, through fear   separated
Dismounting, down the rough and stony moor
I led my horse, and, stumbling on, at length
235   Came to a bottom,† where in former times
A murderer had been hung in iron chains.
The gibbet-mast† had mouldered down, the bones
And iron case† were gone; but on the turf,
Hard by, soon after that fell* deed was wrought,   terrible
240   Some unknown hand had carved the murderer's name.
The monumental letters were inscribed
In times long past; but still, from year to year,
By superstition of the neighbourhood,
The grass is cleared away, and to that hour
245   The characters* were fresh and visible: letters
A casual glance had shown them, and I fled,
Faltering and faint, and ignorant of the road:
Then, reascending the bare common, saw
A naked pool that lay beneath the hills,
250   The beacon† on its summit, and, more near,
A girl, who bore a pitcher on her head,
And seemed with difficult steps to force her way
Against the blowing wind. It was, in truth,
An ordinary sight; but I should need
255   Colours and words that are unknown to man,
To paint the visionary dreariness
Which, while I looked all round for my lost guide,
Invested moorland waste, and naked pool,
The beacon crowning the lone eminence,
260   The female and her garments vexed and tossed
By the strong wind. When, in the blessed hours
Of early love, the loved one† at my side,

---

bottom   bottom of a valley
gibbet-mast   gallows post from which
  criminals were hanged
iron case   metal barred cage in which bodies

were hanged
beacon   a stone signal beacon built on the hill
  above Penrith, 1719
loved one   Mary Hutchinson, his future wife

to take care, that whatever passions he communicates to his reader,
80   those passions, if his reader's mind be sound and vigorous, should
always be accompanied with an overbalance of pleasure. Now the music
of harmonious metrical language, the sense of difficulty overcome, and
the blind association of pleasure which has been previously received
from works of rhyme or metre of the same or similar construction, an
85   indistinct perception perpetually renewed of language closely resembling
that of real life, and yet, in the circumstance of metre, differing from it
so widely, all these imperceptibly make up a complex feeling of delight,
which is of the most important use in tempering the painful feeling
which will always be found intermingled with powerful descriptions of
90   the deeper passions. This effect is always produced in pathetic[†] and
impassioned poetry; while, in lighter compositions, the ease and
gracefulness with which the poet manages his numbers[†] are themselves
confessedly a principal source of the gratification of the reader. I might
perhaps include all which it is *necessary* to say upon this subject by
95   affirming, what few persons will deny, that, of two descriptions, either
of passions, manners, or characters, each of them equally well executed,
the one in prose and the other in verse, the verse will be read a hundred
times where the prose is read once.

1800–2   1802

---

pathetic full of pathos, the quality which   *numbers* verses, metrical feet
excites pity or sadness

Sir Walter Scott

1771–1832

The nineteenth-century cleric and critic, John Keble, thought Scott, 'the noblest of all poets in our own day,' and regretted that Scott had given up writing poetry in the belief that Byron outshone him. It is as a novelist that Scott is now primarily known.

He was born in Edinburgh and educated at the High School and the university. He was called to the bar in 1792, but his leisure was spent in exploring the Scottish border country. His earliest published works are translations from German such as Geothe's *Götz von Berlichingen*.

In 1797 he married Marget Charpentier of Lyon and in 1799 he was made Sheriff-depute of Selkirkshire. He was firstly a poet and quickly established his reputation with the publication of *Minstrelsy of the Scottish Border* (1803), and *The Lay of the Last Minstrel* (1805). He became a partner in James Ballantyne's printing firm, and in 1809 a partner in John Ballantyne's book-selling business. Two years later he bought Abbotsford on the Tweed, and eventually built a large residence there. Dissatisfied with the Whig bias of the *Edinburgh Review* he was influential in founding the Tory *Quarterly Review*.

The height of his poetic career was when he was offered the Laureateship in 1813. He declined, and recommended Southey. Thereafter he turned to the novel as his chosen form of literary expression which proved an admirable vehicle for his sympathies and learning. He wrote busily between 1814 and 1831, urged on after 1826 by a £114,000 debt incurred when James Ballantyne & Co. were involved in the bankruptcy of Constable and Co. After Scott's death all the creditors were paid in full. Among his most famous novels, which were published anonymously at first, are *Waverley* (1814), *Old Mortality* (1816), *The Heart of Midlothian* (1818) and *Redgauntlet* (1824). In 1820 he was made baronet, and in 1827 he acknowledged the authorship of his novels.

He wrote in most literary forms, but was not a successful dramatist. He made valuable contributions, however, to history, criticism and antiquarian writing. He established the historical novel as a popular literary form, and some critics think he established the short story genre with such tales as *The Two Drovers* and *The Highland Widow*.

LOCHINVAR†

O, young Lochinvar is come out of the west,
Through all the wide Border† his steed was the best;
And save his good broadsword he weapons had none,
He rode all unarmed, and he rode all alone.
5   So faithful in love, and so dauntless in war,
There never was knight like the young Lochinvar.

He stayed not for brake,† and he stopped not for stone,
He swam the Eske river where ford there was none;
But ere he alighted at Netherby† gate,
10   The bride had consented, the gallant came late:
For a laggard in love, and a dastard in war,
Was to wed the fair Ellen of brave Lochinvar.

So boldly he entered the Netherby Hall,
Among bride's-men, and kinsmen, and brothers, and all:
15   Then spoke the bride's father, his hand on his sword,
(For the poor craven bridegroom said never a word,)
'O come ye in peace here, or come ye in war,
Or to dance at our bridal, young Lord Lochinvar?'

'I long wooed your daughter, my suit you denied; –
20   Love swells like the Solway, but ebbs like its tide –
And now am I come, with this lost love of mine,
To lead but one measure, drink one cup of wine.
There are maidens in Scotland more lovely by far,
That would gladly be bride to the young Lochinvar.'

25   The bride kissed the goblet: the knight took it up,
He quaffed off the wine, and he threw down the cup.
She looked down to blush, and she looked up to sigh,
With a smile on her lips, and a tear in her eye.
He took her soft hand, ere her mother could bar, –
30   'Now tread we a measure!' said young Lochinvar.

So stately his form, and so lovely her face,
That never a hall such a galliard† did grace;

Lochinvar the poem forms stanza XII, Canto V of *Marmion*, in which it is sung by Lady Heron of Ford in Holyrood Palace
Border the borderlands of Scotland and England
brake thicket, hedge

Netherby a hamlet on the river Esk in Cumberland, adjacent to the boundary with Scotland. Netherbury Hall was the seat of the Graemes of Cumberland
galliard a man of courage and spirit

While her mother did fret; and her father did fume,
And the bridegroom stood dangling his bonnet and plume;
35   And the bride-maidens whispered, "Twere better by far,
To have matched our fair cousin with young Lochinvar.'

One touch to her hand, and one word in her ear,
When they reached the hall-door, and the charger stood near;
So light to the croupe† the fair lady he swung,
40   So light to the saddle before her he sprung!
'She is won! we are gone, over bank, bush, and scaur,†
They'll have fleet steeds that follow,' quoth young Lochinvar.

There was mounting 'mong Græmes of the Netherby clan;
Forsters, Fenwicks, and Musgraves, they rode and they ran:
45   There was racing and chasing on Cannonbie† Lee,
But the lost bride of Netherby ne'er did they see.
So daring in love, and so dauntless in war,
Have ye e'er heard of gallant like young Lochinvar?

1807–8   1808

From THE LADY OF THE LAKE†

Canto First, Section 34

                                                                    XXXIV
At length, with Ellen in a grove
695   He seemed to walk, and speak of love;
She listened with a blush and sigh,
His suit was warm, his hopes were high.
He sought her yielded hand to clasp,
And a cold gauntlet met his grasp:
700   The phantom's sex was changed and gone,
Upon its head a helmet shone;
Slowly enlarged to giant size,
With darkened cheek and threatening eyes,

---

croupe   animal's hindquarters
scaur   precipitous ridge of earth
Cannonbie   border village in south
  Dumfriesshire
The Lady of the Lake   a huntsman knight,

James Fitz-James, is afforded hospitality in
the home on Loch Katrine of Roderick Dhu,
a warrior Highland chief. He meets, and falls
in love with, Ellen, daughter of the outlawed
Lord James of Douglas, who is lodged there

The grisly visage, stern and hoar,
705   To Ellen still a likeness bore.
He woke, and, panting with affright,
Recalled the vision of the night.
The hearth's decaying brands were red,
And deep and dusky lustre shed,
710   Half-showing, half concealing, all
The uncouth[†] trophies of the hall.
'Mid those the stranger fixed his eye,
Where that huge falchion[†] hung on high,
And thoughts on thoughts, a countless throng,
715   Rushed, chasing countless thoughts along,
Until, the giddy whirl to cure,
He rose, and sought the moonshine pure.

1810   1810

PIBROCH OF DONUIL DHU[†]

Pibroch of Donuil Dhu,
   Pibroch of Donuil,
Wake thy wild voice anew,
   Summon Clan-Conuil.
5   Come away, come away,
   Hark to the summons!
Come in your war array,
   Gentles and commons.

Come from deep glen, and
10   From mountain so rocky,
The war-pipe and pennon[†]
   Are at Inverlochy.
Come every hill-plaid, and
   True heart that wears one,
15   Come every steel blade, and
   Strong hand that bears one.

---

uncouth   unknown, unusual
falchion   broad, curved, convex-edged sword
Pibroch of Donuil Dhu   Donald the Black's
   bagpipe-summons: the poem was written to
   the air *Piobair of Donuil Dhuibh* for *Albyn's
   Anthology*, 1816. The event referred to here
   is the expedition of Donald Balloch, who in

1413 launched from the Isles with a
considerable force, invaded Lochaber, and at
Inverlochy defeated and put to flight the
army of the earls of Mar and Caithness
pennon   long narrow, triangular or swallow-
   tailed, flag

Leave untended the herd,
    The flock without shelter;
Leave the corpse uninterred,
20   The bride at the altar;
Leave the deer, leave the steer,
    Leave nets and barges:
Come with your fighting gear,
    Broadswords and targes.*   shields

25   Come as the winds come, when
        Forests are rended,
    Come as the waves come, when
        Navies are stranded:
    Faster come, faster come,
30   Faster and faster,
    Chief, vassal, page and groom,
        Tenant and master.

    Fast they come, fast they come;
        See how they gather!
35   Wide waves the eagle plume,
        Blended with heather.
    Cast your plaids,† draw your blades,
        Forward, each man, set!
    Pibroch of Donuil Dhu,
40   Knell for the onset!

    1816   1816

---

plaid   outer article of Highland costume,
    consisting of long length of chequered tartan-
    patterned cloth

71

From OLD MORTALITY†

[The Archbishop of St Andrews, and the Place he now Worthily Holds]

CHAPTER 4

At fairs he play'd before the spearmen,	
And gaily graithed* in their gear then,	prepared
Steel bonnets, pikes and swords shone clear then	
As ony bead;*	any ornament
Now wha* sall play before sic weir men,	who
Since Habbie's dead!	
Elegy on Habbie Simpson	

The cavalcade of horsemen on their road to the little borough-town
were preceded by Niel Blane, the town-piper, mounted on his white
galloway,† armed with his dirk¹ and broadsword, and bearing a chanter†
streaming with as many ribbons as would deck out six country belles
5 for a fair or preaching. Niel, a clean, tight, well-timbered, long-winded
fellow, had gained the official situation of town-piper of — by his merit,
with all the emoluments thereof; namely, the Piper's Croft, as it is still
called, a field of about an acre in extent, five marks, and a new livery-
coat of the town's colours, yearly; some hopes of a dollar upon the day
10 of the election of magistrates, providing the provost were able and
willing to afford such a gratuity,† and the privilege of paying, at all the
respectable houses in the neighbourhood, an annual visit at spring-time,
to rejoice their hearts with his music, to comfort his own with their ale
and brandy, and to beg from each a modicum† of seed-corn.
15   In addition to these inestimable advantages, Niel's personal, or
professional, accomplishments won the heart of a jolly widow, who
then kept the principal change-house† in the borough. Her former
husband having been a strict presbyterian† of such note that he usually
went among his sect by the name of Gaius† the publican, many of the
20 more rigid were scandalized by the profession of the successor whom
his relict† had chosen for a second help-mate. As the *browst* (or brewing)

Old Mortality the novel is particularly
concerned with the fortunes of Henry
Morton of Milnwood, a courageous young
man, who harbours the fanatical Covenanter
John Balfour of Burley, an old friend of his
father, not knowing that this man has just
taken part in the assassination of the
Archbishop of St Andrews. For this, Morton
is arrested
galloway breed of small horse from Galloway,
SW Scotland

dirk Highlander's dagger
chanter melody pipe of the bagpipes
gratuity present of money
modicum small quantity
change-house small inn
presbyterian a person belonging to the
Scottish church governed by its ministers
Gaius in reference to Romans 16. 23
relict widow

of the Howff[†] retained, nevertheless, its unrivalled reputation, most of
the old customers continued to give it a preference. The character of
the new landlord, indeed, was of that accommodating kind, which
25   enabled him, by close attention to the helm, to keep his little vessel
pretty steady amid the contending tides of faction. He was a good-
humoured, shrewd, selfish sort of fellow, indifferent alike to the disputes
about church and state and only anxious to secure the good-will of
customers of every description. But his character, as well as the state of
30   the country, will be best understood by giving the reader an account of
the instructions which he issued to his daughter, a girl about eighteen,
whom he was initiating in those cares which had been faithfully
discharged by his wife, until about six months before our story
commences, when the honest woman had been carried to the kirkyard.[†]
35   'Jenny,' said Niel Blane, as the girl assisted to disencumber him of
his bagpipes, 'this is the first day that ye are to take the place of your
worthy mother in attending to the public; a douce[†] woman she was,
civil to the customers, and had a good name wi' Whig and Tory, baith[†]
up the street and down the street. It will be hard for you to fill her
40   place, especially on sic[†] a thrang[†] day as this; but Heaven's will maun[†]
be obeyed. – Jenny, whatever Milnwood ca's for, be sure he maun hae't,
for he's the Captain o' the Popinjay,[†] and auld customs maun be
supported; if he canna pay the lawing[†] himsell, as I ken he's keepit
unco[†] short by the head, I'll find a way to shame it out o' his uncle. –
45   The curate[†] is playing at dice wi' Cornet[†] Grahame. Be eident[†] and civil
to them baith – clergy and captains can gie an unco[†] deal o' fash[†] in
thae times, where they take an ill-will. – The dragoons will be crying
for ale, and they wunna want it, and maunna want it – they are unruly
chields[†] but they pay ane[†] some gate[†] or other. I gat the humle[†]-cow,
50   that's the best in the byre,[†] frae black Frank Inglis and Sergeant
Bothwell, for ten pund Scots, and they drank out the price at ae
downsitting.'
'But, father,' interrupted Jenny, 'they say the twa reiving loons[†] drave
the cow frae the gudewife o' Bell's-moor, just because she gaed to hear
55   a field-preaching ae Sabbath afternoon.'

Howff   see l.272, the name of Blane's public
   house
kirkyard   churchyard
douce   pleasant
baith   both
sic   such
thrang   busy
maun   must
Captain o' the Popinjay   champion
lawing   a tavern-bill
unco   remarkably
curate   Episcopalians who replaced ministers

deprived of their livings for not accepting the
   1662 settlement of the church
Cornet   standard-bearer in a troop of cavalry
eident   attentive
unco   great
fash   trouble
chields   young fellows
ane   one
gate   way
humle   hornless
byre   stable
reiving loons   wandering rogues

'Whisht! ye silly tawpie'[†] said her father, 'we have naething to do
how they come by the bestial they sell – be that atween them and their
consciences. – Aweel – Take notice, Jenny, of that dour, stour-looking[†]
carle[†] that sits by the cheek o' the ingle,[†] and turns his back on a' men.
60   He looks like ane o' the hill-folk, for I saw him start a wee when he
saw the red-coats, and I jalouse[†] he wad had liked to hae ridden by,
but his horse (it's a gude gelding) was ower sair[†] travailed; he behoved[†]
to stop whether he wad or no. Serve him cannily, Jenny, and wi' little
din, and dinna bring the sodgers[†] on him by speering ony questions at
65   him; but let na him hae a room to himsell, they wad say we were hiding
him. – For yoursell, Jenny, ye'll be civil to a' the folk, and take nae
heed o' ony nonsense and daffing[†] the young lads may say t'ye. Folk in
the hostler line maun put up wi' muckle.[†] Your mither, rest her saul,
could pit up wi' as muckle as maist women – but aff hands is fair play;
70   and if ony body be uncivil ye may gie me a cry – Aweel, – when the
malt[†] begins to get aboon the meal, they'll begin to speak about
government in kirk and state, and then, Jenny, they are like to quarrel –
let them be doing – anger's a drouthy[†] passion, and the mair they
dispute, the mair ale they'll drink; but ye were best serve them wi' a
75   pint o' the sma' browst, it will heat them less, and they'll never ken the
difference.'
    'But, father,' said Jenny, 'if they come to lounder ilk ither,[†] as they
did last time, suldna I cry on you?'
    'At no hand, Jenny; the redder[†] gets aye the warst lick[†] in the fray.
80   If the sodgers draw their swords, ye'll cry on the corporal and the
guard. If the country folk tak the tangs and poker, ye'll cry on the
bailie[†] and town-officers. But in nae event cry on me, for I am wearied
wi' doudling[†] the bag o' wind a' day, and I am gaun to eat my dinner
quietly in the spence.[†] – And, now I think on't, the Laird of Lickitup
85   (that's him that was the laird) was speering for sma' drink and a saut[†]
herring – gie him a pu' be the sleeve, and round into his lug[†] I wad be
blithe o' his company to dine wi' me; he was a gude customer anes[†] in
a day, and wants naething but means to be a gude ane again – he likes
drink as weel as e'er he did. And if ye ken[†] ony puir body o' our

tawpie foolish girl	*drouthy* thirsty
stour-looking rough-looking	*lounder ilk ither* beat each other
carle common countryman	*redder* person who separates combatants
cheek o' the ingle side or jamb of the fireplace	*lick* blow
jalouse suspect	*bailie* chief magistrate
ower sair over sore	*doudling* playing (the bagpipes)
behoved had to	*spence* larder
sodgers soldiers	*saut* salt
daffing fooling	*round . . . lug* whisper in his ear
muckle much	*anes* once
malt liquor brewed or distilled from malt	*ken* know

90   acquaintance that's blate[†] for want o' siller,[†] and has far to gang hame,
      ye needna stick to gie them a waught[†] o' drink and a bannock[†] – we'll
      ne'er miss't, and it looks creditable in a house like ours. And now,
      hinny, gang awa', and serve the folk, but first bring me my dinner, and
      two chappins[†] o' yill[†] and the mutchkin[†] stoup[†] o' brandy.'
95   Having thus devolved his whole cares on Jenny as prime minister,
      Niel Blane and the ci-devant[†] laird, once his patron, but now glad to
      be his trencher-companion, sate down to enjoy themselves for the
      remainder of the evening, remote from the bustle of the public room.
      All in Jenny's department was in full activity. The knights of the
100   popinjay received and requited the hospitable entertainment of their
      captain, who, though he spared the cup himself, took care it should go
      round with due celerity[†] among the rest, who might not have otherwise
      deemed themselves handsomely treated. Their numbers melted away by
      degrees, and were at length diminished to four or five, who began to
105   talk of breaking up their party. At another table, at some distance, sat
      two of the dragoons, whom Niel Blane had mentioned, a sergeant and
      a private in the celebrated John Grahame of Claverhouse's regiment of
      Life-Guards. Even the non-commissioned officers and privates in these
      corps were not considered as ordinary mercenaries, but rather
110   approached to the rank of the French mousquetaires, being regarded in
      the light of cadets, who performed the duties of rank-and-file with the
      prospect of obtaining commissions in case of distinguishing themselves.
      Many young men of good families were to be found in the ranks, a
      circumstance which added to the pride and self-consequence of these
115   troops. A remarkable instance of this occurred in the person of the non-
      commissioned officer in question. His real name was Francis Stewart,
      but he was universally known by the appellation of Bothwell, being
      lineally descended from the last earl of that name, not the infamous
      lover of the unfortunate Queen Mary, but Francis Stewart, Earl of
120   Bothwell, whose turbulence and repeated conspiracies embarrassed the
      early part of James Sixth's reign, and who at length died in exile in
      great poverty. The son of this Earl had sued to Charles I for the
      restitution of part of his father's forfeited estates, but the grasp of the
      nobles to whom they had been allotted was too tenacious to be
125   unclenched. The breaking out of the civil wars utterly ruined him, by
      intercepting a small pension which Charles I had allowed him, and he
      died in the utmost indigence.[†] His son, after having served as a soldier

---

blate   spiritless
siller   silver
waught   large draught
bannock bread, oatmeal cake
chappin a Scotch liquid measure (a quart of
   English wine-measure)
yill   ale

mutchkin a quarter of a Scotch pint (three-
   quarters of an imperial pint)
stoup   drinking vessel
ci-devant former
celerity speed
indigence poverty

abroad and in Britain, and passed through several vicissitudes[†] of
fortune, was fain[†] to content himself with the situation of a non-
130 commissioned officer in the Life-Guards, although lineally descended
from the royal family, the father of the forfeited Earl of Bothwell having
been a natural son of James VI.[†] Great personal strength, and dexterity
in the use of his arms, as well as the remarkable circumstances of his
descent, had recommended this man to the attention of his officers. But
135 he partook in a great degree of the licentiousness[†] and oppressive
disposition, which the habit of acting as agents for government in
levying fines, extracting free quarters, and otherwise oppressing the
Presbyterian recusants,[†] had rendered too general among these soldiers.
They were so much accustomed to such missions, that they conceived
140 themselves at liberty to commit all manner of license with impunity, as
if totally exempted from all law and authority, excepting the command
of their officers. On such occasions Bothwell was usually the most
forward.
It is probable that Bothwell and his companions would not so long
145 have remained quiet, but for respect to the presence of their Cornet,
who commanded the small party quartered in the borough, and who
was engaged in a game at dice with the curate of the place. But both of
these being suddenly called from their amusement to speak with the
chief magistrate upon some urgent business, Bothwell was not long of
150 evincing[†] his contempt for the rest of the company.
'Is it not a strange thing, Halliday,' he said to his comrade, 'to see a
set of bumpkins sit carousing here this whole evening, without having
drank the king's health?'
'They have drank the king's health,' said Halliday. 'I heard that green
155 kail-worm[†] of a lad name his majesty's health.'
'Did he?' said Bothwell. 'Then, Tom, we'll have them drink the
Archbishop of St Andrew's health, and do it on their knees too.'
'So we will, by G—,' said Halliday; 'and he that refuses it, we'll have
him to the guard-house, and teach him to ride the colt foaled of an
160 acorn,[†] with a brace of carabines at each foot to keep him steady.'
'Right, Tom,' continued Bothwell; 'and, to do all things in order, I'll
begin with that sulky blue-bonnet in the ingle-nook.'
He rose accordingly, and taking his sheathed broadsword under his
arm to support the insolence which he meditated, placed himself in
165 front of the stranger noticed by Niel Blane, in his admonitions[†] to his

vicissitudes alterations
fain willing
James VI Scott's slip for James V
licentiousness disregard of accepted rules, lewdness
recusants people who refused to attend Church of England services

evincing showing
kail-worm the caterpillar of the cabbage-white butterfly
colt . . . acorn wooden horse (relating to a form of military punishment)
admonitions warnings

daughter, as being, in all probability, one of the hill-folk, or refractory[†] presbyterians.

'I make so bold as to request of your precision, beloved,' said the trooper, in a tone of affected solemnity, and assuming the snuffle of a
170   country preacher, 'that you will arise from your seat, beloved, and, having bent your hams until your knees do rest upon the floor, beloved, that you will turn over this measure (called by the profane a gill) of the comfortable creature, which the carnal[†] denominate brandy, to the health and glorification of his Grace the Archbishop of St Andrews, the
175   worthy primate of all Scotland.'

All waited for the stranger's answer. – His features, austere even to ferocity, with a cast of eye, which, without being actually oblique, approached nearly to a squint, and which gave a very sinister expression to his countenance, joined to a frame, square, strong, and muscular,
180   though something under the middle size, seemed to announce a man unlikely to understand rude jesting, or to receive insults with impunity.

'And what is the consequence,' said he, 'if I should not be disposed to comply with your uncivil request?'

'The consequence thereof, beloved,' said Bothwell, in the same tone
185   of raillery,[†] 'will be, firstly, that I will tweak thy proboscis or nose. Secondly, beloved, that I will administer my fist to thy distorted visual optics; and will conclude, beloved, with a practical application of the flat of my sword to the shoulders of the recusant.'

'Is it even so?' said the stranger; 'then give me the cup;' and, taking
190   it in his hand, he said, with a peculiar expression of voice and manner. 'The Archbishop of St Andrews, and the place he now worthily holds; – may each prelate in Scotland soon be as the Right Reverend James Sharpe!'

'He has taken the test,' said Halliday, exultingly.
195   'But with a qualification,' said Bothwell; 'I don't understand what the devil the crop-eared whig[†] means.'

'Come, gentlemen,' said Morton, who became impatient of their insolence, 'we are here met as good subjects, and on a merry occasion; and we have a right to expect we shall not be troubled with this sort of
200   discussion.'

Bothwell was about to make a surly answer, but Halliday reminded him in a whisper, that there were strict injunctions[†] that the soldiers should give no offence to the men who were sent out to the musters[†] agreeably to the council's orders. So, after honouring Morton with a

---

refractory   stubborn
carnal   worldly, wicked
raillery   banter, ridicule
whig   member of the political party that, after the revolution of 1688, aimed at

subordinating the power of the crown to that of Parliament and the upper classes
injunctions   authoritative orders
musters   assemblies of men for inspection

205 broad and fierce stare, he said, 'Well, Mr Popinjay, I shall not disturb
your reign; I reckon it will be out by twelve at night. – Is it not an odd
thing, Halliday,' he continued, addressing his companion, 'that they
should make such a fuss about cracking off their birding-pieces† at a
mark which any woman or boy could hit at a day's practice? If Captain
210 Popinjay now, or any of his troop, would try a bout, either with the
broadsword, backsword, single rapier, or rapier and dagger, for a gold
noble, the first-drawn blood, there would be some soul in it, – or,
zounds, would the bumpkins but wrestle, or pitch the bar, or putt the
stone, or throw the axle-tree, if (touching the end of Morton's sword
215 scornfully with his toe) they carry things about them that they are afraid
to draw.'

Morton's patience and prudence now gave way entirely, and he was
about to make a very angry answer to Bothwell's insolent observations,
when the stranger stepped forward.

220 'This is my quarrel,' he said, 'and in the name of the good cause, I
will see it out myself. – Hark thee, friend,' (to Bothwell,) 'wilt thou
wrestle a fall with me?'

'With my whole spirit, beloved,' answered Bothwell; 'yea I will strive
with thee, to the downfall of one or both.'

225 'Then, as my trust is in Him that can help,' retorted his antagonist,
'I will forthwith make thee an example to all such railing Rabshakehs.'†

With that he dropped his coarse grey horseman's coat from his
shoulders, and extending his strong brawny arms, with a look of
determined resolution, he offered himself to the contest. The soldier
230 was nothing abashed by the muscular frame, broad chest, square
shoulders, and hardy look of his antagonist, but, whistling with great
composure, unbuckled his belt, and laid aside his military coat. The
company stood round them, anxious for the event.

In the first struggle the trooper seemed to have some advantage, and
235 also in the second, though neither could be considered as decisive. But
it was plain he had put his whole strength too suddenly forth, against
an antagonist possessed of great endurance, skill, vigour, and length of
wind. In the third close, the countryman lifted his opponent fairly from
the floor, and hurled him to the ground with such violence, that he
240 lay for an instant stunned and motionless. His comrade Halliday
immediately drew his sword; 'You have killed my sergeant,' he
exclaimed to the victorious wrestler, 'and by all that is sacred you shall
answer it!'

'Stand back!' cried Morton and his companions, 'it was all fair play;
245 your comrade sought a fall, and he has got it.'

---

birding-pieces guns
Rabshakehs after the loud-mouthed officer of
Sennacherib, King of Assyria, who rails, or

abuses, the people of Jerusalem in II Kings
18. It was a favourite word of the
Covenanters

'That is true enough', said Bothwell, as he slowly rose; 'put up your
bilbo,† Tom. I did not think there was a crop-ear of them all could have
laid the best cap and feather in the King's Life-Guards on the floor of a
rascally change-house. – Hark ye, friend, give me your hand.' The
250 stranger held out his hand. 'I promise you,' said Bothwell, squeezing
his hand very hard, 'that the time will come when we shall meet again,
and try this game over in a more earnest manner.'

'And I'll promise you,' said the stranger, returning the grasp with
equal firmness, 'that when we next meet, I will lay your head as low as
255 it lay even now, when you shall lack the power to lift it up again.'

'Well, beloved,' answered Bothwell, 'if thou be'st a whig, thou art a
stout and a brave one, and so good even to thee – Hadst best take thy
nag before the Cornet makes the round; for, I promise thee, he has
stay'd less suspicious-looking persons.'

260 The stranger seemed to think that the hint was not to be neglected;
he flung down his reckoning, and going into the stable, saddled and
brought out a powerful black horse, now recruited by rest and forage,
and turning to Morton, observed, 'I ride towards Milnwood, which I
hear is your home; will you give me the advantage and protection of
265 your company?'

'Certainly,' said Morton; although there was something of gloomy
and relentless severity in the man's manner from which his mind
recoiled. His companions, after a courteous good-night, broke up and
went off in different directions, some keeping them company for about
270 a mile, until they dropped off one by one, and the travellers were left
alone.

The company had not long left the Howff, as Blane's public-house
was called, when the trumpets and kettle-drums sounded. The troopers
got under arms in the market-place at this unexpected summons, while,
275 with faces of anxiety and earnestness, Cornet Grahame, a kinsmen of
Claverhouse, and the Provost† of the borough, followed by half-a-dozen
soldiers, and town-officers with halberts,† entered the apartment of Niel
Blane.

'Guard the doors!' were the first words which the Cornet spoke; 'let
280 no man leave the house. – So, Bothwell, how comes this? Did you not
hear them sound boot and saddle?'

'He was just going to quarters, sir,' said his comrade; 'he has had a
bad fall.'

'In a fray, I suppose?' said Grahame. 'If you neglect duty in this way,
285 your royal blood will hardly protect you.'

'How have I neglected duty?' said Bothwell, sulkily.

---

bilbo   sword   municipal corporation
Provost   Head of a Scottish borough, or   *halberts*   combined spear and battle-axe

'You should have been at quarters, Sergeant Bothwell,' replied the officer; 'you have lost a golden opportunity. Here are news come that the Archbishop of St Andrews has been strangely and foully assassinated
290   by a body of the rebel whigs, who pursued and stopped his carriage on Magus-Muir, near the town of St Andrews, dragged him out, and dispatched[†] him with their swords and daggers.'

All stood aghast at the intelligence.

'Here are their descriptions,' continued the Cornet, pulling out a
295   proclamation, 'the reward of a thousand merks is on each of their heads.'

'The test, the test, and the qualification!' said Bothwell to Halliday; 'I know the meaning now – Zounds, that we should not have stopt him! Go saddle our horses, Halliday. – Was there one of the men,
300   Cornet, very stout and square-made, double-chested, thin in the flanks, hawk-nosed?'

'Stay, stay,' said Cornet Grahame, 'let me look at the paper. – Hackston of Raithillet, tall, thin, black-haired.'

'That is not my man,' said Bothwell.

305   'John Balfour, called Burley, aquiline nose, red-haired, five feet eight inches in height' –

'It is he – it is the very man!' said Bothwell, – 'skellies[†] fearfully with one eye?'

'Right,' continued Grahame, 'rode a strong black horse, taken from
310   the primate at the time of the murder.'

'The very man,' exclaimed Bothwell, 'and the very horse! he was in this room not a quarter of an hour since.'

A few hasty enquiries tended still more to confirm the opinion, that the reserved and stern stranger was Balfour of Burley, the actual
315   commander of the band of assassins, who, in the fury of misguided zeal, had murdered the primate, whom they accidentally met, as they were searching for another person[†] against whom they bore enmity. In their excited imagination the casual rencounter had the appearance of a providential interference, and they put to death the archbishop, with
320   circumstances of great and cold-blooded cruelty, under the belief, that the Lord, as they expressed it, had delivered him into their hands.

'Horse, horse, and pursue, my lads!' exclaimed Cornet Grahame; 'the murdering dog's head is worth its weight in gold.'

1816   1816

---

dispatched killed
skellies squints

another person Carmichael, sheriff-depute in Fife

Samuel Taylor Coleridge
1772–1834

Coleridge was a major poet and critic of extraordinary genius. His friendship with Wordsworth was most influential on the development of English Romanticism. After his father's early death he went to school at Christ's Hospital where he was noted as an inspired talker, and soon had accumulated a prodigious and precocious learning. Amongst his friends there were Leigh Hunt and Charles Lamb.

He proceeded to Jesus College, Cambridge, but his attention to his studies was diverted by interest in the politics of the French Revolution. Politics, drink and a disappointing love affair led him to give up Cambridge temporarily, and enlist in the 15th Light Dragoons under the name of Comberbache: he was eventually bought out by his brothers, returned to Cambridge but did not take a degree.

In 1794 he went on a walking tour and met Robert Southey, an Oxford student, and together they worked out a scheme of social and political ideas which they called Pantisocracy, to be established as a commune in America. Before the scheme could come to fruition, he quarrelled with Southey, and married Sara Fricker, who had been involved in the venture. They resided at Clevedon and a son, Hartley, was born. Their love lasted only a few years and by 1796 Coleridge was becoming addicted to opium which he took as medicine for depression and sickness.

He published *Poems on Various Subjects* (1796), preached in the Unitarian Church (1797), and the next year met Wordsworth at Racedown which marked the beginning of fourteen years of friendship. The year 1797–8 was an *annus mirabilis* for Coleridge while he lived at Nether Stowey close to the Wordsworths at Alfoxden: he wrote his best poetry, much of it constituting the 'conversation' poems addressed to his friends, such as 'This Lime-Tree Bower My Prison' and 'Frost at Midnight': he composed, too, the opium-induced vision poem, 'Kubla Khan', *The Ancient Mariner*, and the unfinished 'Christabel'. He collaborated with Wordsworth in *Lyrical Ballads* (1798).

For ten months, 1798–9, disillusioned with France, he lived and travelled in Germany, after which he returned to the Lake District. His marriage unstable, he fell in love with Sara Hutchinson, Wordsworth's future sister-in-law. By this time, he was chronically addicted to opium. He wrote 'Dejection: an Ode' (1802), and started writing his *Notebooks*, daily reflections on his life, writing and dreams.

In the years leading up to 1811 Coleridge went abroad again, for a period as Secretary to the Governor of Malta. He gave lectures on poetry and drama and wrote *Shakespearian Criticism* (1808). His second series of Shakespeare lectures derived from those given by A. W. Schlegel in Vienna. He wrote, and edited with Sara Hutchinson, *The Friend*, a weekly journal of literary, philosophical, and political issues which ran for 28 numbers. He quarrelled seriously with Wordsworth and lived in London, 1811–14, often contemplating suicide.

He recovered his Christian beliefs in 1814, and in 1817 published one of his most important works, *Biographia Literaria*, a discursive tract dealing with philosophy, poetic theory and autobiography. The benevolence of Dr James Gillman allowed Coleridge to take up residence in his Highgate house in 1816 and to live and write in security for the rest of his life. He published his collected poems under the title *Sibylline Leaves* (1817, 1828, 1834).

Coleridge espoused German Romanticism against British Utilitarianism, and devoted some of his final years to religious writing, the most notable of which is *On the Constitution of Church and State* (1830). *Table Talk*, a record of many of his conversations, was published in 1836.

THE EOLIAN HARP[†]

Composed at Clevedon, Somersetshire

My pensive Sara! thy soft cheek reclined
Thus on mine arm, most soothing sweet it is
To sit beside our cot, our cot o'ergrown
With white-flowered jasmin, and the broad-leaved myrtle,
5   (Meet emblems they of Innocence and Love!)
And watch the clouds, that late were rich with light,
Slow saddening round, and mark the star of eve

Eolian Harp   outdoor musical instrument: strings stretched across a sounding board   which produce a variable wailing noise when the wind blows through them

Serenely brilliant (such should wisdom be)
Shine opposite! How exquisite the scents
10   Snatched from yon bean-field! and the world so hushed!
The stilly murmur of the distant sea
Tells us of silence.
                                    And that simplest lute,
Placed length-ways in the clasping casement, hark!
How by the desultory breeze caressed,
15   Like some coy maid half yielding to her lover,
It pours such sweet upbraiding,* as must needs   reproach
Tempt to repeat the wrong! And now, its strings
Boldlier swept, the long sequacious† notes
Over delicious surges sink and rise,
20   Such a soft floating witchery of sound
As twilight Elfins make, when they at eve
Voyage on gentle gales from Fairy-Land,
Where Melodies round honey-dropping flowers,
Footless and wild, like birds of Paradise,
25   Nor pause, nor perch, hovering on untamed wing!
O the one life within us and abroad,
Which meets all motion and becomes its soul,
A light in sound, a sound-like power in light
Rhythm in all thought, and joyance every where –
30   Methinks, it should have been impossible
Not to love all things in a world so filled;
Where the breeze warbles, and the mute still air
Is Music slumbering on her instrument.

      And thus, my love! as on the midway slope
35   Of yonder hill I stretch my limbs at noon,
Whilst through my half-closed eye-lids I behold
The sunbeams dance, like diamonds, on the main,
And tranquil muse upon tranquillity;
Full many a thought uncalled and undetained,
40   And many idle flitting phantasies,
Traverse my indolent* and passive brain,   lazy
As wild and various as the random gales
That swell and flutter on this subject lute!
      And what if all of animated nature
45   Be but organic harps diversely framed,
That tremble into thought, as o'er them sweeps
Plastic† and vast, one intellectual breeze,

---

sequacious   inclined to follow   *plastic*   pliant, supple

At once the Soul of each, and God of All?
   But thy more serious eye a mild reproof
50 Darts, O beloved woman! nor such thoughts
Dim and unhallowed dost thou not reject,
And biddest me walk humbly with my God.
Meek daughter in the family of Christ!
Well hast thou said and holily dispraised
55 These shapings of the unregenerate† mind;
Bubbles that glitter as they rise and break
On vain Philosophy's aye-babbling spring.
For never guiltless may I speak of him,
The Incomprehensible! save when with awe
60 I praise him, and with Faith that inly feels;
Who with his saving mercies healed me,
A sinful and most miserable man,
Wildered* and dark, and gave me to possess   *bewildered*
Peace, and this cot,* and thee, heart-honoured Maid!   *cottage*

1795   1796

ON A RUINED HOUSE IN A ROMANTIC COUNTRY†

And this reft* house is that the which he built,   *ruined*
Lamented Jack! And here his malt* he pil'd,   *grain*
Cautious in vain! These rats that squeak so wild,
Squeak, not unconscious of their father's guilt.
5 Did ye not see her gleaming thro' the glade?
Belike, 'twas she, the maiden all forlorn.
What though she milk no cow with crumpled horn,
Yet *aye* she haunts the dale where *erst* she stray'd;
And *aye* beside her stalks her amorous knight!
10 Still on his thighs their wonted* brogues* are worn,   *usual*   *trousers*
And thro' those brogues, still tatter'd and betorn,
His hindward charms gleam an unearthly white;
As when thro' broken clouds at night's high noon
Peeps in fair fragments forth the full-orb'd harvest-moon!

1797   1797

---

unregenerate incapable of being improved
  morally
*On a Ruined House in a Romantic
  Country* this poem, based on *The House*

that Jack Built, is Coleridge's parody of his
own early poetic style. It was published under
the pseudonym of Nehemiah Higginbottom

From THE RIME OF THE ANCIENT MARINER†

PART IV

'I fear thee, ancient Mariner!
I fear thy skinny hand!
And thou art† long, and lank, and brown,
As is the ribbed sea-sand.

The wedding guest feareth that a spirit is talking to him.

220   I fear thee and thy glittering eye,
And thy skinny hand, so brown.' –
Fear not, fear not, thou wedding-guest!
This body dropt not down.

But the ancient Mariner assureth him of his bodily life, and proceedeth to relate his horrible penance.

    Alone, alone, all, all alone,
225   Alone on a wide wide sea!
And never a saint took pity on
My soul in agony.

    That many men, so beautiful!
And they all dead did lie:
230   And a thousand thousand slimy things
Lived on; and so did I.

He despiseth the creatures of the calm.

    I looked upon the rotting sea,
And drew my eyes away;
I looked upon the rotting deck,
235   And there the dead men lay.

And envieth that they should live, and so many lie dead.

    I looked to heaven, and tried to pray;
But or ever a prayer had gusht,
A wicked whisper came, and made
My heart as dry as dust.

The Rime of the Ancient Mariner 'Rime' is archaic spelling of 'rhyme'. The marginal notes describe the activities of a parallel spirit world. In this extract, the mariner, who has killed an albatross in an act of cruelty for which the dead bird is hung round his neck in penance, suddenly perceives the natural beauty of watersnakes in the moonlight. He blesses them and the albatross, his penitential burden, falls from his neck
And thou art Coleridge wrote: 'For the last two lines of this stanza, I am indebted to Mr Wordsworth. It was on a delightful walk from Nether Stowey to Dulverton, with him and his sister, in the autumn of 1797, that this poem was planned, and in part composed'

240   I closed my lids, and kept them close,
And the balls like pulses beat;
For the sky and the sea, and the sea and the sky
Lay like a load on my weary eye,
And the dead were at my feet.

245   The cold sweat melted from their limbs,
Nor rot nor reek did they:
The look with which they looked on me
Had never passed away.

An orphan's curse would drag to hell
250   A spirit from on high;
But oh! more horrible than that
Is the curse in a dead man's eye!
Seven days, seven nights, I saw that curse,
And yet I could not die.
255   The moving Moon went up the sky,
And no where did abide;
Softly she was going up,
And a star or two beside –

Her beams bemocked the sultry† main,†
260   Like April hoar-frost spread;
But where the ship's huge shadow lay,
The charmed water burnt alway
A still and awful red.

Beyond the shadow of the ship,
265   I watched the water-snakes:
They moved in tracks of shining white,
And when they reared, the elfish light
Fell off in hoary† flakes.

But the curse liveth for him in the eye of the dead men.

In his loneliness and fixedness he yearneth towards the journeying Moon, and the stars that still sojourn, yet still move onward; and every where the blue sky belongs to them, and is their appointed rest, and their native country and their own natural homes, which they enter unannounced, as lords that are certainly expected and yet there is a silent joy at their arrival.

By the light of the Moon he beholdeth God's creatures of the great calm.

---

sultry hot and oppressive   *hoary* white
main sea

Within the shadow of the ship
270   I watched their rich attire:
Blue, glossy green, and velvet black,
They coiled and swam; and every track
Was a flash of golden fire.

O happy living things! no tongue
275   Their beauty might declare:
A spring of love gushed from my heart,
And I blessed them unaware:
Sure my kind saint took pity on me,
And I blessed them unaware.

*Their beauty
and their
happiness.*

*He blesseth
them in his
heart.*

280   The selfsame moment I could pray;
And from my neck so free
The Albatross fell off, and sank
Like lead into the sea.

*The spell begins
to break.*

He prayeth best, who loveth best
285   All things both great and small;
For the dear God who loveth us,
He made and loveth all.

The Mariner, whose eye is bright,
Whose beard with age is hoar,
290   Is gone: and now the Wedding-Guest†
Turned from the bridegroom's door.

He went like one that hath been stunned,
And is of sense forlorn:
A sadder and a wiser man,
295   He rose the morrow morn.

1797–8   1798

FROST AT MIDNIGHT

The frost performs its secret ministry,
Unhelped by any wind. The owlet's cry
Came loud – and hark, again! loud as before.

Wedding-Guest   the guest has been button-
holed by the mariner, and has listened to his
tale

The inmates of my cottage, all at rest,
5. Have left me to that solitude, which suits
Abstruser† musings: save that at my side
My cradled infant slumbers peacefully.
'Tis calm indeed! so calm, that it disturbs
And vexes meditation with its strange
10 And extreme silentness, Sea, hill, and wood,
This populous village! Sea, and hill, and wood,
With all the numberless goings on of life,
Inaudible as dreams! the thin blue flame
Lies on my low burnt fire, and quivers not;
15 Only that film, which fluttered on the grate,
Still flutters there, the sole unquiet thing.
Methinks, its motion in this hush of nature
Gives it dim sympathies with me who live,
Making it a companionable form,
20 Whose puny flaps and freaks the idling Spirit
By its own moods interprets, every where
Echo or mirror seeking of itself,
And makes a toy of Thought.
                              But O! how oft,
How oft, at school, with most believing mind,
25 Presageful,† have I gazed upon the bars,
To watch that fluttering stranger!† and as oft
With unclosed lids, already had I dreamt
Of my sweet birth-place, and the old church-tower,
Whose bells, the poor man's only music, rang
30 From morn to evening, all the hot Fair-day,
So sweetly, that they stirred and haunted me
With a wild pleasure, falling on mine ear
Most like articulate sounds of things to come!
So gazed I, till the soothing things I dreamt
35 Lulled me to sleep, and sleep prolonged my dreams!
And so I brooded all the following morn,
Awed by the stern preceptor's* face, mine eye   teacher
Fixed with mock study on my swimming book:
Save if the door half opened, and I snatched
40 A hasty glance, and still my heart leaped up,
For still I hoped to see the stranger's face,
Townsman, or aunt, or sister more beloved,
My play-mate when we both were clothed alike!

---

abstruser more profound
presageful full of portent or foreboding
stranger Coleridge noted: 'In all parts of the
kingdom these films (soot on the grate) are
called *strangers* and supposed to portend the
arrival of some absent friend'

Dear Babe,[†] that sleepest cradled by my side,
45 Whose gentle breathings, heard in this deep calm,
Fill up the interspersed vacancies
And momentary pauses of the thought!
My babe so beautiful! it thrills my heart
With tender gladness, thus to look at thee,
50 And think that thou shalt learn far other lore
And in far other scenes! For I was reared
In the great city, pent* 'mid cloisters dim,   confined
And saw nought lovely but the sky and stars.
But thou, my babe! shalt wander like a breeze
55 By lakes and sandy shores, beneath the crags
Of ancient mountain, and beneath the clouds,
Which image in their bulk both lakes and shores
And mountain crags: so shalt thou see and hear
The lovely shapes and sounds intelligible
60 Of that eternal language, which thy God
Utters, who from eternity doth teach
Himself in all, and all things in himself.
Great universal Teacher! he shall mould
Thy spirit, and by giving make it ask.

65   Therefore all seasons shall be sweet to thee,
Whether the summer clothe the general earth
With greenness, or the redbreast sit and sing
Betwixt the tufts of snow on the bare branch
Of mossy apple-tree, while the nigh* thatch   near
70 Smokes in the sun-thaw; whether the eve-drops fall
Heard only in the trances of the blast,
Or if the secret ministry of frost
Shall hang them up in silent icicles,
Quietly shining to the quiet Moon.

1798   1798

Dear Babe   Coleridge's sleeping child, Hartley,
born in 1796

THIS LIME-TREE BOWER MY PRISON

In the June of 1797, some long-expected Friends paid a visit to the author's cottage; and on the morning of their arrival, he met with an accident, which disabled him from walking, during the whole time of their stay. One evening, when they had left him for a few hours, he composed the following lines in the garden-bower.

Well, they are gone, and here must I remain,
This lime-tree bower my prison! I have lost
Beauties and feelings, such as would have been
Most sweet to my remembrance even when age
5   Had dimmed mine eyes to blindness! They, meanwhile,
Friends, whom I never more may meet again,
On springy heath, along the hill-top edge,
Wander in gladness, and wind down, perchance,
To that still roaring dell, of which I told;
10   The roaring dell, o'erwooded, narrow, deep,
And only speckled by the mid-day sun;
Where its slim trunk the ash from rock to rock
Flings arching like a bridge; — that branchless ash,
Unsunned and damp, whose few poor yellow leaves
15   Ne'er tremble in the gale, yet tremble still,
Fanned by the water-fall! and there my friends
Behold the dark green file of long lank weeds,
That all at once (a most fantastic sight!)
Still nod and drip beneath the dripping edge
20   Of the blue clay-stone.

                Now, my friends emerge
Beneath the wide wide Heaven — and view again
The many-steepled tract magnificent
Of hilly fields and meadows, and the sea,
With some fair bark,[1] perhaps, whose sails light up
25   The slip of smooth clear blue betwixt two Isles
Of purple shadow! Yes! they wander on
In gladness all; but thou, methinks, most glad,
My gentle-hearted Charles![t] for thou hast pined
And hungered after Nature, many a year,
30   In the great City pent,[t] winning thy way
With sad yet patient soul, through evil and pain
And strange calamity! Ah! slowly sink

---

bark barque, ship or boat   *pent* confined, shut in
Charles Charles Lamb

Behind the western ridge, thou glorious sun!
Shine in the slant beams of the sinking orb,
35   Ye purple heath-flowers! richlier burn, ye clouds!
Live in the yellow light, ye distant groves!
And kindle, thou blue ocean! So my Friend
Struck with deep joy may stand, as I have stood,
Silent with swimming sense; yea, gazing round
40   On the wide landscape, gaze till all doth seem
Less gross than bodily; and of such hues
As veil the Almighty Spirit, when yet he makes
Spirits perceive his presence.
                                        A delight
Comes sudden on my heart, and I am glad
45   As I myself were there! Nor in this bower,
This little lime-tree bower, have I not marked
Much that has soothed me. Pale beneath the blaze
Hung the transparent foliage; and I watched
Some broad and sunny leaf, and loved to see
50   The shadow of the leaf and stem above
Dappling its sunshine! And that walnut-tree
Was richly tinged, and a deep radiance lay
Full on the ancient ivy, which usurps
Those fronting elms, and now, with blackest mass
55   Makes their dark branches gleam a lighter hue
Through the late twilight: and though now the bat
Wheels silent by, and not a swallow twitters,
Yet still the solitary humble bee
Sings in the bean-flower! Henceforth I shall know
60   That Nature ne'er deserts the wise and pure;
No plot so narrow, be but Nature there,
No waste so vacant, but may well employ
Each faculty of sense, and keep the heart
Awake to Love and Beauty! and sometimes
65   'Tis well to be bereft* of promised good,   dispossessed
That we may lift the Soul, and contemplate
With lively joy the joys we cannot share.
My gentle-hearted Charles! when the last rook
Beat its straight path along the dusky air
70   Homewards, I blest it! deeming, its black wing
(Now a dim speck, now vanishing in light)
Had crossed the mighty orb's dilated* glory,   enlarged
While thou stood'st gazing; or when all was still,

Flew creeking† o'er thy head, and had a charm
75 For thee, my gentle-hearted Charles, to whom
No sound is dissonant* which tells of Life.　　　harsh-toned

1797　　　　　　　　　　　　　　1800

KUBLA KHAN†

In Xanadu did Kubla Khan
A stately pleasure-dome decree:
Where Alph, the sacred river, ran
Through caverns measureless to man
5　　Down to a sunless sea.
So twice five miles of fertile ground
With walls and towers were girdled round:
And there were gardens bright with sinuous† rills
Where blossomed many an incense-bearing tree;
10　And here were forests ancient as the hills,
Enfolding sunny spots of greenery.

flew creeking Coleridge wrote: 'Some months after I had written this line, it gave me pleasure to find that Bartram had observed the same circumstance of the Savanna Crane. "When these Birds move their wings in flight, their strokes are slow, moderate and regular; and even when at a considerable distance or high above us, we plainly hear the quill-feathers; their shafts and webs upon one another creek as the joints or working of a vessel in a tempestuous sea"'

Kubla Khan Coleridge prefaced the poem with the following note:

KUBLA KHAN
Or, a Vision in a Dream. A Fragment.

The following fragment is here published at the request of a poet of great and deserved celebrity [Lord Byron], and, as far as the Author's own opinions are concerned, rather as a psychological curiosity, than on the ground of any supposed *poetic* merits.

In the summer of the year 1797, the Author, then in ill health, had retired to a lonely farm-house between Porlock and Linton, on the Exmoor confines of Somerset and Devonshire. In consequence of a slight indisposition, an anodyne had been prescribed, from the effects of which he fell asleep in his chair at the moment that he was reading the following sentence, or words of the same substance, in 'Purchas's

Pilgrimage': 'Here the Khan Kubla commanded a palace to be built, and a stately garden thereunto. And thus ten miles of fertile ground were enclosed with a wall.' The Author continued for about three hours in a profound sleep, at least of the external senses, during which time he has the most vivid confidence, that he could not have composed less than from two to three hundred lines; if that indeed can be called composition in which all the images rose up before him as *things*, with a parallel production of the correspondent expressions, without any sensation or consciousness of effort. On awaking he appeared to himself to have a distinct recollection of the whole, and taking his pen, ink, and paper, instantly and eagerly wrote down the lines that are here preserved. At this moment he was unfortunately called out by a person on business from Porlock, and detained by him above an hour, and on his return to his room, found, to his no small surprise and mortification, that though he still retained some vague and dim recollection of the general purport of the vision, yet, with the exception of some eight or ten scattered lines and images, all the rest had passed away like the images on the surface of a stream into which a stone has been cast, but, alas! without the after-restoration of the latter!

sinuous with many curves

But oh! that deep romantic chasm which slanted
Down the green hill athwart a cedarn cover!
A savage place! as holy and enchanted
15 As e'er beneath a waning moon was haunted
By woman wailing for her demon-lover!
And from this chasm, with ceaseless turmoil seething,
As if this earth in fast thick pants were breathing,
A mighty fountain momently was forced:
20 Amid whose swift half-intermitted burst
Huge fragments vaulted like rebounding hail,
Or chaffy grain beneath the thresher's flail:
And mid these dancing rocks at once and ever
It flung up momently the sacred river.
25 Five miles meandering* with a mazy motion   *wandering
Through wood and dale the sacred river ran,
Then reached the caverns measureless to man,
And sank in tumult to a lifeless ocean:
And 'mid this tumult Kubla heard from far
30 Ancestral voices prophesying war!

    The shadow of the dome of pleasure
    Floated midway on the waves;
    Where was heard the mingled measure
    From the fountain and the caves.
35 It was a miracle of rare device,
A sunny pleasure-dome with caves of ice!

    A damsel with a dulcimer†
    In a vision once I saw:
    It was an Abyssinian maid,
40   And on her dulcimer she played,
    Singing of Mount Abora.
    Could I revive within me
    Her symphony and song,
    To such a deep delight 'twould win me
45 That with music loud and long,
I would build that dome in air,
That sunny dome! those caves of ice!
And all who heard should see them there,
And all should cry, Beware! Beware!
50 His flashing eyes, his floating hair!
Weave a circle round him thrice,
And close your eyes with holy dread,

---

dulcimer stringed musical instrument, prototype piano

For he on honey-dew hath fed,
And drunk the milk of Paradise.

1798   1816

METRICAL FEET[1]

Lesson for a Boy

Trŏchĕe trīps frŏm lōng tŏ shōrt;
From long to long in solemn sort*   manner
Slōw Spōndēe stālks; strōng fōot! yet ill able
Ēvĕr to cōme ŭp wĭth Dāctўl trĭsȳllăblĕ.
5   Ĭāmbĭcs mārch frŏm shōrt tŏ lōng; –
With ă lēap ănd ă bōund thĕ swĭft Ănăpæ̆sts thrōng;
One syllable long, with one short at each side,
Ămphībrăchўs hāstes with ă stātelў stride; –
Fīrst ănd lāst bĕing lōng, mĭddlĕ shōrt, Ămphĭmācer
10 Strīkes hĭs thūndĕrĭng hōofs līke ă prōud hĭgh-brĕd Rācer.
If Derwent be innocent, steady, and wise,
And delight in the things of earth, water, and skies;
Tender warmth at his heart, with these metres to show it,
With sound sense in his brains, may make Derwent a poet, –
15 May crown him with fame, and must win him the love
Of his father on earth and his Father above.
          My dear, dear child!
Could you stand upon Skiddaw,† you would not from its whole ridge
See a man who so loves you as your fond s. t. coleridge.

1806   1834

Metrical Feet this poem was an exercise begun   technical mastery are necessary for the
for Hartley Coleridge and concluded for his   accomplished poet
brother Derwent. Both sensibility and a   *Skiddaw* Lake District peak

From BIOGRAPHIA LITERARIA, Chapter XIII

The imagination then I consider either as primary, or secondary. The primary imagination I hold to be the living power and prime agent of all human perception, and as a repetition in the finite mind of the eternal act of creation in the infinite I AM. The secondary I consider as
5   an echo of the former, co-existing with the conscious will, yet still as identical with the primary in the kind of its agency, and differing only in degree, and in the mode of its operation. It dissolves, diffuses, dissipates,† in order to recreate; or where this process is rendered impossible, yet still, at all events, it struggles to idealize and to unify. It
10   is essentially *vital*, even as all objects (as objects) are essentially fixed and dead.

Fancy, on the contrary, has no other counters to play with but fixities and definites. The fancy is indeed no other than a mode of memory emancipated from the order of time and space; and blended with, and
15   modified by that empirical† phaenomenon of the will which we express by the word *choice*. But equally with the ordinary memory it must receive all its materials ready made from the law of association.

CHAPTER XIV

Occasion of the *Lyrical Ballads*,† and the objects originally proposed – Preface to the second edition – The ensuing controversy, its causes and acrimony – Philosophic definitions of a poem and poetry with scholia.†

During the first year that Mr Wordsworth and I were neighbours our conversations turned frequently on the two cardinal points of poetry, the power of exciting the sympathy of the reader by a faithful adherence to the truth of nature, and the power of giving the interest of novelty
5   by the modifying colours of imagination. The sudden charm which accidents of light and shade, which moonlight or sunset diffused over a known and familiar landscape, appeared to represent the practicability of combining both. These are the poetry of nature. The thought suggested itself (to which of us I do not recollect) that a series of poems
10   might be composed of two sorts. In the one, the incidents and agents were to be, in part at least, supernatural; and the excellence aimed at was to consist in the interesting of the affections by the dramatic truth

---

diffuses, dissipates   spreads out, disperses
empirical   based, or acting, on observation and
   experiment
Lyrical Ballads   the volume developed as an
   idea on a walking tour to Lynton which

Coleridge and Wordsworth took in
November 1797. In the first edition of 1798,
nineteen poems were composed by
Wordsworth and four by Coleridge
scholia   commentary

of such emotions as would naturally accompany such situations, supposing them real. And real in this sense they have been to every
15 human being who, from whatever source of delusion, has at any time believed himself under supernatural agency. For the second class, subjects were to be chosen from ordinary life; the characters and incidents were to be such as will be found in every village and its vicinity where there is a meditative and feeling mind to seek after them, or to
20 notice them when they present themselves.

In this idea originated the plan of the *Lyrical Ballads*; in which it was agreed that my endeavours should be directed to persons and characters supernatural, or at least romantic; yet so as to transfer from our inward nature a human interest and a semblance of truth sufficient
25 to procure for these shadows of imagination that willing suspension of disbelief for the moment, which constitutes poetic faith. Mr Wordsworth, on the other hand, was to propose to himself as his object to give the charm of novelty to things of every day, and to excite a feeling analogous† to the supernatural, by awakening the mind's
30 attention from the lethargy of custom and directing it to the loveliness and the wonders of the world before us; an inexhaustible treasure, but for which, in consequence of the film of familiarity and selfish solicitude, we have eyes yet see not, ears that hear not, and hearts that neither feel nor understand.
35 With this view I wrote the 'Ancient Mariner,' and was preparing among other poems, the 'Dark Ladie,' and the 'Christabel,'† in which I should have more nearly realized my ideal than I had done in my first attempt. But Mr Wordsworth's industry had proved so much more successful and the number of his poems so much greater, that my
40 compositions, instead of forming a balance, appeared rather an interpolation† of heterogeneous matter. Mr Wordsworth added two or three poems written in his own character, in the impassioned, lofty and sustained diction which is characteristic of his genius. In this form the *Lyrical Ballads* were published; and were presented by him, as an
45 experiment, whether subjects which from their nature rejected the usual ornaments and extra-colloquial† style of poems in general might not be so managed in the language of ordinary life as to produce the pleasurable interest which it is the peculiar business of poetry to impart. To the second edition he added a preface of considerable length; in which,
50 notwithstanding some passages of apparently a contrary import, he was understood to contend for the extension of this style to poetry of all

---

analogous similar
Christabel the two parts of *Christabel* were composed 1797 (1798?) and 1800, but Coleridge did not finish the poem in time for the second edition of *Lyrical Ballads* (1800).

The poem remains incomplete and was not published until 1816
interpolation insertion of matter of a different kind
extra-colloquial beyond ordinary speech

kinds, and to reject as vicious and indefensible all phrases and forms of style that were not included in what he (unfortunately, I think, adopting an equivocal[†] expression) called the language of *real* life. From this
55 preface, prefixed to poems in which it was impossible to deny the presence of original genius, however mistaken its direction might be deemed, arose the whole long continued controversy. For from the conjunction of perceived power with supposed heresy I explain the inveteracy[†] and in some instances I grieve to say, the acrimonious
60 passions with which the controversy has been conducted by the assailants.

Had Mr Wordsworth's poems been the silly, the childish things which they were for a long time described as being; had they been really distinguished from the compositions of other poets merely by meanness
65 of language and inanity[†] of thought; had they indeed contained nothing more than what is found in the parodies and pretended imitations of them; they must have sunk at once, a dead weight, into the slough[†] of oblivion, and have dragged the preface along with them. But year after year increased the number of Mr Wordsworth's admirers. They were
70 found too not in the lower classes of the reading public, but chiefly among young men of strong sensibility and meditative minds; and their admiration (inflamed perhaps in some degree by opposition) was distinguished by its intensity, I might almost say, by its religious fervour. These facts, and the intellectual energy of the author, which was more
75 or less consciously felt where it was outwardly and even boisterously denied, meeting with sentiments of aversion to his opinions and of alarm at their consequences, produced an eddy of criticism which would of itself have borne up the poems by the violence with which it whirled them round and round. With many parts of this preface, in the sense
80 attributed to them and which the words undoubtedly seem to authorize, I never concurred; but, on the contrary objected to them as erroneous in principle, and as contradictory (in appearance at least) both to other parts of the same preface and to the author's own practice in the greater number of the poems themselves. Mr Wordsworth in his recent
85 collection[†] has, I find, degraded this prefatory disquisition[†] to the end of his second volume, to be read or not at the reader's choice. But he has not, as far as I can discover, announced any change in his poetic creed. At all events, considering it as the source of a controversy in which I have been honoured more than I deserve by the frequent
90 conjunction of my name with his, I think it expedient to declare once

equivocal ambiguous
inveteracy obstinacy
inanity emptiness
slough quagmire

recent collection Wordsworth's *Poems,*
  including Lyrical Ballads and Miscellaneous
  Pieces, with Additional Poems, a New Preface
  and a Supplementary Essay, 2 vols (1815)
disquisition enquiry

for all in what points I coincide with his opinions, and in what points I altogether differ. But in order to render myself intelligible I must previously, in as few words as possible, explain my ideas, first, of a poem; and secondly, of poetry itself, in kind and in essence.

95 The office[†] of philosophical disquisition consists in just distinction; while it is the privilege of the philosopher to preserve himself constantly aware that distinction is not division. In order to obtain adequate notions of any truth, we must intellectually separate its distinguishable parts; and this is the technical *process* of philosophy. But having so
100 done, we must then restore them in our conceptions to the unity in which they actually co-exist; and this is the *result* of philosophy. A poem contains the same elements as a prose composition; the difference therefore must consist in a different combination of them, in consequence of a different object proposed. According to the difference of the object
105 will be the difference of the combination. It is possible that the object may be merely to facilitate the recollection of any given facts or observations by artificial arrangement; and the composition will be a poem, merely because it is distinguished from prose by metre, or by rhyme, or by both conjointly. In this, the lowest sense, a man might
110 attribute the name of a poem to the well-known enumeration of the days in the several months:

Thirty days hath September
April, June, and November, etc.

and others of the same class and purpose. And as a particular pleasure
115 is found in anticipating the recurrence of sounds and quantities, all compositions that have this charm superadded, whatever be their contents, *may* be entitled poems.

So much for the superficial form. A difference of object and contents supplies an additional ground of distinction. The immediate purpose
120 may be the communication of truths; either of truth absolute and demonstrable, as in works of science; or of facts experienced and recorded, as in history. Pleasure, and that of the highest and most permanent kind, may result from the attainment of the end; but it is not itself the immediate end. In other works the communication of
125 pleasure may be the immediate purpose; and though truth, either moral or intellectual, ought to be the ultimate end, yet this will distinguish the character of the author, not the class to which the work belongs. Blest indeed is that state of society in which the immediate purpose would be baffled by the perversion of the proper ultimate end; in which
130 no charm of diction or imagery could exempt the Bathyllus[†] even of an

office function

Bathyllus the beautiful youth of Samos whom Anacreon celebrated in his twenty-ninth ode

Anacreon, or the Alexis[†] of Virgil, from disgust and aversion!

But the communication of pleasure may be the immediate object of a work not metrically composed; and that object may have been in a high degree attained, as in novels and romances. Would then the mere
135 superaddition of metre, with or without rhyme, entitle these to the name of poems? The answer is that nothing can permanently please which does not contain in itself the reason why it is so, and not otherwise. If metre be superadded, all other parts must be made consonant with it. They must be such as to justify the perpetual and
140 distinct attention to each part which an exact correspondent recurrence of accent and sound are calculated to excite. The final definition then, so deduced, may be thus worded. A poem is that species of composition which is opposed to works of science by proposing for its *immediate* object pleasure, not truth; and from all other species (having this object
145 in common with it) it is discriminated by proposing to itself such delight from the whole as is compatible with a distinct gratification from each component part.

Controversy is not seldom excited in consequence of the disputants attaching each a different meaning to the same word; and in few
150 instances has this been more striking than in disputes concerning the present subject. If a man chooses to call every composition a poem which is rhyme, or measure, or both, I must leave his opinion uncontroverted. The distinction is at least competent to characterize the writer's intention. If it were subjoined that the whole is likewise
155 entertaining or affecting as a tale or as a series of interesting reflections, I of course admit this as another fit ingredient of a poem and an additional merit. But if the definition sought for be that of a legitimate poem, I answer it must be one of the parts of which mutually support and explain each other; all in their proportion harmonizing with, and
160 supporting the purpose and known influences of metrical arrangement. The philosophic critics of all ages coincide with the ultimate judgment of all countries in equally denying the praises of a just poem on the one hand to a series of striking lines or distichs,[†] each of which absorbing the whole attention of the reader to itself disjoins it from its context
165 and makes it a separate whole, instead of a harmonizing part; and on the other hand, to an unsustained composition, from which the reader collects rapidly the general result unattracted by the component parts. The reader should be carried forward, not merely or chiefly by the mechanical impulse of curiosity, or by a restless desire to arrive at the
170 final solution; but by the pleasurable activity of mind excited by the attractions of the journey itself. Like the motion of a serpent, which

---

Alexis another beautiful youth wooed by the   *distichs* couplets
shepherd Corydon in Virgil's second eclogue

the Egyptians made the emblem of intellectual power; or like the path
of sound through the air; at every step he pauses and half recedes, and
from the retrogressive movement collects the force which again carries
175   him onward. 'Praecipitandus est liber spiritus,'[†] says Petronius Arbiter
most happily. The epithet *liber*[†] here balances the preceding verb; and
it is not easy to conceive more meaning condensed in fewer words.

But if this should be admitted as a satisfactory character of a poem,
we have still to seek for a definition of poetry. The writings of Plato,
180   and Bishop Taylor,[†] and the *Theoria Sacra* of Burnet,[†] furnish undeniable
proofs that poetry of the highest kind may exist without metre, and
even without the contradistinguishing objects of a poem. The first
chapter of Isaiah (indeed a very large proportion of the whole book) is
poetry in the most emphatic sense; yet it would be not less irrational
185   than strange to assert that pleasure, and not truth, was the immediate
object of the prophet. In short, whatever specific import we attach to
the word poetry, there will be found involved in it, as a necessary
consequence, that a poem of any length neither can be, nor ought to
be, all poetry. Yet if a harmonious whole is to be produced, the
190   remaining parts must be preserved *in keeping* with the poetry; and this
can be no otherwise effected than by such a studied selection and
artificial arrangement as will partake of one, though not a peculiar,
property of poetry. And this again can be no other than the property
of exciting a more continuous and equal attention than the language of
195   prose aims at, whether colloquial or written.

My own conclusions on the nature of poetry, in the strictest use of
the word, have been in part anticipated in the preceding disquisition
on the fancy and imagination. What is poetry? is so nearly the same
question with, what is a poet? that the answer to the one is involved in
200   the solution of the other. For it is a distinction resulting from the poetic
genius itself, which sustains and modifies the images, thoughts and
emotions of the poet's own mind. The poet, described in ideal perfection,
brings the whole soul of man into activity, with the subordination of
its faculties to each other, according to their relative worth and dignity.
205   He diffuses a tone and spirit of unity that blends and (as it were) fuses,
each into each, by that synthetic[†] and magical power to which we have
exclusively appropriated the name of imagination. This power, first put
in action by the will and understanding and retained under their
irremissive,[†] though gentle and unnoticed, control (*laxis effertur hab-*

Praecipitandus . . . spiritus The free spirit (of
the epic poet) must be hurried on (by
digressions etc.): *Satyricon*, 118
liber it balances the *must* contained in
precipitandus
Bishop Taylor Jeremy Taylor (1613–67),
bishop of Down and Connor and

subsequently of Dromore
Burnet Thomas Burnet (?1635–1715),
Yorkshire divine and Master of the
Charterhouse
synthetic blending
irremissive unalterably binding

210   *enis*[†]) reveals itself in the balance or reconciliation of opposite or
discordant qualities: of sameness, with difference; of the general, with
the concrete; the idea, with the image; the individual, with the
representative; the sense of novelty and freshness, with old and familiar
objects; a more than usual state of emotion, with more than usual order;
215   judgement ever awake and steady self-possession, with enthusiasm and
feeling profound or vehement; and while it blends and harmonizes the
natural and the artificial, still subordinates art to nature; the manner
to the matter; and our admiration of the poet to our sympathy with
the poetry. 'Doubtless,' as Sir John Davies[†] observes of the soul (and
220   his words may with slight alteration be applied, and even more
appropriately, to the poetic imagination):

> Doubtless this could not be, but that she turns
> Bodies to spirit by sublimation[†] strange,
> As fire converts to fire the things it burns,
225   > As we our food into our nature change.
>
> From their gross matter she abstracts their forms,
> And draws a kind of quintessence from things;
> Which to her proper nature she transforms
> To bear them light on her celestial wings.
>
230   > Thus does she,[†] when from individual states
> She doth abstract the universal kinds;
> Which then re-clothed in divers names and fates
> Steal access through our senses to our minds.

Finally, good sense is the body of poetic genius, fancy its drapery,
235   motion its life, and imagination the soul that is every where, and in
each; and forms all into one graceful and intelligent whole.

1815   1817

---

laxis . . . habenis is borne onwards with loose
   reins: Virgil, *Georgics*, II. 364
Sir John Davies (1569–1626), lawyer
   (solicitor- and attorney-general for Ireland)
   and poet
sublimation refining process

Thus does she . . . minds the third stanza
   should read:
   This doth she, when from things particular
   She doth abstract the universal kinds,
   Which bodiless and immaterial are,
   And can be lodg'd but only in our minds.

DEJECTION†

A LETTER

Well! if the Bard was weatherwise, who made
The grand old Ballad of Sir Patrick Spence,†
This Night, so tranquil now, will not go hence
Unrous'd by winds, that ply a busier trade
5   Than that, which moulds yon clouds in lazy flakes,
Or the dull sobbing Draft, that drones and rakes
Upon the Strings of this Eolian Lute,†
Which better far were mute.
For, lo! the New Moon, winter-bright!
10   And overspread with phantom Light
(With swimming phantom Light o'erspread
But rimm'd and circled with a silver Thread)
I see the Old Moon in her Lap, foretelling
The coming-on of Rain and squally Blast —
15   O! Sara! that the Gust ev'n now were swelling,
And the slant Night-shower driving loud and fast!

A Grief without a pang, void, dark and drear,
A stifling, drowsy, unimpassion'd Grief
That finds no natural outlet, no Relief
20   In word, or sigh, or tear —
This, Sara! well thou know'st,
Is that sore Evil, which I dread the most,
And oft'nest suffer! In this heartless Mood,
To other thoughts by yonder Throstle* woo'd,   thrush
25   That pipes within the Larch tree, not unseen,
(The Larch, which pushes out in tassels green
Its bundled Leafits) woo'd to mild Delights
By all the tender Sounds and gentle Sights
Of this sweet Primrose-month* — and *vainly* woo'd   April
30   O dearest Sara! in this heartless Mood
All this long Eve, so balmy† and serene,
Have I been gazing on the western Sky
And its peculiar Tint of Yellow Green —

Dejection This is the original verse-letter poem
written on 4 April 1802, and sent to Sara
Hutchinson. The poem published in *Sybilline
Leaves* called *Dejection: an Ode* is a 139 line
version, condensed and reshaped
Ballad . . . Spence a traditional ballad, one
stanza of which is as follows:

Late, late yestreen, I saw the New Moon,
With the old Moon in her arms;
And I fear, I fear, my Master dear!
We shall have a deadly storm.
Eolian Lute cf. poem *The Eolian Harp*, above
balmy gentle, fragrant

And still I gaze – and with how blank an eye!
35   And those thin Clouds above, in flakes and bars,
That give away their Motion to the Stars;
Those Stars, that glide behind them, or between,
Now sparkling, now bedimm'd, but always seen;
Yon crescent Moon, as fix'd as if it grew
40   In its own cloudless, starless Lake of Blue –
A boat becalm'd! dear William's* Sky Canoe!†   Wordsworth's
– I see them all, so excellently fair!
I see, not feel, how beautiful they are.

My genial* Spirits fail –   enlivening
45   And what can these avail
To lift the smoth'ring Weight from off my Breast?
It were a vain Endeavor,
Tho' I should gaze for ever
On that Green Light that lingers in the West!
50   I may not hope from outward Forms to win
The Passion and the Life, whose Fountains are within!

These lifeless Shapes, around, below, Above,
   O what can they impart?
When even the gentle Thought, that thou, my Love!
55   Art gazing, now, like me,
And see'st the Heaven, I see –
Sweet Thought it is – yet feebly stirs my Heart!
Feebly! O feebly! – Yet
(I well remember it)
60   In my first Dawn of Youth that Fancy stole
With many secret Yearnings on my Soul.
At eve, sky-gazing in 'ecstatic fit'
(Alas! for cloister'd in a city School
The Sky was all, I knew, of Beautiful)
65   At the barr'd window often did I sit,
And oft upon the leaded School-roof lay,
And to myself would say –
There does not live the Man so stripp'd of good affections
As not to love to see a Maiden's quiet Eyes
70   Uprais'd, and linking on sweet Dreams by dim Connections
To Moon, or Evening Star, or glorious western Skies –
While yet a Boy, this Thought would so pursue me,
That often it became a kind of Vision to me!

Sky Canoe   crescent moon

Sweet Thought! and dear of old
75   To Hearts of finer Mould!
Ten thousand times by Friends and Lovers blest!
I spake with rash Despair,
And ere I was aware,
The Weight was somewhat lifted from my Breast!
80   O Sara! in the weather-fended[†] Wood,
Thy lov'd haunt! where the Stock-doves coo at Noon
I guess, that thou hast stood
And watch'd yon Crescent, and its ghost-like Moon.
And yet, far rather in my present Mood
85   I would, that thou'dst been sitting all this while
Upon the sod-built Seat of Camomile —[†]
And tho' thy Robin may have ceas'd to sing,
Yet needs for *my* sake must thou love to hear
The Bee-hive murmuring near,
90   That ever-busy and most quiet Thing
Which I have heard at Midnight murmuring.

I feel my spirit moved.
And whereso'er thou be,
O Sister! O Beloved!
95   Those dear mild Eyes, that see
Even now the Heaven, *I* see —
There is a Prayer in them! It is for *me* —
And I, dear Sara, *I* am blessing *thee*!

It was as calm as this, that happy night
100   When Mary,[†] thou, and I together were,
The low decaying Fire our only Light,
And listen'd to the Stillness of the Air!
O that affectionate and blameless Maid,
Dear Mary! on her Lap my head she lay'd —
105   Her Hand was on my Brow,
Even as my own is now;
And on my Cheek I felt the eye-lash play.
Such joy I had, that I may truly say,
My spirit was awe-stricken with the Excess
110   And trance-like Depth of its brief Happiness.

---

weather-fended the wood acts as a defence   which bears flowers like daisies
  against weather   *Mary* Sara's sister Mary who married
sod . . . Camomile a seat built with turf   Wordsworth
  covered with the creeping plant camomile

Ah fair Remembrances, that so revive
The Heart, and fill it with a living Power,
Where were they, Sara? – or did I not strive
To win them to me? – on the fretting Hour
115 Then when I wrote thee that complaining Scroll,*   letter
Which even to bodily Sickness bruis'd thy Soul!
And yet thou blam'st thyself alone! And yet
Forbidd'st me all Regret!
And must I not regret, that I distress'd
120 Thee, best belov'd, who lovest me the best?
My better mind had fled, I know not whither,
For O! was this an absent Friend's Employ
To send from far both Pain and Sorrow thither
Where still his Blessings should have call'd down Joy!
125 I read thy guileless Letter o'er again –
I hear thee of thy blameless Self complain –
And only this I learn – and this, alas! I know –
Thou thou art weak and pale with Sickness, Grief, and Pain –
And I, – I made thee so!

130 O for my own sake I regret perforce†
Whatever turns thee, Sara! from the course
Of calm Well-being and a Heart at rest!
When thou, and with thee those, whom thou lov'st best,
Shall dwell together in one happy Home,
135 One House, the dear *abiding* Home of All,
I too will crown me with a Coronal –†
Nor shall this Heart in idle Wishes roam
        Morbidly soft!
No! let me trust, that I shall wear away
140 In no inglorious Toils the manly Day,
And only now and then, and not too oft,
Some dear and memorable Eve will bless
Dreaming of all your Loves and Quietness.
Be happy, and I need thee not in sight.
145 Peace in thy Heart, and Quiet in thy Dwelling,
Health in thy Limbs, and in thine eyes the Light
Of Love and Hope and honorable Feeling –
Where e'er I am, I shall be well content!
Not near thee, haply shall be more content!
150 To all things I prefer the Permanent.
And better seems it, for a Heart, like mine,
Always to *know*, than sometimes to behold,

---

perforce of necessity   *Coronal* wreath, garland

Their Happiness and thine –
For Change doth trouble me with pangs untold!
155 To see thee, hear thee, feel thee – then to part
   Oh! it weighs down the heart!
To *visit* those, I love, as I love thee,
Mary, and William, and dear Dorothy,†
It is but a temptation to repine –*   fret
160 The transientness† is Poison in the Wine,
Eats out the pith of Joy, makes all Joy hollow,
All Pleasure a dim Dream of Pain to follow!
My own peculiar Lot, my house-hold Life
It is, and will remain, Indifference or Strife.
165 While *Ye* are *well* and *happy*, 'twould but wrong you
If I should fondly yearn to be among you –
Wherefore, O wherefore! should I wish to be
A wither'd branch upon a blossoming Tree?

But (let me say it! for I vainly strive
170 To beat away the Thought), but if thou pin'd
Whate'er the Cause, in body or in mind,
I were the miserablest Man alive
To know it and be absent! Thy Delights
Far off, or near, alike I may partake –
175 But O! to mourn for thee, and to forsake
All power, all hope, of giving comfort to thee –
To know that thou art weak and worn with pain,
And not to hear thee, Sara! not to view thee –
   Not sit beside thy Bed,
180   Not press thy aching Head,
   Not bring thee Health again –
   At least to hope, to try –
By this Voice, which thou lov'st, and by this earnest Eye –
Nay, wherefore did I let it haunt my Mind
185 The dark distressful Dream!
I turn from it, and listen to the Wind
Which long has rav'd unnotic'd! What a Scream
Of agony, by Torture lengthen'd out
That Lute sent forth! O thou wild Storm without!
190 Jagg'd Rock, or mountain Pond, or blasted Tree,
Or Pine-Grove, whither Woodman never clomb,*   climbed
Or lonely House, long held the Witches' Home,
Methinks were fitter Instruments for Thee,

Dorothy Wordsworth's sister   *transientness* transience, impermanence

Mad Lutanist! that in this month of Showers,
195 Of dark brown Gardens and of peeping Flowers,
Mak'st Devil's Yule with worse than wintry Song
The Blossoms, Buds, and timorous Leaves among!
Thou Actor, perfect in all tragic Sounds!
Thou mighty Poet, even to frenzy bold!
200 What tell'st thou now about?
'Tis of the Rushing of an Host in Rout
And many groans for men with smarting Wounds –
At once they groan with smart, and shudder with the cold!
'Tis hush'd! there is a Trance of deepest Silence,
205 Again! but all that Sound, as of a rushing Crowd,
And Groans and tremulous Shudderings, all are over.
And it has other Sounds, and all less deep, less loud!
A Tale of less Affright,
And tempered with Delight,
210 As William's self had made the tender Lay –
'Tis of a little Child
Upon a heathy Wild,
Not far from home, but it has lost its way –
And now moans low in utter grief and fear –
215 And now screams loud, and hopes to make its Mother hear!

'Tis Midnight! and small Thoughts have I of Sleep.
Full seldom may my Friend such Vigils keep –
O breathe She softly in her gentle Sleep!
Cover her, gentle sleep! with wings of Healing.
220 And be this Tempest but a Mountain Birth!
May all the Stars hang bright above her Dwelling,
Silent, as though they *watch'd* the sleeping Earth!
Healthful and light, my Darling! may'st thou rise
With clear and cheerful Eyes –
225 And of the same good Tidings to me send!
For oh! beloved Friend!
I am not the buoyant Thing I was of yore
When like an own Child, I to Joy belong'd:
For others mourning oft, myself oft sorely wrong'd,
230 Yet bearing all things then, as if I nothing bore!

Yes, dearest Sara, yes!
There *was* a time when tho' my path was rough,
The Joy within me dallied with Distress;
And all Misfortunes were but as the Stuff
235 Whence Fancy made me Dreams of Happiness;

For Hope grew round me, like the climbing Vine,
And Leaves and Fruitage, not my own, seem'd mine!
But now Ill Tidings bow me down to earth,
Nor care I that they rob me of my Mirth –
240   But Oh! each Visitation
Suspends what nature gave me at my Birth,
My shaping spirit of Imagination!

Speak not now of those habitual Ills
That wear out Life, when two unequal Minds
245   Meet in one House and two discordant Wills –
    This leaves me, where it finds,
Past Cure, and past Complaint, – a fate austere
Too fix'd and hopeless to partake of Fear!
But thou, dear Sara! (dear indeed thou art,
250   My Comforter, a Heart within my Heart!)
Thou, and the Few, we love, tho' few ye be,
Make up a World of Hopes and Fears for me.
And if Affliction, or distemp'ring Pain,
Or wayward Chance befall you, I complain
255   Not that I mourn – O Friends, most dear! most true!
    Methinks to weep with you
Were better far than to rejoice alone –
But that my coarse domestic Life has known
No Habits of heart-nursing Sympathy,
260   No Griefs but such as dull and deaden me,
No mutual mild Enjoyments of its own,
No Hopes of its own Vintage, None O! none –
Whence when I mourn'd for you, my Heart might borrow
Fair forms and living Motions for its Sorrow.
265   For not to think of what I needs must feel,
But to be still and patient all I can;
And haply by abstruse* Research to steal   profound
From my own Nature, all the Natural man –
This was my sole Resource, my wisest plan!
270   And that, which suits a part, infects the whole,
And now is almost grown the Temper of my Soul.

My little Children are a Joy, a Love,
    A good Gift from above!
But what is Bliss, that still calls up a Woe,
275   And makes it doubly keen
Compelling me to *feel*, as well as *know*,
What a most blessed Lot mine might have been.

Those little Angel Children (woe is me!)
There have been hours when feeling how they bind
280   And pluck out the Wing-feathers of my Mind.
Turning my Error to Necessity,
I have half-wish'd they never had been born!
That seldom! but sad Thoughts they always bring
And like the Poet's Philomel,* I sing   nightingale
285   My Love-song, with my breast against a Thorn.

With no unthankful Spirit I confess,
This clinging Grief, too, in its turn, awakes
That Love, and Father's Joy; but O! it makes
The Love the greater, and the Joy far less.
290   These Mountains too, these Vales, these Woods, these Lakes,
Scenes full of Beauty and of Loftiness
Where all my Life I fondly hop'd to live –
I were sunk low indeed, did they *no* solace* give;   comfort
But oft I seem to feel, and evermore I fear,
295   They are not to me now the Things, which once they were.

O Sara! we receive but what we give,
And in *our* life alone does Nature live
Our's is her Wedding Garment, our's her Shroud –
And would we aught behold of higher Worth
300   Than that inanimate cold World allow'd
To that poor loveless ever anxious Crowd,
·   Ah! from the Soul itself must issue forth
A Light, a Glory, and a luminous* Cloud   shining
Enveloping the Earth!
305   And from the Soul itself must there be sent
A sweet and potent Voice, of its own Birth,
Of all sweet Sounds, the Life and Element.
O pure of Heart! thou need'st not ask of me
What this strong music in the Soul may be,
310   What and wherin it doth exist,
This Light, this Glory, this fair luminous Mist,
This beautiful and beauty-making Power!
Joy, innocent Sara! Joy, that ne'er was given
Save to the pure, and in their purest Hour,
315   *Joy*, Sara! is the Spirit and the Power,
That wedding Nature to us gives in Dower*   gift
         A new Earth and new Heaven,
Undreamt of by the Sensual and the Proud!
Joy is that strong Voice, Joy that luminous Cloud –

320   We, we ourselves rejoice!
        And thence flows all that charms or ear or sight,
        All melodies, the Echoes of that Voice,
        All Colours a Suffusion* of that Light.   welling up
        Sister and Friend of my devoutest Choice
325   Thou being innocent and full of love,
        And nested with the Darlings of thy Love,
        And feeling in thy Soul, Heart, Lips and Arms
        Even what the conjugal* and mother Dove,   married
        That borrows genial Warmth from those, she warms,
330   Feels in the thrill'd wings, blessedly outspread –
        Thou free'd awhile from Cares and human Dread
        By the Immenseness of the Good and Fair
            Which thou seest everywhere –
        Thus, thus, should'st thou rejoice!
335   To thee would all things live from Pole to Pole;
        Their Life the Eddying of thy living Soul –
        O dear! O Innocent! O full of Love!
        A very Friend! A Sister of my Choice –
        O dear, as Light and Impulse from above,
340   Thus may'st thou ever, evermore rejoice!

        1802   1947

Robert Southey
1774–1843

Southey, Poet Laureate from 1813 to 1843, was very much like his successor to the Laureateship, William Wordsworth, in one respect: he started off sympathetic to radical, revolutionary policies, and finished as a diehard conservative. Early on he was expelled from Westminster School for instigating a magazine called *The Flagellant*. He proceeded to Balliol College, a devotee of Rousseau and an admirer of Goethe's romantic hero, Werther.

While at Oxford, he met S. T. Coleridge who was on a walking tour, and their subsequent friendship produced the Utopian scheme of Pantisocracy, the establishment of an ideal community on the banks of the Susquehanna in Pennsylvania. Although the project never made headway, Coleridge and Southey each married one of the Fricker sisters who were also involved in the scheme. Southey's marriage took place in 1795, and during the years 1796–78 he wrote many ballads and other poems, such as *The Inchcape Rock* and *The Holly Tree*. In 1800 he visited Spain, and on return to England settled in the Lake District. The following year he wrote *Thalaba*, the first of a number of epic, romantic poems.

Above all things, Southey was a professional writer who decided to make his living from letters. In 1807 he was rewarded by a government pension, and published *Letters from England by Don Manual Alvarez Espriella*, a fictional account of life and manners in England.

He cut his roots with his radical past when, in 1809, he began writing for the *Quarterly Review*, hoping that its establishment character, and ministerial tone, would lend authority to his own views. He was made Poet Laureate in 1813, an office which, as the years passed, became increasingly distasteful to him; but there followed some of his most famous work: his *Life of Nelson* (1813), *Life of John Wesley* (1820), and his edition of Cowper (1835–7). He had already published another epic romance, *The Curse of Kehama* (1810), and the first volume of his *History of Brazil* in the same year: the other two volumes were published in 1817 and 1819.

His greatest misjudgement and absurdity was to publish *A Vision of Judgement* (1821), composed in hexameters, and celebrating the supposed arrival of George III in heaven: in the preface, he attacked

Byron and the 'Satanic school' of poetry. Byron subsequently avenged himself by ridiculing Southey in his own poem *The Vision of Judgement*, and in many places in *Don Juan*.

In 1837 Southey's wife died. Two years later he married Caroline Bowles, but his final years were spent in mental confusion 'patting his books with both hands affectionately' as though they were his children. It was a sad end for a man of dedication to writing, and of prodigious output.

THE EBB TIDE

Slowly thy flowing tide
Came in, old Avon! scarcely did mine eyes,
As watchful I roam'd thy green-wood side,
Perceive its gentle rise.

5   With many a stroke and strong
The labouring boatmen upward plied their oars,
Yet little way they made, though labouring long
Between thy winding shores.

Now down thine ebbing tide
10 The unlaboured boat falls rapidly along;
The solitary helms-man sits to guide,
And sings an idle song.

Now o'er the rocks, that lay
So silent late, the shallow current roars;
15 Fast flow thy waters on their sea-ward way
Thro' wider-spreading shores.

Avon! I gaze and know
The lesson emblemed in thy varying way;
It speaks of human joys that rise so slow,
20   So rapidly decay.

Kingdoms that long have stood,
And slow to strength and power attain'd at last,
Thus from the summit of high fortune's flood
Ebb to their ruin fast.

25   Thus like thy flow appears
          Time's tardy course to manhood's envied stage;
          Alas! how hurryingly the ebbing years
              Then hasten to old age!

      c. 1799   1799

From THE CURSE OF KEHAMA

              I charm thy life
145   From the weapons of strife,
          From stone and from wood,
              From fire and from flood,
              From the serpent's tooth,
              And the beasts of blood:
150   From Sickness I charm thee,
          And Time shall not harm thee;
              But Earth which is mine,
              Its fruits shall deny thee;
              And Water shall hear me,
155   And know thee and fly thee;
      And the Winds shall not touch thee
              When they pass by thee,
          And the Dews shall not wet thee,
              When they fall nigh thee:
160   And thou shalt seek Death
              To release thee, in vain;
          Thou shalt live in thy pain
              While Kehama shall reign,
              With a fire in thy heart,
165   And a fire in thy brain;
          And Sleep shall obey me,
              And visit thee never,
          And the Curse shall be on thee
              For ever and ever.

      1801–9   1810

Jane Austen
1775–1817

Jane Austen led a reserved and quiet life, but she was a woman of remarkably sharp intellect, and a keen observer of human nature. She was born into a clerical family: her father was Rector of Steventon, Hampshire. The farthest afield she went in the first twenty-five years of her uneventful life, was on quiet journeys made to London, or to resorts such as Bath or Lyme, or to her brothers' houses. She did, however, live in a number of different places. In 1801 she moved to Bath; from there, in 1806, to Southampton; and, in 1809, back to Hampshire, to Chawton. She died in Winchester while she was staying in lodgings.

She is regarded as a major novelist, noted for six novels in particular. Three of them are generally judged to be minor works: *Sense and Sensibility*, begun in 1795 and published 1811, *Pride and Prejudice*, begun 1796–7, published 1813, and *Northanger Abbey*, begun in 1798–9, published 1817. Three are her major novels, all written between 1811 and 1816: *Mansfield Park* (1813), *Emma* (1815) and *Persuasion* (1817).

The range of society which she presented in her novels was small and confined. She was essentially a miniaturist, who looked at people and events, behaviour and surroundings, with an analytical, detailed attention and a firm moral grasp. She was a perspicacious satirist of subtlety, elegance and wit; although some of her letters show her to be capable of a surprising coarseness. Her restrained domestic life did not restrict her large intellectual scope.

From EMMA†

[Emma's Matchmaking]

CHAPTER 1

Emma Woodhouse, handsome, clever, and rich, with a comfortable home and happy disposition, seemed to unite some of the best blessings of existence; and had lived nearly twenty-one years in the world with very little to distress or vex her.

5   She was the youngest of the two daughters of a most affectionate, indulgent father, and had, in consequence of her sister's marriage, been mistress of his house from a very early period. Her mother had died too long ago for her to have more than an indistinct remembrance of her caresses, and her place had been supplied by an excellent woman
10   as governess, who had fallen little short of a mother in affection.

Sixteen years had Miss Taylor been in Mr Woodhouse's family, less a governess than a friend, very fond of both daughters, but particularly of Emma. Between *them* it was more the intimacy of sisters. Even before Miss Taylor had ceased to hold the nominal office of governess, the
15   mildness of her temper had hardly allowed her to impose any restraint; and the shadow of authority being now long passed away, they had been living together as friend and friend very mutually attached, and Emma doing just what she liked; highly esteeming Miss Taylor's judgment, but directed chiefly by her own.

20   The real evils indeed of Emma's situation were the power of having rather too much her own way, and a disposition to think a little too well of herself; these were the disadvantages which threatened alloy† to her many enjoyments. The danger, however, was at present so unperceived, that they did not by any means rank as misfortunes with
25   her.

Sorrow came – a gentle sorrow – but not at all in the shape of any disagreeable consciousness. Miss Taylor married. It was Miss Taylor's loss which first brought grief. It was on the wedding-day of this beloved friend that Emma first sat in mournful thought of any continuance. The
30   wedding over and the bride-people gone, her father and herself were left to dine together, with no prospect of a third to cheer a long evening. Her father composed himself to sleep after dinner, as usual, and she had then only to sit and think of what she had lost.

The event had every promise of happiness for her friend. Mr Weston
35   was a man of unexceptionable character, easy fortune, suitable age and

---

Emma Emma is a clever, pretty, self-confident young woman who looks after her father, Mr Woodhouse. Her former governess and companion, Anne Taylor, has just left them to marry a neighbour, Mr Weston
alloy moderation

pleasant manners; and there was some satisfaction in considering with
what self-denying, generous friendship she had always wished and
promoted the match; but it was a black morning's work for her. The
want of Miss Taylor would be felt every hour of every day. She recalled
40   her past kindness – the kindness, the affection of sixteen years – how
she had taught and how she had played with her from five years old –
how she had devoted all her powers to attach and amuse her in health –
and how nursed her through the various illnesses of childhood. A large
debt of gratitude was owing here; but the intercourse of the last seven
45   years, the equal footing and perfect unreserve which had soon followed
Isabella's marriage on their being left to each other, was yet a dearer,
tenderer recollection. It had been a friend and companion such as few
possessed, intelligent, well-informed, useful, gentle, knowing all the
ways of the family, interested in all its concerns, and peculiarly interested
50   in herself, in every pleasure, every scheme of hers; – one to whom she
could speak every thought as it arose, and who had such an affection
for her as could never find fault.
How was she to bear the change? – It was true that her friend was
going only half a mile from them; but Emma was aware that great
55   must be the difference between a Mrs Weston only half a mile from
them, and a Miss Taylor in the house; and with all her advantages,
natural and domestic, she was now in great danger of suffering from
intellectual solitude. She dearly loved her father, but he was no
companion for her. He could not meet her in conversation, rational or
60   playful.
The evil of the actual disparity in their ages (and Mr Woodhouse had
not married early) was much increased by his constitution and habits;
for having been a valetudinarian[†] all his life, without activity of mind
or body, he was a much older man in ways than in years; and though
65   everywhere beloved for the friendliness of his heart and his amiable
temper, his talents could not have recommended him at any time.
Her sister, though comparatively but little removed by matrimony,
being settled in London, only sixteen miles off, was much beyond her
daily reach; and many a long October and November evening must be
70   struggled through at Hartfield, before Christmas brought the next visit
from Isabella and her husband and their little children to fill the house
and give her pleasant society again.
Highbury, the large and populous village almost amounting to a
town, to which Hartfield, in spite of its separate lawns and shrubberies
75   and name, did really belong, afforded her no equals. The Woodhouses
were first in consequence there. All looked up to them. She had many

valetudinarian   a person of infirm health
(especially one much concerned with his own health)

acquaintances in the place, for her father was universally civil, but not one among them who could be accepted in lieu of Miss Taylor for even half a day. It was a melancholy change; and Emma could not but sigh
80   over it and wish for impossible things, till her father awoke, and made it necessary to be cheerful. His spirits required support. He was a nervous man, easily depressed; fond of every body that he was used to, and hating to part with them; hating change of every kind. Matrimony, as the origin of change, was always disagreeable; and he was by no
85   means yet reconciled to his own daughter's marrying, nor could ever speak of her but with compassion, though it had been entirely a match of affection, when he was now obliged to part with Miss Taylor too; and from his habits of gentle selfishness and of being never able to suppose that other people could feel differently from himself, he was
90   very much disposed to think Miss Taylor had done as sad a thing for herself as for them, and would have been a great deal happier if she had spent all the rest of her life at Hartfield. Emma smiled and chatted as cheerfully as she could, to keep him from such thoughts; but when tea came, it was impossible for him not to say exactly as he had said at
95   dinner,

'Poor Miss Taylor! – I wish she were here again. What a pity it is that Mr Weston ever thought of her!'

'I cannot agree with you, papa; you know I cannot. Mr Weston is such a good-humoured, pleasant, excellent man that he thoroughly
100   deserves a good wife; – and you would not have had Miss Taylor live with us for ever and bear all my odd humours, when she might have a house of her own?'

'A house of her own! – but where is the advantage of a house of her own? This is three times as large. – And you have never any odd
105   humours,† my dear.'

'How often we shall be going to see them and they coming to see us! – We shall be always meeting! We must begin, we must go and pay our wedding-visit very soon.'

'My dear, how am I to get so far? Randalls is such a distance. I could
110   not walk half so far.'

'No, papa, nobody thought of your walking. We must go in the carriage to be sure.'

'The carriage! But James will not like to put the horses to for such a little way; – and where are the poor horses to be while we are paying
115   our visit?'

'They are to be put into Mr Weston's stable, papa. You know we have settled all that already. We talked it all over with Mr Weston last night. And as for James, you may be very sure he will always like going

_____

humours physical conditions

to Randalls, because of his daughter's being housemaid there. I only
doubt whether he will ever take us anywhere else. That, was your doing,
papa. You got Hannah that good place. Nobody thought of Hannah
till you mentioned her – James is so obliged to you!'
'I am very glad I did think of her. It was very lucky, for I would not
have had poor James think himself slighted upon any account; and I
am sure she will make a very good servant; she is a civil, pretty-spoken
girl; I have a great opinion of her. Whenever I see her, she always
curtseys and ask me how I do, in a pretty manner; and when you have
had her here to do needlework, I observe she always turns the lock of
the door the right way and never bangs it. I am sure she will be an
excellent servant; and it will be a great comfort to poor Miss Taylor to
have somebody about her that she is used to see. Whenever James goes
over to see his daughter you know, she will be hearing of us. He will
be able to tell her how we all are.'
Emma spared no exertions to maintain this happier flow of ideas,
and hoped, by the help of backgammon,† to get her father tolerably
through the evening, and be attacked by no regrets but her own. The
backgammon-table was placed; but a visitor immediately afterwards
walked in and made it unnecessary.
Mr Knightley, a sensible man about seven or eight-and-thirty, was
not only a very old and intimate friend of the family, but particularly
connected with it as the elder brother of Isabella's husband. He lived
about a mile from Highbury, was a frequent visitor and always welcome,
and at this time more welcome than usual, as coming directly from
their mutual connections in London. He had returned to a late dinner
after some days absence, and now walked up to Hartfield to say that
all were well in Brunswick-square. It was a happy circumstance and
animated Mr Woodhouse for some time. Mr Knightley had a cheerful
manner which always did him good; and his many inquiries after 'poor
Isabella' and her children were answered most satisfactorily. When this
was over, Mr Woodhouse gratefully observed.
'It is very kind of you, Mr Knightley, to come out at this late hour to
call upon us. I am afraid you must have had a shocking walk.'
'Not at all, sir. It is a beautiful, moonlight night; and so mild that I
must draw back from your great fire.'
'But you must have found it very damp and dirty. I wish you may
not catch cold.'
'Dirty, sir! Look at my shoes. Not a speck on them.'
'Well! that is quite surprising for we have had a vast deal of rain
here. It rained dreadfully hard for half an hour, while we were at
breakfast. I wanted them to put off the wedding.'

backgammon   a board game played with draughts and dice

'By the bye – I have not wished you joy. Being pretty well aware of what sort of joy you must both be feeling, I have been in no hurry with my congratulations. But I hope it all went off tolerably well. How did you all behave? Who cried most?'

165   'Ah! poor Miss Taylor! 'tis a sad business.'

'Poor Mr and Miss Woodhouse, if you please; but I cannot possibly say "poor Miss Taylor." I have a great regard for you and Emma; but when it comes to the question of dependence or independence! – At any rate, it must be better to have only one to please, than two.'

170   'Especially when *one* of those two is such a fanciful, troublesome creature!' said Emma playfully. 'That, is what you have in your head, I know – and what you would certainly say if my father were not by.'

'I believe it is very true, my dear, indeed,' said Mr Woodhouse with a sigh. 'I am afraid I am sometimes very fanciful and troublesome.'

175   'My dearest papa! You do not think I could mean *you*, or suppose Mr Knightley to mean *you*. What a horrible idea! Oh, no! I meant only myself. Mr Knightley loves to find fault with me you know – in a joke – it is all a joke. We always say what we like to one another.'

Mr Knightley, in fact, was one of the few people who could see faults
180 in Emma Woodhouse, and the only one who ever told her of them: and though this was not particularly agreeable to Emma herself, she knew it would be so much less so to her father, that she would not have him really suspect such a circumstance as her not being thought perfect by every body.

185   'Emma knows I never flatter her,' said Mr Knightley; 'but I meant no reflection on any body. Miss Taylor has been used to have two persons to please; she will now have but one. The chances are that she must be a gainer.'

'Well,' said Emma, willing to let it pass – 'you want to hear about
190 the wedding, and I shall be happy to tell you, for we all behaved charmingly. Every body was punctual, every body in their best looks. Not a tear, and hardly a long face to be seen. Oh! no, we all felt that we were going to be only half a mile apart, and were sure of meeting every day.'

195   'Dear Emma bears every thing so well,' said her father. 'But, Mr Knightley, she is really very sorry to lose poor Miss Taylor, and I am sure she *will* miss her more than she thinks for.'

Emma turned away her head, divided between tears and smiles.

'It is impossible that Emma should not miss such a companion,' said
200 Mr Knightley. 'We should not like her so well as we do, sir, if we could suppose it. But she knows how much the marriage is to Miss Taylor's advantage; she knows how very acceptable it must be at Miss Taylor's time of life to be settled in a home of her own, and how important to her to be secure of a comfortable provision, and therefore cannot allow

205   herself to feel so much pain as pleasure. Every friend of Miss Taylor
      must be glad to have her so happily married.'
          'And you have forgotten one matter of joy to me,' said Emma, 'and
      a very considerable one – that I made the match myself. I made the
      match, you know, four years ago; and to have it take place, and be
210   proved in the right, when so many people said Mr Weston would never
      marry again, may comfort me for any thing.'
          Mr Knightley shook his head at her. Her father fondly replied, 'Ah!
      my dear, I wish you would not make matches and foretel things, for
      whatever you say always comes to pass. Pray do not make any more
215   matches.'
          'I promise you to make none for myself, papa; but I must, indeed,
      for other people. It is the greatest amusement in the world! And after
      such success you know! – Every body said that Mr Weston would never
      marry again. Oh dear, no! Mr Weston, who had been a widower so
220   long, and who seemed so perfectly comfortable without a wife, so
      constantly occupied either in his business in town or among his friends
      here, always acceptable wherever he went, always cheerful – Mr Weston
      need not spend a single evening in the year alone if he did not like it.
      Oh, no! Mr Weston certainly would never marry again. Some people
225   even talked of a promise to his wife on her death-bed, and others of
      the son and the uncle not letting him. All manner of solemn nonsense
      was talked on the subject, but I believed none of it. Ever since the day
      (about four years ago) that Miss Taylor and I met with him in Broadway-
      lane, when, because it began to mizzle,[†] he darted away with so much
230   gallantry, and borrowed two umbrellas for us from Farmer Mitchell's,
      I made up my mind on the subject. I planned the match from that hour;
      and when such success has blessed me in this instance, dear papa, you
      cannot think that I shall leave off match-making.'
          'I do not understand what you mean by "success;" ' said Mr Knightley.
235   'Success supposes endeavour. Your time had been properly and delicately
      spent, if you have been endeavouring for the last four years to bring
      about this marriage. A worthy employment for a young lady's mind!
      But if, which I rather imagine, your making the match, as you call it,
      means only your planning it, your saying to yourself one idle day, "I
240   think it would be a very good thing for Miss Taylor if Mr Weston were
      to marry her," and saying it again to yourself every now and then
      afterwards, – why do you talk of success? where is your merit? – what
      are you proud of? – you made a lucky guess; and *that* is all that can be
      said.'
245   'And have you ever known the pleasure and triumph of a lucky
      guess? – I pity you. – I thought you cleverer – for depend upon it, a

mizzle   drizzle with rain

lucky guess is never merely luck. There is always some talent in it. And as to my poor word "success," which you quarrel with, I do not know that I am so entirely without any claim to it. You have drawn two 250 pretty pictures – but I think there may be a third – a something between the do-nothing and the do-all. If I had not promoted Mr Weston's visits here, and given many little encouragements, and smoothed many little matters, it might not have come to any thing after all. I think you must know Hartfield enough to comprehend that.'

255 'A straight-forward, open-hearted man, like Weston, and a rational unaffected woman, like Miss Taylor, may be safely left to manage their own concerns. You are more likely to have done harm to yourself, than good to them, by interference.'

'Emma never thinks of herself, if she can do good to others;' rejoined 260 Mr Woodhouse, understanding but in part. 'But, my dear, pray do not make any more matches, they are silly things, and break up one's family circle grievously.'

'Only one more, papa; only for Mr Elton. Poor Mr Elton! You like Mr Elton, papa, – I must look about for a wife for him. There is nobody 265 in Highbury who deserves him – and he has been here a whole year, and has fitted up his house so comfortably that it would be a shame to have him single any longer – and I thought when he was joining their hands to-day, he looked so very much as if he would like to have the same kind office done for him! I think very well of Mr Elton, and this 270 is the only way I have of doing him a service.'

'Mr Elton is a very pretty young man to be sure, and a very good young man, and I have a great regard for him. But if you want to shew him any attention, my dear, ask him to come and dine with us some day. That will be a much better thing. I dare say Mr Knightley will be 275 so kind as to meet him.'

'With a great deal of pleasure, sir, at any time,' said Mr Knightley laughing; 'and I agree with you entirely that it will be a much better thing. Invite him to dinner, Emma, and help him to the best of the fish and the chicken, but leave him to choose his own wife. Depend upon 280 it, a man of six or seven-and-twenty can take care of himself.'

1814–16   1816

From PERSUASION†

[Captain Wentworth's Resolution]

CHAPTER 7

A very few days more, and Captain Wentworth was known to be at Kellynch, and Mr Musgrove had called on him, and come back warm in his praise, and he was engaged with the Crofts to dine at Uppercross, by the end of another week. It had been a great disappointment to Mr
5 Musgrove, to find that no earlier day could be fixed, so impatient was he to shew his gratitude, by seeing Captain Wentworth under his own roof, and welcoming him to all that was strongest and best in his cellars. But a week must pass; only a week, in Anne's reckoning, and then, she supposed, they must meet; and soon she began to wish that she could
10 feel secure even for a week.

Captain Wentworth made a very early return to Mr Musgrove's civility, and she was all but calling there in the same half hour! – She and Mary were actually setting forward for the great house, where, as she afterwards learnt, they must inevitably have found him, when they
15 were stopped by the eldest boy's being at that moment brought home in consequence of a bad fall. The child's situation put the visit entirely aside, but she could not hear of her escape with indifference, even in the midst of the serious anxiety which they afterwards felt on his account.
20 His collar-bone was found to be dislocated, and such injury received in the back, as roused the most alarming ideas. It was an afternoon of distress, and Anne had every thing to do at once – the apothecary† to send for – the father to have pursued and informed – the mother to support and keep from hysterics – the servants to control – the youngest
25 child to banish, and the poor suffering one to attend and soothe; – beside sending, as soon as she recollected it, proper notice to the other house, which brought her an accession rather of frightened, enquiring companions, than of very useful assistants.

Her brother's return was the first comfort; he could take best care of
30 his wife, and the second blessing was the arrival of the apothecary. Till he came and had examined the child, their apprehensions were the worse for being vague; – they suspected great injury, but knew not where; but now the collar-bone was soon replaced, and though Mr

Persuasion Anne, a daughter of Sir Walter Elliot, has been persuaded by a trusted friend, Lady Russell, to break off her engagement to Frederick Wentworth, a young naval officer, much to his indignation. Sir Walter, who has been spendthrift with his inheritance, has been forced to let his seat, Kellynch Hall, to Wentworth's sister and brother-in-law, Admiral and Mrs Croft. Sir Walter's youngest daughter, Mary, is married to Charles Musgrove, heir to a neighbouring landowner

apothecary druggist, chemist

Robinson felt and felt, and rubbed, and looked grave, and spoke low
35   words both to the father and the aunt, still they were all to hope the
best, and to be able to part and eat their dinner in tolerable ease of
mind; and then it was, just before they parted, that the two young
aunts were able so far to digress from their nephew's state, as to give
the information of Captain Wentworth's visit; – staying five minutes
40   behind their father and mother, to endeavour to express how perfectly
delighted they were with him, how much handsomer, how infinitely
more agreeable they thought him than any individual among their male
acquaintance, who had been at all a favourite before – how glad they
had been to hear papa invite him to stay dinner – how sorry when he
45   said it was quite out of his power – and how glad again, when he had
promised in reply to papa and mamma's farther pressing invitations,
to come and dine with them on the morrow, actually on the morrow! –
And he had promised it in so pleasant a manner, as if he felt all the
motive of their attention just as he ought! – And, in short, he had
50   looked and said every thing with such exquisite grace, that they could
assure them all, their heads were both turned by him! – And off they
ran, quite as full of glee as of love, and apparently more full of Captain
Wentworth than of little Charles.
     The same story and the same raptures were repeated, when the two
55   girls came with their father, through the gloom of the evening, to make
enquiries; and Mr Musgrove, no longer under the first uneasiness about
his heir, could add his confirmation and praise, and hope there would
be now no occasion for putting Captain Wentworth off, and only be
sorry to think that the cottage party, probably, would not like to leave
60   the little boy, to give him the meeting. – 'Oh, no! as to leaving the little
boy!' – both father and mother were in much too strong and recent
alarm to bear the thought; and Anne, in the joy of the escape, could
not help adding her warm protestations to theirs.
     Charles Musgrove, indeed, afterwards shewed more of inclination;
65   'the child was going on so well – and he wished so much to be introduced
to Captain Wentworth, that, perhaps, he might join them in the evening;
he would not dine from home, but he might walk in for half an hour.'
But in this he was eagerly opposed by his wife, with 'Oh, no! indeed,
Charles, I cannot bear to have you go away. Only think, if any thing
70   should happen!'
     The child had a good night, and was going on well the next day. It
must be a work of time to ascertain that no injury had been done to
the spine, but Mr Robinson found nothing to increase alarm, and
Charles Musgrove began consequently to feel no necessity for longer
75   confinement. The child was to be kept in bed, and amused as quietly as
possible; but what was there for a father to do? This was quite a female
case, and it would be highly absurd in him, who could be of no use at

home, to shut himself up. His father very much wished him to meet
Captain Wentworth, and there being no sufficient reason against it, he
80   ought to go; and it ended in his making a bold public declaration, when
he came in from shooting, of his meaning to dress directly, and dine at
the other house.

'Nothing can be going on better than the child,' said he, 'so I told
my father just now that I would come, and he thought me quite right.
85   Your sister being with you, my love, I have no scruple at all. You would
not like to leave him yourself, but you see I can be of no use. Anne will
send for me if any thing is the matter.'

Husbands and wives generally understand when opposition will be
vain. Mary knew, from Charles's manner of speaking, that he was quite
90   determined on going, and that it would be of no use to tease him. She
said nothing, therefore, till he was out of the room, but as soon as there
was only Anne to hear,

'So! You and I are to be left to shift by ourselves, with this poor sick
child – and not a creature coming near us all the evening! I knew how
95   it would be. This is always my luck! If there is any thing disagreeable
going on, men are always sure to get out of it, and Charles is as bad as
any of them. Very unfeeling! I must say it is very unfeeling of him, to
be running away from his poor little boy; talks of his being going on
so well! How does he know that he is going on well, or that there may
100   not be a sudden change half an hour hence? I did not think Charles
would have been so unfeeling. So, here he is to go away and enjoy
himself, and because I am the poor mother, I am not to be allowed to
stir; – and yet, I am sure, I am more unfit than any body else to be
about the child. My being the mother is the very reason why my feelings
105   should not be tried. I am not at all equal to it. You saw how hysterical
I was yesterday.'

'But that was only the effect of the suddenness of your alarm – of
the shock. You will not be hysterical again. I dare say we shall have
nothing to distress us. I perfectly understand Mr Robinson's directions,
110   and have no fears; and indeed, Mary, I cannot wonder at your husband.
Nursing does not belong to a man, it is not his province. A sick child is
always the mother's property, her own feelings generally make it so.'

'I hope I am as fond of my child as any mother – but I do not know
that I am of any more use in the sick-room than Charles, for I cannot
115   be always scolding, and teasing a poor child when it is ill; and you
saw, this morning, that if I told him to keep quiet, he was sure to begin
kicking again. I have not nerves for the sort of thing.'

'But, could you be comfortable yourself, to be spending the whole
evening away from the poor boy?'

120   'Yes; you see his papa can, and why should not I? – Jemima is so
careful! And she could send us word every hour how he was. I really

think Charles might as well have told his father we would all come. I
am not more alarmed about little Charles now than he is. I was
dreadfully alarmed yesterday, but the case is very different to-day.'
125 'Well – if you do not think it too late to give notice for yourself,
suppose you were to go, as well as your husband. Leave little Charles
to my care. Mr and Mrs Musgrove cannot think it wrong, while I
remain with him.'
    'Are you serious?' cried Mary, her eyes brightening. 'Dear me! that's
130 a very good thought, very good indeed. To be sure I may just as well
go as not, for I am of no use at home – am I? and it only harasses me.
You, who have not a mother's feelings, are a great deal the properest
person. You can make little Charles do any thing; he always minds you
at a word. It will be a great deal better than leaving him with only
135 Jemina. Oh! I will certaintly go; I am sure I ought if I can, quite as
much as Charles, for they want me excessively to be acquainted with
Captain Wentworth, and I know you do not mind being left alone. An
excellent thought of yours, indeed, Anne! I will go and tell Charles,
and get ready directly. You can send for us, you know, at a moment's
140 notice, if any thing is the matter; but I dare say there will be nothing
to alarm you. I should not go, you may be sure, if I did not feel quite
at ease about my dear child.'
    The next moment she was tapping at her husband's dressing-room
door, and as Anne followed her up stairs, she was in time for the whole
145 conversation, which began with Mary's saying, in a tone of great
exultation.
    'I mean to go with you, Charles, for I am of no more use at home
than you are. If I were to shut myself up for ever with the child, I
should not be able to persuade him to do any thing he did not like.
150 Anne will stay; Anne undertakes to stay at home and take care of him.
It is Anne's own proposal, and so I shall go with you, which will be a
great deal better, for I have not dined at the other house since Tuesday.'
    'This very kind of Anne,' was her husband's answer, 'and I should
be very glad to have you go; but it seems rather hard that she should
155 be left at home by herself, to nurse our sick child.'
    Anne was now at hand to take up her own cause, and the sincerity
of her manner being soon sufficient to convince him, where conviction
was at least very agreeable, he had no farther scruples as to her being
left to dine alone, though he still wanted her to join them in the evening,
160 when the child might be at rest for the night, and kindly urged her to
let him come and fetch her; but she was quite unpersuadable; and this
being the case, she had ere long the pleasure of seeing them set off
together in high spirits. They were gone, she hoped, to be happy,
however oddly constructed such happiness might seem; as for herself,
165 she was left with as many sensations of comfort, as were, perhaps, ever

likely to be hers. She knew herself to be of the first utility to the child;
and what was it to her, if Frederick Wentworth were only half a mile
distant, making himself agreeable to others!

She would have liked to know how he felt as to a meeting. Perhaps
170 indifferent, if indifference could exist under such circumstances. He
must be either indifferent or unwilling. Had he wished ever to see her
again, he need not have waited till this time; he would have done what
she could not but believe that in his place she should have done long
ago, when events had been early giving him the independence which
175 alone had been wanting.

Her brother and sister came back delighted with their new acquaintance, and their visit in general. There had been music, singing, talking,
laughing, all that was most agreeable; charming manners in Captain
Wentworth, no shyness or reserve; they seemed all to know each other
180 perfectly, and he was coming the very next morning to shoot with
Charles. He was to come to breakfast, but not at the Cottage, though
that had been proposed at first; but then he had been pressed to come
to the Great House instead, and he seemed afraid of being in Mrs
Charles Musgrove's way, on account of the child; and therefore,
185 somehow, they hardly knew how, it ended Charles's being to meet him
to breakfast at his father's.

Anne understood it. He wished to avoid seeing her. He had enquired
after her, she found, slightly, as might suit a former slight acquaintance,
seeming to acknowledge such as she had acknowledged, actuated,
190 perhaps, by the same view of escaping introduction when they were to
meet.

The morning hours of the Cottage were always later than those of
the other house; and on the morrow the difference was so great, that
Mary and Anne were not more than beginning breakfast when Charles
195 came in to say that they were just setting off, that he was come for his
dogs, that his sisters were following with Captain Wentworth, his sisters
meaning to visit Mary and the child, and Captain Wentworth proposing
also to wait on her for a few minutes, if not inconvenient; and though
Charles had answered for the child's being in no such state as could
200 make it inconvenient, Captain Wentworth would not be satisfied
without his running on to give notice.

Mary, very much gratified by this attention, was delighted to receive
him; while a thousand feelings rushed on Anne, of which this was the
most consoling, that it would soon be over. And it was soon over. In
205 two minutes after Charles's preparation, the others appeared; they were
in the drawing-room. Her eye half met Captain Wentworth's; a bow, a
curtsey passed; she heard his voice – he talked to Mary, said all that
was right; said something to the Miss Musgroves, enough to mark an
easy footing: the room seemed full – full of persons and voices – but a

210   few minutes ended it. Charles shewed himself at the window, all was
ready, their visitor had bowed and was gone; the Miss Musgroves were
gone too, suddenly resolving to walk to the end of the village with the
sportsmen: the room was cleared, and Anne might finish her breakfast
as she could.

215   'It is over! it is over!' she repeated to herself again, and again, in
nervous gratitude. 'The worst is over!'

Mary talked, but she could not attend. She had seen him. They had
met. They had been once more in the same room!

Soon, however, she began to reason with herself, and try to be feeling
220   less. Eight years, almost eight years had passed, since all had been given
up. How absurd to be resuming the agitation which such an interval
had banished into distance and indistinctness! What might not eight
years do! Events of every description, changes, alienations, removals, –
all, all must be comprised in it; and oblivion of the past – how natural,
225   how certain too! It included nearly a third part of her own life.

Alas! with all her reasonings, she found, that to retentive feelings
eight years may be little more than nothing.

Now, how were his sentiments to be read? Was this like wishing to
avoid her? And the next moment she was hating herself for the folly
230   which asked the question.

On one other question, which perhaps her utmost wisdom might not
have prevented, she was soon spared all suspense; for after the Miss
Musgroves had returned and finished their visit at the Cottage, she had
this spontaneous information from Mary:

235   'Captain Wentworth is not very gallant by you, Anne, though he was
so attentive to me. Henrietta asked him what he thought of you, when
they went away; and he said, 'You were so altered he should not have
known you again.'

Mary had no feelings to make her respect her sister's in a common
240   way; but she was perfectly unsuspicious of being inflicting any peculiar
wound.

'Altered beyond his knowledge!' Anne fully submitted, in silent, deep
mortification.† Doubtless it was so; and she could take no revenge, for
he was not altered, or not for the worse. She had already acknowledged
245   it to herself, and she could not think differently, let him think of her as
he would. No; the years which had destroyed her youth and bloom
had only given him a more glowing, manly, open look, in no respect
lessening his personal advantages. She had seen the same Frederick
Wentworth.

250   'So altered that he should not have known her again!' These were
words which could not but dwell with her. Yet she soon began to

---

mortification   subjection of the self, humiliation

rejoice that she had heard them. They were of sobering tendency; they allayed† agitation; they composed, and consequently must make her happier.

255   Frederick Wentworth had used such words, or something like them, but without an idea that they would be carried round to her. He had thought her wretchedly altered, and, in the first moment of appeal, had spoken as he felt. He had not forgiven Anne Elliot. She had used him ill; deserted and disappointed him; and worse, she had shewn a
260 feebleness of character in doing so, which his own decided, confident temper could not endure. She had given him up to oblige others. It had been the effect of overpersuasion. It had been weakness and timidity.

    He had been most warmly attached to her, and had never seen a woman since whom he thought her equal; but, except from some
265 natural sensation of curiosity, he had no desire of meeting her again. Her power with him was gone for ever.

    It was now his object to marry. He was rich, and being turned on shore, fully intended to settle as soon as he could be properly tempted; actually looking round, ready to fall in love with all the speed which a
270 clear head and quick taste could allow. He had a heart for either of the Miss Musgroves, if they could catch it; a heart, in short, for any pleasing young woman who came in his way, excepting Anne Elliot. This was his only secret exception, when he said to his sister, in answer to her suppositions,
275   'Yes, here I am, Sophia, quite ready to make a foolish match. Any body between fifteen and thirty may have me for asking. A little beauty, and a few smiles, and a few compliments to the navy, and I am a lost man. Should not this be enough for a sailor, who has had no society among women to make him nice?'
280   He said it, she knew, to be contradicted. His bright, proud eye spoke the conviction that he was nice;† and Anne Elliot was not out of his thoughts, when he more seriously described the woman he should wish to meet with. 'A strong mind, with sweetness of manner,' made the first and the last of the description.
285   'This is the woman I want, said he. Something a little inferior I shall of course put up with, but it must not be much. If I am a fool, I shall be a fool indeed, for I have thought on the subject more than most men.'

1815–16   1818

---

allayed   alleviated   *nice*   discriminating

Charles Lamb
1775–1834

At Christ's Hospital, Lamb met Coleridge with whom he became a life-long friend. Subsequently, Lamb's various London homes were the meeting-places for a number of literary figures, which included Coleridge himself, Wordsworth, Hunt, Hazlitt, De Quincey and Southey.

Lamb's first professional position was in South Sea House, then at the age of seventeen he was employed by East India House: he remained there until 1825. In 1795–6 Lamb became mentally ill, recovered but was always afterwards anxious that he might be a victim of hereditary insanity. This feeling was reinforced in 1796, when, in a fit of madness, his sister Mary killed their mother. He saved her from a life in institutions by undertaking to care for her. They lived in London, and after 1823 in Islington, Enfield and Edmonton.

Lamb was an accomplished poet and essayist who became famous for his conversational, familiar but polished style. His first literary attempts met with little success: his poetic drama was unsuccessful and a farce, *Mr. H*, failed at Drury Lane in 1806. In 1807, together with Mary, he composed *Tales from Shakespeare* which were intended to make Shakespeare's plays more accessible to children. In 1808 he published *Specimens of English Dramatic Poets who lived about the time of Shakespeare*, and *Mrs. Leicester's School*, a collection of stories, was published a year later. From 1810–20 he wrote much for journals, for Leigh Hunt's *Reflector* and *Examiner*, for the *Quarterly Review* and the *London Magazine*. During this period he produced his essays 'On the Tragedies of Shakespeare' and 'On the Genius and Character of Hogarth'. It was for the *London Magazine* that he wrote *Essays of Elia*. The first series were collected and published together in 1823; the second series in 1833.

From ELIA: ESSAYS WHICH HAVE APPEARED UNDER THAT SIGNATURE IN THE LONDON MAGAZINE

From The Old and the New Schoolmaster

I lately got into a dilemma of this sort. –

In one of my daily jaunts between Bishopsgate and Shacklewell, the coach stopped to take up a staid-looking† gentleman, about the wrong side of thirty, who was giving his parting directions (while the steps
5 were adjusting), in a tone of mild authority, to a tall youth, who seemed to be neither his clerk, his son, nor his servant, but something partaking of all three. The youth was dismissed, and we drove on. As we were the sole passengers, he naturally enough addressed his conversations to me; and we discussed the merits of the fare, the civility and punctuality
10 of the driver; the circumstance of an opposition coach having been lately set up, with the probabilities of its success – to all which I was enabled to return pretty satisfactory answers, having been drilled into this kind of etiquette† by some years' daily practice of riding to and fro in the stage aforesaid – when he suddenly alarmed me by a startling
15 question, whether I had seen the show of prize cattle that morning in Smithfield? Now as I had not seen it, and do not greatly care for such sort of exhibitions, I was obliged to return a cold negative. He seemed a little mortified, as well as astonished, at my declaration, as (it appeared) he was just come fresh from the sight and doubtless had hoped to
20 compare notes on the subject. However he assured me that I had lost a fine treat, as it far exceeded the show of last year. We were now approaching Norton Falgate, when the sight of some shop-goods *ticketed* freshened him up into a dissertation upon the cheapness of cottons this spring. I was now a little in heart, as the nature of my
25 morning avocations† had brought me into some sort of familiarity with the raw material; and I was surprised to find how eloquent I was becoming on the state of the India market – when, presently, he dashed my incipient vanity to the earth at once, by inquiring whether I had ever made any calculation as to the value of the rental of all the retail
30 shops in London. Had he asked of me, what song the Sirens sang, or what name Achilles assumed when he hid himself among women, I might, with Sir Thomas Browne, have hazarded a 'wide solution'.†
My companion saw my embarrassment, and, the almshouses beyond Shoreditch just coming in view, with great good-nature and dexterity

---

staid-looking steady-, sober-looking
etiquette code of behaviour

avocations occupations
'wide solution' from Browne's *Urn Burial*

35 shifted his conversation to the subject of public charities; which led to
the comparative merits of provision for the poor in past and present
times, with observations on the old monastic institutions, and charitable
orders; – but, finding me rather dimly impressed with some glimmering
notions from old poetic associations, than strongly fortified with any
40 speculations reducible to calculation on the subject, he gave the matter
up; and, the country beginning to open more and more upon us, as we
approached the turnpike[†] at Kingsland (the destined termination of his
journey), he put a home thrust upon me, in the most unfortunate
position he could have chosen, by advancing some queries relative to
45 the North Pole Expedition. While I was muttering out something about
the Panorama[†] of those strange regions (which I had actually seen), by
way of parrying the question, the coach stopping relieved me from any
further apprehensions. My companion getting out, left me in the
comfortable possession of my ignorance; and I heard him, as he went
50 off, putting questions to an outside passenger, who had alighted with
him, regarding an epidemic disorder, that had been rife about Dalston;
and which, my friend assured him, had gone through five or six schools
in that neighbourhood. The truth now flashed upon me, that my
companion was a schoolmaster, and that the youth, whom he had
55 parted from at our first acquaintance, must have been one of the bigger
boys, or the usher.[†] – He was evidently a kind-hearted man, who did
not seem so much desirous of provoking a discussion by the questions
which he put, as of obtaining information at any rate. It did not appear
that he took any interest, either, in such kind of inquiries, for their own
60 sake; but that he was in some way bound to seek for knowledge. A
greenish-coloured coat, which he had on, forbade me to surmise that
he was a clergyman. The adventure gave birth to some reflections on
the difference between persons of his profession in past and present
times.
65   Rest to the souls of those fine old Pedagogues;[†] the breed, long since
extinct, of the Lilys,[†] and the Linacres:[†] who believing that all learning
was contained in the languages which they taught, and despising every
other acquirement as superficial and useless, came to their task as to a
sport! Passing from infancy to age, they dreamed away all their days
70 as in a grammar-school. Revolving in a perpetual cycle of declensions,
conjugations, syntaxes, and prosodies; renewing constantly the occupations which had charmed their studious childhood; rehearsing continually the part of the past; life must have slipped from them at last

turnpike   a road-gate at which a toll is paid
Panorama   continuous passing scene
usher   assistant teacher
Pedagogues   teachers
Lily   William Lily (c. 1468–1522), revived

Greek studies in England: first high master
of St Paul's School
Linacre   Thomas Linacre (1460?–1524),
physician and classical scholar: Latin tutor
to Princess Mary

like one day. They were always in their first garden, reaping harvests
75   of their golden time, among their *Flori*[†] and their *Spici-legia*;[†] in Arcadia
still, but kings; the ferule[†] of their sway not much harsher, but of like
dignity with that mild sceptre attributed to king Basileus;[†] the Greek
and Latin, their stately Pamela and their Philoclea; with the occasional
duncery of some untoward Tyro, serving for a refreshing interlude of a
80   Mopsa, or a clown Damætas!

With what a savour doth the Preface to Colet's, or (as it is sometimes
called) Paul's Accidence,[†] set forth! 'To exhort every man to the learning
of grammar, that intendeth to attain the understanding of the tongues,
wherein is contained a great treasury of wisdom and knowledge, it
85   would seem but vain and lost labour; for so much as it is known, that
nothing can surely be ended, whose beginning is either feeble or faulty;
and no building be perfect, whereas the foundation and ground-work
is ready to fall, and unable to uphold the burden of the frame.' How
well doth this stately preamble (comparable to those which Milton
90   commendeth as 'having been the usage to prefix to some solemn law,
then first promulgated by Solon,[†] or Lycurgus'[†]) correspond with and
illustrate that pious zeal for conformity, expressed in a succeeding
clause, which would fence about grammar-rules with the severity of
faith-articles! – as for the diversity of grammars, it is well profitably
95   taken away by the King's Majesties wisdom, who foreseeing the
inconvenience, and favourably providing the remedie, caused one kind
of grammar by sundry learned men to be diligently drawn, and so to
be set out, only everywhere to be taught for the use of learners, and for
the hurt in changing of schoolmaisters.' What a *gusto* in that which
100 follows: 'wherein it is profitable that he can orderly decline his noun,
and his verb.' *His* noun!

The fine dream is fading away fast; and the least concern of a teacher
in the present day is to inculcate[†] grammar-rules.

The modern schoolmaster is expected to know a little of every thing,
105 because his pupil is required not to be entirely ignorant of any thing.
He must be superficially, if I may say so, omniscient.[†] He is to know
something of pneumatics;[†] of chemistry; of whatever is curious, or
proper to excite the attention of the youthful mind; an insight into
mechanics is desirable, with a touch of statistics; the quality of soils,

---

Flori   Florilegia: literally collections of
   flowers: by analogy a literary selection or
   anthology
Spici-legia   gleaning of corn: an anthology
ferule   flat ruler with widened pierced end for
   punishing pupils
Basileus etc.   see Sir Philip Sidney's *The
   Arcadia*, 1581

Accidence   a grammar-book dealing with
   inflexions
Solon   Athenian statesman (*c.* 638–*c.* 558BC),
   a great lawgiver
Lycurgus   King of Thrace
inculcate   impress persistently
omniscient   all knowing
pneumatics   science of mechanical property of
   air or other elastic fluids or gases

110 &c. botany, the constitution of his country, *cum multis aliis* [along with many other things]. You may get a notion of some part of his expected duties by consulting the famous Tractate on Education[†] addressed to Mr. Hartlib.

All these things – these, or the desire of them – he is expected to
115 instil, not by set lessons from professors, which he may charge in the bill, but at school-intervals, as he walks the streets, or saunters through green fields (those natural instructors), with his pupils. The least part of what is expected from him, is to be done in school-hours. He must insinuate knowledge at the *mollia tempora fandi*.[†] He must seize every
120 occasion – the season of the year – the time of the day – a passing cloud – a rainbow – a waggon of hay – a regiment of soldiers going by – to inculcate something useful. He can receive no pleasure from a casual glimpse of Nature, but must catch at it as an object of instruction. He must interpret beauty into the picturesque. He cannot relish a
125 beggar-man, or a gipsy, for thinking of the suitable improvement. Nothing comes to him, not spoiled by the sophisticating medium of moral uses. The Universe – that Great Book, as it has been called – is to him indeed, to all intents and purposes, a book, out of which he is doomed to read tedious homilies[†] to distasting schoolboys. – Vacations
130 themselves are none to him, he is only rather worse off than before; for commonly he has some intrusive upper-boy fastened upon him at such times; some cadet of a great family; some neglected lump of nobility, or gentry; that he must drag after him to the play, to the Panorama, to Mr. Bartley's Orrery,[†] to the Panopticon,[†] or into the
135 country, to a friend's house, or to his favourite watering-place. Wherever he goes, this uneasy shadow attends him. A boy is at his board, and in his path, and in all his movements. He is boy-rid, sick of perpetual boy.

Boys are capital fellows in their own way, among their mates; but they are unwholesome companions for grown people. The restraint is
140 felt no less on the one side, than on the other. – Even a child, that 'plaything for an hour', tires *always*. The noises of children, playing their own fancies – as I now hearken to them by fits, sporting on the green before my window, while I am engaged in these grave speculations at my neat surburban retreat at Shacklewell – by distance made more
145 sweet – inexpressibly take from the labour of my task. It is like writing to music. They seem to modulate my periods. They ought at least to do so – for in the voice of that tender age there is a kind of poetry, far

Tractate on Education John Milton addressed his *Of Education* to Samuel Hartlib, d. 1662. Hartlib was of Prussian origin, settled in England, and was a patron of invention, science and reform
mollia tempora fandi subtle, easy moments for speaking: Virgil, *Aeneid*, IV, 293–4

'molissima fandi tempora'
homilies sermons, discourses
Orrery clockwork model of the planetary system
Panopticon circular prison with cells around central warders' well

unlike the harsh prose-accents of man's conversation. – I should but spoil their sport, and diminish my own sympathy for them, by mingling in their pastime. . . .

150

1821   1821

Walter Savage Landor
1775–1864

Intemperate moods and the adoption of extreme views marred some of Landor's personal relationships. Yet his writings were admired in his time: Browning, in particular, thought highly of his work.

Landor was educated at Rugby and Trinity College, Oxford, from which he was rusticated. He wrote much poetry; his first published volume was *Poems* (1795), soon followed by an epic poem, *Gebir*. His 1806 volume *Simonidea* included the celebrated 'Rose Aylmer'. In 1812 he had to withdrawn the vituperative *Commentary on the Memoirs of Mr. Fox*.

From 1815 to 1835 he lived in Italy. He continued writing and his most interesting productions were *Citation and Examination of William Shakespare Touching Deer Stealing* (1834), his trilogy (1839–40) *Andrea of Hungary, Giovani of Naples* and *Fra Rupert*, and his 1853 *Imaginary Conversations of Greeks and Romans*.

Charles Dickens caricatured him in the person of Boythorn in *Bleak House*.

ROSE AYLMER, 1779–1800

Ah what avails the sceptred race,
  Ah what the form divine!
What every virtue, every grace!
  Rose Aylmer, all were thine.
5 Rose Aylmer, whom these wakeful eyes
  May weep, but never see,
A night of memories and of sighs
  I consecrate to thee.

1780   1806

PROGRESS OF EVENING

From yonder wood, mark blue-eyed Eve proceed:
First through the deep and warm and secret glens,
Through the pale glimmering privet-scented lane,

And through those alders by the river-side:
5   Now the soft dust impedes her, which the sheep
Have hollow'd out beneath their hawthorn shade.
But ah! look yonder! see a misty tide
Rise up the hill, lay low the frowning grove,
Enwrap the gay white mansion, sap its sides
10   Until they sink and melt away like chalk;
Now it comes down against our village-tower,
Covers its base, floats o'er its arches, tears
The clinging ivy from the battlements,
Mingles in broad embrace the obdurate stone,
15   (All one vast ocean) and goes swelling on
In slow and silent, dim and deepening waves.

1806

LINES TO A DRAGON FLY

Life (priest and poet say) is but a dream;
    I wish no happier one than to be laid
    Beneath some cool syringa's scented shade
Or wavy willow, by the running stream,
5   Brimful of Moral, where the Dragon Fly,
    Wanders as careless and content as I.
Thanks for this fancy, insect king,
Of purple crest and filmy wing,
Who with indifference givest up
10   The water-lily's golden cup,
To come again and overlook
What I am writing in my book.
Believe me, most who read the line
Will read with hornier eyes than thine;
15   And yet their souls shall live for ever,
And thine drop dead into the river!
God pardon them, O insect king,
Who fancy so unjust a thing!

1834   1837

William Hazlitt
1778–1830

Hazlitt was one of the most able essayists of his age, and emerged as a powerful critic of English Letters. His father was a Unitarian minister who in 1783 took his family to New England on missionary work. Returning to Wenn, in Shropshire, he sent his son William to the Unitarian New College, at Hackney. William soon exerted his independence and decided not to enter the ministry. He met Coleridge, became a member of the Lamb circle, 1804–5, staunchly supported the principles of the French Revolution, and grew into an influential political lecturer and journalist. His radical, Jacobin sympathies destroyed many of his friendships: that with Charles Lamb survived.

In 1815 he was invited to write for the influential *Edinburgh Review*. His intellectual embrace took in philosophy, religion, manners, politics, literature and art: he was an admirer of Poussin, Rembrandt and Titian, but eschewed the new wave of Turner and Constable.

Hazlitt's major literary criticism is contained in *Lectures on the English Poets* (1818), *Lectures on the English Comic Writers* (1819) and *Lectures chiefly on the Dramatic Literature of the Age of Elizabeth* (1820). The work which established his contemporary reputation, and which is generally judged his best, is contained in his periodical essays collected in *Table Talk* (1821–2), and *The Plain Speaker* (1826). *Liber Amoris* (1823), brought him some notoriety. It was a gesture of homage towards Rousseau and is an account of his infatuation with his landlord's daughter, Sarah Walker, an habitual flirt. It reveals him as self-analytically perceptive, but unbalanced by his total preoccupation with her.

Hazlitt's writing is characterised by its incisiveness, straightforward-ness and spirit. He should be read along with De Quincey and Lamb.

From THE ROUND TABLE

On Good-Nature

Lord Shaftesbury† somewhere remarks, that a great many people pass for very good-natured persons, for no other reason than because they care about nobody but themselves; and, consequently, as nothing annoys them but what touches their own interest, they never irritate
5 themselves unnecessarily about what does not concern them, and seem to be made of the very milk of human kindness.

Good-nature, or what is often considered as such, is the most selfish of all the virtues: it is nine times out of ten mere indolence of disposition. A good-natured man is, generally speaking, one who does not like to
10 be put out of his way; and as long as he can help it, that is, till the provocation comes home to himself, he will not. He does not create fictitious uneasiness out of the distresses of others; he does not fret and fume, and make himself uncomfortable about things he cannot mend, and that no way concern him, even if he could: but then there is no
15 one who is more apt to be disconcerted by what puts him to any personal inconvenience, however trifling; who is more tenacious of his selfish indulgences, however unreasonable; or who resents more violently any interruption of his ease and comforts, the very trouble he is put to in resenting it being felt as an aggravation of the injury. A
20 person of this character feels no emotions of anger or detestation, if you tell him of the devastation of a province, or the massacre of the inhabitants of a town, or the enslaving of a people; but if his dinner is spoiled by a lump of soot falling down the chimney, he is thrown into the utmost confusion, and can hardly recover a decent command of his
25 temper for the whole day. He thinks nothing can go amiss, so long as he is at his ease, though a pain in his little finger makes him so peevish and quarrelsome, that nobody can come near him. Knavery and injustice in the abstract are things that by no means ruffle his temper, or alter the serenity of his countenance, unless he is to be the sufferer by them;
30 nor is he ever betrayed into a passion in answering a sophism, if he does not think it immediately directed against his own interest.

On the contrary, we sometimes meet with persons who regularly heat themselves in an argument, and get out of humour on every occasion, and make themselves obnoxious to a whole company about nothing.
35 This is not because they are ill-tempered, but because they are in earnest. Good-nature is a hypocrite: it tries to pass off its love of its own ease and indifference to everything else for a particular softness and mildness of disposition. All people get in a passion, and lose their temper, if you

Shaftesbury from *Characteristics, an Inquiry concerning Virtue or Merit* 3 vols (London, 1711)

offer to strike them, or cheat them of their money, that is, if you
40   interfere with that which they are really interested in. Tread on the heel
of one of these good-natured persons, who do not care if the whole
world is in flames, and see how he will bear it. If the truth were known,
the most disagreeable people are the most amiable. They are the only
persons who feel an interest in what does not concern them. They have
45   as much regard for others as they have for themselves. They have as
many vexations and causes of complaint as there are in the world. They
are general righters of wrongs, and redressers of grievances. They not
only are annoyed by what they can help, by an act of inhumanity done
in the next street, or in a neighbouring country by their own countrymen,
50   they not only do not claim any share in the glory, and hate it the more,
the more brilliant the success, – but a piece of injustice done three
thousand years ago touches them to the quick. They have an unfortunate
attachment to a set of abstract phrases, such as *liberty, truth, justice,
humanity, honour,* which are continually abused by knaves, and
55   misunderstood by fools, and they can hardly contain themselves for
spleen.[†] They have something to keep them in perpetual hot water. No
sooner is one question set at rest than another rises up to perplex them.
They wear themselves to the bone in the affairs of other people, to
whom they can do no manner of service, to the neglect of their own
60   business and pleasure. They tease themselves to death about the morality
of the Turks, or the politics of the French. There are certain words that
afflict their ears, and things that lacerate their souls, and remain a
plague-spot there forever after. They have a fellow-feeling with all that
has been done, said, or thought in the world. They have an interest in
65   all science and in all art. They hate a lie as much as a wrong, for truth
is the foundation of all justice. Truth is the first thing in their thoughts,
then mankind, then their country, last themselves. They love excellence,
and bow to fame, which is the shadow of it. Above all, they are anxious
to see justice done to the dead, as the best encouragement to the living,
70   and the lasting inheritance of future generations. They do not like to
see a great principle undermined, or the fall of a great man. They would
sooner forgive a blow in the face than a wanton attack on acknowledged
reputation. The contempt in which the French hold Shakespeare is a
serious evil to them; nor do they think the matter mended, when they
75   hear an Englishman, who would be thought a profound one, say that
Voltaire[†] was a man without wit. They are vexed to see genius playing
at Tom Fool, and honesty turned bawd. It gives them a cutting sensation[†]
to see a number of things which, as they are unpleasant to see, we shall

---

spleen   ill temper
Voltaire   assumed name of François Marie
   Arouet (1694–1778) French philosopher,
   poet and dramatist

cutting sensation   the sentence originally read;
   'It gives them a cutting sensation to see Mr
   Southey, poet laureate; Mr Wordsworth, an
   exciseman, and Mr Coleridge, nothing.'

not here repeat. In short, they have a passion for truth; they feel the
80   same attachment to the idea of what is right, that a knave does to his
interest, or that a good-natured man does to his ease; and they have as
many sources of uneasiness as there are actual or supposed deviations
from this standard in the sum òf things, or as there is a possibility of
folly and mischief in the world.
85   Principle is a passion for truth: an incorrigible attachment to a general
proposition. Good-nature is humanity that costs nothing. No good-
natured man was ever a martyr to a cause, in religion or politics. He
has no idea of striving against the stream, He may become a good
courtier and a loyal subject; and it is hard if he does not, for he has
90   nothing to do in that case but to consult his ease, interest, and outward
appearances. The Vicar of Bray† was a good-natured man. What a pity
he was but a vicar! A good-natured man is utterly unfit for any situation
or office in life that requires integrity, fortitude, or generosity, – any
sacrifice, except of opinion, or any exertion, but to please. A good-
95   natured man will debauch his friend's mistress, if he has an opportunity;
and betray his friend, sooner than share disgrace or danger with him.
He will not forego the smallest gratification to save the whole world.
He makes his own convenience the standard of right and wrong. He
avoids the feeling of pain in himself, and shuts his eyes to the sufferings
100   of others. He will put a malefactor or an innocent person (no matter
which) to the rack, and only laugh at the uncouthness of the gestures,
or wonder that he is so unmannerly as to cry out. There is no villainy
to which he will not lend a helping hand with great coolness and
cordiality, for he sees only the pleasant and profitable side of things.
105   He will assent to a falsehood with a leer of complacency, and applaud
any atrocity that comes recommended in the garb of authority. He will
betray his country to please a Minister, and sign the death-warrant of
thousands of wretches, rather than forfeit the congenial smile, the well-
known squeeze of the hand. The shrieks of death, the torture of mangled
110   limbs, the last groans of despair, are things that shock his smooth
humanity too much ever to make an impression on it: his good-nature
sympathizes only with the smile, the bow, the gracious salutation, the
fawning answer: vice loses its sting, and corruption its poison, in the
oily gentleness of his disposition. He will not hear of any thing wrong
115   in Church or State. He will defend every abuse by which any thing is
to be got, every dirty job, every act of every Minister. In an extreme
case, a very good-natured man indeed may try to hang twelve honester

---

Vicar of Bray   hero of an anonymous
eighteenth-century song: the vicar is a time-
serving parson, a trimmer, who boasts that
he has accommodated himself to the religious
views prevalent in different reigns, of Charles,
James, William, Anne, and George: no
matter 'whatsoever king may reign', he will
remain Vicar of Bray

men than himself to rise at the Bar,[†] and forge the seal of the realm to
continue his colleagues a week longer in office. He is a slave to the will
120   of others, a coward to their prejudices, a tool of their vices. A good-
natured man is no more fit to be trusted in public affairs, than a coward
or a woman is to lead an army. Spleen is the soul of patriotism and of
public good. Lord Castlereagh[†] is a good-natured man, Lord Eldon[†] is
a good-natured man, Charles Fox[†] was a good-natured man. The last
125   instance is the most decisive. The definition of a true patriot is *a good
hater*.[†]

A king, who is a good-natured man, is in a fair way of being a great
tyrant. A king ought to feel concern for all to whom his power extends;
but a good-natured man cares only about himself. If he has a good
130   appetite, eats and sleeps well, nothing in the universe besides can disturb
him. The destruction of the lives or liberties of his subjects will not stop
him in the least of his caprices, but will concoct well with his bile, and
'good digestion wait on appetite, and health on both.' He will send out
his mandate to kill and destroy with the same indifference or satisfaction
135   that he performs any natural function of his body. The consequences
are placed beyond the reach of his imagination, or would not affect
him if they were not, for he is a fool, and good-natured. A good-natured
man hates more than any one else whatever thwarts his will, or
contradicts his prejudices; and if he has the power to prevent it, depend
140   upon it, he will use it without remorse and without control.

There is a lower species of this character which is what is usually
understood by a *well-meaning man*. A well-meaning man is one who
often does a great deal of mischief without any kind of malice. He
means no one any harm, if it is not for his interest. He is not a knave,
145   nor perfectly honest. He does not easily resign a good place. Mr
Vansittart[†] is a well-meaning man.

The Irish are a good-natured people; they have many virtues, but
their virtues are those of the heart, not of the head. In their passions
and affections they are sincere, but they are hypocrites in understanding.
150   If they once begin to calculate the consequences, self-interest prevails.
An Irishman who trusts to his principles, and a Scotchman who yields
to his impulses, are equally dangerous. The Irish have wit, genius,
eloquence, imagination, affections: but they want coherence of understanding, and consequently have no standard of thought or action.
155   Their strength of mind does not keep pace with the warmth of their

---

at the Bar   in the legal profession
Castereagh   Robert Stewart, Viscount
Castlereagh (1769–1822) chief secretary for
Ireland 1799–1801; foreign secretary 1812–
22
Eldon   John Scott, first earl of Eldon (1751–
1838): lord chancellor, 1801–6 and 1807–27

Fox   Charles James Fox (1749–1806): Whig
statesman and orator
a good hater   Dr Samuel Johnson's expression,
which became a favourite of Hazlitt's
Vansittart   Nicholas Vansittart, chancellor of
the exchequer 1812–22

feelings, or the quickness of their conceptions. Their animal spirits run away with them: their reason is a jade.[†] There is something crude, indigested, rash, and discordant, in almost all that they do or say. They have no system, no abstract ideas. They are 'everything by starts, and
160 nothing long.'[†] They are a wild people. They hate whatever imposes a law on their understandings, or a yoke on their wills. To betray the principles they are most bound by their own professions and the expectations of others to maintain, is with them a reclamation of their original rights, and to fly in the face of their benefactors and friends,
165 an assertion of their natural freedom of will. They want consistency and good faith. They unite fierceness with levity. In the midst of their headlong impulses, they have an undercurrent of selfishness and cunning, which in the end gets the better of them. Their feelings, when no longer excited by novelty or opposition, grow cold and stagnant. Their blood,
170 if not heated by passion, turns to poison. They have a rancour in their hatred of any object they have abandoned, proportioned to the attachment they have professed to it. Their zeal, converted against itself, is furious. The late Mr Burke[†] was an instance of an Irish patriot and philosopher. He abused metaphysics,[†] because he could make nothing
175 out of them, and turned his back upon liberty, when he found he could get nothing more by her. – See to the same purpose the winding up of the character of *Judy* in Miss Edgeworth's[†] *Castle Rackrent*.

1816   1816

From THE FIGHT[†]

'– The *fight*, the *fight's* the thing,[†]
Wherein I'll catch the conscience of the king.'

Where there's a will, there's a way – I said to myself, as I walked down Chancery-lane, about half-past six o'clock on Monday the 10th of December, to inquire at Jack Randall's where the fight the next day was to be; and I found 'the proverb' nothing 'musty' in the present
5 instance, I was determined to see this fight, come what would, and see

---

jade   worn out work-horse
'everything . . . long'   from Dryden's *Absolom and Achitophel*
Burke   Edmund Burke (1729–97): writer, philosopher, politician
metaphysics   theoretical philosophy of being and knowing

Edgeworth   see p. 27
The Fight   published February 1822 in *The New Monthly Magazine*, and reprinted by Hazlitt's son in *Literary Remains*, 1836
Epigraph   an adaptation of *Hamlet*, II. 2, 641 'The play, the play's the thing . . .'

it I did, in great style. It was my *first fight*, yet it more than answered my expectations. Ladies – it is to you I dedicate this description; nor let it seem out of character for the fair to notice the exploits of the brave. Courage and modesty are the old English virtues; and may they
10   never look cold and askance on one another! Think, ye fairest of the fair, loveliest of the lovely kind, ye practisers of soft enchantment, how many more ye kill with poisoned baits than ever fell in the ring: and listen with subdued air and without shuddering, to a tale tragic only in appearance, and sacred to the FANCY!
15   I was going down Chancery-lane, thinking to ask at Jack Randall's where the fight was to be, when looking through the glass-door of the *Hole in the Wall*, I heard a gentleman asking the same question *at* Mrs Randall, as the author of Waverley[†] would express it. Now Mrs Randall stood answering the gentleman's question, with the authenticity of the
20   lady of the Champion of the Light Weights. Thinks I, I'll wait till this person comes out, and learn from him how it is. For to say a truth, I was not fond of going into this house of call for heroes and philosophers, ever since the owner of it (for Jack is no gentleman) threatened once upon a time to kick me out of doors for wanting a mutton-chop at his
25   hospitable board, when the conqueror in thirteen battles was more full of *blue ruin*[†] than of good manners. I was the more mortified at this repulse, inasmuch as I had heard Mr James Simpkins, hosier[†] in the Strand, one day when the character of the *Hole in the Wall* was brought in question, observe – 'The house is a very good house, and the company
30   quite genteel: I have been there myself!' Remembering this unkind treatment of mine host, to which mine hostess was also a party, and not wishing to put her in unquiet thoughts at a time jubilant like the present, I waited at the door, when, who should issue forth but my friend Joe Toms, and turning suddenly up Chancery-lane with that
35   quick jerk and impateint stride which distinguishes a lover of the FANCY, I said, 'I'll be hanged if that fellow is not going to the fight, and is on his way to get me to go with him.' So it proved in effect, and we agreed to adjourn to my lodgings to discuss measures with that cordiality which makes old friends like new, and new friends like old, on great
40   occasions. We are cold to others only when we are dull in ourselves, and have neither thoughts nor feelings to impart to them. Give a man a topic in his head, a throb of pleasure in his heart, and he will be glad to share it with the first person he meets. Toms and I, though we seldom meet, were an *alter idem*[†] on this memorable occasion, and had not an
45   idea that we did not candidly impart; and 'so carelessly did we fleet the

---

author of Waverley Sir Walter Scott
blue ruin gin
hosier dealer in socks, stockings and
underwear

alter idem another thing which is yet the same,
i.e. as one

time,' that I wish no better, when there is another fight, than to have
him for a companion on my journey down, and to return with my
friend Jack Pigott talking of what was to happen or of what did happen,
with a noble subject always at hand, and liberty to digress to others
50   whenever they offered. Indeed, on my repeating the lines from Spenser
in an involuntary fit of enthusiasm,

> 'What more felicity can fall to creature,
> Than to enjoy delight with liberty?'

my last-named ingenious friend stopped me by saying that this, translated
55   into the vulgate, meant *'Going to see a fight.'*
    Joe Toms and I could not settle about the method of going down.
He said there was a caravan,[†] he understood, to start from Tom
Belcher's at two, which would go there *right out* and back again the
next day. Now I never travel at night, and said I should get a cast[†] to
60   Newbury by one of the mails.[†] Joe swore the thing was impossible, and
I could only answer that I had made up my mind to it. In short, he
seemed to me to waver, said he only came to see if I was going, had
letters to write, a cause coming on the day after, and faintly said at
parting (for I was bent on setting out that moment) – 'Well, we meet at
65   Philippi!' I made the best of my way to Piccadilly. The mail coach stand
was bare. 'They are all gone,' said I – 'this is always the way with me –
in the instant I lose the future – if I had not stayed to pour out that last
cup of tea, I should have been just in time' – and cursing my folly and
ill-luck together, without inquiring at the coach-office whether the mails
70   were gone or not, I walked on in despite, and to punish my own
dilatoriness and want of determination. At any rate, I would not turn
back: I might get to Hounslow, or perhaps farther, to be on my road
the next morning. I passed Hyde Park Corner (my Rubicon[†]), and
trusted to fortune. Suddenly I heard the clattering of a Brentford stage,
75   and the fight rushed full upon my fancy. I argued (not unwisely) that
even a Brentford coachman was better company than my own thoughts
(such as they were just then), and at his invitation mounted the box
with him. I immediately stated my case to him – namely, my quarrel
with myself for missing the Bath or Bristol mail, and my determination
80   to get on in consequence as well as I could, without any disparagement
or insulting comparison between longer or shorter stages. It is a maxim
with me that stage-coaches, and consequently stage-coachmen, are
respectable in proportion to the distance they have to travel: so I said
nothing on that subject to my Brentford friend. Any incipient tendency

---

caravan a company of merchants, or pilgrims,
    travelling together
cast casual lift
mails mail-coaches

Rubicon the stream limiting Caesar's
    province. By crossing it he committed himself
    to war with Pompey

85   to an abstract proposition, or (as he might have construed it) to a
      personal reflection of this kind, was however nipped in the bud; for I
      had no sooner declared indignantly that I had missed the mails, than
      he flatly denied that they were gone along, and lo! at the instant three
      of them drove by in rapid, provoking, orderly succession, as if they
90   would devour the ground before them. Here again I seemed in the
      contradictory situation of the man in Dryden who exclaims,

                'I follow Fate, which does too hard pursue!'

      If I had stopped to inquire at the White Horse Cellar, which would not
      have taken me a minute, I should now have been driving down the
95   road in all the dignified unconcern and *ideal* perfection of mechanical
      conveyance. The Bath mail I had set my mind upon, and I had missed
      it, as I missed everything else, by my own absurdity, in putting the will
      for the deed, and aiming at ends without employing means. 'Sir,' said
      he of the Brentford, 'The Bath mail will be up presently, my brother-in-
100   law drives it, and I will engage to stop him if there is a place empty.' I
      almost doubted my good genius; but, sure enough, up it drove like
      lightning, and stopped directly at the call of the Brentford Jehu.† I
      would not have believed this possible, but the brother-in-law of a mail-
      coach driver is himself no mean man. I was transferred without loss of
105   time from the top of one coach to that of the other, desired the guard
      to pay my fare to the Brentford coachman for me as I had no change,
      was accommodated with a great coat, put up my umbrella to keep off
      a drizzling mist, and we began to cut through the air like an arrow.
      The mile-stones disappeared one after another, the rain kept off; Tom
110   Turtle, the trainer, sat before me on the coach-box, with whom I
      exchanged civilities as a gentleman going to the fight; the passion that
      had transported me an hour before was subdued to pensive regret and
      conjectural musing on the next day's battle; I was promised a place
      inside at Reading, and upon the whole, I thought myself a lucky fellow.
115   Such is the force of imagination! On the outside of any other coach on
      the 10th of December, with a Scotch mist drizzling through the cloudy
      moonlight air, I should have been cold, comfortless, impatient, and, no
      doubt, wet through; but seated on the Royal mail, I felt warm and
      comfortable, the air did me good, the ride did me good, I was pleased
120   with the progress we had made, and confident that all would go well
      through the journey. When I got inside at Reading, I found Turtle and
      a stout valetudinarian,† whose costume bespoke him one of the FANCY,
      and who had risen from a three months' sick bed to get into the mail
      to see the fight. They were intimate, as we fell into a lively discourse.
125   My friend the trainer was confined in his topics to fighting dogs and

---

Jehu a furious driver (II Kings 10. 20)   *valetudinarian* a person of infirm health

men, to bears and badgers; beyond this he was 'quite chap-fallen,'[†] had
not a word to throw at a dog, or indeed very wisely fell asleep, when
any other game was started. The whole art of training (I, however,
learnt from him) consists in two things, exercise and abstinence,
130   abstinence and exercise, repeated alternately and without end. A yolk
of an egg with a spoonful of rum in it is the first thing in a morning,
and then a walk of six miles till breakfast. This meal consists of a
plentiful supply of tea and toast and beef-steaks. Then another six or
seven miles till dinner-time, and another supply of solid beef or mutton
135   with a pint of porter, and perhaps, at the utmost, a couple of glasses of
sherry. Martin trains on water, but this increases his infirmity on
another very dangerous side. The Gas-man takes now and then a
chirping glass (under the rose[†]) to console him, during a six weeks'
probation, for the absence of Mrs Hickman – an agreeable woman,
140   with (I understand) a pretty fortune of two hundred pounds. How matter
presses on me! What stubborn things are facts! How inexhaustible is
nature and art! 'It is well,' as I once heard Mr Richmond[†] observe, 'to
see a variety.' He was speaking of cock-fighting as an edifying spectacle.
I cannot deny but that one learns more of what *is* (I do not say of what
145   *ought to be*) in this desultory mode of practical study, than from reading
the same book twice over, even though it should be a moral treatise.
Where was I? I was sitting at dinner with the candidate for the honours
of the ring, 'where good digestion waits on appetite, and health on
both.' Then follows an hour of social chat and native glee; and
150   afterwards, to another breathing over healthy hill or dale. Back to
supper, and then to bed, and up by six again – Our hero

> 'Follows so the ever-running sun
> With profitable *ardour*' –

to the day that brings him victory or defeat in the green fairy circle. Is
155   not this life more sweet than mine? I was going to say; but I will not
libel any life by comparing it to mine, which is (at the date of these
presents) bitter as coloquintida[†] and the dregs of aconitum![†]
   The invalid in the Bath mail soared a pitch above the trainer, and
did not sleep so sound, because he had 'more figures and more fantasies.'
160   We talked the hours away merrily. He had faith in surgery, for he had
had three ribs set right, that had been broken in a *turn-up*[†] at Belcher's,
but thought physicians old women, for they had no antidote in their
catalogue for brandy. An indigestion is an excellent common-place for

---

chap-fallen with hanging jaw: dejected
under the rose secretly, privately (sub rosa)
Mr Richmond Bill Richmond, a coloured
  boxer who might have taught Hazlitt to box

coloquintida bitter-apple, pulped and used as
  a purgative drug
aconitum monk's-hood or wolf's-bane, a
  poisonous plant
turn-up fight, fracas

two people that never met before. By way of ingratiating myself, I told
165 him the story of my doctor, who, on my earnestly representing to him
that I thought his regimen had done me harm, assured me that the
whole pharmacopeia† contained nothing comparable to the prescription
he had given me; and, as a proof of its undoubted efficacy, said that,
'he had had one gentleman with my complaint under his hands for the
170 last fifteen years.' This anecdote made my companion shake the rough
sides of his three great coats with boisterous laughter; and Turtle,
starting out of his sleep, swore he knew how the fight would go, for he
had had a dream about it. Sure enough the rascal told us how the three
first rounds went off, but 'his dream,' like others, 'denoted a foregone
175 conclusion.' He knew his men. The moon now rose in silver state, and
I ventured, with some hesitation, to point out this object of placid
beauty, with the blue serene beyond, to the man of science, to which
his ear he 'seriously inclined,' the more as it gave promise *d'un beau
jour*† for the morrow, and showed the ring undrenched by envious
180 showers, arrayed in sunny smiles. Just then, all going on well, I thought
on my friend Toms, whom I had left behind, and said innocently. 'There
was a blockhead of a fellow I left in town, who said there was no
possibility of getting down by the mail, and talked of going by a caravan
from Belcher's at two in the morning, after he had written some letters.'
185 'Why,' said he of the lapels, 'I should not wonder if that was the very
person we saw running about like mad from one coach-door to another,
and asking if any one had seen a friend of his, a gentleman going to
the fight, whom he had missed stupidly enough by staying to write a
note.' 'Pray, Sir,' said my fellow-traveller, 'had he a plaid-cloak on?' –
190 'Why, no,' said I, 'not at the time I left him, but he very well might
afterwards, for he offered to lend me one.' The plaid-cloak and the
letter decided the thing. Joe, sure enough, was in the Bristol mail, which
preceded us by about fifty yards. This was droll enough. We had now
but a few miles to our place of destination, and the first thing I did on
195 alighting at Newbury, both coaches stopping at the same time, was to
call out, 'Pray, is there a gentleman in that mail of the name of Toms?'
'No,' said Joe, borrowing something of the vein of Gilpin, 'for I have
just got out.' 'Well!' says he, 'this is lucky; but you don't know how
vexed I was to miss you; for,' added he, lowering his voice, 'do you
200 know when I left you I went to Belcher's to ask about the caravan, and
Mrs Belcher said very obligingly she couldn't tell about that, but there
were two gentlemen who had taken places by the mail and were gone
on in a landau,† and she could frank† us. It's a pity I didn't meet with

---

pharmacopeia book containing lists of drugs
and directions for use
d'un beau jour of a fine day

landau four-wheeled horse-drawn carriage.
The front and back halves of its canopy can
be raised and lowered independently
frank give signed tickets

you; we could then have got down for nothing. But *mum's the word.'*
205 It's the devil for any one to tell me a secret, for it's sure to come out in print. I do not care so much to gratify a friend, but the public ear is too great a temptation to me.

Our present business was to get beds and a supper at an inn: but this was no easy task. The public-houses were full, and where you saw
210 a light at a private house, and people poking their heads out of the casement to see what was going on, they instantly put them in and shut the window, the moment you seemed advancing with a suspicious overture for accommodation. Our guard and coachman thundered away at the outer gate of the Crown for some time without effect – such was
215 the greater noise within; – and when the doors were unbarred, and we got admittance, we found a party assembled in the kitchen around a good hospitable fire, some sleeping, others drinking, other talking on politics and on the fight. A tall English yeoman† (something like Matthews in the face, and quite as great a wag) –

220   'A lusty man to ben an abbot able,' –†

was making such a prodigious noise about rent and taxes, and the price of corn now and formerly, that he had prevented us from being heard at the gate. The first thing I heard him say was to a shuffling fellow who wanted to be off a bet for a shilling glass of brandy and water –
225 'Confound it, man, don't be *insipid!*'† Thinks I, that is a good phrase. It was a good omen. He kept it so all night, nor flinched with the approach of morning. He was a fine fellow, with sense, wit, and spirit, a hearty body and a joyous mind, free-spoken, frank, convivial – one of that true English breed that went with Harry the Fifth to the siege
230 of Harfleur – 'standing like greyhounds in the slips,' &c. We ordered tea and eggs (beds soon found to be out of the question) and this fellow's conversation was *sauce piquante*.† It did one's heart good to see him brandish his oaken towel† and to hear him talk. He made mince-meat of a drunken, stupid, red-faced, quarrelsome, *frowsy*†
235 farmer, whose nose 'he moralised into a thousand similes,' making it out a firebrand like Bardolph's.† 'I'll tell you what, my friend,' says he, 'the landlady has only to keep you here to save fire and candle. If one was to touch your nose, it would go off like a piece of charcoal.' At this the other only grinned like an idiot, the sole variety in his purple
240 face being his little peering eyes and yellow teeth; called for another glass, swore he would not stand it; and after many attempts to provoke

---

yeoman   a small landowner
A lusty man . . . able   from Chaucer's Prologue
   to the *Canterbury Tales*
insipid   tasteless, dull
piquante   sharply stimulating

oaken towel   cudgel
frowsy   fusty, unkempt
Bardolph   minor character in Shakespeare's
   Henry V

his humorous antagonist to single combat, which the other turned off (after working him up to a ludicrous pitch of choler) with great adroitness, he fell quietly asleep with a glass of liquor in his hand,

245   which he could not lift to his head. His laughing persecutor made a speech over him, and turning to the opposite side of the room, where they were all sleeping in the midst of his 'loud and furious fun,' said, 'There's a scene, by G—d, for Hogarth[†] to paint. I think he and Shakespear were our two best men at copying life.' This confirmed me

250   in my good opinion of him. Hogarth, Shakespear, and Nature, were just enough for him (indeed for any man) to know. I said, 'You read Cobbett,[†] don't you? At least,' says I, 'you talk just as well as he writes.' He seemed to doubt this. But I said, 'We have an hour to spare: if you'll get pen, ink, and paper, and keep on talking, I'll write down

255   what you say; and if it doesn't make a capital Political Register, I'll forfeit my head. You have kept me alive to-night, however. I don't know what I should have done without you.' He did not dislike this view of the thing, nor my asking if he was not about the size of Jem Belcher; and told me soon afterwards, in the confidence of friendship,

260   that 'the circumstance which had given him nearly the greatest concern in his life, was Cribb's beating Jem after he had lost his eye by racket-playing.' – The morning dawns; that dim but yet clear light appears, which weighs like solid bars of metal on the sleepless eyelids; the guests drop down from their chambers one by one – but it was too late to

265   think of going to bed now (the clock was on the stroke of seven), we had nothing for it but to find a barber's (the pole that glittered in the morning sun lighted us to his shop), and then a nine miles' march to Hungerford. The day was fine, the sky was blue, the mists were retiring from the marshy ground, the path was tolerably dry, the sitting-up all

270   night had not done us much harm – at least the cause was good; we talked of this and that with amicable difference, roving and sipping of many subjects, but still invariably we returned to the fight. At length, a mile to the left of Hungerford, on a gentle eminence, we saw the ring surrounded by covered carts, gigs, and carriages, of which hundreds

275   had passed us on the road: Toms gave a youthful shout, and we hastened down a narrow lane to the scene of action.

Reader, have you ever seen a fight? If not, you have a pleasure to come, at least if it is a fight like that between the Gas-man and Bill Neate. The crowd was very great when we arrived on the spot: open

280   carriages were coming up, with streamers flying and music playing, and the countrypeople were pouring in over hedge and ditch in all directions, to see their hero beat or be beaten. The odds were still on Gas, but

---

Hogarth   William Hogarth (1697–1764),   *Cobbett*   William Cobbett (1763–1835; see
    painter and engraver   pp. 23–4)

only about five to four. Gully had been down to try Neate, and
had backed him considerably, which was a damper to the sanguine
285 confidence of the adverse party. About two hundred thousand pounds
were pending. The Gas says, he has lost 3000*l*[†] which were promised
him by different gentlemen if he had won. He had presumed too much
on himself, which had made others presume on him. This spirited and
formidable young fellow seems to have taken for his motto the old
290 maxim, that 'there are three things necessary to success in life –
Impudence! Impudence! Impudence!' It is so in matters of opinion,
but not in the FANCY, which is the most practical of all things, though
even here confidence is half the battle, but only half. Our friend had
vapoured and swaggered too much, as if he wanted to grin and bully
295 his adversary out of the fight. 'Alas! the Bristol man was not so tamed!' –
'This is *the grave-digger*' (would Tom Hickman exclaim in the moments
of intoxication from gin and success, shewing his tremendous right
hand), 'this will send many of them to their long homes; I haven't done
with them yet!' Why should he – though he had licked four of the best
300 men within the hour, yet why should he threaten to inflict dishonourable
chastisement on my old master Richmond, a veteran going off the stage,
and who has borne his sable[†] honours meekly? Magnanimity, my dear
Tom, and bravery, should be inseparable. Or why should he go up to
his antagonist, the first time he ever saw him at the Fives Court, and
305 measuring him from head to foot with a glance of contempt, as Achilles
surveyed Hector, say to him, 'What, are you Bill Neate? I'll knock more
blood out of that great carcase of thine, this day fortnight, than you
ever knock'd out of a bullock's!' It was not manly, 'twas not fighter-
like. If he was sure of the victory (as he was not), the less said about it
310 the better. Modesty should accompany the FANCY as its shadow. The
best men were always the best behaved. Jem Belcher, the Game Chicken
(before whom the Gas-man could not have lived) were civil, silent men.
So is Cribb, so is Tom Belcher, the most elegant of sparrers, and not a
man for every one to take by the nose. I enlarged on this topic in the
315 mail (while Turtle was asleep), and said very wisely (as I thought) that
impertinence was a part of no profession. A boxer was bound to beat
his man, but not to thrust his fist, either actually or by implication, in
every one's face. Even a highwayman, in the way of trade, may blow
out your brains, but if he uses foul language at the same time, I should
320 say he was no gentleman. A boxer, I would infer, need not be a
blackguard or a coxcomb, more than another. Perhaps I press this point
too much on a fallen man – Mr Thomas Hickman has by his time learnt
that first of all lessons. 'That man was made to mourn.' He has lost
nothing by the late fight but his presumption; and that every man may

---

3000*l*   £3000 sterling   *sable*   black or brown colour of mourning

325   do as well without! By an over-display of this quality, however, the public had been prejudiced against him, and the *knowing-ones* were taken in. Few but those who had bet on him wished Gas to win. With my own prepossession on the subject, the result of the 11th of December appeared to me as fine a piece of poetical justice as I had ever witnessed.

330   The difference of weight between the two combatants (14 stone to 12) was nothing to the sporting men. Great, heavy, clumsy, long-armed Bill Neate kicked the beam† in the scale of the Gas-man's vanity. The amateurs were frightened at his big words, and thought that they would make up the difference of six feet and five feet nine. Truly, the FANCY

335   are not men of imagination. They judge of what has been, and cannot conceive of any thing that is to be. The Gas-man had won hitherto, therefore he must beat a man half as big again as himself – and that to a certainty. Besides, there are as many feuds, factions, prejudices, pedantic notions in the FANCY as in the state or in the schools. Mr Gully

340   is almost the only cool, sensible man among them, who exercises an unbiassed discretion, and is not a slave to his passions in these matters. But enough of reflections, and to our tale. The day, as I have said, was fine for a December morning. The grass was wet, and the ground miry, and ploughed up with multitudinous feet, except that, within the ring

345   itself, there was a spot of virgin-green closed in and unprofaned by vulgar tread, that shone with dazzling brightness in the mid-day sun. For it was now noon, and we had an hour to wait. This is the trying time. It is then the heart sickens, as you think what the two champions are about, and how short a time will determine their fate. After the first

350   blow is struck, there is no opportunity for nervous apprehensions; you are swallowed up in the immediate interest of the scene – but

'Between the acting† of a dreadful thing
And the first motion, all the interim is
Like a phantasma, or a hideous dream.'

355   I found it so as I felt the sun's rays clinging to my back, and saw the white wintry clouds sink below the verge of the horizon. 'So,' I thought, 'my fairest hopes have faded from my sight! – so will the Gas-man's glory, or that of his adversary, vanish in an hour.' The *swells*† were parading in their white box-coats, the outer ring was cleared with some

360   bruises on the heads and shins of the rustic assembly (for the *cockneys* had been distanced by the sixty-six miles); the time drew near, I had got a good stand; a bustle, a buzz, ran through the crowd, and from the opposite side entered Neate, between his second and bottle-holder. He rolled along, swathed in his loose great coat, his knock-knees

---

kicked the beam   proved the lighter   *Caesar*, II. 1, 63
Between the acting . . .   Shakespeare's *Julius*   *swells*   dandies, men of fashion

365 bending under his huge bulk; and, with a modest cheerful air, threw
his hat into the ring. He then just looked around, and began quietly to
undress: when from the other side there was a similar rush and an
opening made, and the Gas-man came forward with a conscious air of
anticipated triumph, too much like the cock-of-the-walk. He strutted
370 about more than became a hero, sucked oranges with a supercilious
air, and threw away the skin with a toss of his head, and went up and
looked at Neate, which was an act of supererogation. The only sensible
thing he did was, as he strode away from the modern Ajax, to fling out
his arms, as if he wanted to try whether they would do their work that
375 day. By this time they had stripped, and presented a strong contrast in
appearance. If Neate was like Ajax, 'with Atlantean shoulders, fit to
bear' the pugilistic reputation of all Bristol, Hickman might be compared
to Diomed, light, vigorous, elastic, and his back glistened in the sun, as
he moved about, like a panther's hide. There was now a dead pause –
380 attention was awe-struck. Who at that moment, big with a great event,
did not draw his breath short – did not feel his heart throb? All was
ready. They tossed up for the sun, and the Gas-man won. They were
led up to the *scratch*† – and shook hands, and went at it.
 In the first round every one thought it was all over. After making
385 play a short time, the Gas-man flew at his adversary like tiger, struck
five blows in as many seconds, three first, and then following him as he
staggered back, two more, right and left, and down he fell, a mighty
ruin. There was a shout, and I said, 'There is no standing this.' Neate
seemed like a lifeless lump of flesh and bone, round which the Gas-
390 man's blows played with the rapidity of electricity or lightning, and
you imagined he would only be lifted up to be knocked down again. It
was as if Hickman held a sword or a fire in that right hand of his, and
directed it against an unarmed body. They met again, and Neate seemed,
not cowed, but particularly cautious. I saw his teeth clenched together
395 and his brows knit close against the sun. He held out both his arms at
full length straight before him, like two sledge-hammers, and raised his
left an inch or two higher. The Gas-man could not get over this guard –
they struck mutually and fell, but without advantage on either side. It
was the same in the next round; but the balance of power was thus
400 restored – the fate of the battle was suspended. No one could tell how
it would end. This was the only moment in which opinion was divided;
for, in the next, the Gas-man aiming a mortal blow at his adversary's
neck, with his right hand, and failing from the length he had to reach,
the other returned it with his left at full swing, planted a tremendous
405 blow on his cheek-bone and eyebrow, and made a red ruin of that side
of his face. The Gas-man went down, and there was another shout – a

---

scratch mark or line from which competitors start

roar of triumph as the waves of fortune rolled tumultuously from side to side. This was a settler. Hickman got up, and 'grinned horrible a ghastly smile,' yet he was evidently dashed in his opinion of himself; it was the first time he had ever been so punished; all one side of his face was perfect scarlet, and his right eye was closed in dingy blackness, as he advanced to the fight, less confident, but still determined. After one or two rounds, not receiving another such remembrancer, he rallied and went at it with his former impetuosity. But in vain. His strength had been weakened, – his blows could not tell at such a distance, – he was obliged to fling himself at his adversary, and could not strike from his feet; and almost as regularly as he flew at him with his right hand, Neate warded the blow, or drew back out of his reach, and felled him with the return of his left. There was little cautious sparring – no half-hits – no tapping and trifling, none of the *petit-maîtreship*† of the art – they were almost all knock-down blows: – the fight was a good stand up fight. The wonder was the half-minute time. If there had been a minute or more allowed between each round, it would have been intelligible how they should by degrees recover strength and resolution; but to see two men smashed to the ground, smeared with gore, stunned, senseless, the breath beaten out of their bodies; and then, before you recover from the shock, to see them rise up with new strength and courage, stand steady to inflict or receive mortal offence, and rush upon each other 'like two clouds over the Caspian' – this is the most astonishing thing of all: – this is the high and heroic state of man! From this time forward the event became more certain every round; and about the twelfth it seemed as if it must have been over. Hickman generally stood with his back to me; but in the scuffle, he had changed positions, and Neate just then made a tremendous lunge at him, and hit him full in the face. It was doubtful whether he would fall backwards or forwards; he hung suspended for a second or two, and then fell back, throwing his hands in the air, and with his face lifted up to the sky. I never saw any thing more terrific than his aspect just before he fell. All traces of life, of natural expression, were gone from him. His face was like a human skull, a death's head, spouting blood. The eyes were filled with blood, the nose streamed with blood, the mouth gaped blood. He was not like an actual man, but like a preternatural, spectral appearance, or like one of the figures in Dante's *Inferno*. Yet he fought on after this for several rounds, still striking the first desperate blow, and Neate standing on the defensive, and using the same cautious guard to the last, as if he had still all his work to do; and it was not till the Gas-man was so stunned in the seventeenth or eighteenth round, that his senses forsook him, and he could not come to time, that the battle

---

petit-maîtreship   effeminacy, foppishness

was declared over.[†] Ye who despise the FANCY, do something to shew
450   as much *pluck*, or as much self-possession as this, before you assume a
superiority which you have never given a single proof of by any one
action in the whole course of your lives! – When the Gas-man came to
himself, the first words he uttered were, 'Where am I? What is the
matter?' 'Nothing is the matter, Tom – you have lost the battle, but
455   you are the bravest man alive.' And Jackson whispered to him, 'I am
collecting a purse for you, Tom.' – Vain sounds, and unheard at that
moment! Neate instantly went up and shook him cordially by the hand,
and seeing some old acquaintance, began to flourish with his fists, called
out, 'Ah, you always said I couldn't fight – What do you think now?'
460   But all in good humour, and without any appearance of arrogance;
only it was evident Bill Neate was pleased that he had won the fight.
When it was over, I asked Cribb if he did not think it was a good one?
He said, '*Pretty well!*' The carrier pigeons now mounted into the air,
and one of them flew with the news of her husband's victory to the
465   bosom of Mrs Neate. Alas, for Mrs Hickman!

1822   1822

---

battle . . . over   Hazlitt notes: 'Scroggins said
of the Gas-man, that he thought he was a man
of that courage, that if his hands were cut
off, he would still fight on with the stumps –
like that of Widrington, –

– "In doleful dumps,
Who, when his legs were smitten off
Still fought upon his stumps." '

Leigh Hunt
1784–1859

A number of influential magazines owed their existence to Leigh Hunt. He is important in the history of literature for his energy, enthusiasm and optimism. He acted as a catalyst for many writers, detected their talents and propagated them.

Hunt was the son of a clergyman and attended Christ's Hospital as a charity boy. Together with his brother John, he founded the *Examiner* magazine in 1808. He himself flourished in a minor way as a poet – his first collection was published in 1807 – and as an essayist. In his *Reflector* he first published Lamb's essays on Shakespeare. Around him, at various times, moved Byron, Moore, the Lambs, Bentham, Mill, Keats, Shelley and Hazlitt. His magazines included the *Indicator*, the *Companion*, the *Tatler* and the *London Journal*.

His most famous poem 'Jenny Kissed Me' appeared in an anthology, *Book of Gems* (1838). His poetical works were published in 1844.

TO THE GRASSHOPPER AND THE CRICKET

Green little vaulter in the sunny grass
Catching your heart up at the feel of June,
Sole voice that's heard amidst the lazy noon,
When ev'n the bees lag at the summoning brass;
5   And you, warm little housekeeper, who class
With those who think the candles come too soon,
Loving the fire, and with your tricksome tune
Nick the glad silent moments as they pass;
Oh sweet and tiny cousins, that belong,
10   One to the fields, the other to the hearth,
Both have your sunshine; both though small are strong
At your clear hearts; and both were sent on earth
To sing in thoughtful ears this natural song, –
In doors and out, summer and winter, Mirth.

1816   1817

From THE NYMPHS
Part I

Those are the Naiads,† who keep neat
195 The banks from sedge,* and from the dull-dropp'd feet   marsh-grass
Of cattle that break down the fibrous mould.
They snap the selfish nets, that, overbold,
Cross the whole river, and might trip the keels
Of summer boats. Theirs are the kind appeals
200 And unseen beckoning, holding baits of grass,
That win the sheep into their washing-place;
And they too, in their gentleness, uphold
The sighing nostrils of the stag, when he
Takes to the wrapping water wretchedly;
205 And tow'rds the amorous noon, when some young poet
Comes there to bathe, and yet half thrills to do it,
Hovering with his ripe locks, and fair light limbs,
And trying with cold foot the banks and brims,
They win him to the water with sweet fancies,
210 Till in the girdling stream he pants and dances.
There's a whole bevy there in that recess
Rounding from the main stream: some sleep, some dress
Each other's locks, some swim about, some sit
Parting their own moist hair, or fingering it
215 Lightly, to let the curling air go through:
Some make them green and lilied coronets new;
And one there from her tender instep shakes
The matted sedge; a second, as she swims,
Looks round with pride upon her easy limbs;
220 A third, just holding by a bough, lets float
Her slumberous body like an anchored boat,
Looking with level eye at the glib flakes
And the strange crooked quivering which it makes,
Seen through the weltering of the watery glass:
225 Others (which make the rest look at them) pass,
Nodding and smiling, in the middle tide,
And luring swans on, which like fondled things
Eye poutingly their hands; yet following, glide
With unsuperfluous lift of their proud wings.

c. 1817   1818

Naiads in classical mythology, nymphs of
  lake, fountain, river or stream

RONDEAU

Jenny kissed me when we met,
　Jumping from the chair she sat in;
Time, you thief, who love to get
　Sweets into your list, put that in!
5 Say I'm weary, say I'm sad,
　Say that health and wealth have missed me,
Say I'm growing old, but add,
　Jenny kissed me.

1838

Thomas De Quincey
1785–1859

The possessor of 'a prodigious memory' and an 'inexhaustible fertility of topics' in his own estimation, De Quincey was able to make a substantial living from his writings. He was born in Manchester, educated at Bath, Winkfield, and Manchester Grammar School, from which he ran away, and at Worcester College, Oxford. He became a friend of Wordsworth and Coleridge, and took up residence at Grasmere.

As early as 1804 he had taken opium at Oxford, and by 1812 he was an addict: he described it as that 'dread agent of unimaginable pleasure and pain'. In 1817 he married Margaret Simpson, who bore him eight children. He wrote articles for various magazines and journals, and published *Confessions of an English Opium-Eater* (1822).

For the rest of his life he lived mostly in Edinburgh where he made his living by writing stories, articles and reviews: he published mainly in *Blackwood's*, and Tait's *Edinburgh Magazine*. *Recollections of the Lake Poets* appeared 1834–9, and *The English Mail Coach* in 1849. In 1853 he started supervising the collected edition of his works, *Selections Grave and Gay*, which was published a year after his death.

De Quincey wrote with an elaborate, lucid, analytical style and made considerable use of what he described as his 'capacity for detecting remote analogies'. He particularly influenced Edgar Allan Poe and Charles Baudelaire.

From CONFESSIONS OF AN ENGLISH OPIUM-EATER
[Triumph over Addiction]

But I am now called upon to wind up a narrative which has already extended to an unreasonable length. Within more spacious limits, the materials which I have used might have been better unfolded; and much which I have not used might have been added with effect. Perhaps,

5   however, enough has been given. It now remains that I should say
    something of the way in which this conflict of horrors was finally
    brought to its crisis. The reader is already aware (from a passage near
    the beginning of the introduction to the first part) that the opium-eater
    has, in some way or other, 'unwound, almost to its final links, the
10 accursed chain which bound him'. By what means? To have narrated
    this, according to the original intention, would have far exceeded the
    space which can now be allowed. It is fortunate, as such a cogent reason
    exists for abridging it, that I should on a maturer view of the case, have
    been exceedingly unwilling to injure, by any such unaffecting details,
15 the impression of the history itself, as an appeal to the prudence and
    the conscience of the yet unconfirmed opium-eater – or even (though a
    very inferior consideration) to injure its effect as a composition. The
    interest of the judicious reader will not attach itself chiefly to the subject
    of the fascinating spells, but to the fascinating power. Not the opium-
20 eater, but the opium, is the true hero of the tale; and the legitimate
    centre on which the interest revolves. The object was to display the
    marvellous agency of opium, whether for pleasure or for pain: if that
    is done, the action of the piece has closed.
        However, as some people, in spite of all laws to the contrary, will
25 persist in asking what became of the opium-eater, and in what state he
    now is, I answer for him thus: The reader is aware that opium had
    long ceased to found its empire on spells of pleasure; it was solely by
    the tortures connected with the attempt to abjure it, that it kept its
    hold. Yet, as other tortures, no less it may be thought, attended the
30 non-abjuration† of such a tyrant, a choice only of evils was left: and
    that might as well have been adopted, which, however terrific in itself,
    held out a prospect of final restoration to happiness. This appears true;
    but good logic gave the author no strength to act upon it. However, a
    crisis arrived for the author's life, and a crisis for other objects still
35 dearer to him – and which will always be far dearer to him than his
    life, even now that it is again a happy one – I saw that I must die if I
    continued the opium: I determined, therefore, if that should be required,
    to die in throwing it off. How much I was at the time taking I cannot
    say; for the opium which I used had been purchased for me by a friend
40 who afterwards refused to let me pay him; so that I could not ascertain
    even what quantity I had used within the year. I apprehend, however,
    that I took it very irregularly: and that I varied from about fifty or sixty
    grains, to 150 a-day. My first task was to reduce it to forty, to thirty,
    and, as fast as I could, to twelve grains.
45   I triumphed: but think not, reader, that therefore my sufferings were
    ended; nor think of me as of one sitting in a *dejected* state. Think of

---

non-abjuration   failure to renouce (on oath)

me as of one, even when four months had passed, still agitated, writing, throbbing, palpitating, shattered; and much, perhaps, in the situation of him who has been racked, as I collect the torments of that state from
50 the affecting account of them left by the most innocent sufferer[†] (of the times of James I). Meantime, I derived no benefit from any medicine, except one prescribed to me by an Edinburgh surgeon of great eminence, viz. ammoniated tincture of Valerian.[†] Medical account, therefore, of my emancipation I have not much to give: and even that little, as
55 managed by a man so ignorant of medicine as myself, would probably tend only to mislead. At all events, it would be misplaced in this situation. The moral of the narrative is addressed to the opium-eater; and therefore, of necessity, limited in its application. If he is taught to fear and tremble, enough has been effected. But he may say, that the
60 issue of my case is at least a proof that opium, after a seventeen years' use, and an eight years' abuse of its powers, may still be renounced: and that *he* may chance to bring to the task greater energy than I did, or that with a stronger constitution than mine he may obtain the same results with less. This may be true: I would not presume to measure
65 the efforts of other men by my own: I heartily wish him more energy: I wish him the same success. Nevertheless, I had motives external to myself which he may unfortunately want: and these supplied me with conscientious supporters which mere personal interests might fail to supply to a mind debilitated[†] by opium.
70 Jeremy Taylor[†] conjectures that it may be as painful to be born as to die: I think it probable: and, during the whole period of diminishing the opium, I had the torments of a man passing out of one mode of existence into another. The issue was not death, but a sort of physical regeneration: and I may add, that ever since, at intervals, I have had a
75 restoration of more than youthful spirits, though under the pressure of difficulties, which, in a less happy state of mind, I should have called misfortunes.
One memorial of my former condition still remains: my dreams are not yet perfectly calm: the dread swell and agitation of the storm have
80 not wholly subsided: the legions that encamped in them are drawing off, but not all departed: my sleep is still tumultuous, and, like the gates

---

sufferer De Quincey's note reads: William Lithgow: his book (*Travels*, etc.) is ill and pedantically written; but the account of his own sufferings on the rack at Malaga is overpoweringly affecting
Valerian herb: its root was used as a stimulant
debilitated weakened
Taylor Jeremy Taylor (1613–67). Chaplain to

Archbishop Laud and Charles I: Bishop of Down and Connor, and later of Dromore. Author of *The Rule and Exercise of Holy Living* (1650), and *The Rule and Exercise of Holy Dying* (1651).
In 1856 De Quincey corrected this reference: it was really to an essay on *Death* by Bacon

of Paradise to our first parents when looking back from afar, it is still
(in the tremendous line of Milton) –
    With dreadful faces throng'd and fiery arms.

1821   1822

From SOCIETY OF THE LAKES – I

[Inhabitants of the Lake District]

My cottage was ready in the summer; but I was playing truant
amongst the valleys of Somersetshire; and, meantime, different families,
throughout the summer, borrowed the cottage of the Wordsworths as
my friends. They consisted chiefly of ladies; and some, by the delicacy
5   of their attentions to the flowers, &c., gave me reason to consider their
visit during my absence as a real honour; others – such is the difference
of people in this world – left the rudest memorials of their careless
habits impressed upon house, furniture, garden, &c. In November, at
last, I, the long-expected, made my appearance. Some little sensation
10   did really and naturally attend my coming, for most of the draperies
belonging to beds, curtains, &c., had been sewed by the young women
of that or the adjoining vales. This had caused me to be talked of.
Many had seen me on my visit to the Wordsworths. Miss Wordsworth
had introduced the curious to a knowledge of my age, name, prospects,
15   and all the rest of what can be interesting to know. Even the old people
of the vale were a little excited by the accounts (somewhat exaggerated,
perhaps) of the never ending books that continued to arrive in packing-
cases for several months in succession. Nothing in these vales so much
fixes the attention and respect of the people as the reputation of being
20   a 'far learn'd' man. So far, therefore, I had already bespoke† the
favourable opinion of the Dalesmen. And a separate kind of interest
arose amongst mothers and daughters, in the knowledge that I should
necessarily want what – in a sense somewhat different from the general
one – is called a 'housekeeper'; that is, not an upper servant to
25   superintend others, but one who could undertake, in her own person,
all the duties of the house. It is not discreditable to these worthy people
that several of the richest and most respectable families were anxious
to secure the place for a daughter. Had I been a dissipated young man,
I have good reason to know that there would have been no canvassing
30   at all for the situation. But partly my books spoke for the character of
my pursuits with these simple-minded people – partly the introduction
of the Wordsworths guaranteed the safety of such a service. Even then,

---

bespoke   ordered, or settled, beforehand

had I persisted in my original intention of bringing a man-servant, no
respectable young woman would have accepted the place. As it was,
35   and it being understood that I had renounced this intention, many, in a
gentle, diffident way, applied for the place, or their parents on their
behalf. And I mention the fact, because it illustrates one feature in
the manners of this primitive and peculiar people, the Dalesmen of
Westmoreland. However wealthy, they do not think it degrading to
40   permit even the eldest daughter to go out a few years to service. The
object is not to gain a sum of money in wages, but that sort of household
experience which is supposed to be unattainable upon a suitable scale
out of a gentleman's family. So far was this carried, that, amongst the
offers made to myself, was one from a young woman whose family was
45   amongst the very oldest in the country, and who was at that time under
an engagement of marriage to the very richest young man in the vale.
She and her future husband had a reasonable prospect of possessing
ten thousand pounds in land; and yet neither her own family nor her
husband's objected to her seeking such a place as I could offer. Her
50   character and manners, I ought to add, were so truly excellent, and
won respect so inevitably from everybody, that nobody could wonder
at the honourable confidence reposed in her by her manly and spirited
young lover. The issue of the matter, as respected my service, was, why
I do not know, that Miss Wordsworth did not accept of her: and she
55   fulfilled her purpose in another family, a very grave and respectable
one, in Kendal. She stayed about a couple of years, returned, and
married the young man to whom she had engaged herself, and is now
the prosperous mother of a fine handsome family; and she together
with her mother-in-law are the two leading matrons of the vale.
60   It was on a November night, about ten o'clock, that I first found
myself installed in a house of my own – this cottage, so memorable
from its past tenant to all men, so memorable to myself from all which
has since passed in connexion with it. A writer in *The Quarterly Review*,
in noticing the autobiography of Dr Watson, the Bishop of Llandaff,
65   has thought fit to say that the Lakes, of course, afforded no society
capable of appreciating this commonplace, coarse-minded man of
talents. The person who said this I understand to have been Dr Whitaker,
the respectable antiquary.[1] Now, that the reader may judge of the
propriety[†] with which this was asserted, I shall slightly rehearse the
70   muster-roll of our Lake society, as it existed at the time when I seated
myself in my Grasmere cottage. I will undertake to say that the
meanest person in the whole scattered community was more extensively
accomplished than the good bishop, was more conscientiously true to
his duties, and had more varied powers of conversation. Wordsworth

---

antiquary   student, collector, of antiquities   *propriety*   fitness

75   and Coleridge, then living at Allan Bank, in Grasmere, I will not notice
in such a question. Southey, living thirteen miles off at Keswick, I have
already noticed, and he needs no *prôneur*.[†] I will begin with Windermere.
        At Clappersgate, a little hamlet of perhaps six houses, on its north-
west angle, and about five miles from my cottage, resided two Scottish
80   ladies, daughters of Dr Cullen, the famous physician and nosologist.[†]
They were universally beloved for their truly kind dispositions and the
firm independence of their conduct. They had been reduced from great
affluence to a condition of rigorous poverty. Their father had made
what should have been a fortune by his practice. The good doctor,
85   however, was careless of his money in proportion to the facility with
which he made it. All was put into a box, open to the whole family.
Breach of confidence, in the most thoughtless use of this money, there
could be none; because no restraint in that point, beyond what honour
and good sense imposed, was laid upon any of the elder children. Under
90   such regulations, it may be imagined that Dr Cullen would not
accumulate any very large capital; and, at his death, the family, for the
first time, found themselves in embarrassed circumstances. Of the two
daughters who belonged to our Lake population, one had married a
Mr Millar, son to the celebrated Professor Millar of Glasgow. This
95   gentleman had died in America; and Mrs Millar was now a childless
widow. The other still remained unmarried. Both were equally independent; and independent even with regard to their nearest relatives; for
even from their brother – who had risen to rank and affluence as a
Scottish judge, under the title of Lord Cullen – they declined to receive
100   assistance; and except for some small addition made to their income
by a novel called 'Home' (in as many as seven volumes, I really believe)
by Miss Cullen, their expenditure was rigorously shaped to meet that
very slender income which they drew from their shares of the patrimonial
wrecks. More honourable and modest independence, or poverty more
105   gracefully supported, I have rarely known.
        Meantime, these ladies, though literary and very agreeable in conver-
sation, could not be classed with what now began to be known as the
lake community of literati;[†] for they took no interest in any one of the
lake poets; did not affect to take any; and I am sure they were not
110   aware of so much value in any one thing these poets had written as
could make it worth while even to look into their books and, accordingly,
as well-bred women, they took the same course as was pursued for
several years by Mrs Hannah More,[†] viz. cautiously to avoid mentioning

---

prôneur   praiser, extoller
nosologist   a doctor concerned with the
    classification of diseases
literati   people of letters: the learned
Hannah More   Hannah More (1745–1833):
writer of tragedies and tracts, the latter
directed towards reform of conditions of the
poor. She was a friend of Dr Johnson, Burke,
Richardson, Reynolds, and an eminent
member of the Blue-Stocking Circle

their names in my presence. This was natural enough in women who
115   had probably built their early admiration upon French models (for Mrs
Millar used to tell me that she regarded the 'Mahomet' of Voltaire as
the most perfect of human compositions), and still more so at a period
when almost all the world had surrendered their opinions and their
literary consciences (so to speak) into the keeping of *The Edinburgh*
120   *Review*; in whose favour, besides, those ladies had the pardonable
prepossessions of national pride, as a collateral[†] guarantee of that
implicit faith which, in those days, stronger-minded people than they
took a pride in professing. Still, in defiance of prejudices mustering so
strongly to support their blindness, and the still stronger support which
125   this blindness drew from their total ignorance of everything either done
or attempted by the lake poets, these amiable women persisted in one
uniform tone of courteous forbearance, as often as any question arose
to implicate the names either of Wordsworth or Coleridge, – any
question about them, their books, their families, or anything that was
130   theirs. They thought it strange, indeed (for so much I heard by a
circuitous course), that promising and intellectual young men – men
educated at great Universities, such as Mr Wilson of Elleray, or myself,
or a few others who had paid us visits, – should possess so deep a
veneration for these writers; but evidently this was an infatuation – a
135   craze, originating, perhaps, in personal connexions, and, as the craze
of valued friends, to be treated with tenderness. For us therefore – for
our sakes – they took a religious care to suppress all allusion to these
disreputable names; and it is pretty plain how sincere their indifference
must have been with regard to these neighbouring authors, from the
140   evidence of one fact, viz. that when, in 1810, Mr Coleridge began to
issue, in weekly numbers, his *Friend*, which, by the prospectus, held
forth a promise of meeting all possible tastes – literary, philosophic,
political – even this comprehensive field of interest, combined with the
adventitious[†] attraction (so very unusual, and so little to have been
145   looked for in that thinly-peopled region) of a local origin, from the
bosom of those very hills at the foot of which (though on a different
side) they were themselves living, failed altogether to stimulate their
torpid[†] curiosity; so perfect was their persuasion beforehand that no
good thing could by possibility come out of a community that had
150   fallen under the ban of the Edinburgh critics.

At the same time, it is melancholy to confess that, partly from the
dejection of Coleridge, his constant immersion in opium at that period,
his hatred of the duties he had assumed, or at least of their too frequent
and periodical recurrence, and partly also from the bad selection of

---

collateral parallel   *torpid* dull, sluggish
adventitious accidental, casual

155 topics for a miscellaneous audience, from the heaviness and obscurity
with which they were treated, and from the total want of variety, in
consequence of defective arrangements on his part for ensuring the co-
operation of his friends, no conceivable act of authorship that Coleridge
could have perpetrated, no possible overt act of dulness and somnolent
160 darkness that he *could* have authorized, was so well fitted to sustain
the impression, with regard to him and his friends, that had preoccupied
these ladies' minds. *Habes confitentem reum!* [you have a confessing
defendant] I am sure they would exclaim; not perhaps confessing to
that form of delinquency which they had been taught to expect – trivial
165 or extravagant sentimentalism, *Germanity*† alternating with tumid
inanity;† not this, but something quite as bad or worse, viz. palpable
dulness – dulness that could be felt and handled – rayless obscurity as
to the thoughts – and communicated in language that, according to the
Bishop of Llandaff's complaint, was not always English. For, though
170 the particular words cited for blame were certainly known to the
vocabulary of metaphysics, and had even been employed by a writer of
Queen Anne's reign (Leibnitz),† who, if any, had the gift of translating
dark thoughts into plain ones – still it was intolerable, in point of good
sense, that one who had to win his way into the public ear should begin
175 by bringing before a popular and miscellaneous audience themes that
could require such startling and revolting words. *The Delphic Oracle*
was the kindest of the nicknames which the literary taste of Windermere
conferred upon the new journal. This was the laughing suggestion of a
clever young lady, a daughter of the Bishop of Llandaff, who stood in
180 a neutral position with regard to Coleridge. But others there were
amongst his supposed friends who felt even more keenly than this young
lady the shocking want of adaptation to his audience in the choice of
matter, and, even to an audience better qualified to meet such matter,
the want of adaptation in the mode of publication, – viz. periodically,
185 and by weekly recurrence; a mode of soliciting the public attention
which even authorizes the expectation of current topics – topics arising
each with its own week or day. One in particular I remember of these
disapproving friends: a Mr Blair, an accomplished scholar, and a
frequent visitor at Elleray, who started the playful scheme of a satirical
190 rejoinder to Coleridge's *Friend*, under the name of *The Enemy*, which
was to follow always in the wake of its leader, and to stimulate
Coleridge (at the same time that it amused the public) by attic banter,
or by downright opposition and showing fight in good earnest. It was
a plan that might have done good service to the world, and chiefly

Germanity characteristic German qualities   1716), German philosopher and
tumid inanity swollen emptiness   mathematician
Leibnitz Gottfried Wilhelm Leibnitz (1646–

195 through a seasonable irritation (never so much wanted as then) applied
to Coleridge's too lethargic state: in fact, throughout life, it is most
deeply to be regretted that Coleridge's powers and peculiar learning
were never forced out into a large display by intense and almost
persecuting opposition. However, this scheme, like thousands of other
200 day-dreams and bubbles that rose upon the breath of morning spirits
and buoyant youth, fell to the ground; and, in the meantime, no enemy
to *The Friend* appeared that was capable of matching *The Friend* when
left to itself and its own careless or vagrant[†] guidance. *The Friend*
ploughed heavily along for nine-and-twenty numbers; and our fair
205 recusants[†] and noncomformists in all that regarded the lake poetry or
authorship, the two Scottish ladies of Clappersgate, found no reasons
for changing their opinions; but continued, for the rest of my acquaintance with them, to practise the same courteous and indulgent silence,
whenever the names of Coleridge or Wordsworth happened to be
210 mentioned.

c. 1839   1840

---

vagrant wandering
recusants persons who refuse to submit to
  authority or regulation

166

Thomas Love Peacock
1785–1866

Peacock was a satirist, essayist and poet, particularly noted for his seven novels, the most famous of which is *Nightmare Abbey* (1818), in which he depicts cultural and political aspects of society. He later added a romantic element to his stories, as in *Crotchet Castle* (1831) and *Gryll Grange* (1860–1).

He was fortunate in inheriting independent means. In 1812 he met Shelley and became a close friend. In 1818 he wrote a mythological poem, *Rhododaphne*, in the mode of Keats's *Lamia*, and published a critical work, *Essay on Fashionable Literature*: he followed this piece of criticism two years later with *The Four Ages of Poetry*, which inspired Shelley's response in *A Defence of Poetry*. He started work for the East India Company in 1819, under J. S. Mill whom he succeeded to the responsible position of Examiner in 1836. His favourite daughter was Mary Ellen, who became the first wife of George Meredith and appears in his sonnet sequence, *Modern Love*.

From NIGHTMARE ABBEY,[†] Chapter 3
[The Temporary Supremacy of the Devil]

Marionetta listened a long time in silence, till her lover had exhausted his eloquence and paused for a reply. She then said, with a very arch look, 'I prithee deliver thyself like a man of this world.' The levity[†] of this quotation, and of the manner in which it was delivered, jarred
5 so discordantly on the high-wrought enthusiasm of the romantic inamorato,[†] that he sprang upon his feet, and beat his forehead with his clenched fists. The young lady was terrified; and, deeming it expedient to soothe him, took one of his hands in hers, placed the other

---

Nightmare Abbey the son of the house, Scythrop Glowry, a young writer resembling Shelley, cannot decide between the charms of his frivolous cousin, Marionetta, and the seductive Stella, daughter of the pessimistic Mr Toobad. Peacock mocks the mood of

gloomy despondency which had become a vogue in literature. Coleridge's German transcendentalism and Byron's self-dramatisation were particular targets
levity frivolity
inamorato lover

hand on his shoulder, looked up in his face with a winning seriousness,
10 and said, in the tenderest possible tone, 'What would you have,
Scythrop?'

Scythrop was in heaven again. 'What would I have? What but you,
Marionetta? You, for the companion of my studies, the partner of my
thoughts, the auxiliary of my great designs for the emancipation of
15 mankind.'

'I am afraid I should be but a poor auxiliary, Scythrop. What would
you have me do?'

'Do as Rosalia does with Carlos, divine Marionetta. Let us each open
a vein in the other's arm, mix our blood in a bowl, and drink it as a
20 sacrament of love. Then we shall see visions of transcendental[1] illumi-
nation, and soar on the wings of ideas into the space of pure intelligence.'

Marionetta could not reply; she had not so strong a stomach as
Rosalia, and turned sick at the proposition. She disengaged herself
suddenly from Scythrop, sprang through the door of the tower, and
25 fled with precipitation along the corridors. Scythrop pursued her, crying,
'Stop, stop, Marionetta – my life, my love!' and was gaining rapidly on
her flight, when, at an ill-omened corner, where two corridors ended in
an angle, at the head of a staircase, he came into sudden and violent
contact with Mr Toobad, and they both plunged together to the foot
30 of the stairs, like two billiard-balls into one pocket. This gave the young
lady time to escape, and enclose herself in her chamber; while Mr.
Toobad, rising slowly, and rubbing his knees and shoulders, said, 'You
see, my dear Scythrop, in this little incident, one of the innumerable
proofs of the temporary supremacy of the devil; for what but a
35 systematic design and concurrent contrivance of evil could have made
the angles of time and place coincide in our unfortunate persons at the
head of this accursed staircase?'

'Nothing else, certainly,' said Scythrop: 'you are perfectly in the right,
Mr Toobad. Evil, and mischief, and misery, and confusion, and vanity,
40 and vexation of spirit, and death, and disease, and assassination,
and war, and poverty, and pestilence, and famine, and avarice, and
selfishness, and rancour, and jealousy, and spleen,[†] and malevolence,
and the disappointments of philanthropy, and the faithlessness of
friendship, and the crosses of love – all prove the accuracy of your
45 views, and the truth of your system; and it is not impossible that the
infernal interruption of this fall down stairs may throw a colour of evil
on the whole of my future existence.'

'My dear boy,' said Mr Toobad, 'you have a fine eye for consequences.'

So saying, he embraced Scythrop, who retired, with a disconsolate
50 step, to dress for dinner; while Mr Toobad stalked across the hall,

---

transcendental surpassing   *spleen* ill temper

repeating, 'Woe to the inhabiters of the earth, and of the sea! for the devil is come among you, having great wrath.'

1817–18   1818

From THE MISFORTUNES OF ELPHIN

The War Song of Dinas Vawr†

The mountain sheep are sweeter,
But the valley sheep are fatter;
We therefore deemed it meeter
To carry off the latter.
5   We made an expedition;
We met a host and quelled it;
We forced a strong position,
And killed the men who held it.

On Dyfed's richest valley,
10   Where herds of kine† were browsing,
We made a mighty sally,
To furnish our carousing.
Fierce warriors rushed to meet us;
We met them, and o'erthrew them;
15   They struggled hard to beat us;
But we conquered them, and slew them.

As we drove our prize at leisure,
The king marched forth to catch us:
His rage surpassed all measure,
20   But his people could not match us.
He fled to his hall-pillars;
And, ere our force we led off,
Some sacked his house and cellars,
While others cut his head off.

25   We there, in strife bewildering,
Spilt blood enough to swim in:

The War Song of Dinas Vawr in its context, the song is a criticism of political opportunism, and is a mockery of the

Romantic fashion for escapist themes
kine cattle

We orphaned many children,
And widowed many women.
The eagles and the ravens
30   We glutted with our foemen;
The heroes and the cravens,
The spearmen and the bowmen.

We brought away from battle,
And much their land bemoaned them,
35   Two thousand head of cattle,
And the head of him who owned them:
Ednyfed, King of Dyfed,
His head was borne before us;
His wine and beasts supplied our feasts,
40   And his overthrow, our chorus.

1828–9   1829

George Gordon (Lord) Byron
1788–1824

A life of action and scandal, of alternative lionisation and ostracism, was Byron's lot. According to Shelley, everything Byron did was 'influenced by his personal defect', the club foot, with which he was born. Thus he sought to excel in manly actions and hold his own with the most physically active. While on his foreign tour of 1809–11, he swam the Hellespont.

Byron inherited his title and the Gothic Newstead Abbey in 1798. His upbringing had been mostly in Scotland, and he was initiated very young into worldly ways of sexual practice by his forward nurse. After his inheritance he went to Harrow, did well in sport, and had many a passionate friendship. From there, he proceeded to Cambridge in 1805 and indulged in various debauches in the university and in London.

His first volume of poetry, *Hours of Idleness*, appeared in 1807 and was generally well received, but attacked by the *Edinburgh Review*. Two years later he took his seat in the House of Lords, espoused a number of liberal causes, and during that year began *Childe Harold*. It was not until after his continental tour, when he visited Portugal, Spain, Malta and Greece, that he published the first two cantos of *Childe Harold's Pilgrimage* (1812): it made him a favourite with cultured, literary society in London. A year before he had renewed his intense friendship with his half-sister, Augusta, and in 1812 enjoyed a tempestuous affair with Lady Caroline Lamb. He succeeded in fathering two daughters, one by Annabella Milbanke whom he married in 1815, another by his mistress Clare Claremont, Shelley's sister-in-law, in 1817, and almost certainly a third, by Augusta, in 1814.

In 1813 Byron had published *The Bride of Abydos*, *The Corsair* and *The Giaour*. By 1816 he was heavily in debt, and the general public was scandalised by the news that he had committed incest. Aristocratic and literary society shunned and ostracised him. He left England and made to visit the Shelleys in Genoa. That year produced *The Prisoner of Chillon* and *Manfred*, and *Childe Harold* was completed. In 1817 he visited Venice and Rome: *Beppo* was composed, and Byron found himself financially solvent when Newstead Abbey was sold. In 1818 he began *Don Juan*, a rambling, personal, satirical, reflective poem, and when the first two cantos were published in 1819, *Blackwood's* condemned them: Goethe, on the other hand, praised them. In that year he met Teresa, Countess Guiccioli, who two years later left her husband for him. They lived in Ravenna for a time and he became absorbed in the composition of plays, among them *Sardanapalus*, most of which the modern reader finds unreadable.

In 1821 he published *The Vision of Judgement* and while staying in Genoa was preoccupied with the composition of *Don Juan*. He then became convinced that action was more important than poetry. His 1809–11 tour had convinced him that the Greeks should be freed from Turkish domination and he took himself to Greece, committed to its cause for independence. He landed at Missolonghi in 1824, formed the Byron Brigade, and supported Greek insurgents: he became a Greek national hero, but sadly died by a combination of fever and being bled to death by his doctor.

He was a tireless writer of journals and letters, in one of which, 1822, he wryly observed that his sales were better in Germany than England. Contemporaries and later Victorians often attacked his poetry on moral grounds, but it constitutes one of the most important expressions of Romanticism in English letters.

THE DESTRUCTION OF SENNACHERIB†

Hebrew Melodies, 1815

I

The Assyrian came down like the wolf on the fold,
And his cohorts were gleaming in purple and gold;
And the sheen of their spears was like stars on the sea,
When the blue wave rolls nightly on deep Galilee.

II

5   Like the leaves of the forest when Summer is green,
That host with their banners at sunset were seen:
Like the leaves of the forest when Autumn hath blown,
That host on the morrow lay wither'd and strown.

The Destruction of Sennacherib II Kings 18.19

III

For the Angel of Death spread his wings on the blast,
10   And breathed in the face of the foe as he pass'd;
And the eyes of the sleepers wax'd deadly and chill,
And their hearts but once heaved, and for ever grew still!

IV

And there lay the steed with his nostril all wide,
But through it there roll'd not the breath of his pride;
15   And the foam of his gasping lay white on the turf,
And cold as the spray of the rock-beating surf.

V

And there lay the rider distorted and pale,
With the dew on his brow, and the rust on his mail:
And the tents were all silent, the banners alone,
20   The lances unlifted, the trumpet unblown.

VI

And the widows of Ashur† are loud in their wail,
And the idols are broke in the temple of Baal;
And the might of the Gentile, unsmote by the sword,
Hath melted like snow in the glance of the Lord!

1815   1815

SO WE'LL GO NO MORE A-ROVING

I

So we'll go no more a-roving
   So late into the night,
Though the heart be still as loving,
   And the moon be still as bright.

II

5   For the sword outwears its sheath,
   And the soul wears out the breast,
And the heart must pause to breathe,
   And love itself have rest.

Ashur   Assyria

III

Though the night was made for loving,
10   And the day returns too soon,
Yet we'll go no more a roving
    By the light of the moon.

1817   1830

THE PRISONER OF CHILLON†

1816

SONNET ON CHILLON

Eternal Spirit of the chainless Mind!
    Brightest in dungeons, Liberty! thou art,
    For there thy habitation is the heart –
The heart which love of thee alone can bind;
5   And when thy sons to fetters are consign'd –
    To fetters, and the damp vault's dayless gloom,
    Their country conquers with their martyrdom,
And Freedom's fame finds wings on every wind.
Chillon! thy prison is a holy place,
10   And thy sad floor an altar – for 't was trod,
Until his very steps have left a trace
    Worn, as if thy cold pavement were a sod,
By Bonnivard!† May none those marks efface!
    For they appeal from tyranny to God.

I

My hair is grey, but not with years,
    Nor grew it white
    In a single night,
As men's have grown from sudden fears:
5   My limbs are bow'd, though not with toil,
    But rusted with a vile repose,
For they have been a dungeon's spoil,
    And mine has been the fate of those
To whom the goodly earth and air
10   Are bann'd and barr'd – forbidden fare:
But this was for my father's faith

The Prisoner of Chillon   Chillon is at the east end of Lake Geneva, south of Montreux   *Bonnivard*   François de Bonnivard, citizen of Geneva, patriot and reformer. He was imprisoned in Chillon from 1530 to 1536 for his resistance to the Duke of Savoy

I suffer'd chains and courted death;
That father perish'd at the stake
For tenets* he would not forsake;   principles
15   And for the same his lineal race
In darkness found a dwelling-place;
We were seven† – who now are one,
    Six in youth, and one in age,
Finish'd as they had begun,
20   Proud of Persecution's rage;
One in fire, and two in field,
Their belief with blood have seal'd,
Dying as their father died,
For the God their foes denied;
25   Three were in a dungeon cast,
Of whom this wreck is left the last.

II

There are seven pillars of Gothic mould,
In Chillon's dungeons deep and old,
There are seven columns, massy and grey,
30   Dim with a dull imprison'd ray,
A sunbeam which hath lost its way,
And through the crevice and the cleft
Of the thick wall is fallen and left;
Creeping o'er the floor so damp,
35   Like a marsh's meteor lamp:
And in each pillar there is a ring,
    And in each ring there is a chain;
That iron is a cankering thing,
    For in these limbs its teeth remain,
40   With marks that will not wear away,
Till I have done with this new day,
Which now is painful to these eyes,
Which have not seen the sun so rise
For years – I cannot count them o'er,
45   I lost their long and heavy score,
When my last brother droop'd and died,
And I lay living by his side.

III

They chain'd us each to a column stone,
And we were three – yet, each alone;

---

seven   Bonnivard and his brothers

50   We could not move a single pace,
      We could not see each other's face,
      But with that pale and livid light
      That made us strangers in our sight:
      And thus together – yet apart,
55   Fetter'd in hand, but join'd in heart,
      'T was still solace, in the dearth
      Of the pure elements of earth,
      To hearken to each other's speech.
      And each turn comforter to each
60   With some new hope, or legend old,
      Or song heroically bold;
      But even these at length grew cold.
      Our voices took a dreary tone,
      An echo of the dungeon stone,
65   A grating sound, not full and free,
        As they of yore were wont to be:
        It might be fancy, but to me
      They never sounded like our own.

                      IV

      I was the eldest of the three,
70   And to uphold and cheer the rest
        I ought to do, and did, my best –
      And each did well in his degree.
        The youngest, whom my father loved,
      Because our mother's brow was given
75   To him, with eyes as blue as heaven –
        For him my soul was sorely moved:
      And truly might it be distress'd
      To see such bird in such a nest;
      For he was beautiful as day –
80   (When day was beautiful to me
        As to young eagles, being free) –
        A polar day, which will not see
      A sunset till its summer's gone,
        Its sleepless summer of long light,
85   The snow-clad offspring of the sun:
        And thus he was as pure and bright,
      And in his natural spirit gay,
      With tears for nought but others' ills,
      And then they flow'd like mountain rills,
90   Unless he could assuage the woe
      Which he abhorr'd to view below.

V

The other was as pure of mind,
But form'd to combat with his kind;
Strong in his frame, and of a mood
95   Which 'gainst the world in war had stood,
And perish'd in the foremost rank
    With joy: – but not in chains to pine:
His spirit wither'd with their clank,
    I saw it silently decline –
100   And so perchance in sooth* did mine: truth
But yet I forced it on to cheer
Those relics of a home so dear.
He was a hunter of the hills,
    Had follow'd there the deer and wolf;
105   To him his dungeon was a gulf,
And fetter'd feet the worst of ills.

VI

Lake Leman† lies by Chillon's walls:
A thousand feet in depth below
Its massy waters meet and flow;
110   Thus much the fathom-line was sent
From Chillon's snow-white battlement,
    Which round about the wave inthrals:
A double dungeon wall and wave
Have made – and like a living grave
115   Below the surface of the lake
The dark vault lies wherein we lay,
We heard it ripple night and day;
    Sounding o'er our heads it knock'd;
And I have felt the winter's spray
120   Wash through the bars when winds were high
And wanton in the happy sky;
    And then the very rock hath rock'd,
    And I have felt it shake, unshock'd,
Because I could have smiled to see
125   The death that would have set me free.

VII

I said my nearer brother pined,
I said his mighty heart declined,
He loathed and put away his food;

Leman   Lac Leman is the Lake of Geneva

It was not that 't was coarse and rude,
130   For we were used to hunter's fare,
And for the like had little care:
The milk drawn from the mountain goat
Was changed for water from the moat,
Our bread was such as captives' tears
135   Have moisten'd many a thousand years,
Since man first pent† his fellow men
Like brutes within an iron den;
But what were these to us or him?
These wasted not his heart or limb,
140   My brother's soul was of that mould
Which in a palace had grown cold,
Had his free breathing been denied
The range of the steep mountain's side;
But why delay the truth? – he died.
145   I saw, and could not hold his head,
Nor reach his dying hand – nor dead, –
Though hard I strove, but strove in vain,
To rend and gnash my bonds in twain.
He died, and they unlock'd his chain,
150   And scoop'd for him a shallow grave
Even from the cold earth of our cave.
I begg'd them as a boon to lay
His corse in dust whereon the day
Might shine – it was a foolish thought,
155   But then within my brain it wrought,
That even in death his freeborn breast
In such a dungeon could not rest.
I might have spared my idle prayer –
They coldly laugh'd, and laid him there:
160   The flat and turfless earth above
The being we so much did love;
His empty chain above it leant,
Such murder's fitting monument!

VIII

But he, the favourite and the flower,
165   Most cherish'd since his natal hour,
His mother's image in fair face,
The infant love of all his race,
His martyr'd father's dearest thought,

---

pent   shut in

My latest care, for whom I sought
170   To hoard my life, that his might be
Less wretched now, and one day free;
He, too, who yet had held untired
A spirit natural or inspired –
He, too, was struck, and day by day
175   Was wither'd on the stalk away.
Oh, God! It is a fearful thing
To see the human soul take wing
In any shape, in any mood:
I've seen it rushing forth in blood,
180   I've seen it on the breaking ocean
Strive with a swoln convulsive motion,
I've seen the sick and ghastly bed
Of Sin delirious with its dread;
But these were horrors – this was woe
185   Unmix'd with such – but sure and slow:
He faded, and so calm and meek,
So softly worn, so sweetly weak,
So tearless, yet so tender, kind,
And grieved for those he left behind;
190   With all the while a cheek whose bloom
Was a mockery of the tomb,
Whose tints as gently sunk away
As a departing rainbow's ray;
An eye of most transparent light,
195   That almost made the dungeon bright,
And not a word of murmur, not
A groan o'er his untimely lot, –
A little talk of better days,
A little hope my own to raise,
200   For I was sunk in silence – lost
In this last loss, of all the most;
And then the sighs he would suppress
Of fainting nature's feebleness,
More slowly drawn, grew less and less:
205   I listen'd, but I could not hear;
I call'd, for I was wild with fear;
I knew 't was hopeless, but my dread
Would not be thus admonished;[†]
I call'd, and thought I heard a sound –
210   I burst my chain with one strong bound,

---

admonished   exhorted, advised

And rush'd to him: — I found him not,
I only stirr'd in this black spot,
I only lived, *I* only drew
The accursed breath of dungeon-dew;
215 The last, the sole, the dearest link
Between me and the eternal brink,
Which bound me to my failing race,
Was broken in this fatal place.
One on the earth, and one beneath —
220 My brothers — both had ceased to breathe:
I took that hand which lay so still,
Alas! my own was full as chill;
I had not strength to stir, or strive,
But felt that I was still alive —
225 A frantic feeling, when we know
That what we love shall ne'er be so.
      I know not why
      I could not die,
I had no earthly hope but faith,
230 And that forbade a selfish death.

IX

What next befell me then and there
    I know not well — I never knew —
First came the loss of light, and air,
    And then of darkness too:
235 I had no thought, no feeling — none —
Among the stones I stood a stone,
And was, scarce conscious what I wist,*   knew
As shrubless crags within the mist;
For all was blank, and bleak, and grey;
240 It was not night, it was not day;
It was not even the dungeon-light,
So hateful to my heavy sight,
But vacancy absorbing space,
And fixedness without a place;
245 There were no stars, no earth, no time,
No check, no change, no good, no crime,
But silence, and a stirless breath
Which neither was of life nor death;
A sea of stagnant idleness,
250 Blind, boundless, mute, and motionless!

X

A light broke in upon my brain, –
  It was the carol of a bird;
It ceased, and then it came again,
  The sweetest song ear ever heard,
255 And mine was thankful till my eyes
  Ran over with the glad surprise,
  And they that moment could not see
  I was the mate of misery;
  But then by dull degrees came back
260 My senses to their wonted† track;
  I saw the dungeon walls and floor
  Close slowly round me as before,
  I saw the glimmer of the sun
  Creeping as it before had done,
265 But through the crevice where it came
  That bird was perch'd, as fond and tame,
    And tamer than upon the tree;
  A lovely bird, with azure wings,
  And song that said a thousand things,
270   And seem'd to say them all for me!
  I never saw its like before,
  I ne'er shall see its likeness more:
  It seem'd like me to want a mate,
  But was not half so desolate,
275 And it was come to love me when
  None lived to love me so again,
  And cheering from my dungeon's brink,
  Had brought me back to feel and think.
  I know not if it late were free,
280   Or broke its cage to perch on mine,
  But knowing well captivity,
    Sweet bird! I could not wish for thine!
  Or if it were, in winged guise,
  A visitant from Paradise;
285 For – Heaven forgive that thought! the while
  Which made me both to weep and smile –
  I sometimes deem'd that it might be
  My brother's soul come down to me;
  But then at last away it flew,
290 And then 't was mortal well I knew,
  For he would never thus have flown,

wonted usual, accustomed

And left me twice so doubly lone,
Lone as the corse within its shroud,
Lone as a solitary cloud, –
295   A single cloud on a sunny day,
While all the rest of heaven is clear,
A frown upon the atmosphere,
That hath no business to appear
    When skies are blue, and earth is gay.

XI

300   A kind of change came in my fate,
My keepers grew compassionate;
I know not what had made them so,
They were inured to sights of woe,
But so it was: – my broken chain
305   With links unfasten'd did remain,
And it was liberty to stride
Along my cell from side to side,
And up and down, and then athwart,*   across
And tread it over every part;
310   And round the pillars one by one,
Returning where my walk begun,
Avoiding only, as I trod,
My brothers' graves without a sod;
For if I thought with heedless tread
315   My step profaned their lowly bed,
My breath came gaspingly and thick,
And my crush'd heart fell blind and sick.

XII

I made a footing in the wall,
    It was not therefrom to escape,
320   For I had buried one and all
    Who loved me in a human shape;
And the whole earth would henceforth be
A wider prison unto me:
No child, no sire, no kin had I,
325   No partner in my misery;
I thought of this, and I was glad,
For thought of them had made me mad;
But I was curious to ascend
To my barr'd windows, and to bend
330   Once more, upon the mountains high,
The quiet of a loving eye.

XIII

I saw them, and they were the same,
They were not changed like me in frame;
I saw their thousand years of snow
335 On high – their wide long lake below,
And the blue Rhone in fullest flow;
I heard the torrents leap and gush
O'er channell'd rock and broken bush;
I saw the white-wall'd distant town,
340 And whiter sails go skimming down;
And then there was a little isle,†
Which in my very face did smile,
        The only one in view;
A small green isle, it seem'd no more,
345 Scarce broader than my dungeon floor,
But in it there were three tall trees,
And o'er it blew the mountain breeze,
And by it there were waters flowing,
And on it there were young flowers growing,
350   Of gentle breath and hue.
The fish swam by the castle wall,
And they seem'd joyous each and all;
The eagle rode the rising blast,
Methought he never flew so fast
355 As then to me he seem'd to fly;
And then new tears came in my eye,
And I felt troubled – and would fain
I had not left my recent chain;
And when I did descend again,
360 The darkness of my dim abode
Fell on me as a heavy load;
It was as is a new-dug grave,
Closing o'er one we sought to save, –
And yet my glance, too much opprest,
365 Had almost need of such a rest.

XIV

It might be months, or years, or days,
    I kept no count, I took no note,
I had no hope my eyes to raise,
    And clear them of their dreary mote;†

---

little isle Byron noted: 'Between the entrances
of the Rhone and the Villeneuve, not far

from Chillon, is a very small island'
mote speck of dust

370 At last men came to set me free;
       I ask'd not why, and reck'd not where;
    It was at length the same to me,
    Fetter'd or fetterless to be,
       I learn'd to love despair.
375 And thus when they appear'd at last,
    And all my bonds aside were cast,
    These heavy walls to me had grown
    A hermitage – and all my own!
    And half I felt as they were come
380 To tear me from a second home:
    With spiders I had friendship made,
    And watch'd them in their sullen trade,
    Had seen the mice by moonlight play,
    And why should I feel less than they?
385 We were all inmates of one place,
    And I, the monarch of each race,
    Had power to kill – yet, strange to tell!
    In quiet we had learn'd to dwell;
    My very chains and I grew friends,
390 So much a long communion tends
    To make us what we are: – even I
    Regain'd my freedom with a sigh.

1816   1816

From DON JUAN†

Canto I. Stanzas 1, 4–10

I want a hero: an uncommon want,
   When every year and month sends forth a new one,
Till, after cloying* the gazettes with cant;*   satiating   hypocrisy
   The age discovers he is not the true one:
5 Of such as these I should not care to vaunt,
   I 'll therefore take our ancient friend Don Juan –
We all have seen him, in the pantomime,
Sent to the devil somewhat ere his time. . . .

Don Juan   the poem is an unfinished epic satire
written in *ottava rima*. Don Juan,
pronounced as if English, i.e. Don Jūan, is a
young, charming romantic hero who falls in
love with most women he meets. His presence,
and exploits, in the poem constitute the main
thread in a long satirical, social commentary

25   Nelson was once Britannia's god of war,
        And still should be so, but the tide is turn'd;
      There's no more to be said of Trafalgar,
        'Tis with our hero quietly inurn'd;
      Because the army's grown more popular,
30   At which the naval people are concern'd;
      Besides, the prince is all for the land-service,
      Forgetting Duncan, Nelson, Howe, and Jervis.

      Brave men were living before Agamemnon
        And since, exceeding valorous and sage,
35   A good deal like him too, though quite the same none;
        But then they shone not on the poet's page,
      And so have been forgotten: – I condemn none,
        But can't find any in the present age
      Fit for my poem (that is, for my new one);
40   So, as I said, I'll take my friend Don Juan.

      Most epic poets plungs 'in medias res'†
        (Horace makes this the heroic turnpike† road),
      And then your hero tells, whene'er you please,
        What went before – by way of episode,
45   While seated after dinner at his ease,
        Beside his mistress in some soft abode,
      Palace, or garden, paradise, or cavern,
      Which serves the happy couple for a tavern.

      That is the usual method, but not mine –
50   My way is to begin with the beginning;
      The regularity of my design
        Forbids all wandering as the worst of sinning,
      And therefore I shall open with a line
        (Although it cost me half an hour in spinning)
55   Narrating somewhat of Don Juan's father,
      And also of his mother, if you'd rather.

      In Seville was he born, a pleasant city,
        Famous for oranges and women – he
      Who has not seen it will be much to pity,

'in medias res'   into the middle of things   *turnpike*   gated road where a toll must be paid
                                                                    before vehicles pass

60 So says the proverb – and I quite agree;
Of all the Spanish towns is none more pretty,
Cadiz, perhaps – but that you soon may see: –
Don Juan's parents lived beside the river,
A noble stream, and call'd the Guadalquivir.

65 His father's name was José – *Don*, of course,
A true Hidalgo,† free from every stain
Of Moor or Hebrew blood, he traced his source
Through the most Gothic gentlemen of Spain;
A better cavalier ne'er mounted horse,
70 Or, being mounted, e'er got down again,
Than José, who begot our hero, who
Begot – but that's to come – Well, to renew:

His mother was a learned lady, famed
For every branch of every science known –
75 In every Christian language ever named,
With virtues equall'd by her wit alone:
She made the cleverest people quite ashamed,
And even the good with inward envy groan,
Finding themselves so very much exceeded
80 In their own way by all the things that she did.

I. Stanzas 200–5

My poem's epic, and is meant to be
Divided in twelve books; each book containing,
1595 With love, and war, a heavy gale at sea,
A list of ships, and captains, and kings reigning,
New characters; the episodes are three:
A panoramic view of hell's in training,
After the style of Virgil and of Homer,
1600 So that my name of Epic's no misnomer.

All these things will be specified in time,
With strict regard to Aristotle's rules,†
The *Vade Mecum*† of the true sublime,
Which makes so many poets, and some fools:
1605 Prose poets like blank-verse, I'm fond of rhyme,

Hidalgo Spanish gentleman
Aristotle's rules based on a renaissance
  misconception of passages in Aristotle's
  Poetics. Aristotle stresses the importance of
  the Unity of Action in drama: from incidental

references in *Poetics* it was deduced that the
Unity of Time and the Unity of Place were
equally important
Vade Mecum lit. 'go with me': a handbook
or guide

Good workmen never quarrel with their tools;
I've got new mythological machinery,
And very handsome supernatural scenery.

There's only one slight difference between
1610   Me and my epic brethren gone before,
And here the advantage is my own, I ween*   expect
    (Not that I have not several merits more,
But this will more peculiarly be seen);
    They so embellish, that 't is quite a bore
1615 Their labyrinth of fables to thread through,
Whereas this story's actually true.

If any person doubt it, I appeal
    To history, tradition, and to facts,
To newspapers, whose truth all know and feel,
1620   To plays in five, and operas in three acts;
All these confirm my statement a good deal,
    But that which more completely faith exacts
Is, that myself, and several now in Seville,
Saw Juan's last elopement with the devil.

1625 If ever I should condescend to prose,
    I'll write poetical commandments, which
Shall supersede beyond all doubt all those
    That went before: in these I shall enrich
My text with many things that no one knows,
1630   And carry precept† to the highest pitch:
I'll call the work 'Longinus† o'er a Bottle,
Or, Every Poet his *own* Aristotle.'

Thou shalt believe in Milton, Dryden, Pope;
    Thou shalt not set up Wordsworth, Coleridge, Southey;
1635 Because the first is crazed beyond all hope,
    The second drunk, the third so quaint and mouthy:
With Crabbe† it may be difficult to cope,
    And Campbell's† Hippocrene is somewhat drouthy:*   dry
Thou shalt not steal from Samuel Rogers,† nor
1640 Commit – flirtation with the muse of Moore.†

---

precept moral instruction
Longinus the name given by scribal error to
  the author of a Greek critical treatise, *On*

the Sublime, written in first century AD
Crabbe, Campbell, Rogers, Moore all
  contemporary minor poets

The Isles of Greece

Don Juan, III. Stanzas 1–10

1

The isles of Greece, the isles of Greece!
690   Where burning Sappho loved and sung,
Where grew the arts of war and peace,
    Where Delos rose, and Phœbus† sprung!
Eternal summer gilds them yet,
But all, except their sun, is set.

2

695   The Scian† and the Teian† muse,
    The hero's harp, the lover's lute,
Have found the fame your shores refuse:
    Their place of birth alone is mute
To sounds which echo further west
700   Than your sires' 'Islands of the Blest.'

3

The mountains look on Marathon —†
    And Marathon looks on the sea;
And musing there an hour alone,
    I dream'd that Greece might still be free;
705   For standing on the Persians' grave,
I could not deem myself a slave.

4

A king† sate on the rocky brow
    Which looks o'er sea-born Salamis;
And ships, by thousands, lay below,
710   And men in nations; – all were his!
He counted them at break of day –
And when the sun set where were they?

5

And where are they? and where art thou,
    My country? On thy voiceless shore

Delos . . . Phoebus Delos is the smallest isle of the Cyclades. It is supposed to have been called out of the deep by Poseidon, god of the sea. It was the legendary birthplace of Phoebus Apollo, god of the sun
Scian Chios (Scios) was a reputed birthplace of Homer

Teian Teos in Ionia was the birthplace of Anacreon
Marathon on the east coast of Attica where the Greeks checked the invasion of the Persians, 490 BC
king Xerxes watched the battle of Salamis, 480 BC from Mount Aegaleos, on the mainland north of Athens

715   The heroic lay is tuneless now –
       The heroic bosom beats no more!
       And must thy lyre, so long divine,
       Degenerate into hands like mine?

                                        6
       'Tis something, in the dearth of fame,
720   Though link'd among a fetter'd race,
       To feel at least a patriot's shame,
          Even as I sing, suffuse my face;
       For what is left the poet here?
       For Greeks a blush – for Greece a tear.

                                        7
725   Must *we* weep o'er days more blest?
          Must *we* but blush? – Our fathers bled.
       Earth! render back from out thy breast
          A remnant of our Spartan dead!
       Of the three hundred grant but three,
730   To make a new Thermopylæ!†

                                        8
       What, silent still? and silent all?
          Ah! no; – the voices of the dead
       Sound like a distant torrent's fall,
          And answer, 'Let one living head,
735   But one arise, – we come, we come!'
       'Tis but the living who are dumb.

                                        9
       In vain – in vain: strike other chords;
          Fill high the cup with Samian wine!
       Leave battles to the Turkish hordes,
740   And shed the blood of Scio's vine!
       Hark! rising to the ignoble call –
       How answers each bold Bacchanal!†

                                       10
       You have the Pyrrhic† dance as yet;
          Where is the Pyrrhic phalanx gone?

Thermopylae   the pass of Thermopylae was
where the Spartan Leonidas and his 300
heroes resisted to the death the attack of the
Persians, 480 BC

Bacchanal   a revel, or dance, in honour of
Bacchus, god of wine
Pyrrhic   famous war dance of the Greeks
invented by Pyrrhicos, a Dorian

745   Of two such lessons, why forget
    The nobler and the manlier one?
    You have the letters Cadmus[†] gave –
    Think ye he meant them for a slave?

11

    Fill high the bowl with Samian wine!
750   We will not think of themes like these!
    It made Anacreon's[†] song divine:
    He served – but served Polycrates –
    A tyrant; but our masters then
    Were still, at least, our countrymen.

12

755   The tyrant of the Chersonese[†]
    Was freedom's best and bravest friend;
    That tyrant was Miltiades![†]
    Oh! that the present hour would lend
    Another despot of the kind!
760   Such chains as his were sure to bind.

13

    Fill high the bowl with Samian wine!
    On Suli's rock, and Parga's[†] shore,
    Exists the remnant of a line
    Such as the Doric[†] mothers bore;
765   And there, perhaps, some seed is sown,
    The Heracleidan[†] blood might own.

14

    Trust not for freedom to the Franks –[†]
    They have a king who buys and sells;
    In native swords, and native ranks,
770   The only hope of courage dwells:
    But Turkish force, and Latin fraud,
    Would break your shield, however broad.

Cadmus   King of Phoenicia and founder of
  Thebes, introduced the sixteen simple Greek
  letters from Phoenicia
Anacreon   Greek lyric poet (born *c.* 570 BC)
  who wrote chiefly in praise of love and wine
the Chersonese   now Gallipoli
Miltiades   the victor of Marathon

Suli's . . . Parga's   a district and a town in west
  Epirus
Doric   one of the four main divisions of ancient
  Greeks
Heracleidon   of Heracles from whom the
  Dorian aristocracy claimed its descent
Franks   name given in eastern Mediterranean
  to men of western race

15

Fill high the bowl with Samian wine!
Our virgins dance beneath the shade –
775   I see their glorious black eyes shine;
But gazing on each glowing maid,
My own the burning tear-drop laves,
To think such breasts must suckle slaves.

16

Place me on Sunium's† marbled steep,
780   Where nothing, save the waves and I,
May hear our mutual murmurs sweep;
There, swan-like, let me sing and die:
A land of slaves shall ne'er be mine –
Dash down yon cup of Samian wine!

Canto XIII. Stanzas 101–11

The gentlemen got up betimes to shoot,
Or hunt: the young, because they liked the sport –
The first thing boys like after play and fruit;
The middle-aged, to make the day more short;
805   For *ennui*† is a growth of English root,
Though nameless in our language: – we retort
The fact for words, and let the French translate
That awful yawn which sleep cannot abate.

The elderly walk'd through the library,
810   And tumbled books, or criticised the pictures,
Or saunter'd through the gardens piteously,
And made upon the hot-house several strictures,
Or rode a nag which trotted not too high,
Or on the morning papers read their lectures,
815   Or on the watch their longing eyes would fix,
Longing at sixty for the hour of six.

But none were 'gêné':† the great hour of union
Was rung by dinner's knell; till then all were
Masters of their own time – or in communion,
820   Or solitary, as they chose to bear
The hours, which how to pass is but to few known.

Sunium   Athena's temple was at Sunium, the
promontory at the extreme south of Attica:
its modern name is Cape Colonna, derived
from its ruined columns. Byron is reputed to
have inscribed his own name there
ennui   boredom, mental and spiritual
weariness
gêné   ill at ease

Each rose up at his own, and had to spare
What time he chose for dress, and broke his fast
When, where, and how he chose for that repast.

825 The ladies – some rouged, some a little pale –
Met the morn as they might. If fine, they rode,
Or walk'd; if foul, they read, or told a tale,
Sung, or rehearsed the last dance from abroad;
Discuss'd the fashion which might next prevail,
830 And settled bonnets by the newest code,
Or cramm'd twelve sheets into one little letter,
To make each correspondent a new debtor.

For some had absent lovers, all had friends.
The earth has nothing like a she epistle,
835 And hardly heaven – because it never ends.
I love the mystery of a female missal,
Which, like a creed, ne'er says all it intends,
But full of cunning as Ulysses' whistle,
When he allured poor Dolon:† – you had better
840 Take care what you reply to such a letter.

Then there were billiards; cards, too, but *no* dice; –
Save in the clubs no man of honour plays; –
Boats when 't was water, skating when 't was ice,
And the hard frost destroy'd the scenting days:
845 And angling, too, that solitary vice,
Whatever Izaak Walton† sings or says:
The quaint, old, cruel coxcomb,† in his gullet
Should have a hook, and a small trout to pull it.

With evening came the banquet and the wine;
850 The conversazione,† the duet,
Attuned by voices more or less divine
(My heart or head aches with the memory yet).
The four Miss Rawbolds in a glee† would shine;
But the two youngest loved more to be set
855 Down to the harp – because to music's charms
They added graceful necks, white hands and arms.

Dolon   *Iliad*, X, 341ff
Izaak Walton (1593–1683), author of *The*
  Compleat Angler
coxcomb   conceited, showy person

conversazione   an evening social gathering
  given over to conversation about art,
  literature, etc.
glee   an arranged song of three or more parts

Sometimes a dance (though rarely on field days,
   For then the gentlemen were rather tired)
Display'd some sylph-like figures in its maze;
860   Then there was small-talk ready when required;
Flirtation – but decorous; the mere praise
   Of charms that should or should not be admired.
The hunters fought their fox-hunt o'er again,
And then retreated soberly – at ten.

865   The politicians, in a nook apart,
   Discuss'd the world, and settled all the spheres;
The wits watch'd every loophole for their art,
   To introduce a bon-mot[†] head and ears;
Small is the rest of those who would be smart,
870   A moment's good thing may have cost them years
Before they find an hour to introduce it;
And then, even *then*, some bore may make them lose it.

But all was gentle and aristocratic
   In this our party; polish'd, smooth, and cold,
875   As Phidian[†] forms cut out of marble Attic.
   There now are no Squire Westerns[†] as of old;
And our Sophias are not so emphatic,
   But fair as then, or fairer to behold.
We have no accomplish'd blackguards, like Tom Jones,
880   But gentlemen in stays, as stiff as stones.

They separated at an early hour;
   That is, ere midnight – which is London's noon;
But in the country ladies seek their bower
   A little earlier than the waning moon.
885   Peace to the slumbers of each folded flower –
   May the rose call back its true colour soon!
Good hours of fair cheeks are the fairest tinters,
And lower the price of rouge – at least some winters.

---

bon mot   witty saying
Phidian   like the work of the most famous
   ancient Greek sculptor, Phidias

Squire Westerns, Sophias, Tom
   Jones   characters in Henry Fielding's novel
   Tom Jones

From LETTERS

890

TO THOMAS MOORE

July 10, 1817

Last week I had a row on the road (I came up to Venice from my
casino,[†] a few miles on the Paduan road, this blessed day, to bathe)
with a fellow in a carriage, who was impudent to my horse. I gave him
a swinging box on the ear, which sent him to the police, who dismissed
5 his complaint. Witnesses had seen the transaction. He first shouted, in
an unseemly way, to frighten my paltrey. I wheeled round, rode up to
the window, and asked him what he meant. He grinned, and said some
foolery, which produced him an immediate slap in the face, to his utter
discomfiture. Much blasphemy ensued, and some menace, which I
10 stopped by dismounting and opening the carriage door, and intimating
an intention of mending the road with his immediate remains, if he did
not hold his tongue. He held it.

TO JOHN MURRAY

Ravenna, February 21, 1821

Dear Sir, – In the 44th page, vol. 1st, of Turner's travels (which you
lately sent me), it is stated that 'Lord Byron, when he expressed such
confidence of its practicability, seems to have forgotten that Leander[†]
swam both ways, with and *against* the tide, whereas *he* (L[d]. B.) only
5 performed the easiest part of the task by swimming *with* it from Europe
to Asia.' I certainly could not have forgotten what is known to every
schoolboy, that Leander crossed in the night and returned towards the
morning. My object was to ascertain that the Hellespont could be
crossed *at all* by swimming, and in this Mr Ekenhead and myself both
10 succeeded, the one in an hour and ten minutes, and the other in one
hour and five minutes. The *tide* was *not* in our favour: on the contrary,
the great difficulty was to bear up against the current, which, so far
from helping us to the Asiatic side, set us down right towards the
Archipelago. Neither Mr Ekenhead, myself, nor, I will venture to add,
15 any person on board the frigate, from Captain (now Admiral) Bathurst
downwards, had any notion of a difference of the current on the Asiatic
side, of which Mr Turner speaks. I never heard of it till this moment,
or I would have taken the other course. Lieutenant Ekenhead's sole
motive, and mine also, for setting out from the European side was, that
20 the little Cape above Sestos was a more prominent starting place, and
the frigate, which lay below, close under the Asiatic castle, formed a

---

casino small house
Leander in Greek mythology, Leander swam

across the Hellespont (now Dardanelles)
every night to visit Hero, a priestess of Venus

better point of view for us to swim towards, and in fact we landed immediately below it.

Mr Turner says, 'Whatever is thrown into the stream on this part of
25 the European bank *must* arrive at the Asiatic shore.' This is so far from being the case, that it *must* arrive in the Archipelago, if left to the current, although a strong wind in the Asiatic direction might have such an effect occasionally.

Mr Turner attempted the passage from the Asiatic side, and failed.
30 'After five and twenty minutes, in which he did not advance a hundred yards, he gave it up from complete exhaustion.' This is very possible, and might have occurred to him just as readily on the European side. He should have set out a couple of miles higher, and could then have come out below the European castle. I particularly stated, and Mr
35 Hobhouse has done so also, that we were obliged to make the real passage of one mile extend to between *three* and *four*, owing to the force of the stream. I can assure Mr Turner that his success would have given me great pleasure, as it would have added one more instance to the proofs of the practicability. It is not quite fair in him to infer, that
40 because *he* failed, Leander could not succeed. There are still four instances on record: a Neapolitan, a young Jew, Mr Ekenhead, and myself; the two last done in the presence of hundreds of *English* witnesses.

With regard to the difference of the *current*, I perceived none: it is
45 favourable to the swimmer on neither side, but may be stemmed by plunging into the sea a considerable way above the opposite point of the coast which the swimmer wishes to make, but still bearing up against it: it is strong, but if you *calculate* well, you may reach land. My own experience and that of others bids me pronounce the passage
50 of Leander perfectly practicable; any young man in good health and [of] tolerable skill in swimming might succeed in it from *either* side. I was three hours in swimming across the Tagus, which is much more hazardous, being two hours longer than the passage of the Hellespont. Of what may be done in swimming, I will mention one more instance.
55 In 1818 the Chevalier Mengaldo (a Gentleman of Bassano), a good swimmer, wished to swim with my friend Mr Alexander Scott and myself. As he seemed particularly anxious on the subject, we indulged him. We all three started from the Island of the Lido and swam to Venice. At the entrance of the Grand Canal Scott and I were a good
60 way ahead, and we saw no more of our foreign friend, which however was of no consequence, as there was a Gondola to hold his clothes and pick him up. Scott swum in till past the Rialto, where he got out, less from fatigue than from *chill*, having been *four hours* in the water, without rest or stay, except what is to be obtained by floating on one's
65 back – this being the *condition* of our performance. I continued my

course on to Santa Chiara, comprising the whole of the Grand Canal (besides the distance from the Lido), and got out where the Laguna once more opens to Fusina. I had been in the water, by my watch, without help or rest, and never touching ground or boat, *four hours*
70 and *twenty minutes*. To this match, and during the greater part of its performance, Mr Hoppner, the Consul General, was witness; and it is well known to many others. Mr Turner can easily verify the fact, if he thinks it worth while, by referring to Mr Hoppner. The distance we could not *accurately* ascertain; it was of course considerable.
75 I crossed the *Hellespont* in *one* hour and ten minutes only. I am now ten years older in time, and twenty in constitution, than I was when I passed the Dardanelles; and yet two years ago I was capable of swimming four hours and twenty minutes; and I am sure that I could have continued two hours longer, though I had on a pair of trousers,
80 an accoutrement which by no means assists the [swimmer]. My two companions were also *four* hours in the water. Mengaldo might be about thirty years of age; Scott about six and twenty.
With this experience in swimming at different periods of life, not only upon the *Spot*, but elsewhere, of various persons, what is there to
85 make me doubt that Leander's exploit was perfectly practicable? If three individuals did more than the passage of the Hellespont, why should he [have done] less? But Mr Turner failed, and, naturally seeking a plausible reason for his failure, lays the blame on the *Asiatic* side of the Strait. To me the cause is evident. He tried to swim *directly* across,
90 instead of going higher up to take the vantage. He might as well have tried to *fly* over Mount Athos.
That a young Greek of the heroic times, in love, and with his limbs in full vigour, might have *succeeded* in such an attempt is neither wonderful nor doubtful. Whether he *attempted* it or *not* is another
95 question, because he might have had a small *boat* to save him the trouble.

I am yours very truly,
Byron.

PS. – Mr Turner says that the swimming from Europe to Asia was
100 'the *easiest* part of the task.' I doubt whether Leander found it so, as it was the return; however, he had several hours between the intervals. The argument of Mr T., 'that higher up or lower down, the strait widens so considerably that he would save little labour by his starting,' is only good for indifferent swimmers: a man of any practice or skill
105 will always consider the distance less than the strength of the stream. If Ekenhead and myself had thought of crossing at the *narrowest point*, instead of going up to the Cape above it, we should have been swept down to Tenedos. The strait is, however, not extremely wide, even where it broadens above and below the forts. As the frigate was

110   stationed some time in the Dardanelles waiting for the firman,[†] I bathed
often in the straight subsequently to our traject, and generally on the
Asiatic side, without perceiving the greater strength of the opposing
steam by which the diplomatic traveller palliates his own failure. An
amusement in the small bay which opens immediately below the Asiatic
115   fort was to *dive* for the *Land* tortoises, which we flung in on purpose,
as they amphibiously crawled along the bottom. *This* does not argue
any vaster violence of current than on the European shore. With regard
to the modest insinuation that we chose the European side as 'easier,' I
appeal to Mr Hobhouse and Admiral Bathurst if it be true or no (poor
120   Ekenhead being since dead): had we been aware of any such difference
of current as is asserted, we would at least have proved it, and were
not likely to have given it up in the twenty-five minutes of Mr T.'s own
experiment. The secret of all this is, that Mr Turner failed, and that we
succeeded; and he is consequently disappointed, and seems not unwilling
125   to overshadow whatever little merit there might be in our success. Why
did he not try the European side? If he had succeeded there after failing
on the Asiatic, his plea would have been more graceful and gracious.
Mr T. may find what fault he pleases with my poetry, or my politics;
but I recommend him to leave aquatic reflections, till he is able to swim
130   'five and twenty minutes' without being '*exhausted*,' though I believe
he is the first modern Tory who ever swam '*against* the stream' for half
the time.

---

firman   Oriental sovereign's licence or passport

Percy Bysshe Shelley
1792–1822

The writings of Percy Bysshe Shelley reveal a revolutionary, radical, tempestuous cast of mind. Much of his poetry combines romantic idealism and emotionalism: most typical is 'Ode to the West Wind' (1820).

He was born in 1792 at Field Place, Sussex, son of a wealthy landowner, and was given a privileged education at Eton, which he did not enjoy, and at University College, Oxford, from which he was expelled with his friend T. J. Hogg in 1811 for publishing *The Necessity of Atheism*. He circulated the controversial pamphlet to bishops and the heads of Oxford Colleges. In the same year he married Harriet Westbrook, and resided for short times in many different places, including Dublin where he espoused the cause of Roman Catholic emancipation. During the three years leading up to his separation from Harriet he composed *Queen Mab*.

In 1814, he visited Switzerland with Mary Godwin, daughter of William Godwin and Mary Wollstonecraft. In 1816 Harriet committed suicide by drowning herself in the London Serpentine, and in that same year *Alastor and Other Poems* was published. In the year before, although Shelley's relations with his father were uneasy because of his political views, he became heir by the death of his grandfather to the equivalent of a multi-million pound fortune.

In 1816, too, his friendship with Lord Byron began, and *Laon and Cynthia* (later entitled *The Revolt of Islam*) was begun while Shelley lived at Marlow. Italy attracted him, and in 1818 he removed there, meeting Byron in Venice, and living successively in Rome and Pisa. Political ferment at home, particularly the Peterloo massacre, inspired him to compose the *Masque of Anarchy* which condemned Castlereagh's administration; and he wrote a satirical poem on Wordsworth, *Peter Bell the Third*. In 1819 he composed *The Cenci*, a dull tragedy in Shakespearean blank verse: the following year *Prometheus Unbound* was published.

He became one of Lamb's 'Pisan circle', of which Byron and the Cornish adventurer Edward Trelawny were members. In Pisa he wrote most of his best lyrics such as 'Ode to the West Wind', 'To a Skylark', and the elegy 'Adonais', ostensibly about Keats but more truly about himself. To this time belongs his long essay *The Defence of Poetry*, not published until 1840.

In 1821 he went to live at Lerici on the shores of the bay of Spezia. He identified himself with the struggle for Greek independence and in 1822 wrote *Hellas*. In July 1822, in his thirtieth year, he was drowned when caught in a storm while sailing near La Spezia.

The best of his poetry has an elevated, romantic, lyrical beauty, but many critics have seen it as artificial, exaggerated, and contaminated by too much enthusiasm. His poetic reputation has been re-established over the last thirty years.

From ALASTOR

50	There was a Poet whose untimely tomb
	No human hands with pious reverence reared,
	But the charmed eddies of autumnal winds
	Built o'er his mouldering bones a pyramid
	Of mouldering leaves in the waste wilderness: —
55	A lovely youth, — no mourning maiden decked

With weeping flowers, or votive* cypress† wreath,   consecrated
The lone couch of his everlasting sleep: —
Gentle, and brave, and generous, — no lorn† bard
Breathed o'er his dark fate one melodious sigh:
60   He lived, he died, he sung, in solitude.
Strangers have wept to hear his passionate notes,
And virgins, as unknown he passed, have pined
And wasted for fond love of his wide eyes.
The fire of those soft orbs has ceased to burn,
65   And Silence, too enamoured of that voice,
Locks its mute music in her rugged cell.

By solemn vision, and bright silver dream,
His infancy was nurtured. Every sight
And sound from the vast earth and ambient* air,   surrounding
70   Sent to his heart its choicest impulses.
The fountains of divine philosophy
Fled not his thirsting lips, and all of great,

---

cypress coniferous tree of dark foliage, the   *lorn* forlorn, desolate
  symbol of mourning

Or good, or lovely, which the sacred past
In truth or fable consecrates, he felt
75 And knew. When early youth had passed, he left
His cold fireside and alienated home
To seek strange truths in undiscovered lands.
Many a wide waste and tangled wilderness
Has lured his fearless steps; and he has bought
80 With his sweet voice and eyes, from savage men,
His rest and food. Nature's most secret steps
He like her shadow has pursued, where'er
The red volcano overcanopies
Its fields of snow and pinnacles of ice
85 With burning smoke, or where bitumen† lakes
On black bare pointed islets ever beat
With sluggish surge, or where the secret caves
Rugged and dark, winding among the springs
Of fire and poison, inaccessible
90 To avarice or pride, their starry domes
Of diamond and of gold expand above
Numberless and immeasurable halls,
Frequent with crystal column, and clear shrines
Of pearl, and thrones radiant with chrysolite.†
95 Nor had that scene of ampler majesty
Than gems or gold, the varying roof of heaven
And the green earth lost in his heart its claims
To love and wonder; he would linger long
In lonesome vales, making the wild his home,
100 Until the doves and squirrels would partake
From his innocuous* hand his bloodless food,   harmless
Lured by the gentle meaning of his looks,
And the wild antelope, that starts whene'er
The dry leaf rustles in the brake, suspend
105 Her timid steps to gaze upon a form
More graceful than her own.
                              His wandering step
Obedient to high thoughts, has visited
The awful ruins of the days of old:
Athens, and Tyre, and Balbec, and the waste
110 Where stood Jerusalem, the fallen towers
Of Babylon, the eternal pyramids,
Memphis and Thebes, and whatsoe'er of strange

---

bitumen pitch, asphalt   *chrysolite* green gem

Sculptured on alabaster† obelisk,†
Or jasper† tomb, or mutilated sphynx,†
115 Dark Æthiopia in her desert hills
Conceals. Among the ruined temples there,
Stupendous columns, and wild images
Of more than man, where marble daemons watch
The Zodiac's† brazen mystery, and dead men
120 Hang their mute* thoughts on the mute walls around,   silent
He lingered, poring† on memorials
Of the world's youth, though the long burning day
Gazed on those speechless shapes, nor, when the moon
Filled the mysterious halls with floating shades
125 Suspended he that task, but ever gazed
And gazed, till meaning on his vacant mind
Flashed like strong inspiration, and he saw
The thrilling secrets of the birth of time.

1815   1816

OZYMANDIAS†

I met a traveller from an antique land
Who said: Two vast and trunkless legs of stone
Stand in the desert . . . Near them, on the sand,
Half sunk, a shattered visage lies, whose frown,
5 And wrinkled lip, and sneer of cold command,
Tell that its sculptor well those passions read
Which yet survive, stamped on these lifeless things,
The hand that mocked them, and the heart that fed:
And on the pedestal these words appear:
10 'My name is Ozymandias, king of kings:
Look on my works, ye Mighty, and despair!'
Nothing beside remains. Round the decay
Of that colossal wreck, boundless and bare
The lone and level sands stretch far away.

1817   1818

---

alabaster   carbonated limestone
obelisk   tapering, monolithic shaft of square
   or rectangular stone, with a pyramidal apex
jasper   opaque quartz, red, yellow or brown in
   colour
sphynx   carved figure with lion's body and
   woman's head

Zodiac   the imaginary belt of the heavens,
   extending about 8 degrees each side of the
   ecliptic, which the sun traverses annually
poring   thinking intently
Ozymandias   or Rameses II of Egypt,
   thirteenth century BC whose great tomb at
   Thebes was shaped as a male sphinx

From PROMETHEUS UNBOUND

DRAMATIS PERSONÆ

PROMETHEUS.	APOLLO.	HERCULES.
DEMOGORGON.	MERCURY	THE PHANTASM OF JUPITER.
JUPITER.	ASIA	THE SPIRIT OF THE EARTH.
THE EARTH.	PANTHEA } Oceanides.	THE SPIRIT OF THE MOON.
OCTAN.	IONE.	SPIRITS OF THE HOURS.

SPIRITS. ECHOES. FAUNS. FURIES.

ACT I

20 Scene. – *A Ravine of Icy Rocks in the Indian Caucasus.* PROMETHEUS *is
discovered bound to the Precipice.* PANTHEA *and* IONE *are seated at
his feet. Time, night. During the Scene, morning slowly breaks.*

Prometheus. Monarch of Gods and Dæmons, and all Spirits
But One, who throng those bright and rolling words
Which Thou and I alone of living things
Behold with sleepless eyes! regard this Earth
5 Made multitudinous with thy slaves, whom thou
Requitest* for knee-worship, prayer, and praise,   repay
And toil, and hecatombs† of broken hearts,
With fear and self-contempt and barren hope.
Whilst me, who am thy foe, eyeless in hate,
10 Hast thou made reign and triumph, to thy scorn,
O'er mine own misery and thy vain revenge.
Three thousand years of sleep-unsheltered hours,
And moments aye divided by keen pangs
Till they seemed years, torture and solitude,
15 Scorn and despair, – these are mine empire: –
More glorious far than that which thou surveyest
From thine unenvied throne, O Mighty God!
Almighty, had I deigned to share the shame
Of thine ill tyranny, and hung not here
20 Nailed to this wall of eagle-baffling* mountain,   thwarting
Black, wintry, dead, unmeasured; without herb,
Insect, or beast, or shape or sound of life.
Ah me! alas, pain, pain ever, for ever!

---

hecatombs   great public sacrifices

No change, no pause, no hope! Yet I endure.
25 I ask the Earth, have not the mountains felt?
I ask yon Heaven, the all-beholding Sun,
Has it not seen? The Sea, in storm or calm,
Heaven's ever-changing Shadow, spread below,
Have its deaf waves not heard my agony?
30 Ah me! alas, pain, pain ever, for ever!

The crawling glaciers pierce me with the spears
Of their moon-freezing crystals, the bright chains
Eat with their burning cold into my bones.
Heaven's wingèd hound, polluting from thy lips
35 His beak in poison not his own, tears up
My heart; and shapeless sights come wandering by,
The ghastly people of the realm of dream,
Mocking me: and the Earthquake-fiends are charged
To wrench the rivets from my quivering wounds
40 When the rocks split and close again behind:
While from their loud abysses howling throng
The genii of the storm, urging the rage
Of whirlwind, and afflict me with keen hail.
And yet to me welcome is day and night,
45 Whether one breaks the hoar* frost of the morn,   white
Or starry, dim, and slow, the other climbs
The leaden-coloured east; for then they lead
The wingless, crawling hours, one among whom
– As some dark Priest hales† the reluctant victim
50 Shall drag thee, cruel King, to kiss the blood
From these pale feet, which then might trample thee
If they disdained not such a prostrate† slave.
Disdain! Ah no! I pity thee. What ruin
Will hunt thee undefended through wide Heaven!
55 How will thy soul, cloven to its depth with terror,
Gape like a hell within! I speak in grief,
Not exultation, for I hate no more,
As then ere misery made me wise. The curse
Once breathed on thee I would recall. Ye Mountains,
60 Whose many-voicèd Echoes, through the mist
Of cataracts* flung the thunder of that spell!   waterfalls

---

hales   drags forcibly   *prostrate*   lying full-length on the ground, face
                                                               downwards

Ye icy Springs, stagnant with wrinkling frost,
Which vibrated to hear me, and then crept
Shuddering through India! Thou serenest Air,
65 Through which the Sun walks burning without beams!
And yet swift Whirlwinds, who on poisèd wings
Hung mute and moveless o'er yon hushed abyss,†
As thunder, louder than your own, made rock
The orbèd world! If then my words had power,
70 Though I am changed so that aught evil wish
Is dead within, although no memory be
Of what is hate, let them not lose it now!
What was that curse? for ye all heard me speak.

1818–19   1820

TO A SKYLARK

Hail to thee, blithe† Spirit!
    Bird thou never wert,
    That from Heaven, or near it,
    Pourest thy full heart
5 In profuse strains of unpremeditated art.

Higher still and higher
    From the earth thou springest
Like a cloud of fire;
    The blue deep thou wingest,
10 And singing still dost soar, and soaring ever singest.

In the golden lightning
    Of the sunken sun,
O'er which clouds are bright'ning,
    Thou dost float and run;
15 Like an unbodied joy whose race is just begun.

The pale purple even
    Melts around thy flight;
Like a star of Heaven,
    In the broad daylight
20 Thou art unseen, but yet I hear thy shrill delight,

---

abyss chasm, deep gorge   *blithe* happy, joyous

Keen as are the arrows
Of that silver sphere,
Whose intense lamp narrows
In the white dawn clear
25   Until we hardly see – we feel that it is there.

All the earth and air
With thy voice is loud,
As, when night is bare,
From one lonely cloud
30   The moon rains out her beams, and Heaven is overflowed.

What thou art we know not;
What is most like thee?
From rainbow clouds there flow not
Drops so bright to see
35   As from thy presence showers a rain of melody.

Like a Poet hidden
In the light of thought,
Singing hymns unbidden,
Till the world is wrought
40   To sympathy with hopes and fears it heeded not:

Like a high-born maiden
In a palace-tower,
Soothing her love-laden
Soul in secret hour
45   With music sweet as love, which overflows her bower:

Like a glow-worm golden
In a dell of dew,
Scattering unbeholden
Its aëreal hue
50   Among the flowers and grass, which screen it from the view!

Like a rose embowered†
In its own green leaves,
By warm winds deflowered,
Till the scent it gives
55   Makes faint with too much sweet those heavy-wingèd thieves:

---

embowered   closed around

Sound of vernal[†] showers
On the twinkling grass,
Rain-awakened flowers,
All that ever was
60 Joyous, and clear, and fresh, thy music doth surpass:

Teach us, Sprite or Bird,
What sweet thoughts are thine:
I have never heard
Praise of love or wine
65 That panted forth a flood of rapture so divine.

Chorus Hymeneal,[†]
Or triumphal chant,
Matched with thine would be all
But an empty vaunt,
70 A thing wherein we feel there is some hidden want.

What objects are the fountains
Of thy happy strain?
What fields, or waves, or mountains?
What shapes of sky or plain?
75 What love of thine own kind? what ignorance of pain?

With thy clear keen joyance
Languor cannot be:
Shadow of annoyance
Never came near thee:
80 Thou lovest – but ne'er knew love's sad satiety.*   over-satisfaction

Waking or asleep,
Thou of death must deem
Things more true and deep
Than we mortals dream,
85 Or how could thy notes flow in such a crystal stream?

We look before and after,
And pine for what is not:
Our sincerest laughter

---

vernal occurring in Spring
Hymeneal to do with Hymen, the god of marriage

With some pain is fraught;
90   Our sweetest songs are those that tell of saddest thought.

Yet if we could scorn
Hate, and pride, and fear;
If we were things born
Not to shed a tear,
95   I know not how thy joy we ever should come near.

Better than all measures
Of delightful sound,
Better than all treasures
That in books are found,
100   Thy skill to poet were, thou scorner of the ground!

Teach me half the gladness
That thy brain must know,
Such harmonious madness
From my lips would flow
105   The world should listen then – as I am listening now.

1820   1820

ODE TO THE WEST WIND†

I

O wild West Wind, thou breath of Autumn's being,
Thou, from whose unseen presence the leaves dead
Are driven, like ghosts from an enchanter fleeing,

Yellow, and black, and pale, and hectic† red,
5   Pestilence-stricken multitudes: O thou,
Who chariotest to their dark wintry bed

Ode to the West Wind   Shelley wrote the
following note:
This poem was conceived and chiefly written
in a wood that skirts the Arno, near Florence,
and on a day when that tempestuous wind,
whose temperature is at once mild and
animating, was collecting the vapours which
pour down the autumnal rains. They began,
as I foresaw, at sunset with a violent tempest
of hail and rain, attended by that magnificent
thunder and lightning peculiar to the
Cisalpine regions.
   The phenomenon alluded to at the
conclusion of the third stanza is well known
to naturalists. The vegetation at the bottom
of the sea, of rivers, and of lakes, sympathizes
with that of the land in the change of seasons,
and is consequently influenced by the winds
which announce it. –
hectic   flushed as with a fever

The wingèd seeds, where they lie cold and low,
Each like a corpse within its grave, until
Thine azure sister of the Spring shall blow

10   Her clarion* o'er the dreaming earth, and fill   trumpet
(Driving sweet buds like flocks to feed in air)
With living hues and odours plain and hill:

Wild Spirit, which art moving everywhere;
Destroyer and preserver; hear, oh, hear!

II

15   Thou on whose stream, mid the steep sky's commotion,
Loose clouds like earth's decaying leaves are shed,
Shook from the tangled boughs of Heaven and Ocean,

Angels of rain and lightning: there are spread
On the blue surface of thine aëry surge,
20   Like the bright hair uplifted from the head

Of some fierce Maenad,† even from the dim verge
Of the horizon to the zenith's† height,
The locks of the approaching storm. Thou dirge*   lament

Of the dying year, to which this closing night
25   Will be the dome of a vast sepulchre,*   tomb
Vaulted with all thy congregated might

Of vapours, from whose solid atmosphere
Black rain, and fire, and hail will burst: oh, hear!

III

Thou who didst waken from his summer dreams
30   The blue Mediterranean, where he lay,
Lulled by the coil of his crystalline† streams,

Beside a pumice† isle in Baiae's† bay,
And saw in sleep old palaces and towers
Quivering within the wave's intenser day,

Maenad   a frenzied female attendant of
  Bacchus
zenith   highest point in the heavens above the
  observer

crystalline   clear like crystal
pumice   light, spongy lava-stone
Baiae   resort near Naples frequented by
  emperors

35   All overgrown with azure moss and flowers
      So sweet, the sense faints picturing them! Thou
      For whose path the Atlantic's level powers

      Cleave themselves into chasms, while far below
      The sea-blooms and the oozy† woods which wear
40   The sapless foliage of the ocean, know

      Thy voice, and suddenly grow gray with fear,
      And tremble and despoil* themselves: oh, hear!   ruin

                          IV

      If I were a dead leaf thou mightest bear;
      If I were a swift cloud to fly with thee;
45   A wave to pant* beneath thy power, and share   throb

      The impulse of thy strength, only less free
      Than thou, O uncontrollable! If even
      I were as in my boyhood, and could be

      The comrade of thy wanderings over Heaven,
50   As then, when to outstrip thy skiey speed
      Scarce seemed a vision; I would ne'er have striven

      As thus with thee in prayer in my sore need.
      Oh, lift me as a wave, a leaf, a cloud!
      I fall upon the thorns of life! I bleed!

55   A heavy weight of hours has chained and bowed
      One too like thee: tameless, and swift, and proud.

                          V

      Make me thy lyre,† even as the forest is:
      What if my leaves are falling like its own!
      The tumult of thy mighty harmonies

60   Will take from both a deep, autumnal tone,
      Sweet though in sadness. Be thou, Spirit fierce,
      My spirit! Be thou me, impetuous one!

---

oozy   wet, slimy   *lyre*   small harp-like instrument

Drive my dead thoughts over the universe
Like withered leaves to quicken a new birth!
65   And, by the incantation† of this verse,

Scatter, as from an unextinguished hearth
Ashes and sparks, my words among mankind!
Be through my lips to unawakened earth

The trumpet of a prophecy! O, Wind,
70   If Winter comes, can Spring be far behind?

1819   1820

From ADONAIS†

I weep for Adonais – he is dead!
O, weep for Adonais! though our tears
Thaw not the frost which binds so dear a head!
And thou, sad Hour, selected from all years
5   To mourn our loss, rouse thy obscure compeers,
And teach them thine own sorrow, say: 'With me
Died Adonais; till the Future dares
Forget the Past, his fate and fame shall be
An echo and a light unto eternity!'

II

10   Where wert thou, mighty Mother, when he lay,
When thy Son lay, pierced by the shaft which flies
In darkness? where was lorn Urania†
When Adonais died? With veilèd eyes,
'Mid listening Echoes, in her Paradise
15   She sate, while one, with soft enamoured breath,
Rekindled all the fading melodies,
With which, like flowers that mock the corse* beneath,   corpse
He had adorned and hid the coming bulk of Death.

III

Oh, weep for Adonais – he is dead!
20   Wake, melancholy Mother, wake and weep!

---

incantation spell, charm
Adonais Shelley's elegy on the death of Keats, written at Pisa, published 1821. It is written in Spenserian stanzas and was inspired by the

Greek elegies of Bion and Moscus, and by Milton's *Lycidas*
Urania one of the muses in Greek mythology who presides over astrology

Yet wherefore? Quench within their burning bed
Thy fiery tears, and let thy loud heart keep
Like his, a mute and uncomplaining sleep;
For he is gone, where all things wise and fair
25 Descend; – oh, dream not that the amorous Deep
Will yet restore him to the vital* air;   life-giving
Death feeds on his mute voice, and laughs at our despair.

IV

Most musical of mourners, weep again!
Lament anew, Urania! – He died,
30 Who was the Sire of an immortal strain,
Blind, old, and lonely, when his country's pride,
The priest, the slave, and the liberticide,†
Trampled and mocked with many a lothèd rite*   ceremony
Of lust and blood; he went, unterrified,
35 Into the gulf of death; but his clear Sprite
Yet reigns o'er earth; the bird among the sons of light.

V

Most musical of mourners, weep anew!
Not all to that bright station dared to climb;
And happier they their happiness who knew,
40 Whose tapers yet burn through that night of time
In which suns perished; others more sublime,
Struck by the envious wrath of man or god,
Have sunk, extinct in their refulgent* prime;   shining
And some yet live, treading the thorny road,
45 Which leads, through toil and hate, to Fame's serene abode.

VI

But now, thy youngest, dearest one, had perished –
The nursling of thy widowhood, who grew,
Like a pale flower by some sad maiden cherished,
And fed with true-love tears, instead of dew;
50 Most musical of mourners, weep anew!
Thy extreme hope, the loveliest and the last,
The bloom, whose petals nipped before they blew
Died on the promise of the fruit, is waste;
The broken lily lies – the storm is overpast

---

liberticide   destroyer of liberty

VII

55 To that high Capital, where kingly Death
    Keeps his pale court in beauty and decay,
    He came; and bought, with price of purest breath,
    A grave among the eternal. – Come away!
    Haste, while the vault of blue Italian day
60 Is yet his fitting charnel-roof† while still
    He lies, as if in dewy sleep he lay;
    Awake him not! surely he takes his fill
Of deep and liquid rest, forgetful of all ill.

VIII

    He will awake no more, oh, never more! –
65 Within the twilight chamber spreads apace
    The shadow of white Death, and at the door
    Invisible Corruption waits to trace
    His extreme way to her dim dwelling-place;
    The eternal Hunger sits, but pity and awe
70 Soothe her pale rage, nor dares she to deface
    So fair a prey, till darkness, and the law
Of change, shall o'er his sleep the mortal curtain draw.

IX

    Oh, weep for Adonais! – The quick Dreams,
    The passion-wingèd Ministers of thought,
75 Who were his flocks, whom near the living streams
    Of his young spirit he fed, and whom he taught
    The love which was its music, wander not. –
    Wander no more, from kindling† brain to brain,
    But droop there, whence they sprung; and mourn their lot
80 Round the cold heart, where, after their sweet pain,
They ne'er will gather strength, or find a home again.

X

    And one with trembling hands clasps his cold head,
    And fans him with her moonlight wings, and cries;
    'Our love, our hope, or sorrow, is not dead;
85 See, on the silken fringe of his faint eyes,
    Like dew upon a sleeping flower, there lies
    A tear some Dream has loosened from his brain.'
    Lost Angel of a ruined Paradise!

---

charnel-roof roof of the house where corpses   *kindling* coming to life
   or bones are stored

She knew not 'twas her own; as with no stain
90   She faded, like a cloud which had outwept its rain.

1821   1821

AUTUMN: A DIRGE

I

The warm sun is failing, the bleak wind is wailing,
The bare boughs are sighing, the pale flowers are dying,
                    And the Year
On the earth her death-bed, in a shroud of leaves dead,
5   Is lying.
                    Come, Months, come away,
                    From November to May,
                    In your saddest array;
                    Follow the bier†
10   Of the dead cold Year,
And like dim shadows watch by her sepulchre*   tomb

II

The chill rain is falling, the nipped worm is crawling,
The rivers are swelling, the thunder is knelling†
                    For the Year;
15   The blithe swallows are flown, and the lizards each gone
                    To his dwelling;
                    Come Months, come away;
                    Put on white, black, and gray;
                    Let your light sisters play –
20   Ye, follow the bier
                    Of the dead cold Year,
And make her grave green with tear on tear.

1820   1824

---

bier   a movable stand on which a coffin is   *knelling*   ring of a bell for a funeral
carried

From LETTER TO LEIGH HUNT[†]

Florence,
November 3, 1819.

My dear Friend,
       The event of Carlisle's[†] trial has filled me with an indignation that will not, and ought not to be suppressed.

    In the name of all we hope for in human nature what are the people
5 of England about? Or rather how long will they, and those whose hereditary duty it is to lead them, endure the enormous outrages of which they are one day made the victim and the next the instrument? Post succeeds post, and fresh horrors are ever detailed. First we hear that a troop of the enraged master-manufacturers are let loose with
10 sharpened swords upon a multitude of their starving dependents and in spite of the remonstrances of the regular troops that they ride over them and massacre without distinction of sex or age, and cut off women's breasts and dash the heads of infants against the stones. Then comes information that a man has been found guilty of some inexplicable
15 crime, which his prosecutors call blasphemy; one of the features of which, they inform us, is the denying that the massacring of children and the ravishing of women, was done by the immediate command of the author and preserver of all things. And thus at the same time we see on one hand men professing to act by the public authority who put
20 in practise the trampling down and murdering an unarmed multitude without distinction of sex or age, and on the other a tribunal which punishes men for asserting that deeds of the same character, transacted in a distant age and country were not done by the command of God. If not for this, for what was Mr. Carlisle prosecuted? For impugning[†] the
25 Divinity of Jesus Christ? I impugn it. For denying that the whole mass of ancient Hebrew literature is of divine authority? I deny it. I hope this is no blasphemy, and that I am not to be dragged home by the enmity of our political adversaries to be made a sacrifice to the superstitious fury of the ruling sect. But I am prepared both to do my
30 duty and abide by whatever consequences may be attached to its fulfilment.

    It is said that Mr. Carlisle has been found guilty by a jury. Juries are frequently in cases of libel illegally and partially[†] constituted, and whenever this can be proved the party accused has a title to a new trial.
35 A view of the question, so simple that it is in danger of being overlooked

---

Leigh Hunt James Henry Leigh Hunt (1784–1859), poet and editor
Carlisle Richard Carlisle (1790–1843), publisher of free-thought books. He was tried in 1819 for blasphemous libel in Paine's *Age*
of Reason and Palmer's *Principles of Nature*, was fined £1000, and given three years imprisonment
impugn call in question
partially biasedly, unfairly

from its very obviousness, has presented itself to me, by which, I think
it will clearly appear that this illegal and partial character belonged to
the jury which pronounced a verdict of guilty against Mr. Carlisle, and
that he is entitled to a new trial.

40   It is the privilege of an Englishman to be tried not only by a jury,
but by a jury of his peers. Who are the *peers* of any man and what is
the legal import of this word? Let us illustrate the letter by the spirit of
the law. A nobleman has a right to be tried by his peers, a gentleman,
a tradesman, a farmer – the like; the peers of a man are men of the

45   same station, class denomination with himself. The reason on which
this provision is founded is that the persons called upon to determine
the guilt or innocence of the accused might be so alive to a tender
sympathy towards him, through common interests, habits and opinions,
as to render it impossible, either that through neglect or aversion they

50   would commit injustice towards him, or that they might be incapable
of knowing and weighing the merits of the case. Butchers and surgeons
are excluded on this ground from juries; it being supposed by the law
that they are engaged in occupations foreign to that delicate sensibility
respecting human life and suffering exacted in those selected as arbiters[†]

55   for inflicting it. From the dictation of this spirit, in all cases where
foreigners are criminally accused, the jury impanelled are half English-
men and half foreigners. And the reason why they are not all foreigners
is manifest; not that it is theoretically just that any men not strictly his
peers should determine between the accused and the country, but

60   because the practical disadvantage arising from the inexperience of
foreigners in this admirable form peculiar to English law, would
overbalance the advantage of adhering to the shadow, by letting the
substance of justice escape. This therefore is the law, and the spirit of
the law, of juries; and thus plainly and clearly it is illustrated by the

65   ancient and perpetual practice of the English courts of Justice.
      Who were Mr. Carlisle's peers? Mr. Carlisle was a Deist[†] accused of
blaspheming the religion of men professing themselves Christians. Who
were his peers? Christians? Surely not. Such a proposition is refuted by
the very terms of which it is composed. It were to constitute a jury out

70   of the men who are parties to the prosecution; it were to make those
who are offended, judges of the cause of him by whom they profess
themselves to have been offended; it were less absurd to impannell the
nearest relations of a murdered man to try the guilt or innocence of a
person on whom circumstances attach a strong suspicion of the deed.

75   No honest Christian would sit on such a jury; except he felt himself
thoroughly imbued with the universal toleration preached by the alleged

---

arbiters judges   *Deist* a believer in the existence of God
                                      without accepting revelation

founder of his religion; a state of feeling which we are not warranted
by experience to presume to belong except to extraordinary men. He
must know he could not be impartial. He sees before him the enemy of
80 his God; one already predestined to the tortures of Hell and who by
the most specious arguments is seducing every one around him into the
same peril. He probably feels that his own faith is tottering whilst he
listens to the prisoner's defence and this naturally redoubles his
indignation. How is such a person to be considered as the *peer* of the
85 other, if by peer he meant, one who from common habits and interests
would be likely to weigh the merits of the cause dispassionately? He is
a person of the same sect with him who framed the indictment in which
the culprit is accused as a malicious blasphemer. He is evidently less
his *peer* with reference to the circumstances of the case than a ploughman
90 would be the peer of a nobleman, and it is less probable that the one
would give an unconscientious verdict from envy towards rank, that
the other from abhorrence from the speculative opinions of the prisoner.
The Christian may be the peer of the Deist with reference to any matter
not involving a question of his guilt in expressing contumelious[†]
95 sentiments concerning the Christian's own belief (for this if anything is
meant by blasphemy) because he may have those common interests and
feelings which make one man alive to render justice to another; but
with regard to the matter in question he cannot be his peer, because he
is one of the persons whom he is charged as having injured, because
100 what he boasts to consider as his most important interests compel him
to judge harshly of the accused, and to impersonate the character of
the injured party, the accuser and the judge, rather than the impartial
juryman.
   Neither therefore the practice of law, nor the reason of law on which
105 lawyers profess to ground that practice, nor the universal reason of all
men which is the foundation not only of law but of all human society,
admit that a professed Christian should be the peer of a Deist in a case
where the uttering contumelious expressions against the opinions of the
Christian is the crime of which the Deist is accused. Suppose a Deist
110 brought an action against a Christian for reviling *his* opinions, how
would an English court of justice endure to be told that the jury must
not be Christians but Deists, and what weight would they give to the
prosecutor's objections to such and such a juryman because he suspected
that he believed the Bible to be of divine authority. And yet Christianity,
115 or that system which is founded on the maxim of 'Do unto others as
thou wouldst they should do unto thee' has been declared to be part of
the law of the land.
   Who then, are the peers of the Deist? We must admit I fear the

contumelious hateful

existence of a law against *blasphemy*. Let us hope that some legislative
120   enactment will speedily be passed to erase this scandal from our age.
Meanwhile there is a law that men should be censured for what is called
blasphemy. But who are to be the judges of blasphemy? Not the
blasphemer; still less the blasphemed, or the persons who are injured
and provoked by the blasphemy? The peers of the accused. Who are
125   the peers of the Deist? Deists, to be sure. 'No,' objects the Christian
'they will assuredly acquit him.' But the Christian would condemn him
right or wrong. Well, let there be that same compromise between the
theoretical justice and the practical convenience of the case, as already
obtains in the instance of foreigners. Let them be half Deists and half
130   Christians. As in the case of foreigners accused of crimes of universally
acknowledged enormity let there be impannelled a jury one moiety
consisting of such as have interests and feelings common with his own,
and the other of such as are uninfluenced by those interests. Anything
short of this is an open mockery, an unfeeling denial of justice. 'But,'
135   says the Christian, 'you would not insist on impannelling murderers to
try a murderer on the pretence that they are alone his peers, because
they alone have the same interests and feelings. Why impannell Deists
to try a Deist? My reply to the insolent bigot[†] is simple. Deism is no
crime by the law of England any more than Sandimonianism[†] or
140   Unitarianism[†] is a crime. The indictment does not accuse him of Deism
but of blasphemy. He is accused of speaking injuriously of a certain
religious persuasion, and not of avowing his disbelief in that persuasion.
Mere disbelief is perfectly legal. And it is so legal that if a man be asked
in public, 'Do you believe the Bible to be of divine authority?' and he
145   should deliberately answer, 'I am from my soul convinced that it is
not', no legal punishment could be inflicted on him for that avowal.

But, it will be said, a Deist cannot take the oath requisite to being
impannelled – he cannot kiss the book. He cannot feel that the Bible is
of divine sanction and of course cannot appeal to it as a solemn type
150   of the authority and presence of God. Nor can the Mahometan, the
Hindoo, the Chinese, and yet each is sworn, on the codes of their
respective faiths, and no one ever heard of the testimony of one of these
being rejected in an English court of justice on the ground of his religion.
Suppose not a regular Mahometan but a Wahabee were in the question.
155   Suppose a North American Indian, or an Otaheitan or a Tupinambo
or an Hottentot. Some of these are Deists, some Polytheists, some have
obscure and imperfect notions of supernatural agencies in the visible

---

bigot   a prejudiced holder of a view
Sandimonianism   Sandemanians, or Glasites,
were a religious party expelled from the
Church of Scotland for maintaining that
national churches, because they are of this

world, are unscriptural
Unitarianism   a religious sect which denies the
Trinity and believes God exists in one person
only

operations of nature hardly amounting to religion. Would the testimony
of a sensible and intelligent person belonging to any of these classifi-
160   cations of the human species be rejected in a case where he could give
impartial testimony, because he could shew no written code of opinions
respecting the origin and government of the world? No, assuredly. He
would be called upon to make his solemn asseveration† that what he
spoke was true; to declare what his faith in divine agency and attributes
165   was, he would be reminded justly of the great temporal penalties and
infamy attached to perjury,† and his testimony would be admitted.
What of the Unitarian? He openly denies the divinity of Christ, or
rather, if I understand his tenets,† he asserts that every great moral
teacher is divinely inspired in exact proportion to the excellence of the
170   morality which he promulgates, and that Jesus Christ was a moral
teacher of surpassing excellence. He considers whole passages of the
Bible as interpolations and forgeries. He admires the book of Job and
Solomon's song as he admires Æschylus† or Anacreon†, and considers
those models of poetical sublimity and pathos as no more than the
175   uninspired productions of persons of distinguished genius. Yet it can
hardly be said that Sir Samuel Romilly,† a professed Unitarian, would
have been excluded from acting as a juryman not having been excluded
from his seat in parliament.

   . . . A Quaker's† testimony is not indeed admitted in criminal cases,
180   and this disqualification bears with it a sort of appearance of reason.
He protests as it were against the jurisdiction of the court by refusing
to comply with that formality in which it has been the established
practice of every British citizen to acquiesce. Besides, he not only refuses,
but, refusing, acknowledges the divine authority of that code on which
185   he is nevertheless unwilling to pledge the truth of his statement. This
might be interpreted into the leaving himself a loophole through which
to escape. The pretence might be assumed by those who wished to do
evil by a false assertion, and yet to escape what they might fear from
the vengeance of their God in invoking him as the witness of a
190   deliberate untruth. At least all this is plausible. But the truth is that
Jesus Christ forbade in the most express terms the attaching to any one
asseveration rather than to any other a sanction to ensure its credibility.
This the Quaker knows. The grounds on which the Quakers testimony
is rejected might be shown to be futile; at present it seems sufficient to
195   have proved that the same arguments which have been used to exclude

---

asseveration   solemn declaration
perjury   breach of oath
tenents   principles of belief
Aeschylus   (525–456 BC), the earliest of the
  three great Greek tragic poets
Anacreon   sixth century BC Greek lyric poet of
  love and wine

Sir Samuel Romilly   (1757–1818), MP and law
  reformer
Quaker   a member of the *Society of Friends*,
  a religious sect founded by George Fox who
  began preaching in 1647: they believe in no
  fixed creed and have no regular ministry

the Quaker from his rights (for all civil powers are rights) as a witness
and juryman, do not apply to the Deist.

On these grounds I think Mr. Carlisle is entitled to make application
for a new trial; and I am at a loss to conceive how the Judges of the
200   King's Bench can refuse to comply with his demand; unless a few
modern precedents founded on an oversight now corrected, are to
overturn the very foundations of the law of which they have been
perversions.

One point of consideration which was pleaded by Mr. Carlisle on
205   his defence, cannot be too distinctly understood. The same Justice ought
to be dispensed to all. Of two murderers one ought not to be hung
whilst the other having committed the same crime, with the same
evidence notoriously existing against him, is allowed to walk about at
liberty. Of two perjurers one ought not to be pilloried, and the other
210   sent on embassies. Nor are they, for these are real and not conventional
crimes. But is Mr. Carlisle the only Deist and Mr. Paine[†] the only
deistical writer that these heavy penalties are called down on the person
of the one, and these furious execrations started from an indictment
upon the work of the other? What! was Hume[†] not a Deist? Has
215   not Gibbon,[†] without whose work no library is complete, assailed
Christianity with most subtle reasoning, turned it into a bye word and
a joke? Has not Sir William Drummond,[†] the most acute metaphysical
critic of the age, a man of profound learning, high employments in the
state and unblemished integrity of character, controverted Christianity
220   in a manner no less undisguised and bold than Mr. Paine? If Mr.
Godwin[†] in his Political Justice and his Inquirer has abstained from
entering into a detailed argument against it, has he not treated it as an
exploded superstition to which, in the present state of knowledge, it
was unworthy of his high character as a moral philosopher to advert?
225   Has not Mr. Burdon, a gentleman of great fortune, published a book
called 'Materials for thinking' in which he plainly avows his disbelief
in the divine authority of the Bible? Is not Mr. Bentham[†] a Deist? What
men of any rank in society from their talents are not Deists whose
understandings have been unbiassed by the allurements of worldly
230   interest? Which of our great literary characters not receiving emolument
from the advocating a system of religion inseparably connected with
the source of that emolument, is not a Deist? Even some of those very
men who are the loudest to condemn and malign others for rejecting

---

Paine   Tom Paine (1737–1809), politician and
theorist
Hume   David Hume (1711–76), Scottish
philosopher
Gibbon   Edward Gibbon (1737–94), historian
Sir William Drummond   (1770–1828), scholar
and diplomat, Fellow of the Royal Society,

and minister to the court of Naples
Godwin   William Godwin (1756–1836),
novelist and political theorist
Bentham   Jeremy Bentham (1748–1832),
political and economic thinker, and social
reformer

Christianity *I know to be Deists*. But that I disdain to violate the
235   sanctity of private intercourse for good, as others have done for evil, I
would state names. Those already cited – who have publicly professed
themselves Deists – are the names of persons of splendid genius, wealth
and rank, and exercising a great influence through their example and
their reasoning faculties upon the conduct and opinions of their
240   contemporaries. But who is Mr. Carlisle? A bookseller, I imagine, of
small means who with the innocent design of maintaining his wife and
children took advantage of the repeal of the acts against impugning the
Divinity of Jesus Christ to publish some books the main object of which
was to impugn that notion and destroy the authorities on which it is
245   founded. The chief of these works is the Age of Reason, a production
of the celebrated Paine, which the prosecutors were so far unfortunate
in selecting, whatever may be its defects as a piece of argument,
inasmuch as it was written by that great and good man under
circumstances in which only great and good men are ever found; at the
250   bottom of a dungeon under momentary expectation of death for having
opposed a tyrant. It has the solemn sincerity – and that is something in
an age of hypocrites – of a voice from the bed of death.
   Why not brand other works which are more learned and systematically
complete than this work of Paine's; why not brand works which have
255   been written not in a solitary dungeon with no access to any book of
reference, but in convenient and well selected libraries, by a judicial
process? Why not indict Mr. Bentham or Sir William Drummond? Why
crush a starving bookseller, and anathematize[†] a work, which though
perhaps perfect enough for its purpose, must from the very circumstances
260   of its composition be imperfect? Surely; if the tyrants could find any
individual of the higher classes of talent and rank devoted to the cause
of liberty, against whom from any peculiar combination of accidents
they would excite the superstitions of the people, no doubt they would
trample upon him to their hearts' content, especially if circumstances
265   permitted them to trample and to outrage in secret. Tyrants, after all,
are only a kind of demagogues; they must flatter the great Beast. But
in the case of attacking any of the aristocratical[†] Deists the risk of
defeat would be great, and the chances of success small. And the
prosecutors care little for religion, or care for it only as it is the mask
270   and the garment by which they are invested with the symbols of worldly
power. In prosecuting Carlisle they have used the superstition of the
jury as their instrument for crushing a political enemy, or rather they
strike in his person at all their political enemies. They know that the

---

anathematize   curse
aristocratical   Shelley noted: 'This word is not
used in a bad sense; nor is the word

aristocracy susceptible of an ill signification.
Oligarchy is the term for the tyrannical
monopoly of the few'

Established Church is based upon the belief in certain events of a
275 supernatural character having occurred in Judæa eighteen centuries
ago; that but for this belief the farmer would refuse to pay the tenth of
the produce of his labours to maintain its numbers in idleness; that this
class of persons if not maintained in idleness would have something
else to do than to divert the attention of the people from obtaining a
280 Reform in their oppressive government, and that consequently the
government would be reformed, and that the people would receive a
just price for their labours, a consummation† incompatible with the
luxurious idleness in which their rulers esteem it their interest to live.
Economy, – retrenchment, – the disbanding of the standing army, – the
285 gradual abolition of the national debt† by some just yet speedy and
effectual system, – and such a reform in the representation as by
admitting the constitutional presence of the people in the state may
prevent the recurrence of evils which now present us with the alternative
of despotism or revolution, are the objects at which the jury uncon-
290 sciously struck, when from a sentiment of religious intolerance they
delivered a verdict of guilty against Mr. Carlisle.

How such a verdict could ever have been returned by men upon their
oath, whatever might have been their religious abhorrence from the
prisoner, must be matter of astonishment to every sober minded person
295 of what speculative opinions soever.

---

consummation completion
national debt public debt of the central
government of a state and secured on the
national revenue

John Clare
1793–1864

The greatest mistake John Clare made was to forsake his first love, Mary Joyce; her memory was to inspire many of his poems. Clare was the son of a labourer. He was deeply attached to his locality in Northamptonshire, and lived simply as thresher, ploughboy and limeburner. His first volume of poems, *Poems Descriptive of Rural Life and Scenery*, was published in 1820. Having given up Mary Joyce, he soon after married Martha Turner, but it was not a happy affair. He found solace and occupation in poetry: a number of volumes quickly appeared: *The Village Minstrel* (1821), *The Shepherd's Calendar* (1827).

In 1832 he made the fatal decision to leave his native village and move to Northborough. He gradually became disturbed and unsettled. In 1835 *The Rural Muse* was published, but by 1837 he was judged insane and committed to the asylum at High Beech, Epping. He was devastated by being at a distance from his native countryside. He escaped in 1841 and walked home to Northamptonshire under the delusion that he was rejoining his wife Mary Joyce. Again, he was committed, this time to the Northampton General Asylum.

His poetry was immediately popular, but soon lost its appeal. Clare's reputation revived in the twentieth century. His poetry carries great conviction and speaks powerfully and honestly about place, landscape, love, human abilities, and about the state of innocence and its loss. He has been much admired by a number of modern poets.

I AM

I am: yet what I am none cares or knows.
   My friends forsake me like a memory lost,
I am the self-consumer of my woes –
   They rise and vanish in oblivious host,
5   Life shadows in love's frenzied, stifled throes: –
And yet I am, and live – like vapours tost

Into the nothingness of scorn and noise,
  Into the living sea of waking dreams,
  Where there is neither sense of life or joys,
10   But the vast shipwreck of my life's esteems;
  Even the dearest, that I love the best,
  Are strange – nay, rather stranger than the rest.

I long for scenes, where man hath never trod,
  A place where woman never smiled or wept –
15 There to abide with my Creator, God,
  And sleep as I in childhood sweetly slept,
  Untroubling, and untroubled where I lie,
  The grass below – above the vaulted sky.

c. 1844   1865

THE FEAR OF FLOWERS

The nodding oxeye bends before the wind,
The woodbine† quakes lest boys their flowers should find,
And prickly dog-rose, spite of its array,
Can't dare the blossom-seeking hand away,
5 While thistles wear their heavy knobs of bloom
Proud as a war-horse wears its haughty plume,
And by the roadside danger's self defy;
On commons where pined sheep and oxen lie,
In ruddy pomp and ever thronging mood
10 It stands and spreads like danger in a wood,
And in the village street, where meanest weeds
Can't stand untouched to fill their husks with seeds,
The haughty thistle o'er all danger towers,
In every place the very wasp of flowers.

                                             1908

---

woodbine   wild honeysuckle

From REMEMBRANCES: ENCLOSURE

By Langley Bush I roam, but the bush hath left its hill,
On Cowper Green I stray, 'tis a desert strange and chill,
And the spreading Lea Close Oak, ere decay had penned its will,
To the axe of the spoiler and self-interest fell a prey,
5   And Crossberry Way and old Round Oak's narrow lane
With its hollow trees like pulpits I shall never see again,
Enclosure like a Buonaparte let not a thing remain,
It levelled every bush and tree and levelled every hill
And hung the moles for traitors – though the brook is running still
10   It runs a naked stream, cold and chill.

1832–5   1908

SCHOOLBOYS IN WINTER

The schoolboys still their morning ramble take
To neighbouring village school with playing speed,
Loitering with pastime's leisure till they quake,
Oft looking up the wild-geese droves to heed,
5   Watching the letters which their journeys make;
Or plucking haws† on which the fieldfares† feed,
And hips and sloes; and on each shallow lake
Making glib slides, where they like shadows go
Till some fresh pastimes in their minds awake.
10   Then off they start anew and hasty blow
Their numbed and clumpsing† fingers till they glow;
The races with their shadows wildly run
That stride huge giants o'er the shining snow
In the pale splendour of the winter sun.

1924

---

haws fruits of the hawthorn   *clumpsing* awkwardly moving
fieldfares thrushes that winter in Britain

John Keats

1795–1821

The Keats family was doomed to fall victim to the scourge of nineteenth-century society, consumption or tuberculosis of the lungs. Keats's mother died of the disease when he was fourteen. His brother Tom died of it in December 1818 after being nursed by John throughout his illness; and John died of it at the age of twenty-five in Rome.

The poet was well-educated at Clarke's School, Enfield, and became apprenticed to an apothecary-surgeon. After a few years he abandoned his apprenticeship and attended Guy's Hospital as a medical student. Although licensed to act as an apothecary in 1816, he gave up his medical studies and, in precarious financial circumstances, devoted himself to poetry.

He depended very much on close personal relationships, and among these were his school-friend Cowden Clarke, and Leigh Hunt who was the first to publish his work: 'On First Looking into Chapman's Homer' appeared in Hunt's *The Examiner*. Keats's early poetry was greatly influenced by Spenser's gorgeous diction. His first volume of poetry was published in 1817 and included 'I stood tip-toe upon a little hill' and 'Sleep and Poetry' as well as a number of other miscellaneous songs and sonnets. The critic John Lockhart was scathing in his critical attack and named Keats as a member of 'the Cockney school of poets'. It was in December 1817, that another friend of Keats, the artist Benjamin Haydon, held his 'immortal dinner' when the guests included Keats, Wordsworth and Charles Lamb.

In 1818 Keats published *Endymion*, and completed *Isabella, or the Pot of Basil*. With Charles Armitage Brown, he visited the Lake District and went on to Scotland where the natural scenery lifted his spirits and gave him inspiration. To his dismay, he had to endure savage attacks on his *Endymion* by Lockhart in *Blackwood's Magazine* and J. W. Croker in *The Quarterly Review*. That year, 1818, saw his brother Tom die, after which Keats moved to the Hampstead home of Armitage Brown. Unhappily, he began to show signs of the fatal illness himself.

1818 to 1819 was the 'great year' for his poetic muse in which he wrote much of his best poetry: lyrical, luxurious and colourful as in

Lamia, both sensuous and sensual as in *The Eve of St. Agnes* in which
'lucent syrops tinct with cinnamon' are provided for the feast in
Madeline's chamber, and philosophical and reflective as in the great
odes. For most of 1819 Keats was not well, but in 1820 he published
Lamia, Isabella, The Eve of St. Agnes and other Poems. The volume
received a popular welcome and even criticism levelled in *Blackwood's*
was muted.

Shelley invited him to Italy, and he travelled to Rome with his friend
Joseph Severn. He never reached Shelley. Temporarily settling in
Rome, Keats died of consumption in February 1821: Severn nursed
him on his deathbed. Shelley composed his elegy 'Adonais' for Keats,
and when he himself was drowned a year later, Keats's 1820 volume
was found in his pocket.

Keats's poetry puts him in the first rank of English poets. He was a
man of great sensitivity and openness of mind: T. S. Eliot admired
his letters to friends and confidants for their frankness and directness.

ON FIRST LOOKING INTO CHAPMAN'S HOMER

Much have I travell'd in the realms of gold,
    And many goodly states and kingdoms seen;
    Round many western islands have I been
Which bards in fealty[†] to Apollo[†] hold.
5 Oft of one wide expanse had I been told
    That deep-brow'd Homer[†] rules as his demesne;[†]
    Yet did I never breathe its pure serene
Till I heard Chapman[†] speak out loud and bold:
Then felt I like some watcher of the skies
10   When a new planet swims into his ken;
    Or like stout Cortez[†] when with eagle eyes

---

fealty obligation of fidelity to
Apollo son of Zeus: god of poetry, music,
  archery, prophecy and the healing art
Homer ancient Greek poet
demesne land, region
Chapman George Chapman, Elizabethan poet

and dramatist who translated *Iliad* and
Odyssey between 1598 and 1616
Cortez in fact Balboa discovered the Pacific in
  1513; but this passage recalls Titian's
  portrait of Cortez, the conqueror of Mexico

He star'd at the Pacific – and all his men
Look'd at each other with a wild surmise –
Silent, upon a peak in Darien.[†]

1816   1816

From SLEEP AND POETRY

85   Stop and consider! life is but a day;
      A fragile dew-drop on its perilous way
      From a tree's summit; a Poor Indian's sleep
      While his boat hastens to the monstrous steep
      Of Montmorenci. Why so sad a moan?
90   Life is the rose's hope while yet unblown;
      The reading of an ever-changing tale;
      The light uplifting of a maiden's veil;
      A pigeon tumbling in clear summer air;
      A laughing school-boy, without grief or care,
95   Riding the springy branches of an elm,

      O for ten years, that I may overwhelm
      Myself in poesy; so I may do the deed
      That my own soul has to itself decreed.
      Then will I pass the countries that I see
100   In long perspective, and continually
      Taste their pure fountains. First the realm I'll pass
      Of Flora,[†] and old Pan:[†] sleep in the grass,
      Feed upon apples red, and strawberries,
      And choose each pleasure that my fancy sees;
105   Catch the white-handed nymphs[†] in shady places,
      To woo sweet kisses from averted faces, –
      Play with their fingers, touch their shoulders white
      Into a pretty shrinking with a bite
      As hard as lips can make it: till agreed,
110   A lovely tale of human life we'll read.
      And one will teach a tame dove how it best
      May fan the cool air gently o'er my rest;

Darien   the heights of Darien in Panama
Flora   Roman goddess of flowers, especially
    associated with spring
Pan   Greek god of pasture, forests, flocks and
    herds

nymphs   in classical mythology, minor female
    divinities of the countryside, well-disposed
    towards mortals

Another, bending o'er her nimble tread,
Will set a green robe floating round her head,
115 And still will dance with ever varied ease,
Smiling upon the flowers and the trees:
Another will entice me on, and on
Through almond blossoms and rich cinnamon;
Till in the bosom of a leafy world
120 We rest in silence, like two gems uncurl'd
In the recesses of a pearly shell.

And can I ever bid these joys farewell?
Yes, I must pass them for a nobler life,
Where I may find the agonies, the strife
125 Of human hearts: for lo! I see afar,
O'ersailing the blue cragginess, a car
And steeds with steamy manes – the charioteer
Looks out upon the winds with glorious fear:
And now the numerous tramplings quiver lightly
130 Along a huge cloud's ridge; and now with sprightly
Wheel downward come they into fresher skies,
Tipt round with silver from the sun's bright eyes.
Still downward with capacious whirl they glide;
And now I see them on the green-hill's side
135 In breezy rest among the nodding stalks.
The charioteer with wond'rous gesture talks
To the trees and mountains; and there soon appear
Shapes of delight, of mystery, and fear,
Passing along before a dusky space
140 Made by some mighty oaks: as they would chase
Some ever-fleeting music on they sweep.
Lo! how they murmur, laugh, and smile, and weep:
Some with upholden hand and mouth severe;

Some with their faces muffled to the ear
145 Between their arms; some, clear in youthful bloom,
So glad and smilingly athwart the gloom;
Some looking back, and some with upward gaze;
Yes, thousands in a thousand different ways
Flit onward – now a lovely wreath of girls
150 Dancing their sleek hair into tangled curls;
And now broad wings. Most awfully intent
The driver of those steeds is forward bent.
And seems to listen: O that I might know
All that he writes with such a hurrying glow.

155   The visions all are fled – the car is fled
       Into the light of heaven, and in their stead
       A sense of real things comes doubly strong,
       And, like a muddy stream, would bear along
       My soul to nothingness: but I will strive
160   Against all doubtings, and will keep alive
       The thought of that same chariot, and the strange
       Journey it went.

       1816   1817

From THE EVE OF ST AGNES

XXIV

       A casement high and triple-arch'd there was,
       All garlanded with carven imag'ries
       Of fruits, and flowers, and bunches of knot-grass,†
210   And diamonded with panes of quaint device,
       Innumerable of stains and splendid dyes,
       As are the tiger-moth's deep-damask'd† wings;
       And in the midst, 'mong thousand heraldries,
       And twilight saints, and dim emblazonings,†
215   A shielded scutcheon blush'd with blood of queens and kings.

XXV

       Full on his casement shone the wintry moon,
       And threw warm gules† on Madeline's fair breast,
       As down she knelt for heaven's grace and boon;*   favour
       Rose-bloom fell on her hands, together prest,
220   And on her silver cross soft amethyst,†
       And on her hair a glory, like a saint:
       She seem'd a splendid angel, newly drest,
       Save wings, for heaven: – Porphyro grew faint:
       She knelt, so pure a thing, so free from mortal taint.

XXVI

225   Anon his heart revives: her vespers† done,
       Of all its wreathed pearls her hair she frees;

---

knot-grass   common weed with intricate
  creeping stems and pale pink flowers
damask'd   bluish red
emblazonings   heraldic depictions

gules   heraldic colour red
amethyst   precious stone of purple quartz
vespers   evening rituals

Unclasps her warmed jewels one by one;
Loosens her fragrant boddice; by degrees
Her rich attire creeps rustling to her knees:
230   Half-hidden, like a mermaid in sea-weed,
Pensive awhile she dreams awake, and sees,
In fancy, fair St Agnes in her bed,
But dares not look behind, or all the charm is fled.

XXVII

Soon, trembling in her soft and chilly nest,
235   In sort of wakeful swoon, perplex'd she lay,
Until the poppied warmth of sleep oppress'd
Her soothed limbs, and soul fatigued away;
Flown, like a thought, until the morrow-day;
Blissfully haven'd both from joy and pain;
240   Clasp'd like a missal† where swart† Paynims† pray;
Blinded alike from sunshine and from rain,
As though a rose should shut, and be a bud again.

XXVIII

Stol'n to this paradise, and so entranced,
Porphyro gazed upon her empty dress,
245   And listen'd to her breathing, if it chanced
To wake into a slumberous tenderness;
Which when he heard, that minute did he bless,
And breath'd himself: then from the closet crept,
Noiseless as fear in a wide wilderness,
250   And over the hush'd carpet, silent, stept,
And 'tween the curtains peep'd, where, lo! – how fast she slept.

XXIX

Then by the bed-side, where the faded moon
Made a dim, silver twilight, soft he set
A table, and, half anguish'd, threw thereon
255   A cloth of woven crimson, gold, and jet: –
O for some drowsy Morphean† amulet!†
The boisterous, midnight, festive clarion,*   trumpet
The kettle-drum, and far-heard clarinet,
Affray his ears, though but in dying tone: –
260   The hall door shuts again, and all the noise is gone.

---

missal   book of prayers
swart   swarthy, dark
Paynims   pagans, usually Mohammedans

Morphean   sleepy, from Morpheus, god of
sleep
amulet   a charm against evil

XXX

And still she slept an azure†-lidded sleep,
In blanched linen, smooth, and lavender'd,
While he from forth the closet brought a heap
Of candied apple, quince, and plum, and gourd;
265   With jellies soother than the creamy curd,
And lucent* syrops, tinct* with cinnamon;   translucent   flavoured
Manna* and dates, in argosy† transferr'd   food
From Fez; and spiced dainties, every one,
From silken Samarcand to cedar'd Lebanon.

XXXI

270   These delicates he heap'd with glowing hand
On golden dishes and in baskets bright
Of wreathed silver: sumptuous they stand
In the retired quiet of the night,
Filling the chilly room with perfume light. –
275   'And now, my love, my seraph fair, awake!
'Thou art my heaven, and I thine eremite:
'Open thine eyes, for meek St. Agnes' sake,
'Or I shall drowse beside thee, so my soul doth ache.'

XXXII

Thus whispering, his warm, unnerved arm
280   Sank in her pillow. Shaded was her dream
By the dusk curtains: – 'twas a midnight charm
Impossible to melt as iced stream:
The lustrous* salvers* in the moonlight gleam;   shining   trays
Broad golden fringe upon the carpet lies:
285   It seem'd he never, never could redeem
From such a stedfast spell his lady's eyes;
So mus'd awhile, entoil'd in woofed* phantasies.   woven

XXXIII

Awakening up, he took her hollow lute† –
Tumultuous, – and, in chords that tenderest be,
290   He play'd an ancient ditty, long since mute,
In Provence call'd, 'La belle dame sans mercy:'†
Close to her ear touching the melody; –
Wherewith disturb'd, she utter'd a soft moan:
He ceased – she panted quick – and suddenly

---

azure sky-blue: fig. serene
argosy large merchant vessel
lute renaissance guitar-like instrument

La belle dame sans mercy the beautiful woman
without compassion

295   Her blue affrayed* eyes wide open shone: assaulted
       Upon his knees he sank, pale as smooth-sculptured stone.

XXXIV

       Her eyes were open, but she still beheld,
       Now wide awake, the vision of her sleep:
       There was a painful change, that nigh expell'd
300   The blisses of her dream so pure and deep
       At which fair Madeline began to weep,
       And moan forth witless words with many a sigh;
       While still her gaze on Porphyro would keep;
       Who knelt, with joined hands and piteous eye,
305   Fearing to move or speak, she look'd so dreamingly.

XXXV

       'Ah, Porphyro!' said she, 'but even now
       'Thy voice was at sweet tremble in mine ear,
       'Made tuneable with every sweetest vow;
       'And those sad eyes were spiritual and clear:
310   'How chang'd thou art! how pallid, chill, and drear!
       'Give me that voice again, my Porphyro,
       'Those looks immortal, those complainings dear!
       'Oh leave me not in this eternal woe,
       'For if thou diest, my Love, I know not where to go.'

XXXVI

315   Beyond a mortal man impassion'd far
       At these voluptuous* accents, he arose,   sensuous
       Ethereal,† flush'd, and like a throbbing star
       Seen mid the sapphire heaven's deep repose;
       Into her dream he melted, as the rose
320   Blendeth its odour with the violet, –
       Solution sweet: meantime the frost-wind blows
       Like Love's alarum pattering the sharp sleet
       Against the window-panes; St Agnes' moon hath set.

XXXVII

       'Tis dark: quick pattereth the flaw*-blown sleet: squall
325   'This is no dream, my bride, my Madeline!'
       'Tis dark: the iced gusts still rave and beat:
       'No dream, alas! alas! and woe is mine!
       'Porphyro will leave me here to fade and pine. –

ethereal light, airy

'Cruel! what traitor could thee hither bring?
330　'I curse not, for my heart is lost in thine,
'Though thou forsakest a deceived thing; –
'A dove forlorn and lost with sick unpruned wing.'

XXXVIII

'My Madeline! sweet dreamer! lovely bride!
'Say, may I be for aye thy vassal blest?
335　'Thy beauty's shield, heart-shap'd and vermeil[†] dyed?
'Ah, silver shrine, here will I take my rest
'After so many hours of toil and quest,
'A famish'd pilgrim, – sav'd by miracle.
'Though I have found, I will not rob thy nest
340　'Saving of thy sweet self; if thou think'st well
'To trust, fair Madeline, to no rude infidel.

XXXIX

'Hark!' 'tis an elfin-storm from faery land,
'Of haggard* seeming, but a boon indeed:　　　　　　wild
'Arise – arise! the morning is at hand; –
345　'The bloated wassaillers[†] will never heed: –
'Let us away, my love, with happy speed;
'There are no ears to hear, or eyes to see, –
'Drown'd all in Rhenish[†] and the sleepy mead:[†]
'Awake! arise! my love, and fearless be,
350　'For o'er the southern moors I have a home for thee.'

XL

She hurried at his words, beset with fears,
For there were sleeping dragons all around,
At glaring watch, perhaps, with ready spears –
Down the wide stairs a darkling[†] way they found. –
355　In all the house was heard no human sound.
A chain-droop'd lamp was flickering by each door;
The arras,* rich with horseman, hawk, and hound,　　　tapestry
Flutter'd in the besieging wind's uproar;
And the long carpets rose along the gusty floor.

XLI

360　They glide, like phantoms, into the wide hall;
Like phantoms, to the iron porch, they glide;

---

vermeil　vermilion, orange-red　　　　　　　　*mead*　fermented liquor of honey and water
wassailers　drunken merrymakers　　　　　　　*darkling*　in the dark
Rhenish　wine of the Rhine, hock

Where lay the Porter, in uneasy sprawl,
With a huge empty flaggon by his side:
The wakeful bloodhound rose, and shook his hide,
365   But his sagacious[†] eye an inmate owns:
By one, and one, the bolts full easy slide: –
The chains lie silent on the footworn stones; –
The key turns, and the door upon its hinges groans.

XLII

And they are gone: aye, ages long ago
370   These lovers fled away into the storm.
That night the Baron dreamt of many a woe,
And all his warrior-guests, with shade and form
Of witch, and demon, and large coffin-worm,
Were long be-nightmar'd. Angela the old
375   Died palsy-twitch'd, with meagre face deform;
The Beadsman,[†] after thousand aves[†] told,
For aye unsought for slept among his ashes cold.

1819   1820

LA BELLE DAME SANS MERCI[†]

A Ballad

O what can ail thee Knight at arms,
    Alone and palely loitering?
The sedge* has withered from the Lake   marsh-grass
    And no birds sing!

5   O what can ail thee Knight at arms,
    So haggard, and so woe-begone?
The squirrel's granary is full
    And the harvest 's done.

I see a lily on thy brow,
10   With anguish moist and fever dew,

---

sagacious   discerning, acute-minded
Beadsman   pensioner bound to pray for
    benefactor, almsman
aves   Ave Marias, devotional recitations

La Belle Dame Sans Merci   the beautiful
woman without compassion: it was first
written in a letter to George and Georgiana
Keats (1819)

And on thy cheek a fading rose
Fast withereth too —

I met a Lady in the Meads
Full beautiful, a faery's child;
15 Her hair was long, her foot was light,
And her eyes were wild —

I made a garland for her head,
And bracelets too, and fragrant Zone;†
She look'd at me as she did love
20 And made sweet moan —

I set her on my pacing steed,
And nothing else saw all day long;
For sidelong would she bend and sing
A faery's song —

25 She found me roots of relish sweet,
And honey wild, and manna† dew;
And sure in language strange she said
I love thee true —

She took me to her elfin grot,
30 And there she wept and sigh'd full sore,
And there I shut her wild wild eyes
With kisses four.

And there she lulled me asleep,
And there I dream'd, Ah Woe betide!
35 The latest dream I ever dreamt
On the cold hill side.

I saw pale Kings, and Princes too,
Pale warriors, death pale were they all;
They cried 'La belle Dame sans merci
40 Thee hath in thrall.'*   servitude

I saw their starv'd lips in the gloom*   twilight
With horrid warning gaped wide,
And I awoke, and found me here
On the cold hill's side.

Zone girdle, sash   *manna* heavenly food

45   And this is why I sojourn† here
         Alone and palely loitering;
      Though the sedge is withered from the Lake,
         And no birds sing.

ODE TO A NIGHTINGALE

1

My heart aches, and a drowsy numbness pains
   My sense, as though of hemlock I had drunk,
Or emptied some dull opiate† to the drains*   dregs
   One minute past, and Lethe†-wards had sunk:
5   'Tis not through envy of thy happy lot,
      But being too happy in thine happiness, –
         That thou, light-winged Dryad† of the trees,
            In some melodious plot
      Of beechen green, and shadows numberless,
10   Singest of summer in full-throated ease.

2

O, for a draught of vintage! that hath been
   Cool'd a long age in the deep-delved earth,
Tasting of Flora† and the country green,
   Dance, and Provençal song, and sunburnt mirth!
15 O for a beaker full of the warm South,
      Full of the true, the blushful Hippocrene,†
         With beaded bubbles winking at the brim,
            And purple-stained mouth;
      That I might drink, and leave the world unseen,
20   And with thee fade away into the forest dim:

3

Fade far away, dissolve, and quite forget
   What thou among the leaves hast never known,
The weariness, the fever, and the fret
   Here, where men sit and hear each other groan;

---

sojourn   stay temporarily
opiate   drug containing opium
Lethe   in Greek mythology, a river of Hades
   which the souls of the dead must taste in
   order to forget everything experienced while
   alive

Dryad   in classical mythology, a tree-nymph
Flora   Roman goddess of flowers
Hippocrene   fountain of the Muses on Mount
   Helicon

25 Where palsy shakes a few, sad, last gray hairs,
Where youth grows pale, and spectre-thin, and dies;
Where but to think is to be full of sorrow
And leaden-eyed despairs,
Where Beauty cannot keep her lustrous eyes,
30 Or new Love pine at them beyond to-morrow.

4

Away! away! for I will fly to thee,
Not charioted by Bacchus† and his pards,*   leopards
But on the viewless wings of Poesy,
Though the dull brain perplexes and retards:
35 Already with thee! tender is the night,
And haply the Queen-Moon is on her throne,
Cluster'd around by all her starry Fays;*   fairies
But here there is no light,
Save what from heaven is with the breezes blown
40 Through verdurous† glooms and winding mossy ways.

5

I cannot see what flowers are at my feet,
Nor what soft incense hangs upon the boughs,
But, in embalmed darkness, guess each sweet
Wherewith the seasonable month endows
45 The grass, the thicket, and the fruit-tree wild;
White hawthorn, and the pastoral eglantine;*   sweet-briar
Fast fading violets cover'd up in leaves;
And mid-May's eldest child,
The coming musk-rose,† full of dewy wine,
50 The murmurous haunt of flies on summer eves.

6

Darkling* I listen; and, for many a time   in the dark
I have been half in love with easeful Death,
Call'd him soft names in many a mused rhyme,
To take into the air my quiet breath;
55 Now more than ever seems it rich to die,
To cease upon the midnight with no pain,
While thou art pouring forth thy soul abroad
In such an ecstasy!

Bacchus Roman god of wine   *musk-rose* rambling rose with large fragrant
verdurous green with vegetation   white flowers

60   Still wouldst thou sing, and I have ears in vain –
        To thy high requiem† become a sod.†

7

    Thou wast not born for death, immortal Bird!
    No hungry generations tread thee down;
    The voice I hear this passing night was heard
    In ancient days by emperor and clown:
65   Perhaps the self-same song that found a path
        Through the sad heart of Ruth,† when, sick for home,
           She stood in tears amid the alien corn;
              The same that oft-times hath
        Charm'd magic casements, opening on the foam
70   Of perilous seas, in faery lands forlorn.

8

    Forlorn! the very word is like a bell
    To toll me back from thee to my sole self!
    Adieu! the fancy cannot cheat so well
    As she is fam'd to do, deceiving elf.
75   Adieu! adieu! thy plaintive anthem fades
        Past the near meadows, over the still stream,
           Up the hill-side; and now 'tis buried deep
              In the next valley-glades;
        Was it a vision, or a waking dream?
80   Fled is that music: – Do I wake or sleep?

1819   1819

ODE ON A GRECIAN URN

I

    Thou still unravish'd bride of quietness,
        Thou foster-child of silence and slow time,
    Sylvan† historian, who canst thus express
        A flowery tale more sweetly than our rhyme:
5   What leaf-fring'd legend haunts about thy shape
        Of deities or mortals, or of both,

---

requiem special mass for repose of souls of
    the dead
sod earth ('dust to dust' of the Anglican Burial
    service)

Ruth Book of Ruth, Old Testament: see *Ruth*
    I. 9 and 11. 3–17
Sylvan of the woods, rural

In Tempe† or the dales of Arcady?†
What men or gods are these? What maidens loth?
What mad pursuit? What struggle to escape?
10   What pipes and timbrels?* What wild ecstasy?   tambourines

II

Heard melodies are sweet, but those unheard
Are sweeter; therefore, ye soft pipes, play on;
Not to the sensual ear, but, more endear'd,
Pipe to the spirit ditties of no tone:*   sound
15   Fair youth, beneath the trees, thou canst not leave
Thy song, nor even can those trees be bare;
Bold Lover, never, never canst thou kiss
Though winning near the goal – yet, do not grieve;
She cannot fade, though thou hast not thy bliss,
20   For ever wilt thou love, and she be fair!

III

Ah, happy, happy boughs! that cannot shed
Your leaves, nor ever bid the Spring adieu;*   farewell
And, happy melodist, unwearied,
For ever piping songs for ever new;
25   More happy love! more happy, happy love!
For ever warm and still to be enjoy'd,
For ever panting, and forever young;
All breathing human passion far above,
That leaves a heart high-sorrowful and cloyed,*   satiated
30   A burning forehead, and a parching tongue.

IV

Who are these coming to the sacrifice?
To what green altar, O mysterious priest,
Lead'st thou that heifer lowing at the skies,
And all her silken flanks with garlands dressed?
35   What little town by river or sea shore,
Or mountain-built with peaceful citadel,
Is emptied of this folk, this pious morn?
And, little town, thy streets for evermore
Will silent be; and not a soul to tell
40   Why thou art desolate, can e'er return.

Tempe   a valley in Thessaly   associated with shepherds and the worship
Arcady   mountainous district in Greece   of Pan

V

O Attic[†] shape! Fair attitude! with brede[†]
　Of marble men and maidens overwrought,
With forest branches and the trodden weed;
　Thou, silent form, dost tease us out of thought
45　As doth eternity: Cold Pastoral![†]
　　When old age shall this generation waste,
　　　Thou shalt remain, in midst of other woe
Than ours, a friend to man, to whom thou say'st,
　'Beauty is truth, truth beauty,' – that is all
50　　Ye know on earth, and all ye need to know.

1819　　　　　　　　　　　　　　　　　　　1820

ODE ON MELANCHOLY

I

No, no, go not to Lethe,[†] neither twist
　Wolf's-bane,[†] tight-rooted, for its poisonous wine;
Nor suffer thy pale forehead to be kiss'd
　By nightshade, ruby grape of Proserpine;[†]
5　Make not your rosary of yew-berries,
　　Nor let the beetle, nor the death-moth[†] be
　　　Your mournful Psyche,[†] nor the downy owl
A partner in your sorrow's mysteries;
　For shade to shade will come too drowsily,
10　　And drown the wakeful anguish of the soul.

II

But when the melancholy fit shall fall
　Sudden from heaven like a weeping cloud,
That fosters the droop-headed flowers all,
　And hides the green hill in an April shroud;
15　Then glut thy sorrow on a morning rose,

Attic　of Attica, the region around Athens and centre of Greek culture
brede　braid, embroidery
Cold Pastoral　sculptured pastoral scene
Lethe　in Greek mythology, a river of Hades which the souls of the dead must taste in order to forget everything experienced while alive

wolf's bane　poisonous plant named monk's hood or aconite
Proserpine　wife of Pluto and goddess of the underworld
death-moth　death's head moth
Psyche　the soul itself

Or on the rainbow of the salt sand-wave,
Or on the wealth of globed peonies;
Or if thy mistress some rich anger shows,
Emprison her soft hand, and let her rave,
20   And feed deep, deep upon her peerless eyes.

III

She dwells with Beauty — Beauty that must die;
And Joy, whose hand is ever at his lips
Bidding adieu; and aching Pleasure nigh,
Turning to Poison while the bee-mouth sips:
25 Ay, in the very temple of delight
Veil'd Melancholy had her sovran shrine,
Though seen of none save him whose strenuous tongue
Can burst Joy's grape against his palate fine;
His soul shall taste the sadness of her might,
30   And be among her cloudy trophies hung.

1819   1820

TO AUTUMN

I

Season of mists and mellow fruitfulness,
Close bosom-friend of the maturing sun;
Conspiring with him how to load and bless
With fruit the vines that round the thatch-eves run;
5 To bend with apples the moss'd cottage-trees,
And fill all fruit with ripeness to the core;
To swell the gourd, and plump the hazel shells
With a sweet kernel; to set budding more,
And still more, later flowers for the bees,
10 Until they think warm days will never cease,
For Summer has o'er-brimm'd their clammy cells.

II

Who hath not seen thee oft amid thy store?
Sometimes whoever seeks abroad may find
Thee sitting careless on a granary floor,
15   Thy hair soft-lifted by the winnowing wind;
Or on a half-reap'd furrow sound asleep,

Drows'd with the fume of poppies, while thy hook
Spares the next swath[†] and all its twined flowers:
And sometimes like a gleaner thou dost keep
20   Steady thy laden head across a brook;
Or by a cyder-press, with patient look,
Thou watchest the last oozings hours by hours.

III

Where are the songs of Spring? Ay, where are they?
Think not of them, thou hast thy music too, –
25   While barred clouds bloom the soft-dying day,
And touch the stubble-plains with rosy hue;
Then in a wailful choir the small gnats mourn
Among the river sallows,[†] borne aloft
Or sinking as the light wind lives or dies;
30   And full-grown lambs loud bleat from hilly bourn;[†]
Hedge-crickets sing; and now with treble soft
The red-breast whistles from a garden-croft;
And gathering swallows twitter in the skies.

1819   1820

From LETTER TO BENJAMIN BAILEY, 22 November, 1817

I am certain of nothing but of the holiness of the Heart's affections and
the truth of Imagination – What the Imagination seizes as Beauty must
be truth – whether it existed before or not – for I have the same Idea of
all our Passions as of Love they are all in their sublime, creative of
5   essential Beauty. In a Word, you may know my favourite Speculation
by my first Book and the little song I sent in my last – which is a
representation from the fancy of the probable mode of operating in
these Matters. The Imagination may be compared to Adam's dream –
he awoke and found it truth. I am the more zealous[†] in this affair,
10   because I have never yet been able to perceive how any thing can be
known for truth by consequitive reasoning – and yet it must be. Can it
be that even the greatest Philosopher ever arrived at his goal without

---

swath lit. a ridge of grass or corn lying after
   being cut
sallows low-growing willow trees

bourn small stream
zealous earnest

putting aside numerous objections. However it may be, O for a Life of Sensations rather than of Thoughts! It is 'a Vision in the form of Youth'

15 a Shadow of reality to come – and this consideration has further convinced me for it has come as auxiliary to another favourite Speculation of mine, that we shall enjoy ourselves here after by having what we called happiness on Earth repeated in a finer tone and so repeated. And yet such a fate can only befall those who delight in

20 Sensation rather than hunger as you do after Truth. Adam's dream will do here and seems to be a conviction that Imagination and its empyreal† reflection is the same as human Life and its Spiritual repetition. But as I was saying – the simple imaginative Mind may have its rewards in the repetition of its own silent Workings coming continually on the

25 Spirit with a fine Suddenness – to compare great things with small – have you never by being Surprised with an old Melody – in a delicious place – by a delicious voice, felt over again your very Speculation and Surmises at the time it first operated on your soul – do you not remember forming to yourself the singer's face more beautiful than it was possible

30 and yet with the elevation of the moment you do not think so – even then you were mounted on the Wings of Imagination so high – that the Prototype must be here after – that delicious face you will see. What a time! I am continually running away from the subject – sure this cannot be exactly the case with a complex Mind – one that is imaginative and

35 at the same time careful of its fruits – who would exist partly on Sensation partly on thought – to whom it is necessary that years should bring the philosophic Mind – such an one I consider your's and therefore it is necessary to your eternal Happiness that you should not only drink this old Wine of Heaven, which I shall call the redigestion of our most

40 ethereal† Musings on Earth; but also increase in knowledge and know all things. I am glad to hear you are in a fair way for Easter – you will soon get through your unpleasant reading and then! – but the world is full of troubles and I have not much reason to think myself pestered with many – I think Jane or Marianne has a better opinion of me than

45 I deserve – for really and truly I do not think my Brother's illness connected with mine – you know more of the real Cause then they do nor have I any chance of being rack'd as you have been – You perhaps at one time thought there was such a thing as Worldly Happiness to be arrived at, at certain periods of time marked out – you have of necessity

50 from your disposition been thus led away – I scarcely remember counting upon any Happiness – I look not for it if it be not in the present hour – nothing startles me beyond the Moment. The setting Sun will always set me to rights – or if a Sparrow come before my Window I take part in its existence and pick about the Gravel. The first thing that strikes

---

empyreal   visible heavenly   *ethereal*   heavenly

55 me on hearing a Misfortune having befallen another is this. 'Well it
    cannot be helped – he will have the pleasure of trying the resources of
    his spirit' – and I beg now my dear Bailey that hereafter should you
    observe any thing cold in me not to put it to the account of heartlessness
    but abstraction – for I assure you I sometimes feel not the influence of
60 a Passion or affection during the whole week – and so long this
    sometimes continues I begin to suspect myself and the genuineness of
    my feelings at other times – thinking them a few barren Tragedy-tears –
    My Brother Tom is much improved – he is going to Devonshire –
    whither I shall follow him. . . .

From LETTER TO GEORGE AND TOM KEATS, 21 December, 1817

    I dined with Haydon† the Sunday after you left, and had a very pleasant
    day, I dined too (for I have been out too much lately) with Horace
    Smith, and met his two Brothers, with Hill and Kingston, and one Du
    Bois. They only served to convince me, how superior humour is to wit
5   in respect to enjoyment – These men say things which make one start,
    without making one feel; they are all alike; they all know fashionables;
    they have a mannerism in their very eating and drinking, in their mere
    handling a Decanter – They talked of Kean† and his low company –
    Would I were with that Company instead of yours, said I to myself! I
10 know such like acquaintance will never do for me, and yet I am going
    to Reynolds on Wednesday. Brown and Dilke walked with me and
    back from the Christmas pantomime. I had not a dispute but a
    disquisition,† with Dilke on various subjects; several things dovetailed
    in my mind, and at once it struck me what quality went to form a
15 Man of Achievement, especially in Literature, and which Shakespeare
    possessed so enormously – I mean *Negative Capability*, that is, when a
    man is capable of being in uncertainties, mysteries, doubts, without any
    irritable searching after fact and reason – Coleridge, for instance, would
    let go by a fine isolated verisimilitude† caught from the Penetralium† of
20 mystery, from being incapable of remaining content with half-
    knowledge. This pursued through volumes would perhaps take us no
    further than this, that with a great poet the sense of Beauty overcomes
    every other consideration, or rather obliterates all consideration . . .

Haydon Benjamin Haydon (1786–1846) artist   *disquisition* long discourse
    and friend of Keats   *verisimilitude* semblance of truth
Kean Edmund Kean (1787/90–1833) actor   *Penetralium* innermost sanctuary

From A LETTER TO FANNY BRAWNE, 25 July, 1819

25

You cannot conceive how I ache to be with you, how I would die for one hour for what is in the world? I say you cannot conceive it is impossible you should look with such eyes upon me as I have upon you; it cannot be. Forgive me if I wander a little this evening, for I have
5   been all day employed in a very abstract poem, and I am in deep love with you, two things which must excuse me. I have, believe me, not been an age in letting you take possession of me. The very first week I knew you I wrote myself your vassal,[†] but burnt the letter, as the very next time I saw you I thought you manifested some dislike to me. If
10   you should ever feel for man at the first sight what I did for you, I am lost. Yet I should not quarrel with you, but hate myself if such a thing were to happen only I should burst if the thing were not as fine a man as you are as a woman.

Perhaps I am too vehement.[†] Then fancy me on my knees especially
15   when I mention a part of your letter which hurt me. You say, speaking of Mr Severn,[†] 'but you must be satisfied in knowing that I admired you much more than your friend'. My dear love, I cannot believe there ever was or ever could be anything to admire in me, especially as far as sight goes. I cannot be admired; I am not a thing to be admired. You
20   are, I love you; all I can bring you is a swooning admiration of your beauty. I hold that place among men that snub-nosed brunettes with meeting eyebrows do among women they are trash to me unless I find one among them with a fire in her heart like the one that burns in mine. You absorb me in spite of myself, you alone, for I look not forward
25   with any pleasure to what is called being settled in the world. I tremble at domestic cares, yet for you I would meet them, though if it would leave you the happier I would rather die than do so.

I have two luxuries to brood over in my walks, your loveliness and the hour of my death. O that I could have possession of them both in
30   the same minute. I hate the world: it batters too much the wings of my self-will, and would I could take a sweet poison from your lips to send me out of it. From no others would I take it. I am indeed astonished to find myself so careless of all charms but yours, remembering as I do the time when even a bit of ribband was a matter of interest with me.
35   What softer words can I find for you after this? What it is I will not read. Nor will I say more here, but in a postscript answer anything else you may have mentioned in your letter in so many words, for I am

vassal servant, slave
vehement passionate, impetuous

Severn Joseph Severn (1793–1879) painter
and devoted friend of Keats

distracted with a thousand thoughts. I will imagine you Venus tonight and pray, pray, pray to your star like a heathen.

Thomas Carlyle
1795–1881

The Carlyle family belonged to a dissenting branch of the Presbyterian Church. Born at Ecclefechan, Thomas went to school at Dunnan Academy, and then to the University of Edinburgh. He became devoted to the study of German literature, wrote a biography of Schiller (1825), and published translations of Goethe's *Wilhelm Meister's Apprenticeship* (1824) and *Wilhelm Meister's Travels* (1827).

He married Jane Welsh in 1826 and soon moved from Edinburgh to the more isolated Craigenputtock. Socially and politically, he became an articulate critic of Utilitarianism, which was made clear in *Sartor Resartus* (1883–4). In 1834 the Carlyles moved to Cheyne Walk in London: his *History of the French Revolution* appeared in 1837, but not before the manuscript of the first volume, on loan to J. S. Mill, had been used to light a fire. Carlyle published *Chartism* (1839), and gave a popular series of lectures during 1840, *Heroes, Hero-Worship and the Heroic in History*, which were published in 1841. He earned for himself the soubriquet 'sage of Chelsea'. In *Past and Present* (1843), he attacked the political philosophy of 'laissez-faire'.

He exposed increasingly his anti-democratic views, as in *Occasional Discourse on the Nigger Question* (1849) and *Latter-day Pamphlets* (1850). He was an admirer of strong rulers such as Oliver Cromwell and, having spent fourteen years preparing his biography of Frederick the Great of Prussia, published it over the years 1858–65. Prior to the appearance of this great work, he had written a tribute to his old friend John Sterling, his *Life of Sterling* (1851).

The University of Edinburgh elected him Lord Rector in 1865, and the following year his wife died. Her death left him a man broken in spirit and he wrote little thereafter. He was awarded the Prussian Order of Merit in 1874.

Carlyle's literary style is strong and vigorous; and by the 1850s similar writing was described as 'Carlylese'. It is exclamatory, full of apostrophes, italics and archaisms: it often has the rhetoric of a politician's hectoring speech. He coined words from German, such as *maelstrom*, and naturalised words such as *backwoodsman*. He stood high in his contemporaries' esteem as social prophet and critic, although he did not please everyone: Trollope caricatured him in *The Warden* (1855) as Dr Pessimist Anticant.

Carlyle's friend, the historian J. A. Froude, published Carlyle's *Reminiscences* (1881) and a frank and forthright biography in four volumes (1882–4): there is much in it (against the custom of Victorian England) to suggest discord in his married relationship with Jane, and his own sexual inadequacy.

From NOTEBOOKS

Charles Lamb at 56

Charles Lamb I sincerely believe to be in some considerable degree *insane*. A more pitiful, ricketty, gasping, staggering, stammering Tom fool I do not know. He is witty by denying truisms, and abjuring good manners. His speech wriggles hither and thither with an incessant
5   painful fluctuation; not an opinion in it or a fact or even a phrase that you can thank him for: more like a convulsion fit than natural systole[†] and diastole.[†] – Beside he is now a confirmed shameless drunkard: *asks* vehemently[†] for gin-and-water in strangers' houses; tipples until he is utterly mad, and is only not thrown out of doors because he is too
10 much despised for taking such trouble with him. Poor Lamb! Poor England where such a despicable abortion is named genius! – He said: There are just two things I regret in English History; first that Guy Faux's plot did not take effect (there would have been so glorious an *explosion*); second that the Royalists did not hang Milton (then we
15 might have laughed at them); etc., etc.

2 November 1831

---

systole contraction of heart alternate with diastole

diastole dilation of heart alternate with systole
vehemently passionately, forcibly

From THE LIFE OF JOHN STERLING
Samuel Taylor Coleridge at 53

Nothing could be more copious than his talk; and furthermore it was always, virtually or literally, of the nature of a monologue; suffering no interruption, however reverent; hastily putting aside all foreign additions, annotations, or most ingenuous[†] desire for elucidation,[†] as
5   well-meant superfluities which would never do. Besides, it was talk not flowing anywhither like a river, but spreading everywhither in inextricable currents and regurgitations like a lake or sea; terribly deficient in definite goal or aim, nay often in logical intelligibility; *what* you were to believe or do, on any earthly or heavenly thing, obstinately
10   refusing to appear from it. So that, most times, you felt logically lost; swamped near to drowning in this tide of ingenious vocables, spreading out boundless as if to submerge the world.

To sit as a passive bucket and be pumped into, whether you consent or not, can in the long-run be exhilarating to no creature; how eloquent
15   soever the flood of utterance that is descending. But if it be withal a confused unintelligible flood of utterance, threatening to submerge all known landmarks of thought, and drown the world and you! – I have heard Coleridge talk, with eager musical energy, two stricken hours, his face radiant and moist, and communicate no meaning whatsoever
20   to any individual of his hearers, – certain of whom, I for one, still kept eagerly listening in hope; the most had long before given up, and formed (if the rooms were large enough) secondary humming groups of their own. He began anywhere: you put some question to him, made some suggestive observation: instead of answering this, or decidedly setting
25   out towards answer of it, he would accumulate formidable apparatus, logical swim-bladders, transcendental life-preservers and other precautionary and vehiculatory gear, for setting out; perhaps did at last get under way, – but was swiftly solicited, turned aside by the glance of some radiant new game on this hand or that, into new courses; and
30   ever into new; and before long into all the Universe, where it was uncertain what game you would catch, or whether any.

His talk, alas, was distinguished, like himself, by irresolution: it disliked to be troubled with conditions, abstinences, definite fulfilments; – loved to wander at its own sweet will, and make its
35   auditor and his claims and humble wishes a mere passive bucket for itself! He had knowledge about many things and topics, much curious reading; but generally all topics led him, after a pass or two, into the

---

ingenuous   frank   *elucidation*   clarification

high seas of theosophic† philosophy, the hazy infinitude of Kantean
transcendentalism,† with its 'sum-m-mjects' and 'om-m-mjects.' Sad
40 enough; for with such indolent impatience of the claims and ignorances
of others, he had not the least talent for explaining this or anything
unknown to them; and you swam and fluttered in the mistiest wide
unintelligible deluge of things, for most part in a rather profitless
uncomfortable manner.

1851

From THE FRENCH REVOLUTION, III, Book 2, Chapter 7

[The Fate of Louis XVI]

Consider therefore if, on this Wednesday morning, there is an
affluence† of Patriotism; if Paris stands a-tiptoe, and all Deputies are at
their post! Seven-hundred and Forty-nine honourable Deputies; only
some twenty absent on mission, Duchâtel and some seven others absent
5 by sickness. Meanwhile expectant Patriotism and Paris standing a-tiptoe
have need of patience. For this Wednesday again passes in debate and
effervescence; Girondins proposing that a 'majority of three-fourths'
shall be required; Patriots fiercely resisting them. Danton,† who has
just got back from mission in the Netherlands, does obtain 'order of
10 the day' on this Girondin proposal; nay he obtains farther that we
decide *sans désemparer*,† in Permanent-session, till we have done.

And so, finally, at eight in the evening this Third stupendous Voting,
by roll-call or *appel nominal*, does begin. What Punishment? Girondins
undecided, Patriots decided, men afraid of Royalty, men afraid of
15 Anarchy, must answer here and now. Infinite Patriotism, dusky in the
lamp-light, floods all corridors, crowds all galleries; sternly waiting to
hear. Shrill-sounding Ushers summon you by Name and Department;
you must rise to the Tribune, and say.

Eye-witnesses have represented this scene of the Third Voting, and

---

theosophic professing to attain to a knowledge
of God by spiritual ecstasy
Kantean transcendentalism philosophy not
realisable in experience. Immanuel Kant
(1724–1804) German philosopher
affluence free flow
Danton Georges Jacques Danton was the most

colourful and eloquent revolutionary leader.
He opposed the Girondins but voted for the
death of Louis XVI after returning from the
Netherlands, which had been taken by the
French Army
sans désemparer without intermission

20   of the votings that grew out of it, – a scene protracted, like to be endless,
     lasting, with few brief intervals, from Wednesday till Sunday morning, –
     as one of the strangest seen in the Revolution. Long night wears itself
     into day, morning's paleness is spread over all faces; and again the
     wintry shadows sink, and the dim lamps are lit: but through day and
25   night and the vicissitudes of hours, Member after Member is mounting
     continually those Tribune-steps; pausing aloft there, in the clearer upper
     light, to speak his Fate-word; then diving down into the dusk and
     throng again. Like Phantoms in the hour of midnight; most spectral,
     pandemonial!† Never did President Vergniaud, or any terrestrial Presi-
30   dent, superintend the like. A King's Life, and so much else that depends
     thereon, hangs trembling in the balance. Man after man mounts; the
     buzz hushes itself till he have spoken: Death; Banishment; Imprisonment
     till the Peace. Many say, Death; with what cautious well-studied phrases
     and paragraphs they could devise, of explanation, of enforcement, of
35   faint recommendation to mercy. Many too say, Banishment; something
     short of Death. The balance trembles, none can yet guess whitherward.
     Whereat anxious Patriotism bellows; irrepressible by Ushers.
        The poor Girondins, many of them, under such fierce bellowing of
     Patriotism, say Death; justifying, *motivant*, that most miserable word
40   of theirs by some brief casuistry† and jesuitry.† Vergniaud himself says,
     Death; justifying by jesuitry. Rich Lepelletier Saint-Fargeau had been
     of the Noblesse, and then of the Patriot Left Side, in the Constituent;
     and had argued and reported, there and elsewhere, not a little, *against*
     Capital Punishment: nevertheless he now says, Death; a word which
45   may cost him dear. Manuel did surely rank with the Decided in August
     last; but he had been sinking and backsliding ever since September and
     the scenes of September. In this Convention, above all, no word he
     could speak would find favour; he says now, Banishment; and in mute
     wrath quits the place forever, – much hustled in the corridors. Philippe
50   Egalité† votes, in his soul and conscience, Death: at the sound of which
     and of whom, even Patriotism shakes its head; and there runs a groan
     and shudder through this Hall of Doom. Robespierre's vote cannot be
     doubtful; his speech is long. Men see the figure of shrill Sieyes ascend;
     hardly pausing, passing merely, this figure says, '*La Mort sans phrase*,
55   Death without phrases;' and fares onward and downward. Most
     spectral, pandemonial!
        And yet if the Reader fancy it of a funereal, sorrowful or even grave
     character, he is far mistaken: 'the Ushers in the Mountain quarter,' says

---

pandemonial   similar to the place where
   demons live: a state of confusion
casuistry   quibbling: argument in detail
jesuitry   (in the pejorative sense of)
   dissembling: argument as given by a Jesuit

Philippe Egalité   Philippe, Duc D'Orléans, an
   enemy of the king, who identified himself
   with the Revolution by adopting the name
   'Egalité'. Carlyle regarded him as a
   treacherous intriguer

Mercier, 'had become as Box-keepers at the Opera;' opening and
60   shutting of Galleries for privileged persons, for 'D'Orléans Egalité's
mistresses,' or other high-dizened[†] women of condition, rustling with
laces and tricolor. Gallant Deputies pass and repass thitherward, treating
them with ices, refreshments and small-talk; the high-dizened heads
beck responsive; some have their card and pin, pricking down the Ayes
65   and Noes, as at a game of *Rouge-et-Noir*.[†] Farther aloft reigns Mère
Duchesse[†] with her unrouged Amazons; she cannot be prevented making
long *Hahas*, when the vote is not *La Mort*. In these Galleries there is
refection, drinking of wine and brandy 'as in open tavern, *en pleine
tabagie*.' Betting goes on in all coffee-houses of the neighbourhood. But
70   within doors, fatigue, impatience, uttermost weariness sits now on all
visages; lighted up only from time to time by turns of the game.
Members have fallen asleep; Ushers come and awaken them to vote:
other Members calculate whether they shall not have time to run and
dine. Figures rise, like phantoms, pale in the dusky lamp-light; utter
75   from this Tribune, only one word: Death. '*Tout est optique*,' says
Mercier, 'The world is all an optical shadow.' Deep in the Thursday
night, when the Voting is done, and Secretaries are summing it up, sick
Duchâtel, more spectral than another, comes borne on a chair, wrapt
in blankets, in 'nightgown and nightcap,' to vote for Mercy: one vote
80   it is thought may turn the scale.

Ah no! In profoundest silence, President Vergniaud, with a voice full
of sorrow, has to say: 'I declare, in the name of the Convention, that
the punishment it pronounces on Louis Capet is that of Death.' Death
by a small majority of Fifty-three. Nay, if we deduct from the one side,
85   and add to the other, a certain Twenty-six, who said Death but coupled
some faintest ineffectual surmise of mercy with it, the majority will be
but *One*.

Death is the sentence: but its execution? It is not executed yet!
Scarcely is the vote declared when Louis's Three Advocates enter; with
90   Protest in his name, with demand for Delay, for Appeal to the People.
For this do Desèze and Tronchet plead, with brief eloquence: brave old
Malesherbes pleads for it with eloquent want of eloquence, in broken
sentences, in embarrassment and sobs; that brave time-honoured face,
with its gray strength, its broad sagacity and honesty, is mastered with
95   emotion, melts into dumb tears. – They reject the Appeal to the People;
that having been already settled. But as to the Delay, what they call
Sursis, it *shall* be considered; shall be voted for tomorrow: at present

---

dizened   arrayed, decked out, with finery
Rouge-et-Noir   card-game played on a table
    with red and black marks on which money
    staked is laid

Mère Duchesse   a famous mob-orator
    representative of the women in the
    revolutionary crowd

we adjourn. Whereupon Patriotism 'hisses' from the Mountain: but a 'tyrannical majority' has so decided, and adjourns.

100 There is still this *fourth* Vote, then, growls indignant Patriotism: – this vote, and who knows what other votes, and adjournments of voting; and the whole matter still hovering hypothetical! And at every new vote those Jesuit Girondins, even they who voted for Death, would so fain find a loophole! Patriotism must watch and rage. Tyrannical

105 adjournments there have been; one, and now another at midnight on plea of fatigue, – all Friday wasted in hesitation and higgling; in re-counting of the votes, which are found correct as they stood! Patriotism bays fiercer than ever; Patriotism, by long watching, has become red-eyed, almost rabid.

110 'Delay: yes or no?' men do vote it finally, all Saturday, all day and night. Men's nerves are worn out, men's hearts are desperate; now it shall end. Vergniaud, spite of the baying, ventures to say Yes, Delay; though he had voted Death. Philippe Egalité says, in his soul and conscience, No. The next Member mounting: 'Since Philippe says No,

115 I for my part say Yes, *moi je dis Oui.*' The balance still trembles. Till finally, at three o'clock on Sunday morning, we have: *No Delay*, by a majority of Seventy; *Death within four-and-twenty hours!*

Garat, Minister of Justice, has to go to the Temple with this stern message: he ejaculates repeatedly, '*Quelle commission affreuse*, What

120 a frightful function!' Louis begs for a Confessor;[†] for yet three days of life, to prepare himself to die. The Confessor is granted; the three days and all respite are refused.

There is no deliverance, then? Thick stone walls answer, None. Has King Louis no friends? Men of action, of courage grown desperate, in

125 this his extreme need? King Louis's friends are feeble and far. Not even a voice in the coffee-houses rises for him. At Méot the Restaurateur's no Captain Dampmartin[†] now dines: or sees death-doing whiskeran-does[†] on furlough[†] exhibit daggers of improved structure. Méot's gallant Royalists on furlough are far across the marches; they are wandering

130 distracted over the world: or their bones lie whitening Argonne Wood.[†] Only some weak Priests, leave Pamphlets on all the bourne-stones, this night, calling for a rescue: calling for the pious women to rise; or are taken disturbing Pamphlets, and sent to prison.

Nay there is one death-doer, of the ancient Méot sort, who, with

135 effort, has done even less and worse: slain a Deputy, and set all the

---

Confessor priest who hears confession
Dampmartin a Royalist officer who wrote a book about events which he witnessed in the Revolution
whiskerandoes moustachioed, bearded

desperadoes
furlough leave
Argonne Wood Prussian army was defeated in the Battle of Valmy in the Argonne forest, September 1792

Patriotism of Paris on edge! It was five on Saturday evening when
Lepelletier Saint-Fargeau, having given his vote, *No Delay*, ran over to
Février's in the Palais Royal to snatch a morsel of dinner. He had dined,
and was paying. A thickset man 'with black hair and blue beard,' in a
140   loose kind of frock, stept up to him; it was, as Février and the bystanders
bethought them, one Pâris of the old King's-Guard. 'Are you Lepelletier?'
asks he. – 'Yes.' – 'You voted in the King's Business – ?' – 'I voted
Death.' – '*Scélérat*,† take that!' cries Pâris, flashing out a sabre from
under his frock, and plunging it deep in Lepelletier's side. Février
145   clutches him; but he breaks off; is gone.
    The voter Lepelletier lies dead; he has expired in great pain, at one
in the morning; – two hours before that Vote of *No Delay* was fully
summed up. Guardsman Pâris is flying over France; cannot be taken;
will be found some months after, self-shot in a remote inn. – Robespierre
150   sees reason to think that Prince d'Artois himself is privately in Town;
that the Convention will be butchered in the lump. Patriotism sounds
mere wail and vengeance: Santerre doubles and trebles all his patrols.
Pity is lost in rage and fear; the Convention has refused the three days
of life and all respite.

1834–7   1837

From PAST AND PRESENT Book 3, Chapter 2

Gospel of Mammonism†

Reader, even Christian Reader as thy title goes, hast thou any notion
of Heaven and Hell? I rather apprehend, not. Often as the words are
on our tongue, they have got a fabulous or semi-fabulous character for
most of us, and pass on like a kind of transient similitude,† like a sound
5   signifying little.
    Yet it is well worth while for us to know, once and always, that they
are not a similitude, nor a fable nor semi-fable; that they are an
everlasting highest fact! 'No Lake of Sicilian or other sulphur burns
now anywhere in these ages,' sayest thou? Well, and if there did not!
10   Believe that there does not; believe it if thou wilt, nay hold it by as a
real increase, a rise to higher stages, to wider horizons and empires. All

---

Scélérat   villain   *transient similitude*   passing likeness
Mammonism   idolisation of wealth

this has vanished, or has not vanished; believe as thou wilt as to all this. But that an Infinite of Practical Importance, speaking with strict arithmetical exactness, an *Infinite*, had vanished or can vanish from the
15   Life of any Man: this thou shalt not believe! O brother, the Infinite of Terror, of Hope, of Pity, did it not at any moment disclose itself to thee, indubitable, unnameable? Came it never, like the gleam of *preter*natural† eternal Oceans, like the voice of old Eternities, far-sounding through thy heart of hearts? Never? Alas, it was not thy
20   Liberalism, then; it was thy Animalism! The Infinite is more sure than any other fact. But only men can discern it; mere building beavers, spinning arachnes,† much more the predatory vulturous and vulpine† species, do not discern it well! –

'The word Hell,' says Sauerteig,† 'is still frequently in use among the
25   English people: but I could not without difficulty ascertain what they meant by it. Hell generally signifies the Infinite Terror, the thing a man *is* infinitely afraid of, and shudders and shrinks from, struggling with his whole soul to escape from it. There is a Hell therefore, if you will consider, which accompanies man, in all stages of his history, and
30   religious or other development: but the hells of men and Peoples differ notably. With Christians it is the infinite terror of being found guilty before the Just Judge. With old Romans, I conjecture, it was the terror not of Pluto,† for whom probably they cared little, but of doing unworthily, doing unvirtuously, which was their word for un*man*fully.
35   And now what is it, if you pierce through his Cants, his oft-repeated Hearsays, what he calls his Worships and so forth, – what is it that the modern English soul does, in very truth, dread infinitely, and contemplates with entire despair? What *is* his Hell, after all these reputable, oft-repeated Hearsays, what is it? With hesitation, with
40   astonishment, I pronounce it to me: The terror of "Not succeeding;" of not making money, fame, or some other figure in the world, – chiefly of not making money! Is not that a somewhat singular Hell?'

Yes, O Sauerteig, it is very singular. If we do not 'succeed,' where is the use of us? We had better never have been born. 'Tremble intensely,'
45   as our friend the Emperor of China says: *there* is the black Bottomless of Terror; what Sauerteig calls the 'Hell of the English'! – But indeed this Hell belongs naturally to the Gospel of Mammonism, which also has its corresponding Heaven. For there is one Reality among so many Phantasms; about one thing we are entirely in earnest: The making of
50   money. Working Mammonism does divide the world with idle game-

---

preternatural   outside the ordinary course of
   nature
arachnes   spiders
vulpine   fox-like, crafty
Sauerteig   a Carlylean character, 'a sardonic

German writer', whose fictitious history of
England, and various philosophies, provide
the basis for much of Carlyle's comment
Pluto   Roman mythological ruler of the
underworld

preserving Dilettantism,[†] – thank Heaven that there is even a Mammonism, *anything* we are in earnest about! Idleness is worst. Idleness alone
is without hope: work earnestly at anything, you will by degrees learn
to work at almost all things. There is endless hope in work, were it
55 even work at making money.

True, it must be owned, we for the present, with our Mammon-
Gospel, have come to strange conclusions. We call it a Society; and go
about professing openly the totalest separation, isolation. Our life is
not a mutual helpfulness; but rather, cloaked under due laws-of-war,
60 named 'fair competition' and so forth, it is a mutual hostility. We have
profoundly forgotten everywhere that *Cash-payment* is not the sole
relation of human beings; we think nothing doubting, that *it absolves*
and liquidates all engagements of man. 'My starving workers?' answers
the rich mill-owner: 'Did not I hire them fairly in the market? Did I
65 not pay them, to the last sixpence, the sum convenanted for? What
have I to do with them more?' – Verily Mammon-worship is a
melancholy creed. When Cain, for his own behoof,[†] had killed Abel,
and was questioned, 'Where is thy brother?' he too made answer, 'Am
I my brother's keeper?' Did I not pay my brother *his* wages, the thing
70 he had merited from me?

O sumptuous Merchant-Prince, illustrious game-preserving Duke, is
there no way of 'killing' thy brother but Cain's rude way! 'A good man
by the very look of him, by his very presence with us as 'a fellow
wayfarer in this Life-pilgrimage, *promises* so much:' woe to him if he
75 forget all such promises, if he never know that they were given! To a
deadened soul, seared with the brute Idolatry[†] of Sense, to whom going
to Hell is equivalent to not making money, all 'promises,' and moral
duties, that cannot be pleaded for in Courts of Requests,[†] address
themselves in vain. Money he can be ordered to pay, but nothing more.
80 I have not heard in all Past History, and expect not to hear in all Future
History, of any Society anywhere under God's Heaven supporting itself
on such Philosophy. The Universe is not made so; it is made otherwise
than so. The man or nation of men that thinks it is made so, marches
forward nothing doubting, step after step; but marches – whither we
85 know! In these last two centuries of Atheistic Government (near two
centuries now, since the blessed restoration of his Sacred Majesty, and
Defender of the Faith, Charles Second), I reckon that we have pretty
well exhausted what of 'firm earth' there was for us to march on; –
and are now, very ominously, shuddering, reeling, and let us hope
90 trying to recoil, on the cliff's edge! –

Dilettantism dabbling in affairs   *Courts of Requests* courts in which small debts
behoof advantage   were recovered
Idolatry worship of idols

For out of this that we call Atheism come so many other *isms* and falsities, each falsity with its misery at its heels! – A soul is not like wind (*spiritus*, or breath) contained within a capsule; the ALMIGHTY MAKER is not like a Clockmaker[†] that once, in old immemorial ages,
95 having *made* his Horologe[†] of a Universe, sits ever since and sees it go! Not at all. Hence comes Atheism; come, as we say, many other *isms*; and as the sum of all, comes *Valetism*,[†] the *reverse* of Heroism; sad root of all woes whatsoever. For indeed, as no man ever saw the above-said wind-element enclosed within its capsule, and finds it at bottom
100 more deniable than conceivable; so too he finds, in spite of Bridgwater Bequests,[†] your Clockmaker Almighty an entirely questionable affair, a deniable affair; – and accordingly denies it, and along with it so much else. Alas, one knows not what and how much else! For the faith in an Invisible, Unnameable Godlike, present everywhere in all that we see
105 and work and suffer, is the essence of all faith whatsoever; and that once denied, or still worse, asserted with lips only, and out of bound prayerbooks only, what other thing remains believable? That Cant[†] well-ordered is marketable Cant; that Heroism means gas-lighted Histrionism;[†] that seen with 'clear eyes' (as they call Valet-eyes), no
110 man is a Hero, or ever was a Hero, but all men are Valets and Varlets. The accursed practical quintessence of all sorts of Unbelief! For if there be now no Hero, and the Histrio himself begin to be seen into, what hope is there for the seed of Adam here below? We are the doomed everlasting prey of the Quack,[†] who, now in this guise, now in that, is
115 to filch us, to pluck and eat us, by such modes as are convenient for him. For the modes and guises I care little. The Quack once inevitable, let him come swiftly, let him pluck and eat me; – swiftly, that I may at least have done with him; for in his Quack-world I can have no wish to linger. Though he slay me, yet will I not trust in him. Though he
120 conquer nations, and have all the Flunkies of the Universe shouting at his heels, yet will I know well that *he* is an Inanity; that for him and his there is no continuance appointed, save only in Gehenna[†] and the Pool. Alas, the Atheist world, from its utmost summits of Heaven and Westminster-Hall, downwards through poor seven-feet Hats and
125 'Unveracities fallen hungry,' down to the lowest cellars and neglected hunger-dens of it, is very wretched.

Clockmaker   William Paley in *Natural Theology* (1802) had argued that the Almighty Maker was like a clockmaker: the analogy had become a cliché of rationalist theology
Horologe   clock
Valetism   a Carlylean invention: it is a state of mind governed by fashion
Bridgwater Bequests   The eighth Earl of

Bridgwater (1758–1829) bequeathed a prize for the best treatise on the 'Power, Wisdom and Goodness of God, as manifested in the Creation'
Cant   hypocritical language
Histrionism   play-acting
Quack   charlatan
Gehenna   Hell, place of burning torment

One of Dr Alison's Scotch facts[†] struck us much. A poor Irish Widow,
her husband having died in one of the Lanes of Edinburgh, went forth
with her three children, bare of all resource, to solicit help from the
130 Charitable Establishments of that City. At this Charitable Establishment
and then at that she was refused; referred from one to the other, helped
by none; – till she had exhausted them all; till her strength and heart
failed her: she sank down in typhus-fever; died, and infected her Lane
with fever, so that 'seventeen other persons' died of fever there in
135 consequence. The humane Physician asks thereupon, as with a heart
too full for speaking, Would it not have been *economy* to help this
poor Widow? She took typhus fever, and killed seventeen of you! –
Very curious. The forlorn Irish Widow applies to her fellow-creatures,
as if saying, 'Behold I am sinking, bare of help: ye must help me! I am
140 your sister, bone of your bone; one God made us: ye must help me!'
They answer, 'No, impossible; thou art no sister of ours.' But she
proves her sisterhood; her typhus-fever kills *them*: they actually were
her brothers, though denying it! Had human creature ever to go lower
for a proof?
145 For, as indeed was very natural in such case, all government of the
Poor by the Rich has long ago been given over to Supply-and-demand,
Laissez-faire[†] and suchlike, and universally declared to be 'impossible.'
'You are no sister of ours; what shadow of proof is there? Here are
our parchments, our padlocks, proving indisputably our money-safes
150 to be *ours*, and you have no business with them. Depart! It is
impossible!' – Nay, what wouldst thou thyself have us do? cry indignant
readers. Nothing, my friends, – till you have got a soul for yourselves
again. Till then all things are 'impossible.' Till then I cannot even bid
you buy, as the old Spartans would have done, two-pence worth of
155 powder and lead, and compendiously[†] shoot to death this poor Irish
Widow: even that is 'impossible' for you. Nothing is left but that she
prove her sisterhood by dying, and infecting you with typhus. Seventeen
of you lying dead will not deny such proof that she *was* flesh of your
flesh; and perhaps some of the living may lay it to heart.
160 'Impossible:' of a certain two-legged animal with feathers it is said,
if you draw a distinct chalk-circle round him, he sits imprisoned, as if
girt with the iron ring of Fate; and will die there, though within sight
of victuals, – or sit in sick misery there, and be fatted to death. The
name of this poor two-legged animal is – Goose; and they make of him,
165 when well fattened, *Pâté de foie gras*,[†] much prized by some!

1843   1843

Alison's Scotch facts   William Alison (1790–
1859) showed the disparity between
minimum social conditions in England and
Scotland in *Observations on Management of
the Poor in Scotland*, 1840

Laissez-faire   freedom of action for individuals
    in commerce
compendiously   briefly and comprehensively
Pâté de foie gras   pâté made from goose liver

Mary Shelley
1797–1851

A radical background produced Mary Shelley: she was the daughter of William Godwin and Mary Wollstonecraft. In 1814 she eloped with the married poet, Shelley, and they left England for Italy. After Harriet Shelley's suicide in 1816, they married. As a precocious nineteen-year-old she wrote *Frankenstein, or the Modern Prometheus*, published 1818, variously interpreted, but remarkable as an early and dire warning of scientific invention and development unrestrained by the checks of moral considerations; at the same time it is an extravaganza of the Gothic imagination.

In 1822 Shelley was drowned in the Bay of Spezia and Mary returned to England. Her writing continued: she published *Valperga* (1823), *The Last Man* (1826) and *Lodore* (1835). The prevailing tone of her work was Gothic and continental. Her short stories were published under the title, *The Keepsake*. She edited Shelley's poems (1830) and his essays and letters (1840). Her own views were radical and reflected the philosophy of her parents: she believed that the inequalities which people met with in society encouraged selfishness, corruption of the individual, and, inevitably, vindictiveness.

From FRANKENSTEIN, Chapter 5
[Frankenstein's Success]

It was on a dreary night of November, that I beheld the accomplishment of my toils. With an anxiety that almost amounted to agony, I collected the instruments of life around me, that I might infuse a spark of being into the lifeless thing that lay at my feet. It was already one in the morning; the rain pattered dismally against the panes, and my candle was nearly burnt out, when, by the glimmer of the half-extinguished light, I saw the dull yellow eye of the creature open; it breathed hard, and a convulsive motion agitated its limbs.

How can I describe my emotions at this catastrophe, or how delineate
the wretch whom with such infinite pains and care I had endeavoured
to form? His limbs were in proportion, and I had selected his features
as beautiful. Beautiful! – Great God! His yellow skin scarcely covered
the work of muscles and arteries beneath; his hair was of a lustrous
black, and flowing; his teeth of a pearly whiteness; but these luxuriances
only formed a more horrid contrast with his watery eyes, that seemed
almost of the same colour as the dun white sockets in which they were
set, his shrivelled complexion and straight black lips.

The different accidents of life are not so changeable as the feelings of
human nature. I had worked hard for nearly two years, for the sole
purpose of infusing life into an inanimate body. For this I had deprived
myself of rest and health. I had desired it with an ardour that far
exceeded moderation; but now that I had finished, the beauty of the
dream vanished, and breathless horror and disgust filled my heart.
Unable to endure the aspect of the being I had created, I rushed out of
the room, and continued a long time traversing my bedchamber, unable
to compose my mind to sleep. At length lassitude† succeeded to the
tumult I had before endured; and I threw myself on the bed in my
clothes, endeavouring to seek a few moments of forgetfulness. But it
was in vain: I slept, indeed, but I was disturbed by the wildest dreams.
I thought I saw Elizabeth, in the bloom of health, walking in the streets
of Ingolstadt. Delighted and surprised, I embraced her; but as I imprinted
the first kiss on her lips, they became livid with the hue of death; her
features appeared to change, and I thought that I held the corpse of my
dead mother in my arms; a shroud enveloped her form, and I saw the
grave-worms crawling in the folds of the flannel. I started from my
sleep with horror; a cold dew covered my forehead, my teeth chattered,
and every limb became convulsed: when, by the dim and yellow light
of the moon, as it forced its way through the window shutters, I beheld
the wretch – the miserable monster whom I had created. He held up
the curtain of the bed; and his eyes, if eyes they may be called, were
fixed on me. His jaws opened, and he muttered some inarticulate
sounds, while a grin wrinkled his cheeks. He might have spoken, but I
did not hear; one hand was stretched out, seemingly to detain me, but
I escaped, and rushed down stairs. I took refuge in the courtyard
belonging to the house which I inhabited; where I remained during the
rest of the night, walking up and down in the greatest agitation, listening
attentively, catching and fearing each sound as if it were to announce
the approach of the demoniacal corpse to which I had so miserably
given life.

---

lassitude tiredness

50   Oh! no mortal could support the horror of that countenance. A
mummy again endued with animation could not be so hideous as that
wretch. I had gazed on him while unfinished; he was ugly then; but
when those muscles and joints were rendered capable of motion, it
became a thing such as even Dante[†] could not have conceived.

1816–17   1818

Dante   Dante Alighieri (1265–1321) Italian   *Inferno*, the *Purgatorio*, and the *Paradiso*,
poet born in Florence. His most famous work   descriptions of Hell, Purgatory and Paradise
is the *Divina Commedia*, comprising the

Thomas Hood

1799–1845

Hood was a minor literary figure, a poet and editor of magazines, who was a friend of some of the more notable littérateurs of the time such as Lamb, Hazlitt and De Quincey. He edited the *London Magazine* (1821–3), and with J. H. Reynolds brought out *Odes and Addresses to Great People* (1825), a series of satires and parodies which met with general applause.

His reputation has not survived because his satire was not sharp enough. His best poetry is contained in *The Song of the Shirt*, and *The Plea of the Mid-Summer Fairies*: in the latter appears the famous poem 'I remember, I remember'. He was awarded a Civil List pension just before he died.

ODE: AUTUMN

I

I saw old Autumn in the misty morn
Stand shadowless like Silence, listening
To silence, for no lonely bird would sing
Into his hollow ear from woods forlorn,
5   Nor lowly hedge nor solitary thorn; —
Shaking his languid locks all dewy bright
With tangled gossamer† that fell by night,
· Pearling† his coronet of golden corn.

II

Where are the songs of Summer? — With the sun,
10   Oping* the dusky eyelids of the south,   opening
Till shade and silence waken up as one,
And Morning sings with a warm odorous mouth.
Where are the merry birds? — Away, away,
On panting wings through the inclement† skies,

---

gossamer   filmy threads of spider's web   *inclement*   severe, stormy
pearling   sprinkling with pearly drops

15   Lest owls should prey
        Undazzled at noon-day
        And tear with horny beak their lustrous eyes.

                              III
        Where are the blooms of Summer? – in the west,
        Blushing their last to the last sunny hours,
20   When the mild Eve by sudden Night is prest*   oppressed
        Like tearful Proserpine,† snatch'd from her flow'rs
            To a most gloomy breast.
        Where is the pride of Summer, – the green prime, –†
        The many, many leaves all twinkling? – Three
25   On the moss'd elm; three on the naked lime
        Trembling, – and one upon the old oak tree!
            Where is the Dryad's† immortality? –
        Gone into mournful cypress and dark yew,
        Or wearing the long gloomy Winter through
30   In the smooth holly's green eternity.

                              IV
        The squirrel gloats on his accomplish'd hoard,
        The ants have brimm'd their garners† with ripe grain,
            And honey bees have stor'd
        The sweets of Summer in their luscious cells;
35   The swallows all have wing'd across the main;
        But here the Autumn melancholy dwells,
            And sighs her tearful spells
        Amongst the sunless shadows of the plain.
            Alone, alone,
40   Upon a mossy stone,
        She sits and reckons up the dead and gone
        With the last leaves for a love-rosary,†
        Whilst all the wither'd world looks drearily,
        Like a dim picture of the drowned past
45   In the hush'd mind's mysterious far away,
        Doubtful what ghostly thing will steal the last
        Into that distance, grey upon the grey.

Proserpine   Roman equivalent of Greek   *Dryad*   the tree-nymph of classical mythology
   goddess Persephone, queen of Hades, or the   who is supposed to die when the tree dies
   infernal regions, and wife of Pluto   *garners*   granaries, stores
prime   state of perfection   *rosary*   string of beads used for counting

V

O go and sit with her, and be o'ershaded
Under the languid downfall of her hair:
50   She wears a coronal of flowers faded
Upon her forehead, and a face of care; –
There is enough of wither'd every where
To make her bower,[†] – and enough of gloom;
There is enough of sadness to invite,
55   If only for the rose that died, – whose doom
Is Beauty's, – she that with the living bloom
Of conscious cheeks most beautifies the light,
There is enough of sorrowing, and quite
Enough of bitter fruits the earth doth bear, –
60   Enough of chilly droppings for her bowl;
Enough of fear and shadowy despair,
To frame her cloudy prison for the soul!

1823

---

bower   a place closed in with foliage: an arbour

Thomas Babington Macaulay
1800–59

Lord Acton remarked of Macaulay in his maturity: 'He seems to me one of the greatest of all writers and masters, although I think him base, contemptible and odious.' Macaulay was the son of the philanthropist and social reformer, Zachary Macaulay. He was educated at Trinity College, Cambridge, and called to the bar. An essay on Milton written for the *Edinburgh Review* brought him immediate fame. Turning aside from the law and literature, he decided to pursue a political career, and was elected MP for Calne and Leeds successively: he was concerned closely in manoeuvring the Reform Bill through Parliament.

In 1834 he produced *Essays Critical and Historical*, and was appointed to the Supreme Council for India. Both the Indian law and education systems, firmly based on their British originals, owe their existence to Macaulay's Minutes on Law and Education. He returned to England in 1838, began to write a history of England since 1688, and took up politics again. In 1839 he became MP for Edinburgh. He was Secretary of War 1839–41 and Paymaster General 1846–7.

Meanwhile his literary reputation was beginning to eclipse his political one: in 1842 *Lays of Ancient Rome* had appeared and was immensely popular. Then in 1849 the first two volumes of his *History of England* were published, followed by volumes 3 and 4 in 1855. It became a best-seller of the century. Macaulay's aim was to replace the novel on the occasional tables of fashionable ladies by his *History*: he wrote it lucidly, dramatically, and with a detailed narrative power reminiscent of the novelist he most admired, Walter Scott.

The *History* brought him great wealth and a peerage on Palmerston's recommendation: Lord Melbourne, having read it, commented: 'I wish I was as cocksure of anything as Tom Macaulay is of everything.' Macaulay's dogmatic opinions couched in his sweeping narrative style influenced the historian G. M. Trevelyan, and Winston Churchill in his writing of *A History of the English-Speaking Peoples*.

From JOHN BUNYAN

[A review of The Pilgrim's Progress, *with a life of John Bunyan, by Robert Southey, London, 1831]*

The characteristic peculiarity of the Pilgrim's Progress is that it is the only work of its kind which possesses a strong human interest. Other allegories only amuse the fancy. The allegory of Bunyan has been read by many thousands with tears. There are some good allegories in
5   Johnson's[†] works, and some of still higher merit by Addison.[†] In these performances there is, perhaps, as much wit and ingenuity as in the Pilgrim's Progress. But the pleasure which is produced by the Vision of Mirza, the Vision of Theodore, the genealogy of Wit, or the contest between Rest and Labour, is exactly similar to the pleasure which we
10 derive from one of Cowley's[†] odes or from a canto of Hudibras.[†] It is a pleasure which belongs wholly to the understanding, and in which the feelings have no part whatever. Nay, even Spenser[†] himself, though assuredly one of the greatest poets that ever lived, could not succeed in the attempt to make allegory interesting. It was in vain that he lavished
15 the riches of his mind on the House of Pride and the House of Temperance.[†] One unpardonable fault, the fault of tediousness, pervades the whole of the Fairy Queen.[†] We become sick of cardinal virtues and deadly sins, and long for the society of plain men and women. Of the persons who read the first canto, not one in ten reaches the end of the
20 first book, and not one in a hundred perseveres to the end of the poem. Very few and very weary are those who are in at the death of the Blatant Beast. If the last six books, which are said to have been destroyed in Ireland, had been preserved, we doubt whether any heart less stout than that of a commentator would have held out to the end.
25   It is not so with the Pilgrim's Progress. That wonderful book, while it obtains admiration from the most fastidious critics, is loved by those who are too simple to admire it. Doctor Johnson, all whose studies were desultory, and who hated, as he said, to read books through, made an exception in favour of the Pilgrim's Progress. That work was
30 one of the two or three works which he wished longer. It was by no

---

Johnson   Dr Samuel Johnson (1709–84), lexicographer, critic, poet, editor

Addison   Joseph Addison (1672–1719), scholar, writer, editor

Cowley   Abraham Cowley (1618–67), poet and playwright

Hudibras   the lover of Elissa in Spenser's *Faerie Queene* (II. ii, 17); also a satire in three parts, each containing three cantos, by Samuel Butler

Spenser   Edmund Spenser (1552–99), poet and diplomat

House of Pride, House of Temperance passages in the *Faerie Queene*

Fairy Queen   Spenser's major poem, for which he is most famous, is a long, complex poem of moral and political allegories

common merit that the illiterate sectary[†] extracted praise like this from
the most pedantic[†] of critics and the most bigoted[†] of Tories. In the
wildest parts of Scotland the Pilgrim's Progress is the delight of the
peasantry. In every nursery the Pilgrim's Progress is a greater favourite
35   than Jack the Giant-killer. Every reader knows the straight and narrow
path as well as he knows a road in which he has gone backward and
forward a hundred times. This is the highest miracle of genius, that
things which are not should be as though they were, that the imaginations
of one mind should become the personal recollections of another. And
40   this miracle the tinker has wrought. There is no ascent, no declivity, no
resting-place, no turnstile, with which we are not perfectly acquainted.
The wicket gate, and the desolate swamp which separates it from the
City of Destruction, the long line of road, as straight as a rule can make
it, the Interpreter's house and all its fair shows, the prisoner in the iron
45   cage, the palace, at the doors of which armed men kept guard, and on
the battlements of which walked persons clothed all in gold, the cross
and the sepulchre, the steep hill and the pleasant harbour, the stately
front of the House Beautiful by the wayside, the chained lions crouching
in the porch, the low green valley of Humiliation, rich with grass and
50   covered with flocks, all are as well known to us as the sights of our
own street. Then we come to the narrow place where Apollyon strode
right across the whole breadth of the way, to stop the journey of
Christian, and where afterwards the pillar was set up to testify how
bravely the pilgrim had fought the good fight. As we advance, the valley
55   becomes deeper and deeper. The shade of the precipices on both sides
falls blacker and blacker. The clouds gather overhead. Doleful voices,
the clanking of chains, and the rushing of many feet to and fro, are
heard through the darkness. The way, hardly discernible in gloom, runs
close by the mouth of the burning pit, which sends forth its flames, its
60   noisome[†] smoke, and its hideous shapes, to terrify the adventurer.
Thence he goes on, amidst the snares and pitfalls, with the mangled
bodies of those who have perished lying in the ditch by his side. At the
end of the long dark valley he passes the dens in which the old giants
dwelt, amidst the bones of those whom they had slain.
65   Then the road passes straight on through a waste moor, till at length
the towers of a distant city appear before the traveller; and soon he is
in the midst of the innumerable multitudes of Vanity Fair. There are
the jugglers and the apes, the shops and the puppet-shows. There are
Italian Row, and French Row, and Spanish Row, and Britain Row,
70   with their crowds of buyers, sellers, and loungers, jabbering all the
languages of the earth.

sectary member of a religious sect different from the established or orthodox church *pedantic* demandingly learned	*bigoted* blindingly biased *noisome* harmful, offensive

Thence we go on by the little hill of the silver mine, and through the meadow of lilies, along the bank of that pleasant river which is bordered on both sides by fruit-trees. On the left branches off the path leading
75   to the horrible castle, the court-yard of which is paved with the skulls of pilgrims; and right onward are the sheepfolds and orchards of the Delectable Mountains.

From the Delectable Mountains, the way lies through the fogs and briers of the Enchanted Ground, with here and there a bed of soft
80   cushions spread under a green arbour. And beyond is the land of Beulah, where the flowers, the grapes, and the songs of birds never cease, and where the sun shines night and day. Thence are plainly seen the golden pavements and streets of pearl, on the other side of that black and cold river over which there is no bridge.
85   All the stages of the journey, all the forms which cross or overtake the pilgrims, giants, and hobgoblins, ill-favoured ones, and shining ones, the tall, comely, swarthy Madam Bubble, with her great purse by her side, and her fingers playing with the money, the black man in the bright vesture, Mr. Worldly Wiseman and my Lord Hategood, Mr.
90   Talkative, and Mrs. Timorous, all are actually existing beings to us. We follow the travellers through their allegorical progress with interest not inferior to that with which we follow Elizabeth[†] from Siberia to Moscow, or Jeanie Deans[†] from Edinburgh to London. Bunyan is almost the only writer who ever gave to the abstract the interest of the
95   concrete. In the works of many celebrated authors, men are mere personifications. We have not a jealous man, but jealousy, not a traitor, but perfidy; not a patriot, but patriotism. The mind of Bunyan, on the contrary, was so imaginative that personifications, when he dealt with them, became men. A dialogue between two qualities, in his dream, has
100   more dramatic effect than a dialogue between two human beings in most plays. In this respect the genius of Bunyan bore a great resemblance to that of a man who had very little else in common with him, Percy Bysshe Shelley.[†] The strong imagination of Shelley made him an idolator[†] in his own despite. Out of the most indefinite terms of a hard, cold,
105   dark, metaphysical[†] system, he made a gorgeous Pantheon,[†] full of beautiful, majestic, and life-like forms. He turned atheism itself into a mythology, rich with visions as glorious as the gods that live in the marble of Phidias,[†] or the virgin saints that smile on us from the canvas of Murillo.[†] The Spirit of Beauty, the Principle of Good, the Principle

---

Elizabeth   a reference to *Elizabeth, or The Exiles of Siberia* by Mme Cottin
Jeanie Deans   a character from Scott's *Heart of Midlothian*
Shelley   the poet (1792–1822)
idolator   worshipper of idols

metaphysical   based on abstract general reasoning
Pantheon   temple dedicated to all the gods
Phidias   the most famous of ancient Greek sculptors
Murillo   Bartolomé Esteban Murillo, Spanish artist (1617–82)

110 of Evil, when he treated of them, ceased to be abstractions. They took
shape and colour. They were no longer mere words; but 'intelligible
forms;' 'fair humanities;' objects of love, of adoration, or of fear. As
there can be no stronger sign of a mind destitute of the poetical faculty
than that tendency which was so common among the writers of the
115 French school to turn images into abstractions, Venus, for example,
into Love, Minerva into Wisdom, Mars into War, and Bacchus into
Festivity, so there can be no stronger sign of a mind truly poetical than
a disposition to reverse this abstracting process, and to make individuals
out of generalities. Some of the metaphysical and ethical[†] theories of
120 Shelley were certainly most absurd and pernicious. But we doubt
whether any modern poet has possessed in an equal degree some of the
highest qualities of the great ancient masters. The words bard and
inspiration, which seem so cold and affected when applied to other
modern writers, have a perfect propriety when applied to him. He was
125 not an author, but a bard. His poetry seems not to have been an art,
but an inspiration. Had he lived to the full age of man, he might not
improbably have given to the world some great work of the very highest
rank in design and execution. But, alas!

ὁ Δάφνις ἔβα ῥόον ἔκλυσε δίνα
130 τὸν Μώσαις φίλον ἄνδρα, τὸν οὐ Νύμφαισιν ἀπεχθῆ.
['Daphnis has gone down the stream; the eddies have closed over the
man whom the Muses loved and whom the Nymphs did not disdain.'
Theocritus, Idyll i, 140–1]

But we must return to Bunyan. The Pilgrim's Progress undoubtedly
135 is not a perfect allegory. The types are often inconsistent with each
other; and sometimes the allegorical disguise is altogether thrown off.
The river, for example, is emblematic of death; and we are told that
every human being must pass through the river. But Faithful does not
pass through it. He is martyred, not in shadow, but in reality, at Vanity
140 Fair. Hopeful talks to Christian about Esau's birthright and about his
own convictions of sin as Bunyan might have talked with one of his
own congregation. The damsels at the House Beautiful catechize[†]
Christiana's boys as any good ladies might catechize any boys at a
Sunday School. But we do not believe that any man, whatever might
145 be his genius, and whatever his good luck, could long continue a
figurative history without falling into many inconsistencies. We are sure
that inconsistencies, scarcely less gross than the worst into which
Bunyan has fallen, may be found in the shortest and most elaborate

ethical moral   catechize instruct by question and answer

allegories of the Spectator[†] and the Rambler.[†] The Tale of a Tub[†] and
150   the History of John Bull[†] swarm with similar errors, if the name of
error can be properly applied to that which is unavoidable. It is not
easy to make a simile go on all-fours. But we believe that no human
ingenuity could produce such a centipede as a long allegory in which
the correspondence between the outward sign and the thing signified
155   should be exactly preserved. Certainly no writer, ancient or modern,
has yet achieved the adventure. The best thing, on the whole, that an
allegorist can do, is to present to his readers a succession of analogies,
each of which may separately be striking and happy, without looking
very nicely to see whether they harmonize with each other. This Bunyan
160   has done; and though a minute scrutiny may detect inconsistencies in
every page of his Tale, the general effect which the Tale produces on
all persons, learned and unlearned, proves that he has done well. The
passages which it is most difficult to defend are those in which he
altogether drops the allegory, and puts into the mouth of his pilgrims
165   religious ejaculations[†] and disquisitions,[†] better suited to his own pulpit
at Bedford or Reading than to the Enchanted Ground or to the
Interpreter's Garden. Yet even these passages, though we will not
undertake to defend them against the objections of critics, we feel that
we could ill spare. We feel that the story owes much of its charm to
170   these occasional glimpses of solemn and affecting subjects, which will
not be hidden, which force themselves through the veil, and appear
before us in their native aspect. The effect is not unlike that which is
said to have been produced on the ancient stage, when the eyes of the
actor were seen flaming through his mask, and giving life and expression
175   to what would else have been an inanimate and uninteresting disguise.

1831   1831

Spectator   periodical conducted by Richard
   Steele and Joseph Addison in 1711–12, and
   revived in 1714 by Addison
Rambler   twice-weekly periodical issued by Dr
   Johnson in 1750–2
The Tale of a Tub   *A Tale of a Tub*, a play by

Ben Jonson (1572/3–1637), performed 1633
History of John Bull   a collection of pamphlets
   by John Arbuthnot (1667–1735), issued in
   1712
ejaculations   sudden utterances
disquisitions   inquiries

William Barnes
1801–86

The currency and popularity of Barnes's poetry was restricted because he wrote it mostly in Dorsetshire dialect. Nevertheless he was an accomplished lyric poet whose variety of form was much admired by Thomas Hardy.

Born near Sturminster Newton, Barnes developed early an inclination to learning. As a young man, working for a solicitor, he contributed poems to a local newspaper. In 1823 he became a schoolmaster at Mere, and after his marriage in 1827 began to consider moving his flourishing school, which he did, in 1835, to Dorchester. His interest in dialects and languages led him to suggest a number of Saxonised alternatives for words of foreign origin; for example, he anticipated American usage by proposing 'fall-time' for 'autumn'. He entered the books of St John's College, Cambridge, as a ten-year man, gained his BD and was ordained in 1848.

He published *Poems of Rural Life in the Dorset Dialect* (1844) and *Hwomely Rhymes* (1859). In 1868 *Poems of Rural Life* appeared in standard English, and in 1879 *Poems of Rural Life in the Dorset Dialect*, his collected poems.

Barnes was a cultured man of wide intellectual curiosity whose poems are made charming by their moving simplicity. Thomas Hardy learned much from Barnes's poetry.

BE'MI'STER†

Sweet Be'mi'ster, that bist a-bound*	is bounded
By green and woody hills all round,	
Wi' hedges, reachèn* up between	reaching
A thousan' vields o' zummer green,	
5 Where elems' lofty heads do drow*	throw
Their sheädes vor haÿ-meakers below,	
An' wild hedge-flow'rs do charm the souls	
O' maïdens in their evenèn strolls	

Be'mi'ster Beaminster, a Dorsetshire town

When I o' Zunday nights wi' Jeäne
10 Do saunter drough* a vield or leäne,   through
Where elder-blossoms be a-spread
Above the eltrot's* milk-white head,   cow-parsley
An' flow'rs o' blackberries do blow
Upon the brembles, white as snow,
15 To be outdone avore my zight
By Jeäne's gay frock o' dazzlèn white;

Oh! then there's nothèn that's 'ithout
Thy hills that I do ho about,* –   long for
Noo bigger pleäce, noo gaÿer town,
20 Beyond thy sweet bells' dyèn soun',
As they do ring, or strike the hour,
At evenèn vrom thy wold* – red tow'r.   old
No: shelter still my head, an' keep
My bwones when I do vall asleep.

1844

THE BWOAT†

Where cows did slowly seek the brink
O' Stour, drough zunburnt grass, to drink;
Wi' vishèn* float, that there did sink   fishing
   An' rise, I zot* as in a dream.   sat
5 The dazzlèn sun did cast his light
On hedge-row blossom, snowy white,
Though nothèn yet did come in zight,
   A-stirrèn on the straÿen stream;

Till, out by sheädy rocks there show'd
10 A bwoat along his foamy road,
Wi' thik feaïr maïd* at mill, a-row'd   this fair maid
   Wi' Jeane behind her brother's oars.
An' steätely as a queen o' vo'k*   folk
She zot wi' floatèn scarlet cloak,

The Bwoat   the boat

15   An' comèn on, at ev'ry stroke,
        Between my withy* sheäded shores.   willow

      The broken stream did idly try
      To show her sheäpe a-ridèn by,
      The rushes brown-bloomed stems did ply,
20   As if they bow'd to her by will.
      The rings o' water, wi' a sock,*   sobbing noise
      Did break upon the mossy rock,
      An' gi'e my beatèn heart a shock,
        Above my float's up-leapèn quill.*   fishing-float

25   Then, lik' a cloud below the skies,
      A-drifted off, wi' less'nèn size,
      An' lost, she floated vrom my eyes,
        Where down below the stream did wind;
      An' left the quiet weäves woonce mwore*   once more
30   To zink at rest, a sky-blue'd vloor,*   floor
      Wi all so still's the clote* they bore   water-lily
        Ay, all but my own ruffled mind.

                        1879

LYDLINCH BELLS†

      When skies wer peäle wi' twinklèn stars,
      An' whislèn aïr a-risèn keen;
      An' birds did leäve the icy bars*   perches
      To vind, in woods, their mossy screen;
5   When vrozen grass, so white's a sheet,
      Did scrunchy sharp below our veet,
      An' water, that did sparkle red
      At zunset, wer a-vrozen dead;
      The ringers then did spend an hour
10   A-ringèn changes up in tow'r;
      Vor Lydlinch bells be good vor sound,
      An' liked by all the naïghbours round.

Lydlinch Bells   the bells of Lydlinch church

An' while along the leafless boughs
O' ruslèn hedges, win's* did pass,   winds
15   An' orts* ov haÿ, a-left by cows,   remnants
Did russle on the vrozen grass,
An' maïdens' païls, wi' all their work
A-done, did hang upon their vurk,*   fork of a pail-stand
An' they, avore the fleämèn* brand,   flaming
20   Did teäke their needle-work in hand,
The men did cheer their heart an hour
A ringèn changes up in tow'r;
Vor Lydlinch bells be good vor sound,
An' lik'd by all the naïghbours round.

25   There sons did pull the bells that rung
Their mothers' weddèn peals avore,*   before
The while their fathers led em young
An' blushèn vrom the churches door,
An' still did cheem,* wi' happy sound   chime
30   As time did bring the Zundays round,
An' call em to the holy pleäce
Vor heavenly gifts o' peace an' greäce;
An' vo'k did come, a-streamèn slow
Along below the trees in row,
35   While they, in merry peals, did sound
The bells vor all the naïghbours round.

An' when the bells, wi' changèn peal,
Did smite their own vo'ks window-peänes,
Their sof'en'd sound did often steal
40   Wi' west winds drough the Bagber leänes;
Or, as the win' did shift, mid goo*   even went
Where woody Stock do nessle lew,*   nestles low
Or where the risèn moon did light
The walls o' Thornhill on the height;
45   An' zoo, whatever time mid bring
To meäke their vive* clear vaices* zing,   five   voices
Still Lydlinch bells wer good vor sound
An' liked by all the naïghbours round.

1879

SHAFTESBURY FEÄIR†

When hillborne Paladore did show
So bright to me down miles below
As woonce the zun, a-rollèn west,
Did brighten up his hill's high breast
5   Wi' walls a-lookèn dazzlèn white,
Or yollow,* on the grey-topp'd height   *yellow*
Of Paladore, as peäle day wore
    Awaÿ so feäir.
Oh! how I wish'd that I wer there.

10   The pleäce wer too vur off to spy
The livèn vo'k a-passèn by;
The vo'k too vur vor aïr* to bring   *too far for air*
The words that they did speak or zing.
All dum' to me wer each abode,
15   An' empty wer the down-hill road
Vrom Paladore, as peäle day wore
    Awaÿ so feäir;
But how I wish'd that I wer there.

But when I clomb the lofty ground
20   Where livèn veet an' tongues did sound,
At feäir,* bezide your bloomèn feäce,   *at the fair*
The pertiest* in all the pleäce,   *prettiest*
As you did look, wi' eyes as blue
As yonder southern hills in view,
25   Vrom Paladore – O Polly dear,
    Wi' you up there,
How merry then wer I at feäir.

Since vu'st* I trod thik steep hill-zide   *first*
My grievèn soul'v a-been a-tried
30   Wi' pain, an' loss o' worldly geär,
An souls a-gone I wanted near;
But you be here too goo up still,
An' look to Blackmwore vrom the hill
O' Paladore. Zoo,* Polly dear,   *so*
35   We'll goo up there,
An' spend an hour or two at feäir.

Shaftesbury Feäir   Shaftesbury Fair

The wold brown meäre's a-brought vrom grass,
An' rubb'd an' cwombed so bright as glass;
An' now we'll hitch her in, an' start
40   To feäir upon the new green cart,
An' teäke our little Poll between
Our zides, as proud's a little queen,
To Paladore. Aye, Poll a dear,
       Vor now 'tis feäir,
45   An' she's a-longèn to goo there.

While Paladore, on watch, do strain
Her eyes to Blackmwore's blue-hillèd pläin,
While Duncliffe is the traveller's mark;
Or cloty* Stour's a-rollèn dark;   water-lilied
50   Or while our bells do call, vor greäce,
The vo'k avore their Seävior's* feäce,   Saviour's
Mid* Paladore, an' Poll a dear,   may
       Vor ever know
O' peäce an' plenty down below.

1879

John Henry Newman

1801–90

James Joyce admired Newman's 'cloistral, silver-veined' prose; and it is as a stylist that Newman is chiefly remembered in English literature. He was educated at school in Ealing and at Trinity College, Oxford. He became a Fellow of Oriel College, then the most intellectually prestigious college in Oxford, and met and collaborated with, some of the most brilliant men in church and university: John Keble, E. B. Pusey, R. H. Froude. In 1828 he was appointed Vicar of St Mary's Church, from whose pulpit he was generally considered to speak with the voice both of Oxford University and of an important part of the Church of England. He travelled to the Mediterranean in 1832, and while in Rome wrote many poems which were to appear in *Lyra Apostolica* (1836); one of the collection was 'Lead, Kindly Light', written on his return voyage between Sicily and Marseilles.

He arrived back in England to witness the event recognised as the birth of the Oxford Movement, Keble's famous Assize Sermon of 1833 preached in Oxford. Newman founded *Tracts for the Times*, which sought to turn attention to the early Christian church, maintain the integrity of the Book of Common Prayer, and defend catholicity. His tract XC which argued that the 39 Articles are compatible with Catholic theology caused the bishops to ban him from publishing any more.

In 1842 he retreated to Littlemore, a short distance from Oxford, where in 1845 he was received into the Roman Catholic church. He visited Rome in 1846 and returned to England in order to found the Oratory in Birmingham. From 1854–8, in addition to looking after the Oratory, he was Rector of the Catholic University of Ireland in Dublin. From his experiences there, he wrote a series of essays on university education, published finally in 1873 as *The Idea of a University Defined and Illustrated*, which argued that a university's first duty is to instruct rather than to pursue research or teach religion.

Newman's *Apologia pro Vita Sua*, his greatest work, appeared in 1864 as a reply to false accusations made by Charles Kingsley in *Macmillan's Magazine*: Kingsley had misrepresented Newman's views and had maintained that for Newman, and the Roman Catholic clergy in general, truth was not necessarily a virtue. The *Apologia*, Newman's history of his own spiritual development, is his massive rebuttal of Kingsley's charges.

1866 saw the publication in book form of *The Dream of Gerontius*, which had appeared the previous year in the Roman Catholic journal *The Month*. It has been set to music as an Oratorio by Elgar: its most famous lyric is 'Praise to the Holiest in the height'. In 1870 he published his most powerful, and most intellectual, work, *An Essay in aid of the Grammar of Assent*.

Newman wrote two novels, *Loss and Gain* (1848), fundamentally autobiographical, and *Callista* (1856), the story of a third-century martyr.

He was made a cardinal in 1879. His writings survive still as a great influence in the Roman Catholic Church, and as more general examples of an exact, logical, clear, intellectual and inspired English prose-style.

From THE PILLAR OF THE CLOUD

Lead, kindly Light, amid the encircling gloom.
    Lead thou me on;
The night is dark, and I am far from home;
    Lead thou me on.
5 Keep thou my feet; I do not ask to see
The distant scene; one step enough for me.

I was not ever thus, nor prayed that thou
    Shouldst lead me on;
I loved to choose and see my path; but now
10   Lead thou me on,
I loved the garish day, and, spite of fears,
Pride ruled my will: remember not past years.

So long thy power hath blest me, sure it still
    Will lead me on.
15 O'er moor and fen, o'er crag and torrent, till
    The night is gone,
And with the morn those angel faces smile,
Which I have loved long since, and lost a while.

1833   1836

From THE DREAM OF GERONTIUS

1

Praise to the Holiest in the height,
And in the depth be praise:
In all his words most wonderful,
Most sure in all his ways.

2

5   O loving wisdom of our God!
When all was sin and shame,
A second Adam† to the fight
And to the rescue came.

3

O wisest love! that flesh and blood,
10   Which did in Adam fail,
Should strive afresh against the foe,
Should strive and should prevail;

4

And that a higher gift than grace
Should flesh and blood refine,
15   God's presence and his very self,
And essence all-divine.

5

O generous love! that he, who smote
In Man for man the foe,
The double agony in Man
20   For man should undergo;

6

And in the garden secretly,
And on the Cross on high,
Should teach his brethren, and inspire
To suffer and to die.

7

25   Praise to the Holiest in the height,
And in the depth be praise:

A second Adam   Jesus Christ

In all his words most wonderful,
Most sure in all his ways.

1865   1865

From APOLOGIA PRO VITA SUA
Chapter 5
Position of My Mind Since 1845

From the time that I became a Catholic,[†] of course I have no further history of my religious opinions to narrate. In saying this, I do not mean to say that my mind has been idle, or that I have given up thinking on theological subjects; but that I have had no variations to record,
5   and have had no anxiety of heart whatever. I have been in perfect peace and contentment; I never have had one doubt. I was not conscious to myself, on my conversion, of any change, intellectual or moral, wrought in my mind. I was not conscious of firmer faith in the fundamental truths of Revelation,[†] or of more self-command; I had not more fervour;
10 but it was like coming into port after a rough sea; and my happiness on that score remains to this day without interruption.

Nor had I any trouble about receiving those additional articles,[†] which are not found in the Anglican[†] Creed. Some of them I believed already, but not any one of them was a trial to me. I made a profession
15 of them upon my reception with the greatest ease, and I have the same ease in believing them now. I am far of course from denying that every article of the Christian Creed, whether as held by Catholics or by Protestants, is beset with intellectual difficulties; and it is simple fact, that, for myself, I cannot answer those difficulties. Many persons are
20 very sensitive of the difficulties of Religion; I am as sensitive of them as any one; but I have never been able to see a connexion between apprehending those difficulties, however keenly, and multiplying them to any extent, and on the other hand doubting the doctrines to which they are attached. Ten thousand difficulties do not make one doubt, as
25 I understand the subject; difficulty and doubt are incommensurate.[†] There of course may be difficulties in the evidence; but I am speaking of difficulties intrinsic to the doctrines themselves, or to their relations

---

Catholic Roman Catholic
Revelation the revelation of God to mankind
articles separate clauses

Anglican Church of England
incommensurate out of proportion

with each other. A man may be annoyed that he cannot work out a
mathematical problem, of which the answer is or is not given to him,
30   without doubting that it admits of an answer, or that a certain particular
answer is the true one. Of all points of faith, the being of a God is, to
my own apprehension, encompassed with most difficulty, and yet borne
in upon our minds with most power.

People say that the doctrine of Transubstantiation[†] is difficult to
35   believe; I did not believe the doctrine till I was a Catholic. I had no
difficulty in believing it, as soon as I believed that the Catholic Roman
Church was the oracle of God, and that she had declared this doctrine
to be part of the original revelation. It is difficult, impossible, to imagine,
I grant; – but how is it difficult to believe? Yet Macaulay[†] thought it
40   so difficult to believe, that he had need of a believer in it of talents as
eminent as Sir Thomas More,[†] before he could bring himself to conceive
that the Catholics of an enlightened age could resist 'the overwhelming
force of the argument against it.' 'Sir Thomas More,' he says, 'is one of
the choice specimens of wisdom and virtue; and the doctrine of
45   transubstantiation is a kind of proof charge. A faith which stands that
test, will stand any test.' But for myself, I cannot indeed prove it, I
cannot tell *how* it is; but I say, 'Why should it not be? What's to hinder
it? What do I know of substance or matter? just as much as the greatest
philosophers, and that is nothing at all;' – so much is this the case, that
50   there is a rising school of philosophy now, which considers phenomena[†]
to constitute the whole of our knowledge in physics. The Catholic
doctrine leaves phenomena alone. It does not say that the phenomena
go; on the contrary, it says that they remain; nor does it say that the
same phenomena are in several places at once. It deals with what no
55   one on earth knows any thing about, the material substances themselves.
And, in like manner, of that majestic Article of the Anglican as well as
the Catholic Creed, – the doctrine of the Trinity in Unity.[†] What do I
know of the Essence of the Divine Being? I know that my abstract idea
of three is simply incompatible with my idea of one; but when I come
60   to the question of concrete fact, I have no means of proving that there
is not a sense in which one and three can equally be predicated[†] of the
Incommunicable God.

But I am going to take upon myself the responsibility of more than
the mere Creed of the Church; as the parties accusing me are determined
65   I shall do. They say, that now, in that I am a Catholic, though I may

Transubstantiation   conversion of whole
substance of eucharistic bread and wine into
the body and blood of Christ
Macaulay   Thomas Babington Macaulay
(1800–59), politician, administrator, poet
and historian
Sir Thomas More   saint (1477–1535), lawyer,

writer, diplomat and Lord Chancellor of
England
phenomena   immediate objects of perception
Trinity in Unity   God – the Father, the Son
and the Holy Ghost
predicated   asserted

not have offences of my own against honesty to answer for, yet, at least, I am answerable for the offences of others, of my co-religionists, of my brother priests, of the Church herself. I am quite willing to accept the responsibility; and, as I have been able, as I trust, by means of a
70 few words, to dissipate, in the minds of all those who do not begin with disbelieving me, the suspicion with which so many Protestants start, in forming their judgment of Catholics, viz. that our Creed is actually set up in inevitable superstition and hypocrisy, as the original sin of Catholicism; so now I will proceed, as before, identifying myself
75 with the Church and vindicating it, – not of course denying the enormous mass of sin and error which exists of necessity in that world-wide multiform Communion, – but going to the proof of this one point, that its system is in no sense dishonest, and that therefore the upholders and teachers of that system, as such, have a claim to be acquitted in their
80 own persons of that odious imputation.

From note A, *Liberalism*

When, in the beginning of the present century, not very long before my own time, after many years of moral and intellectual declension, the University of Oxford woke up to a sense of its duties, and began to reform itself, the first instruments of this change, to whose zeal and
5 courage we all owe so much, were naturally thrown together for mutual support, against the numerous obstacles which lay in their path, and soon stood out in relief from the body of residents, who, though many of them men of talent themselves, cared little for the object which the others had at heart. These Reformers, as they may be called, were for
10 some years members of scarcely more than three or four Colleges; and their own Colleges, as being under their direct influence, of course had the benefit of those stricter views of discipline and teaching, which they themselves were urging on the University. They had, in no long time, enough of real progress in their several spheres of exertion, and enough
15 of reputation out of doors, to warrant them in considering themselves the *élite*[†] of the place; and it is not wonderful if they were in consequence led to look down upon the majority of Colleges, which had not kept pace with the reform, or which had been hostile to it. And, when those rivalries of one man with another arose, whether personal or collegiate,
20 which befall literary and scientific societies, such disturbances did but tend to raise in their eyes the value which they had already set upon academical distinction, and increase their zeal in pursuing it. Thus was formed an intellectual circle or class in the University, – men, who felt

élite best

they had a career before them, as soon as the pupils, whom they were
25   forming, came into public life; men, whom non-residents, whether
country parsons or preachers of the Low Church, on coming up from
time to time to the old place, would look at, partly with admiration,
partly with suspicion, as being an honour indeed to Oxford, but withal
exposed to the temptation of ambitious views, and to the spiritual evils
30   signified in what is called the 'pride of reason.'

Nor was this imputation altogether unjust; for, as they were following
out the proper idea of a University, of course they suffered more or less
from the moral malady incident to such a pursuit. The very object of
such great institutions lies in the cultivation of the mind and the spread
35   of knowledge; if this object, as all human objects, has its dangers at all
times, much more would these exist in the case of men, who were
engaged in a work of reformation, and had the opportunity of measuring
themselves, not only with those who were their equals in intellect, but
with the many, who were below them. In this select circle or class of
40   men, in various Colleges, the direct instruments and the choice fruit of
real University Reform, we see the rudiments of the Liberal† party.

Whenever men are able to act at all, there is the chance of extreme
and intemperate action; and therefore, when there is exercise of mind,
there is the chance of wayward or mistaken exercise. Liberty of thought
45   is in itself a good; but it gives an opening to false liberty. Now by
Liberalism I mean false liberty of thought, or the exercise of thought
upon matters, in which, from the constitution of the human mind,
thought cannot be brought to any successful issue, and therefore is out
of place. Among such matters are first principles of whatever kind; and
50   of these the most sacred and momentous are especially to be reckoned
the truths of Revelation. Liberalism then is the mistake of subjecting to
human judgment those revealed doctrines which are in their nature
beyond and independent of it, and of claiming to determine on intrinsic
grounds the truth and value of propositions which rest for their reception
55   simply on the external authority of the Divine Word.

Now certainly the party of whom I have been speaking, taken as a
whole, were of a character of mind out of which Liberalism might easily
grow up, as in fact it did; certainly they breathed around an influence
which made men of religious seriousness shrink into themselves. But,
60   while I say as much as this, I have no intention whatever of implying
that the talent of the University, in the years before and after 1820,
was liberal in its theology, in the sense in which the bulk of the educated
classes through the country are liberal now. I would not for the world
be supposed to detract from the Christian earnestness, and the activity
65   in religious works, above the average of men, of many of the persons

---

Liberal   not in a political sense: Newman is concerned with religious doctrine

in question. They would have protested against their being supposed
to place reason before faith, or knowledge before devotion; yet I do
consider that they unconsciously encouraged and successfully introduced
into Oxford a licence of opinion which went far beyond them. In their
70 day they did little more than take credit to themselves for enlightened
views, largeness of mind, liberality of sentiment, without drawing the
line between what was just and what was inadmissible in speculation,†
and without seeing the tendency of their own principles; and engrossing,
as they did, the mental energy of the University, they met for a time
75 with no effectual hindrance to the spread of their influence, except
(what indeed at the moment was most effectual, but not of an intellectual
character) the thorough-going Toryism and traditionary Church-of-
England-ism of the great body of the Colleges and Convocation.†
    Now and then a man of note appeared in the Pulpit or Lecture Rooms
80 of the University, who was a worthy representative of the more religious
and devout Anglicans. These belonged chiefly to the High-Church party;
for the party called Evangelical never has been able to breathe freely in
the atmosphere of Oxford, and at no time has been conspicuous, as a
party, for talent or learning. But of the old High Churchmen several
85 exerted some sort of Anti-liberal influence in the place, at least from
time to time, and that influence of an intellectual nature. Among these
especially may be mentioned Mr. John Miller, of Worcester College,
who preached the Bampton Lecture in the year 1817. But, as far as I
know, he who turned the tide, and brought the talent of the University
90 round to the side of the old theology, and against what was familiarly
called 'march-of-mind,' was Mr. Keble. In and from Keble the mental
activity of Oxford took that contrary direction which issued in what
was called Tractarianism.†

1864–5   1865

---

speculation inquiry
Convocation the corporate body of members
    of Oxford University
Tractarianism called this because tracts were

written, edited and published by Keble,
Newman and others, representing the views
of the High Church party

From THE IDEA OF A UNIVERSITY, Discourse 9, Section 8

[Literature in University Education]

Nay, I am obliged to go further still; even if we could, still we should be shrinking from our plain duty, gentlemen, did we leave out literature from education. For why do we educate, except to prepare for the world? Why do we cultivate the intellect of the many beyond the first
5 elements of knowledge, except for this world? Will it be much matter in the world to come whether our bodily health or whether our intellectual strength was more or less, except of course as this world is in all its circumstances a trial for the next? If then a university is a direct preparation for this world, let it be what it professes. It is not a
10 Convent, it is not a seminary; it is a place to fit men of the world for the world. We cannot possibly keep them from plunging into the world, with all its ways and principles and maxims, when their time comes; but we can prepare them against what is inevitable; and it is not the way to learn to swim in troubled waters, never to have gone into them.
15 Proscribe (I do not merely say particular authors, particular works, particular passages) but secular literature as such; cut out from your class books all broad manifestations of the natural man; and those manifestations are waiting for your pupil's benefit at the very doors of your lecture room in living and breathing substance. They will meet
20 him there in all the charm of novelty, and all the fascination of genius or of amiableness. To-day a pupil, to-morrow a member of the great world: to-day confined to the lives of the Saints, to-morrow thrown upon Babel; – thrown on Babel, without the honest indulgence of wit and humour and imagination having ever been permitted to him,
25 without any fastidiousness of taste wrought into him, without any rule given him for discriminating 'the precious from the vile,' beauty from sin, the truth from the sophistry of nature, what is innocent from what is poison. You have refused him the masters of human thought, who would in some sense have educated him, because of their incidental
30 corruption: you have shut up from him those whose thoughts strike home to our hearts, whose words are proverbs, whose names are indigenous to all the world, who are the standard of their mother tongue, and the pride and boast of their countrymen, Homer, Ariosto, Cervantes, Shakespeare, because the old Adam† smelt rank in them;
35 and for what have you reserved him? You have given him 'a liberty unto' the multitudinous blasphemy of his day; you have made him free

---

the old Adam   Adam, as the fount and head   or man without regenerating grace
of unredeemed man, stands for original sin

of its newspapers, its reviews, its magazines, its novels, its controversial pamphlets, of its parliamentary debates, its law proceedings, its platform speeches, its songs, its drama, its theatre, of its enveloping, stifling
40 atmosphere of death. You have succeeded but in this, – in making the world his university.

Difficult then as the question may be, and much as it may try the judgments and even divide the opinions of zealous and religious Catholics, I cannot feel any doubt myself, gentlemen, that the Church's
45 true policy is not to aim at the exclusion of literature from secular schools, but at her own admission into them. Let her do for literature in one way what she does for science in another; each has its imperfection, and she has her remedy for each. She fears no knowledge, but she purifies all; she represses no element of our nature, but cultivates
50 the whole. Science is grave, methodical, logical; with science then she argues, and opposes reason to reason. Literature does not argue, but declaims and insinuates; it is multiform and versatile: it persuades instead of convincing, it seduces, it carries captive; it appeals to the sense of honour, or to the imagination, or to the stimulus of curiosity;
55 it makes its way by means of gaiety, satire, romance, the beautiful, the pleasurable. Is it wonderful that with an agent like this the Church should claim to deal with a vigour corresponding to its restlessness, to interfere in its proceedings with a higher hand, and to wield an authority in the choice of its studies and of its books which would be tyrannical,
60 if reason and fact were the only instruments of its conclusions? But, any how, her principle is one and the same throughout: not to prohibit truth of any kind, but to see that no doctrines pass under the name of Truth but those which claim it rightfully.

1852–73   1873

Benjamin Disraeli
1804–81

The achievement of Disraeli in the world of letters and politics was remarkable. He became prime minister and statesman, and during the six years (1874–80) he was leading the Tory government, he negotiated the purchase of the Suez Canal, acquired Cyprus, and arranged affairs so that Queen Victoria was crowned Empress of India.

His first literary project was successful at the age of fifteen when Leigh Hunt published *A True Story* in his journal, the *Indicator*. Disraeli's first venture was to publish with John Murray a newspaper, the *Representative*, in opposition, and competition, to *The Times*: it ran for over a year but made a huge loss. His first novel was *Vivian Grey*, published anonymously in 1826. Thereafter he wrote many novels.

By 1834 he was moving in the highest reaches of fashionable political and literary society. His experiences are reflected in the love stories of *Henrietta Temple* and *Venetia* (1837). The 1840s saw the publication of his famous trilogy, *Coningsby* (1844), *Sybil* (1845) and *Tancred* (1847): these were the first English political novels. He wrote a biography of Lord George Bentinck (1852), and in 1870 published *Lothair*. He opined that: 'My works are my life'. He viewed the life of fashionable high society with humour and disdain, and yet he was captivated by it. He was an acute observer of the manners and machinations of politicians. Even as an aged statesman in retirement he found the time and energy to write and publish *Endymion* (1880), for which he was paid £10,000.

From HENRIETTA TEMPLE[†]

Chapter 7: Containing an Unexpected Visit to London, and its Consequences

The day after the conversation in the library to which Glastonbury had been an unwilling listener, he informed his friends that it was necessary for him to visit the metropolis,[†] and as young Ferdinand had never yet seen London, he proposed that he should accompany him. Sir Ratcliffe
5 and Lady Armine cheerfully assented to this proposition; and as for Ferdinand, it is difficult to describe the delight which the anticipation of his visit occasioned him. The three days that were to elapse before his departure did not seem sufficient to ensure the complete packing of his portmanteau[†] and his excited manner, the rapidity of his conversa-
10 tion, and the restlessness of his movements were very diverting.

'Mamma! is London twenty times bigger than Nottingham? How big is it then? Shall we travel all night? What o'clock is it now? I wonder if Thursday will ever come? I think I shall go to bed early, to finish the day sooner. Do you think my cap is good enough to travel
15 in? I shall buy a hat in London. I shall get up early the very first morning, and buy a hat. Do you think my uncle is in London? I wish Augustus were not at Eton, perhaps he would be there. I wonder if Mr Glastonbury will take me to see St. Paul's.[†] I wonder if he will take me to the play. I'd give anything to go to the play. I should like to go the
20 play and St. Paul's! What fun it will be dining on the road!'[†]

It did indeed seem that Thursday would never come; yet it came at last. The travellers were obliged to rise before the sun, and drive over to Nottingham to meet their coach; so they bid their adieus the previous eve. As for Ferdinand, so fearful was he of losing the coach, that he
25 scarcely slept, and was never convinced that he was really in time, until he found himself planted in breathless agitation outside of the Dart, light post coach. It was the first time in his life that he had ever travelled outside of a coach. He felt all the excitement of expanding experience and advancing manhood. They whirled along: at the end of every stage
30 Ferdinand followed the example of his fellow-travellers and dismounted, and then with sparkling eyes hurried to Glastonbury, who was inside, to inquire how he sped. 'Capital travelling, isn't it, sir? Did the ten

---

Henrietta Temple the novel concerns the young, dashing Ferdinand Armine who, impecunious, joins the army, and in fashionable society incurs great debt. He fails to inherit his grandfather's estate, and becomes engaged to his wealthy cousin, Katherine Grandison; but he falls in love with the penniless Henrietta Temple to whom he also becomes engaged
metropolis the capital, London
portmanteau leather case for clothes, opening in two equal parts
St. Paul's St. Paul's Cathedral
on the road on the journey

miles within the hour. You have no idea what a fellow our coachman
is; and the guard, such a fellow our guard! Don't wait here a moment.
35 Can I get anything for you? We dine at Mill-field. What fun!'

Away whirled the dashing Dart over the rich plains of our merry
midland; a quick and dazzling vision of golden cornfields and lawny
pasture land; farmhouses embowered in orchards and hamlets shaded
by the straggling members of some vast and ancient forest. Then rose
40 in the distance the dim blue towers, or the graceful spire, of some old
cathedral, and soon the spreading causeways announce their approach
to some provincial capital. The coachman flanks† his leaders, who break
into a gallop; the guard sounds his triumphant bugle; the coach bounds
over the noble bridge that spans a stream covered with craft; public
45 buildings, guildhalls, and county gaols rise on each side. Rattling
through many an inferior way they at length emerged into the High
Street, the observed of all observers, and mine host of the Red Lion, or
the White Hart, followed by all his waiters, advances from his portal
with a smile to receive the 'gentlemen passengers'.
50 'The coach stops here half an hour, gentlemen: dinner quite ready!'

'Tis a delightful sound. And what a dinner! What a profusion of
substantial delicacies! What mighty and iris-tinted rounds of beef! What
vast and marble-veined ribs! What gelatinous veal pies! What colossal
hams! Those are evidently prize cheeses! And how invigorating is the
55 perfume of those various and variegated pickles! Then the bustle
emulating† the plenty; the ringing of bells, the clash of thoroughfare,
the summoning of ubiquitous waiters, and the all-pervading feeling of
omnipotence, from the guests, who order what they please, to the
landlord, who can produce and execute everything they can desire. 'Tis
60 a wondrous sight. Why should a man go and see the pyramids and
cross the desert, when he has not beheld York Minster or travelled on
the Road!

Our little Ferdinand amid all this novelty heartily enjoyed himself,
and did ample justice to mine host's good cheer. They were soon again
65 whirling along the road; but at sunset, Ferdinand, at the instance of
Glastonbury, availed himself of his inside place, and, wearied by the
air and the excitement of the day, he soon fell soundly asleep.

Several hours had elapsed, when, awaking from a confused dream in
which Armine and all he had lately seen were blended together, he
70 found his fellow-travellers slumbering, and the mail dashing along
through the illuminated streets of a great city. The streets were thickly
thronged. Ferdinand stared at the magnificence of the shops blazing
with lights, and the multitude of men and vehicles moving in all
directions. The guard sounded his bugle with treble energy, and the

---

flanks whips on the flanks   *emulating* rivalling

75   coach suddenly turned through an arched entrance into the court-yard
     of an old-fashioned inn. His fellow-passengers started and rubbed their
     eyes.
         'So! we have arrived, I suppose,' grumbled one of these gentlemen,
     taking off his night-cap.
80   'Yes, gentlemen, I am happy to say our journey is finished,' said a
     more polite voice; 'and a very pleasant one I have found it. Porter, have
     the goodness to call me a coach.'
         'And one for me,' added the gruff voice.
         'Mr Glastonbury,' whispered the awe-struck Ferdinand, 'is this
85   London?'
         'This is London: but we have yet two or three miles to go before we
     reach our quarters. I think we had better alight and look after our
     luggage. Gentlemen, good evening!'
         Mr Glastonbury hailed a coach, into which, having safely deposited
90   their portmanteaus, he and Ferdinand entered; but our young friend
     was so entirely overcome by his feelings and the genius[†] of the place,
     that he was quite unable to make an observation. Each minute the
     streets seemed to grow more spacious and more brilliant, and the
     multitude more dense and more excited. Beautiful buildings, too, rose
95   before him; palaces, and churches, and streets and squares of imposing
     architecture; to his inexperienced eye and unsophisticated spirit their
     route appeared a never-ending triumph. To the hackney-coachman,[†]
     however, who had no imagination, and who was quite satiated with
     metropolitan experience, it only appeared that he had had an exceeding
100 good fare, and that he was jogging up from Bishopsgate Street to
     Charing Cross.
         When Jarvis, therefore, had safely deposited his charge at Morley's
     Hotel, in Cockspur Street, and extorted from them an extra shilling, in
     consideration of their evident rustication,[†] he bent his course towards
105 the Opera House; for clouds were gathering, and, with the favour of
     Providence, there seemed a chance about midnight of picking up some
     helpless beau,[†] or desperate cabless dandy,[†] the choicest victim, in a
     midnight shower, of these public conveyancers.[†]
         The coffee-room at Morley's was a new scene of amusement to
110 Ferdinand, and he watched with great diversion the two evening papers
     portioned out among twelve eager quidnuncs,[†] and the evident anxiety
     which they endured, and the nice diplomacies to which they resorted,
     to obtain the envied journals. The entrance of our two travellers so
     alarmingly increasing the demand over the supply, at first seemed to

---

genius   spirit
hackney coachman   the driver of a coach for
    hire
rustication   countryfied ways

beau, dandy   fashionable young gentleman
conveyancers   carriers
quidnuncs   newsmongers, gossips

115   attract considerable and not very friendly notice; but when a malignant
       half-pay officer,† in order to revenge himself for the restless watchfulness
       of his neighbour, a political doctor of divinity, offered the journal,
       which he had long finished, to Glastonbury, and it was declined, the
       general alarm visibly diminished. Poor Mr Glastonbury had never
120   looked into a newspaper in his life, save the *County Chronicle*, to which
       he occasionally contributed a communication, giving an account of the
       digging up of some old coins, signed Antiquarius; or of the exhumation
       of some fossil remains, to which he more boldly appended his initials.
           In spite of the strange clatter in the streets, Ferdinand slept well, and
125   the next morning, after an early breakfast, himself and his fellow-
       traveller set out on their peregrinations.† Young and sanguine, full of
       health and enjoyment, innocent and happy, it was with difficulty that
       Ferdinand could restrain his spirits as he mingled in the bustle of the
       streets. It was a bright sunny morning, and although the end of June,
130   the town was yet quite full.
           'Is this Charing Cross, sir? I wonder if we shall ever be able to get
       over? Is this the fullest part of the town, sir? What a fine day, sir! How
       lucky we are in the weather! We are lucky in everything! Whose house
       is that? Northumberland House! Is it the Duke of Northumberland's?
135   Does he live there? How I should like to see it! Is it very fine? Who is
       that? What is this? The Admiralty; oh! let me see the Admiralty! The
       Horse Guards! Oh! where, where? Let us set our watches by the Horse
       Guards. The guard of our coach always sets his watch by the Horse
       Guards. Mr Glastonbury, which is the best clock, the Horse Guards,
140   or St. Paul's? Is that the Treasury? Can we go in? That is Downing
       Street, is it? I never heard of Downing Street. What do they do in
       Downing Street? Is this Charing Cross still, or is it Parliament Street?
       Where does Charing Cross end, and where does Parliament Street
       begin? By Jove, I see Westminster Abbey!'
145   After visiting Westminster Abbey and the Two Houses of Parliament,
       Mr Glastonbury, looking at his watch, said it was now time to call
       upon a friend of his who lived in St. James's Square. This was the
       nobleman with whom early in life Glastonbury had been connected,
       and with whom and whose family he had become so great a favourite,
150   that, notwithstanding his retired life, they had never permitted the
       connection entirely to subside. During the very few visits which he had
       made to the metropolis, he always called in St. James's Square, and his
       reception always assured him that his remembrance imparted pleasure.
           When Glastonbury sent up his name he was instantly admitted, and
155   ushered up stairs. The room was full, but it consisted only of a family

---

half-pay officer   an army officer who is neither   *peregrinations*   wanderings
retired nor on active commission

party. The mother of the Duke, who was an interesting personage, with fine grey hair, a clear blue eye, and a soft voice, was surrounded by her great-grandchildren, who were at home for the Midsummer holidays, and who had gathered together at her rooms this morning to consult
160 upon amusements. Among them was the heir presumptive† of the house, a youth of the age of Ferdinand, and of a prepossessing appearance. It was difficult to meet a more amiable and agreeable family, and nothing could exceed the kindness with which they all welcomed Glastonbury. The Duke himself soon appeared. 'My dear, dear Glastonbury,' he said,
165 'I heard you were here, and I would come. This shall be a holiday for us all. Why, man, you bury yourself alive!'
    'Mr Armine,' said the Duchess, pointing to Ferdinand.
    'Mr Armine, how do you do? Your grandfather and I were well acquainted. I am glad to know his grandson. I hope your father, Sir
170 Ratcliffe, and Lady Armine are well. My dear Glastonbury, I hope you have come to stay a long time. You must dine with us every day. You know we are very old-fashioned people, we do not go much into the world; so you will always find us at home, and we will do what we can to amuse your young friend. Why, I should think he was about the
175 same age as Digby? Is he at Eton? His grandfather was. I shall never forget the time he cut off old Barnard's pig-tail. He was a wonderful man, poor Sir Ferdinand! he was indeed.'
    While his Grace and Glastonbury maintained their conversation, Ferdinand conducted himself with so much spirit and propriety towards
180 the rest of the party, and gave them such a lively and graceful narrative of all his travels up to town, and the wonders he had already witnessed, that they were quite delighted with him; and, in short, from this moment, during his visit to London he was scarcely ever out of their society, and every day became a greater favourite with them. His letters
185 to his mother, for he wrote to her almost every day, recounted all their successful efforts for his amusement, and it seemed that he passed his mornings in a round of sight-seeing, and that he went to the play every night of his life. Perhaps there never existed a human being who at this moment more thoroughly enjoyed life than Ferdinand Armine.
190   In the meantime while he thought only of amusement, Mr Glastonbury was not inattentive to his more important interests; for the truth is that this excellent man had introduced him to the family only with the hope of interesting the feelings of the Duke in his behalf. His Grace was a man of a generous disposition. He sympathized with the recital
195 of Glastonbury as he detailed to him the unfortunate situation of this youth, sprung from so illustrious a lineage, and yet cut off by a

---

heir presumptive a person whose right of inheritance is liable to be defeated by the   birth of a nearer heir

combination of unhappy circumstances from almost all those natural sources whence he might have expected support and countenance. And when Glastonbury, seeing that the Duke's heart was moved, added that
200   all he required for him, Ferdinand, was a commission† in the army, for which his parents were prepared to advance the money, his Grace instantly declared that he would exert all his influence to obtain their purpose.

Mr Glastonbury was, therefore, more gratified than surprised when,
205   a few days after the conversation which we have mentioned, his noble friend informed him, with a smile, that he believed all might be arranged, provided his young charge could make it convenient to quit England at once. A vacancy had unexpectedly occurred in a regiment just ordered to Malta, and an ensigncy† had been promised to Ferdinand Armine.
210   Mr Glastonbury gratefully closed with the offer. He sacrificed a fourth part of his moderate independence in the purchase of the commission and the outfit of his young friend, and had the supreme satisfaction, ere the third week of their visit was complete, of forwarding a Gazette† to Armine, containing the appointment of Ferdinand Armine as Ensign
215   in the Royal Fusiliers.

1836–7   1837

---

commission officers' commissions in the army
  were bought
ensigncy traditionally, standard-bearer: the
  lowest officer commission in a regiment of
  foot-soldiers

Gazette London Gazette issued twice-weekly
  which published government and service
  appointments

Elizabeth Barrett Browning

1806–61

Elizabeth Barrett was the eldest of a large family whose landowning father was Edward Moulton Barrett. Her extremely happy childhood was spent at Hope End near Great Malvern where, encouraged by her father, she proved to be at an early age a very able classicist. She read Homer at the age of eight and was later to produce translations of ancient Greek and Byzantine poems. Her childhood happiness was cut short by two events. First the tragically early death of her mother and then her own riding accident at the age of fifteen which left her crippled for years and led to her eventual move to London in 1835 for medical treatment. From London she was sent to Torquay, again ill, where she remained until 1841. It was in Torquay that her eldest brother, Edward, was drowned, and over whose death she was always to grieve. She returned to London and the literary scene still an invalid, where her spirit, sense of humour and liveliness won for her a close circle of admirers.

Robert Browning began a correspondence with her in 1845 and they married secretly the following year when they went to Italy. The marriage was secret because of her father's opposition. The Brownings lived in Florence and in 1849 their only son, 'Penini', was born.

Elizabeth Barrett Browning's two earliest works were published by her father: *The Battle of Marathon* (1820) and *An Essay on Mind* (1826). *The Seraphim, and Other Poems* appeared in 1838 and was well received. This was followed by *Poems* (1844), by which time she had become so popular that her name was suggested for Poet Laureate on the death of Wordsworth in 1850. *Casa Guidi: Windows* was written on the subject of Italian Liberation in which she became passionately involved. In 1856 she wrote the epic *Aurora Leigh*, followed by the 1860 *Poems Before Congress*, a less popular political work. Her *Last Poems* were published posthumously in 1862.

From SONNETS FROM THE PORTUGUESE

I

I thought once how Theocritus[†] had sung
Of the sweet years, the dear and wished-for years,
Who each one in a gracious hand appears
To bear a gift for mortals, old or young:
5   And, as I mused it in his antique tongue,
I saw, in gradual vision through my tears,
The sweet, sad years, the melancholy years,
Those of my own life, who by turns had flung
A shadow across me. Straightway I was 'ware,
10   So weeping, how a mystic Shape did move
Behind me, and drew me backward by the hair;
And a voice said in mastery, while I strove, –
'Guess now who holds thee?' – 'Death,' I said. But, there,
The silver answer rang, – 'Not Death, but Love.'

VI

Go from me. Yet I feel that I shall stand
Henceforward in thy shadow. Nevermore
Alone upon the threshold of my door
Of individual life, I shall command
5   The uses of my soul, nor lift my hand
Serenely in the sunshine as before,
Without the sense of that which I forbore –
Thy touch upon the palm. The widest land
Doom takes to part us, leaves thy heart in mine
10   With pulses that beat double. What I do
And what I dream include thee, as the wine
Must taste of its own grapes. And when I sue
God for myself, He hears that name of thine,
And sees within my eyes the tears of two.

XLIII

How do I love thee? Let me count the ways.
I love thee to the depth and breadth and height
My soul can reach, when feeling out of sight
For the ends of Being and ideal Grace.
5   I love thee to the level of everyday's

Theocritus   Greek poet of Syracuse who lived
in third century BC. He created pastoral

poetry and was imitated by Virgil

Most quiet need, by sun and candle-light.
I love thee freely, as men strive for Right;
I love thee purely, as they turn from Praise.
I love thee with the passion put to use
10   In my old griefs, and with my childhood's faith.
I love thee with a love I seemed to lose
With my lost saints, – I love thee with the breath,
Smiles, tears, of all my life! – and, if God choose,
I shall but love thee better after death.

1845   1850

John Stuart Mill
1806–73

Mill was a precocious child, intensively educated by his father at a tender age. He is reputed to have begun Greek at three, and was fluent in the Latin authors by the age of seven. He became a Clerk at India House, both a disciple and a critic of Jeremy Bentham, and formed the Utilitarian Society which met during the years 1823–6 in order to read and discuss essays and papers. In 1825 he edited Bentham's *Treatise upon Evidence.*

A year later, Mill suffered acute depression which induced a severe intellectual crisis, and forced him into reconsiderations of his philosophical position. He found new inspiration in the writings of Wordsworth and Coleridge, but particularly in the poetry of Wordsworth: he came to the conclusion that it is 'better to be Socrates unhappy, than a pig happy'.

In 1831 he met Harriet Taylor, who was to be his major inspiration over the next twenty years. Mill married her in 1851 when her husband died.

Mill worked tirelessly: he published *System of Logic* (1843), *Principles of Political Economy* (1848), *Liberty* (1859), *Utilitarianism* (1861), *The Subjection of Women* (1869), his autobiography (1873) and many other essays, treaties and papers. He retired from the East India Company on its dissolution in 1858 with a pension, and sat as MP for Westminster (1865–8). He failed to be re-elected because of his support for the atheist MP Charles Bradlaugh.

Mill was a major social and political thinker of the period and is most famous for his felicific calculus which proclaimed 'the greatest happiness of the greatest number'.

From THE SUBJECTION OF WOMEN

[Women's Role in Society]

There is nothing, after disease, indigence,[†] and guilt, so fatal to the pleasurable enjoyment of life as the want of a worthy outlet for the active faculties. Women who have the cares of a family, and while they have the cares of a family, have this outlet, and it generally suffices for

5 them: but what of the greatly increasing number of women, who have had no opportunity of exercising the vocation which they are mocked by telling them is their proper one? What of the women whose children have been lost to them by death or distance, or have grown up, married, and formed homes of their own? There are abundant examples of men

10 who, after a life engrossed by business, retire with a competency to the enjoyment, as they hope, of rest, but to whom, as they are unable to acquire new interests and excitements that can replace the old, the change to a life of inactivity brings ennui,[†] melancholy, and premature death. Yet no one thinks of the parallel case of so many worthy and

15 devoted women, who, having paid what they are told is their debt to society – having brought up a family blamelessly to manhood and womanhood – having kept a house as long as they had a house needing to be kept – are deserted by the sole occupation for which they have fitted themselves; and remain with undiminished activity but with no

20 employment for it, unless perhaps a daughter or daughter-in-law is willing to abdicate in their favour the discharge of the same functions in her younger household. Surely a hard lot for the old age of those who have worthily discharged, as long as it was given to them to discharge, what the world accounts their only social duty. Of such

25 women, and of those others to whom this duty has not been committed at all – many of whom pine through life with the consciousness of thwarted vocations, and activities which are not suffered to expand – the only resources, speaking generally, are religion and charity. But their religion, though it may be one of feeling, and of ceremonial

30 observance, cannot be a religion of action, unless in the form of charity. For charity many of them are by nature admirably fitted; but to practise it usefully, or even without doing mischief, requires the education, the manifold preparation, the knowledge and the thinking powers, of a skilful administrator. There are few of the administrative functions of

35 government for which a person would not be fit, who is fit to bestow charity usefully. In this as in other cases (pre-eminently in that of the education of children), the duties permitted to women cannot be

---

indigence poverty
ennui mental weariness from lack of occupation

performed properly, without their being trained for duties which, to the great loss of society, are not permitted to them. And here let me
40 notice the singular way in which the question of women's disabilities is frequently presented to view, by those who find it easier to draw a ludicrous picture of what they do not like, than to answer the arguments for it. When it is suggested that women's executive capacities and prudent counsels might sometimes be found valuable in affairs of state,
45 these lovers of fun hold up to the ridicule of the world, as sitting in parliament or in the cabinet, girls in their teens, or young wives of two or three and twenty, transported bodily, exactly as they are, from the drawing-room to the House of Commons. They forget that males are not usually selected at this early age for a seat in Parliament, or for
50 responsible political functions. Common sense would tell them that if such trusts were confided to women, it would be to such as having no special vocation for married life, or preferring another employment of their faculties (as many women even now prefer to marriage some of the few honourable occupations within their reach), have spent the best
55 years of their youth in attempting to qualify themselves for the pursuits in which they desire to engage; or still more frequently perhaps, widows or wives of forty or fifty, by whom the knowledge of life and faculty of government which they have acquired in their families, could by the aid of appropriate studies be made available on a less contracted scale.
60 There is no country of Europe in which the ablest men have not frequently experienced, and keenly appreciated, the value of the advice and help of clever and experienced women of the world, in the attainment both of private and of public objects; and there are important matters of public administration to which few men are equally competent
65 with such women; among others, the detailed control of expenditure. But what we are now discussing is not the need which society has of the services of women in public business, but the dull and hopeless life to which it so often condemns them, by forbidding them to exercise the practical abilities which many of them are conscious of, in any
70 wider field than one which to some of them never was, and to others is no longer, open. If there is anything vitally important to the happiness of human beings, it is that they should relish their habitual pursuit. This requisite of an enjoyable life is very imperfectly granted, or altogether denied, to a large part of mankind; and by its absence many
75 a life is a failure, which is provided, in appearance, with every requisite of success. But if circumstances which society is not yet skilful enough to overcome, render such failures often for the present inevitable, society need not itself inflict them. The injudiciousness of parents, a youth's own inexperience, or the absence of external opportunities for the
80 congenial vocation, and their presence for an uncongenial, condemn numbers of men to pass their lives in doing one thing reluctantly and

ill, when there are other things which they could have done well and happily. But on women this sentence is imposed by actual law, and by customs equivalent to law. What, in unenlightened societies, colour,
85 race, religion, or in the case of a conquered country, nationality, are to some men, sex is to all women; a peremptory[†] exclusion from almost all honourable occupations, but either such as cannot be fulfilled by others, or such as those others do not think worthy of their acceptance. Sufferings arising from causes of this nature usually meet with so
90 little sympathy, that few persons are aware of the great amount of unhappiness even now produced by the feeling of a wasted life. The case will be even more frequent, as increased cultivation creates a greater and greater disproportion between the ideas and faculties of women, and the scope which society allows to their activity.
95　　When we consider the positive evil caused to the disqualified half of the human race by their disqualification – first in the loss of the most inspiriting and elevating kind of personal enjoyment, and next in the weariness, disappointment, and profound dissatisfaction with life, which are so often the substitute for it; one feels that among all the lessons
100 which men require for carrying on the struggle against the inevitable imperfections of their lot on earth, there is no lesson which they more need, than not to add to the evils which nature inflicts, by their jealous and prejudiced restrictions on one another. Their vain fears only substitute other and worse evils for those which they are idly apprehen-
105 sive of: while every retraint on the freedom of conduct of any of their human fellow creatures (otherwise than by making them responsible for any evil actually caused by it), dries up pro tanto[†] the principal fountain of human happiness, and leaves the species less rich, to an inappreciable degree, in all that makes life valuable to the individual
110 human being.

1861   1869

---

peremptory absolutely fixed   *pro tanto* on account of so much

Edward Fitzgerald

1809–93

Fitzgerald came from a wealthy, landed background and remained provincial throughout his life, which he spent mostly at Woodbridge, Suffolk. He is chiefly notable for his translation of the *Rubáiyát of Omar Khayyám* (1859), and for his letters to famous literary friends. He knew Thackeray, Tennyson and Carlyle, and preferred to correspond with them rather than meet them. His letters display his kindly, sympathetic temperament, and their anecdotes afford biographers a source of valuable information for the period and its personalities.

He made a disastrous marriage to Lucy Barton which lasted no more than a year. He had published a biography of her father, Bernard, the Quaker poet, in 1849. He published *Euphanor: a Dialogue on Youth*, in the Socratic style (1851), and translated amongst other writers Calderon and Aeschylus. None of his translations made much of a mark, but later he was to add two more esoteric works to his list of translations from the Persian: Attar's *Parliament of Birds* and Jami's *Salaman and Absal*.

From THE RUBÁIYÁT OF OMAR KHAYYÁM†

I

Wake! For the Sun, who scatter'd into flight
The Stars before him from the Field of Night,
   Drives Night along with them from Heav'n, and strikes
The Sultán's Turret with a Shaft of Light.

II

5   Before the phantom of False morning† died,
   Methought a Voice within the Tavern cried,

The Rubáiyát of Omar Khayyám Omar Khayyám was a twelfth-century mathematician, astronomer and teacher from Nishapur in Persia. In Persian, rhymed quatrains constituted a verse form called 'rubā'i'

phantom . . . morning Fitzgerald described a 'transient light on the horizon' which appeared before the true dawn

'When all the Temple is prepared within,
Why nods the drowsy Worshipper outside?'

III

And, as the Cock crew, those who stood before
10   The Tavern shouted – 'Open then the Door!
You know how little while we have to stay,
And, once departed, may return no more.'

IV

Now the New Year† reviving old Desires,
The thoughtful Soul to Solitude retires,
15   Where the WHITE HAND OF MOSES on the Bough
Puts out, and Jesus† from the Ground suspires.†

V

Iram† indeed is gone with all his Rose,
And Jamshýd's† Sev'n-ring'd Cup where no one knows;
    But still a Ruby kindles in the Vine,
20   And many a Garden by the Water blows.

VI

And David's lips are lockt; but in divine
High-piping Pehleví,† with 'Wine! Wine! Wine!
    Red Wine!' – the Nightingale cries to the Rose
That sallow† cheek of hers to incarnadine.†

VII

25   Come, fill the Cup, and in the fire of Spring
Your Winter-garment of Repentance fling:
    The Bird of Time has but a little way
To flutter – and the Bird is on the Wing.

VIII

Whether at Naishápúr or Babylon,
30   Whether the Cup with sweet or bitter run,
    The Wine of Life keeps oozing drop by drop,
The Leaves of Life keep falling one by one.

New Year the beginning of spring in Persia
White . . . Jesus plants named in honour of
  prophets who preceded Mohammed
suspires breathes (Persians believed that the
  healing power of Jesus was in his breath)

Iram a royal garden which has disappeared
  beneath the sands
Jamshýd a legendary king
Pehleví classical language of Persia
sallow sickly yellow
incarnadine make crimson

IX

Each Morn a thousand Roses brings, you say;
Yes, but where leaves the Rose of Yesterday?
35   And this first Summer month that brings the Rose
Shall take Jamshýd and Kaikobád† away.

X

Well, let it take them! What have we to do
With Kaikobád the Great, or Kaikhosrú?†
Let Zál and Rustum† bluster as they will,
40   Or Hátim† call to Supper – heed not you.

XI

With me along the strip of Herbage strown
That just divides the desert from the sown,
Where name of Slave and Sultán is forgot –
And Peace to Mahmúd† on his golden Throne!

. . .

LXVIII

We are no other than a moving row
270   Of Magic Shadow-shapes that come and go
Round with the Sun-illumined Lantern held
In Midnight by the Master of the Show;

LXIX

But helpless Pieces of the Game He plays
Upon this Chequer-board of Nights and Days;
275   Hither and thither moves, and checks, and slays,
And one by one back in the Closet lays.

LXX

The Ball no question makes of Ayes and Noes,
But Here or There as strikes the Player† goes;
And He that toss'd you down into the Field,
280   *He* knows about it all – HE knows – HE knows!

Kaikobád   founder of a line of Persian
  emperors
Kaikhosrú a king
Zál and Rustum   son and father warriors

Hátim   a generous host
Mahmúd   a sultan who conquered India
Player   polo player

LXXI

The Moving Finger writes; and, having writ,
Moves on: nor all your Piety nor Wit
   Shall lure it back to cancel half a line,
Nor all your Tears wash out a Word of it.

LXXII

285   And that inverted Bowl they call the Sky,
Whereunder crawling coop'd we live and die,
   Lift not your hands to *It* for help – for It
As impotently moves as you or I.

1856–9   1879 (1859)

Alfred, Lord Tennyson
1809–92

After Wordsworth, Tennyson was the most famous poet of the nineteenth century. He was admired particularly for his descriptive and narrative poetry, in which he exercised a superb technical mastery. He took notice of adverse criticism and became an habitual reviser of his work, which is best shown in the revision of many 1830 and 1832 poems subsequently published in 1842: good examples of such revisions are the opening, and the ending, of *The Lady of Shalott*.

Tennyson was born in Somersby, Lincolnshire, and brought up and educated in his father's rectory. In spite of his father's having been disinherited by his own father, Tennyson was able to proceed to Trinity College, Cambridge, where in 1829 he won the Chancellor's Medal for English verse and became, with his friend Arthur Hallam, a member of the Apostles, a group dedicated mainly to the discussion of literature, philosophy and politics. It was with Hallam in 1832 that Tennyson made his first visit to the Continent.

Tennyson published *Poems, Chiefly Lyrical* in 1830, and a further volume in 1832 which contained many which were to help establish his reputation, such as *The Two Voices* and *The Lotus Eaters*. Ten years later he published another selection with many of the early poems much revised. Poems such as *Morte D'Arthur*, *Locksley Hall* and *Ulysses* made him deservedly popular, and in 1845 he was awarded a civil list pension of £200.

In 1833 Hallam died abroad. This untimely and tragic event had a profound effect on Tennyson, and for seventeen years he meditated on the loss of his friend; intermittently for ten years he wrote parts of a long elegy, one of the greatest in the history of English literature, and published it in 1850 as *In Memoriam A.H.H.*

That year saw the death of Wordsworth, and Tennyson was made Poet Laureate in his place. Other major poems followed: *Ode on the Death of the Duke of Wellington*, in 1852, *The Charge of the Light Brigade* in 1854. In that year he rented a large country house, Farringford, on the Isle of Wight. Such was the income which he derived from the publication of his poems, that he was soon able to buy Farringford outright; and some years later, in 1868, he commissioned another grand house to be built at Aldworth in Surrey.

In 1855 *Maud* was published. Described by Tennyson as a mono-drama, it is the monologue of a distraught and disappointed lover who escapes to frenzied activity in the Crimean War as a diversion from the obsession with his beloved. It is a poem of uneven achievement, but Tennyson regarded it for a long time as his favourite, and loved to declaim it.

From 1859 to 1872, he published various books of *Idylls of the King*, concerned with the Arthurian legend, which sold to the public extremely well and secured his fortune.

In the 1880s literary taste began to change and Tennyson's poetry lost its unreserved critical acclaim. Matthew Arnold had pointed out that Tennyson's poetry was 'defective in intellectual power'. His friend Carlyle admired the descriptive patches in the *Idylls* but considered that they expressed 'the inward perfection of vacancy'. Swinburne wrote satirically of the 'Morte D'Albert' and 'The Idylls of the Prince Consort'. Tennyson's reputation was in process of being eclipsed by Browning's.

It was not until T. S. Eliot turned his attention to him in the twentieth century that Tennyson's reputation was rehabilitated. Eliot wrote that Tennyson had 'the finest ear of any English poet since Milton'. The new look at Tennyson produced Christopher Ricks's monumental and definitive edition of his poems, first published in 1969.

THE LADY OF SHALOTT

PART I

On either side the river lie
Long fields of barley and of rye,
That clothe the wold and meet the sky;
And through the field the road runs by
5   To many-towered Camelot,[†]
And up and down the people go,
Gazing where the lilies blow
Round an island there below,
     The island of Shalott.

Camelot the legendary town where King
  Arthur held his court

10 Willows whiten, aspens quiver,
Little breezes dusk and shiver
Through the wave that runs for ever
By the island in the river
  Flowing down to Camelot.
15 Four gray walls, and four gray towers,
Overlook a space of flowers,
And the silent isle imbowers
  The Lady of Shalott.

By the margin, willow-veiled,
20 Slide the heavy barges trailed
By slow horses; and unhailed
The shallop† flitteth silken-sailed,
  Skimming down to Camelot:
But who hath seen her wave her hand?
25 Or at the casement seen her stand?
Or is she known in all the land,
  The Lady of Shalott?

Only reapers, reaping early
In among the bearded barley,
30 Hear a song that echoes cheerly
From the river winding clearly,
  Down to towered Camelot:
And by the moon the reaper weary,
Piling sheaves in uplands airy,
35 Listening, whispers "Tis the fairy
  Lady of Shalott.'

       PART II
There she weaves by night and day
A magic web with colours gay.
She has heard a whisper say,
40 A curse on her if she stay
  To look down to Camelot.
She knows not what the curse may be,
And so she weaveth steadily,
And little other care hath she,
45   The Lady of Shalott.

And moving through a mirror clear
That hangs before her all the year,

---

shallop light open boat

Shadows of the world appear.
There she sees the highway near
50   Winding down to Camelot:
There the river eddy whirls,
And there the surly village-churls,*   peasants
And the red cloaks of market girls,
      Pass onward from Shalott.

55 Sometimes a troop of damsels glad,
An abbot on an ambling pad,
Sometimes a curly shepherd-lad,
Or long-haired page in crimson clad,
      Goes by to towered Camelot;
60 And sometimes through the mirror blue
The knights come riding two and two;
She hath no loyal knight and true,
      The Lady of Shalott.

But in her web she still delights
65 To weave the mirror's magic sights,
For often through the silent nights
A funeral, with plumes and lights
      And music, went to Camelot:
Or when the moon was overhead,
70 Came two young lovers lately wed;
'I am half sick of shadows,' said
      The Lady of Shalott.

PART III

A bow-shot from her bower-eaves,
He rode between the barley-sheaves,
75 The sun came dazzling through the leaves,
And flamed upon the brazen greaves†
      Of bold Sir Lancelot,
A red-cross knight for ever kneeled
To a lady in his shield,
80 That sparkled on the yellow field,
      Beside remote Shalott.

The gemmy bridle glittered free,
Like to some branch of stars we see
Hung in the golden Galaxy.

---

greaves armour guards for the shins

85   The bridle bells rang merrily
         As he rode down to Camelot:
     And from his blazoned baldric† slung
     A mighty silver bugle hung,
     And as he rode his armour rung,
90   Beside remote Shalott.

     All in the blue unclouded weather
     Thick-jewelled shone the saddle-leather,
     The helmet and the helmet-feather
     Burned like one burning flame together,
95   As he rode down to Camelot.
     As often through the purple night,
     Below the starry clusters bright,
     Some bearded meteor, trailing light,
         Moves over still Shalott.

100 His broad clear brow in sunlight glowed;
     On burnished hooves his war-horse trode;*   trod
     From underneath his helmet flowed
     His coal-black curls as on he rode,
         As he rode down to Camelot.
105 From the bank and from the river
     He flashed into the crystal mirror,
     'Tirra lirra,' by the river
         Sang Sir Lancelot.

     She left the web, she left the loom,
110 She made three paces through the room,
     She saw the water-lily bloom,
     She saw the helmet and the plume,
         She looked down to Camelot.
     Out flew the web and floated wide;
115 The mirror cracked from side to side;
     'The curse is come upon me,' cried
         The Lady of Shalott.

                         PART IV

     In the stormy east-wind straining,
     The pale yellow woods were waning,
120 The broad stream in his banks complaining.
     Heavily the low sky raining

---

blazoned baldric   heraldically decorated sash
   or belt from which a bugle hangs

Over towered Camelot;
Down she came and found a boat
Beneath a willow left afloat,
125 And round about the prow she wrote
    The Lady of Shallott.

And down the river's dim expanse
Like some bold seër in a trance,
Seeing all his own mischance –
130 With a glassy countenance
    Did she look to Camelot.
And at the closing of the day
She loosed the chain, and down she lay;
The broad stream bore her far away,
135   The Lady of Shalott.

Lying, robed in snowy white
That loosely flew to left and right –
The leaves upon her falling light –
Through the noises of the night
140   She floated down to Camelot:
And as the boat-head wound along
The willowy hills and fields among,
They heard her singing her last song,
    The Lady of Shalott.

145 Heard a carol, mournful, holy,
Chanted loudly, chanted lowly,
Till her blood was frozen slowly,
And her eyes were darkened wholly,
    Turned to towered Camelot.
150 For ere she reached upon the tide
The first house by the water-side,
Singing in her song she died,
    The Lady of Shalott.

Under tower and balcony,
155 By garden-wall and gallery,
A gleaming shape she floated by,
Dead-pale between the houses high,
    Silent into Camelot.
Out upon the wharfs they came,
160 Knight and burgher,* lord and dame,   citizen
And round the prow they read her name,
    The Lady of Shalott.

Who is this? and what is here?
And in the lighted palace near
165   Died the sound of royal cheer;
And they crossed themselves for fear,
      All the knights at Camelot:
But Lancelot mused a little space;
He said, 'She has a lovely face;
170   God in his mercy lend her grace
      The Lady of Shalott.'

1832   1832

From THE LOTUS-EATERS†

Choric Song

I

There is sweet music here that softer falls
Than petals from blown roses on the grass,
Or night-dews on still waters between walls
Of shadowy granite, in a gleaming pass;
5   Music that gentlier on the spirit lies,
Than tired eyelids upon tired eyes;
Music that brings sweet sleep down from the blissful skies.
Here are cool mosses deep,
And through the moss the ivies creep,
10   And in the stream the long-leaved flowers weep,
And from the craggy ledge the poppy hangs in sleep.

II

Why are we weighed upon with heaviness,
And utterly consumed with sharp distress,
While all things else have rest from weariness?
15   All things have rest: why should we toil alone,
We only toil, who are the first of things,
And make perpetual moan,

The Lotus-Eaters in Homeric legend, the
lotus-eaters ate fruit from the lotus tree which
made them forget their friends and native

land. They had no wish to return and were
satisfied to live in ease and luxury

Still from one sorrow to another thrown:
Nor ever fold our wings,
20 And cease from wanderings,
Nor steep our brows in slumber's holy balm;
Nor harken what the inner spirit sings,
'There is no joy but calm!'
Why should we only toil, the roof and crown of things?

III

25 Lo! in the middle of the wood,
The folded leaf is wooed from out the bud
With winds upon the branch, and there
Grows green and broad, and takes no care,
Sun-steeped at noon, and in the moon
30 Nightly dew-fed; and turning yellow
Falls, and floats adown the air.
Lo! sweetened with the summer light,
The full-juiced apple, waxing over-mellow,
Drops in a silent autumn night.
35 All its allotted length of days,
The flower ripens in its place,
Ripens and fades, and falls, and hath no toil,
Fast-rooted in the fruitful soil.

IV

Hateful is the dark-blue sky,
40 Vaulted o'er the dark-blue sea.
Death is the end of life; ah, why
Should life all labour be?
Let us alone. Time driveth onward fast,
And in a little while our lips are dumb.
45 Let us alone. What is it that will last?
All things are taken from us, and become
Portions and parcels of the dreadful Past.
Let us alone. What pleasure can we have
To war with evil? Is there any peace
50 In ever climbing up the climbing wave?
All things have rest, and ripen toward the grave
In silence; ripen, fall and cease:
Give us long rest or death, dark death, or dreamful ease.

V

How sweet it were, hearing the downward stream,
55 With half-shut eyes ever to seem

Falling asleep in a half-dream!
To dream and dream, like yonder amber light,
Which will not leave the myrrh-bush on the height;
To hear each other's whispered speech;
60   Eating the Lotos day by day,
To watch the crisping[†] ripples on the beach,
And tender curving lines of creamy spray;
To lend our hearts and spirits wholly
To the influence of mild-minded melancholy;
65   To muse and brood and live again in memory,
With those old faces of our infancy
Heaped over with a mound of grass,
Two handfuls of white dust, shut in an urn of brass!

VI

Dear is the memory of our wedded lives,
70   And dear the last embraces of our wives
And their warm tears: but all hath suffered change:
For surely now our household hearths are cold:
Our sons inherit us: our looks are strange:
And we should come like ghosts to trouble joy.
75   Or else the island princes over-bold
Have eat our substance, and the minstrel sings
Before them of the ten years' war[†] in Troy,
And our great deeds, as half-forgotten things.
Is there confusion in the little isle?
80   Let what is broken so remain.
The Gods are hard to reconcile:
'Tis hard to settle order once again.
There *is* confusion worse than death,
Trouble on trouble, pain on pain,
85   Long labour unto agèd breath,
Sore task to hearts worn out by many wars
And eyes grown dim with gazing on the pilot-stars.

VII

But, propt on beds of amaranth[†] and moly,[†]
How sweet (while warm airs lull us, blowing lowly)
90   With half-dropt eyelid still,
Beneath a heaven dark and holy,
To watch the long bright river drawing slowly

---

crisping   curling in short, stiff folds
ten years' war   the Graeco-Trojan war lasted
    ten years

amaranth   a mythical unfading flower
moly   a fabulous herb of white flower and
    black root which had magic qualities

His waters from the purple hill –
To hear the dewy echoes calling
95 From cave to cave through the thick-twinèd vine –
To watch the emerald-coloured water falling
Through many a woven acanthus†-wreath divine!
Only to hear and see the far-off sparkling brine,
Only to hear were sweet, stretched out beneath the pine.

VIII

100 The Lotos blooms below the barren peak:
The Lotos blows by every winding creek:
All day the wind breathes low with mellower tone:
Through every hollow cave and alley lone
Round and round the spicy downs the yellow Lotos-dust is blown.
105 We have had enough of action, and of motion we,
Rolled to starboard, rolled to larboard,* when the surge   port
      was seething free,
Where the wallowing monster spouted his foam-fountains in the sea.
Let us swear an oath, and keep it with an equal mind,
In the hollow Lotos-land to live and lie reclined
110 On the hills like Gods together, careless of mankind.
For they lie beside their nectar, and the bolts are hurled
Far below them in the valleys, and the clouds are lightly curled
Round their golden houses, girdled with the gleaming world:
Where they smile in secret, looking over wasted lands,
115 Blight and famine, plague and earthquake, roaring deeps and fiery
      sands,
Clanging fights, and flaming towns, and sinking ships, and praying
      hands.
But they smile, they find a music centred in a doleful song
Streaming up, a lamentation and an ancient tale of wrong,
Like a tale of little meaning though the words are strong;
120 Chanted from an ill-used race of men that cleave the soil,
Sow the seed, and reap the harvest with enduring toil,
Storing yearly little dues of wheat, and wine and oil;
Till they perish and they suffer – some, 'tis whispered – down in hell
Suffer endless anguish, others in Elysian valleys† dwell,
125 Resting weary limbs at last on beds of asphodel.†

---

acanthus a plant whose leaf was the model
  for some plant decoration in Greek
  architecture
Elysian valleys Elysium was the legendary

country where the blessed lived. Elysian
means 'happy' or 'delightful'
asphodel a kind of liliaceous plant: the
immortal flower of Elysium

Surely, surely, slumber is more sweet than toil, the shore
Than labour in the deep mid-ocean, wind and wave and oar;
Oh rest ye, brother mariners, we will not wander more.

1830–2   1832

MORTE D'ARTHUR[†]

So all day long the noise of battle rolled
Among the mountains by the winter sea;
Until King Arthur's table, man by man,
Had fallen in Lyonnesse[†] about their Lord,
5   King Arthur: then, because his wound was deep,
The bold Sir Bedivere[†] uplifted him,
Sir Bedivere, the last of all his knights,
And bore him to a chapel nigh the field,
A broken chancel with a broken cross,
10   That stood on a dark strait of barren land.
On one side lay the Ocean, and on one
Lay a great water, and the moon was full.

Then spake King Arthur to Sir Bedivere:
'The sequel of today unsolders all
15   The goodliest fellowship of famous knights
Whereof this world holds record. Such a sleep
They sleep – the men I loved. I think that we
Shall never more, at any future time,
Delight our souls with talk of knightly deeds,
20   Walking about the gardens and the halls
Of Camelot,[†] as in the days that were.
I perish by this people which I made, –
Though Merlin[†] sware that I should come again
To rule once more – but let what will be, be,
25   I am so deeply smitten through the helm
That without help I cannot last till morn.
Thou therefore take my brand Excalibur,[†]

Morte D'Arthur   Death of Arthur
Lyonnesse   a fabled tract of fertile ground
which lay between Land's End, Cornwall,
and the Scilly Isles. Arthur came from this
mythical country
Sir Bedivere   one of King Arthur's knights of
the Round Table, who was his most loyal
butler

Camelot   the legendary town where Arthur
held his court
Merlin   enchanter and magician of the
Arthurian romance
Excalibur   the name of King Arthur's sword.
By virtue of pulling it from a stone in which
it was magically fixed, he was acclaimed king

Which was my pride: for thou rememberest how
In those old days, one summer noon, an arm
30   Rose up from out the bosom of the lake,
Clothed in white samite,[†] mystic, wonderful,
Holding the sword — and how I rowed across
And took it, and have worn it, like a king:
And, wheresoever I am sung or told
35   In aftertime, this also shall be known:
But now delay not: take Excalibur,
And fling him far into the middle mere:
Watch what thou seëst, and lightly bring me word.'

To him replied the bold Sir Bedivere:
40   'It is not meet, Sir King, to leave thee thus,
Aidless, alone, and smitten through the helm.
A little thing may harm a wounded man.
Yet I thy hest will all perform at full,
Watch what I see, and lightly bring thee word.'

45   So saying, from the ruined shrine he stept
And in the moon athwart the place of tombs,
Where lay the mighty bones of ancient men,
Old knights, and over them the sea-wind sang
Shrill, chill, with flakes of foam. He, stepping down
50   By zig-zag paths, and juts of pointed rock,
Came on the shining levels of the lake.

There drew he forth the brand Excalibur,
And o'er him, drawing it, the winter moon,
Brightening the skirts of a long cloud, ran forth
55   And sparkled keen with frost against the hilt:
For all the haft twinkled with diamond sparks,
Myriads[†] of topaz-lights,[†] and jacinth[†]-work
Of sublest jewellery. He gazed so long
That both his eyes were dazzled, as he stood,
60   This way and that dividing the swift mind,
In act to throw: but at the last it seemed
Better to leave Excalibur concealed
There in the many-knotted waterflags,*   water-iris
That whistled stiff and dry about the marge.
65   So strode he back slow to the wounded King.

---

samite   medieval dress-fabric of rich silk   *topaz-lights*   gleaming pieces of translucent
   sometimes woven with gold   silicate
myriads   ten thousands: huge numbers   *jacinth*   reddish orange gem

Then spake King Arthur to Sir Bedivere:
'Hast thou performed my mission which I gave?
What is it thou hast seen? or what hast heard?'

And answer made the bold Sir Bedivere:
70 'I heard the ripple washing in the reeds,
And the wild water lapping on the crag.'

To whom replied King Arthur, faint and pale:
'Thou hast betrayed thy nature and thy name,
Not rendering true answer, as beseemed
75 Thy fëalty,† nor like a noble knight:
For surer sign had followed, either hand,
Or voice, or else a motion of the mere.
This is a shameful thing for men to lie.
Yet now, I charge thee, quickly go again
80 As thou art lief† and dear, and do the thing
I bad thee, watch, and lightly bring me word'.

Then went Sir Bedivere the second time
Across the ridge, and paced beside the mere,
Counting the dewy pebbles, fixed in thought;
85 But when he saw the wonder of the hilt,
How curiously and strangely chased, he smote
His palms together, and he cried aloud,

'And if indeed I cast the brand away,
Surely a precious thing, one worthy note,
90 Should thus be lost for ever from the earth,
Which might have pleased the eyes of many men.
What good should follow this, if this were done?
What harm, undone? deep harm to disobey,
Seeing obedience is the bond of rule.
95 Were it well to obey then, if a king demand
An act unprofitable, against himself?
The King is sick, and knows not what he does.
What record, or what relic of my lord
Should be to aftertime, but empty breath
100 And rumours of a doubt? but were this kept,
Stored in some treasure-house of mighty kings,
Some one might show it at a joust of arms,
Saying, "King Arthur's sword, Excalibur,

---

fëalty pledged faithfulness   *lief* glad to act

Wrought by the lonely maiden of the Lake.†
105   Nine years she wrought it, sitting in the deeps
Upon the hidden bases of the hills."
So might some old man speak in the aftertime
To all the people, winning reverence.
But now much honour and much fame were lost.'

110   So spake he, clouded with his own conceit,
And hid Excalibur the second time,
And so strode back slow to the wounded King.

Then spoke King Arthur, breathing heavily:
'What is it thou hast seen? or what hast heard?'

115   And answer made the bold Sir Bedivere:
'I heard the water lapping on the crag,
And the long ripple washing in the reeds.'

To whom replied King Arthur, much in wrath:
'Ah, miserable and unkind, untrue,
120   Unknightly, traitor-hearted! Woe is me!
Authority forgets a dying king,
Laid widowed of the power in his eye
That bowed the will. I see thee what thou art,
For thou, the latest-left of all my knights,
125   In whom should meet the offices of all,
Thou wouldst betray me for the precious hilt;
Either from lust of gold, or like a girl
Valuing the giddy pleasure of the eyes.
Yet, for a man may fail in duty twice,
130   And the third time may prosper, get thee hence:
But, if thou spare to fling Excalibur,
I will arise and slay thee with my hands.'

Then quickly rose Sir Bedivere, and ran,
And, leaping down the ridges lightly, plunged
135   Among the bulrush-beds, and clutched the sword,
And strongly wheeled and threw it. The great brand
Made lightnings in the splendour of the moon,
And flashing round and round, and whirled in an arch,
Shot like a streamer of the northern morn,

---

maiden . . . Lake   the Lady of the Lake. Vivien,   of a lake surrounded by knights and damsels
the mistress of Merlin. She lived in the middle

140   Seen where the moving isles of winter shock
      By night, with noises of the northern sea.
      So flashed and fell the brand Excalibur:
      But ere he dipt the surface, rose an arm
      Clothed in white samite, mystic, wonderful,
145   And caught him by the hilt, and brandished him
      Three times, and drew him under in the mere.
      And lightly went the other to the King.

         Then spoke King Arthur, drawing thicker breath:
      'Now see I by thine eyes that this is done.
150   Speak out: what is it thou hast heard, or seen?'

         And answer made the bold Sir Bedivere:
      'Sir King, I closed mine eyelids, lest the gems
      Should blind my purpose, for I never saw,
      Nor shall see, here or elsewhere, till I die,
155   Not though I live three lives of mortal men,
      So great a miracle as yonder hilt.
      Then with both hands I flung him, wheeling him;
      But when I looked again, behold an arm,
      Clothed in white samite, mystic, wonderful,
160   That caught him by the hilt, and brandished him
      Three times, and drew him under in the mere.'

         And answer made King Arthur, breathing hard:
      'My end draws nigh; 'tis time that I were gone.
      Make broad thy shoulders to receive my weight,
165   And bear me to the margin; yet I fear
      My wound hath taken cold, and I shall die.'

         So saying, from the pavement he half rose,
      Slowly, with pain, reclining on his arm,
      And looking wistfully with wide blue eyes
170   As in a picture. Him Sir Bedivere
      Remorsefully regarded through his tears,
      And would have spoken, but he found not words,
      Then took with care, and kneeling on one knee,
      O'er both his shoulders drew the languid hands,
175   And rising bore him through the place of tombs.

         But, as he walked, King Arthur panted hard,
      Like one that feels a nightmare on his bed
      When all the house is mute. So sighed the King,

Muttering and murmuring at his ear, 'Quick, quick!
180   I fear it is too late, and I shall die.'
But the other swiftly strode from ridge to ridge,
Clothed with his breath, and looking, as he walked,
Larger than human on the frozen hills.
He heard the deep behind him, and a cry
185   Before. His own thought drove him, like a goad.
Dry clashed his harness in the icy caves
And barren chasms, and all to left and right
The bare black cliff clanged round him, as he based
His feet on juts of slippery crag that rang
190   Sharp-smitten with the dint of armèd heels –
And on a sudden, lo! the level lake,
And the long glories of the winter moon.
    Then saw they how there hove a dusky barge,
Dark as a funeral scarf from stem to stern,
195   Beneath them; and descending they were ware*   aware
That all the decks were dense with stately forms
Black-stoled, black-hooded, like a dream – by these
Three Queens with crowns of gold – and from them rose
A cry that shivered to the tingling stars,
200   And, as it were one voice, an agony
Of lamentation, like a wind, that shrills
All night in a waste land, where no one comes,
Or hath come, since the making of the world.

    Then murmured Arthur, 'Place me in the barge,'
205   And to the barge they came. There those three Queens
Put forth their hands, and took the King, and wept.
But she, that rose the tallest of them all
And fairest, laid his head upon her lap,
And loosed the shattered casque* and chafed† his hands,   helmet
210   And called him by his name, complaining loud,
And dropping bitter tears against his brow
Striped with dark blood: for all his face was white
And colourless, and like the withered moon
Smote by the fresh beam of the springing east;
215   And all his greaves† and cuisses† dashed with drops
Of onset; and the light and lustrous curls –
That made his forehead like a rising sun
High from the daïs-throne – were parched with dust;

chafed   made warm by rubbing   *cuisses*   thigh armour
greaves   armour which guards the shins

Or, clotted into points and hanging loose,
220 Mixed with the knightly growth that fringed his lips.
So like a shattered column lay the King;
Not like that Arthur who, with lance in rest,
From spur to plume a star of tournament,
Shot through the lists at Camelot, and charged
225 Before the eyes of ladies and of kings.

Then loudly cried the bold Sir Bedivere,
'Ah! my Lord Arthur, whither shall I go?
Where shall I hide my forehead and my eyes?
For now I see the true old times are dead,
230 When every morning brought a noble chance,
And every chance brought out a noble knight.
Such times have been not since the light that led
The holy Elders with the gift of myrrh.
But now the whole ROUND TABLE† is dissolved
235 Which was an image of the mighty world;
And I, the last, go forth companionless,
And the days darken round me, and the years,
Among new men, strange faces, other minds.'

And slowly answered Arthur from the barge:
240 'The old order changeth, yielding place to new,
And God fulfils Himself in many ways,
Lest one good custom should corrupt the world.
Comfort thyself: what comfort is in me?
I have lived my life, and that which I have done
245 May He within Himself make pure! but thou,
If thou shouldst never see my face again,
Pray for my soul. More things are wrought by prayer
Than this world dreams of. Wherefore, let thy voice
Rise like a fountain for me night and day.
250 For what are men better than sheep or goats
That nourish a blind life within the brain,
If, knowing God, they lift not hands of prayer
Both for themselves and those who call them friend?
For so the whole round earth is every way
255 Bound by gold chains about the feet of God.
But now farewell. I am going a long way

ROUND TABLE   the table was made by Merlin for
Uther Pendragon, who gave it to King
Leodegraunce, who, in turn, gave it to King
Arthur, when Arthur married his daughter
Guinevere. It was circular to prevent
argument over precedence. It seated 150
knights and a place was left empty for the
Holy Grail

With these thou seëst – if indeed I go –
(For all my mind is clouded with a doubt)
To the island-valley of Avilion;†
260 Where falls not hail, or rain, or any snow,
Nor ever wind blows loudly; but it lies
Deep-meadowed, happy, fair with orchard-lawns
And bowery hollows crowned with summer sea,
Where I will heal me of my grievous wound.'

265 So said he, and the barge with oar and sail
Moved from the brink, like some full-breasted swan
That, fluting a wild carol ere her death,
Ruffles her pure cold plume, and take the flood
With swarthy webs.† Long stood Sir Bedivere
270 Revolving many memories, till the hull
Looked one black dot against the verge of dawn,
And on the mere the wailing died away.

1833–4   1842

ULYSSES†

It little profits that an idle king,
By this still hearth, among these barren crags,
Matched with an agèd wife, I mete* and dole*   allot   give
Unequal laws unto a savage race,
5 That hoard, and sleep, and feed, and know not me.

I cannot rest from travel: I will drink
Life to the lees:* all times I have enjoyed   dregs
Greatly, have suffered greatly, both with those
That loved me, and alone; on shore, and when
10 Through scudding drifts the rainy Hyades†
Vext the dim sea: I am become a name;

Avilion a legendary paradisal resting-place
  after death
swarthy webs dark sails
Ulysses or Odysseus. Mythical king of Ithaca,
  a small rocky island of Greece. He was a
  leading chieftain in Homer's *Iliad*, and the
  hero of the *Odyssey*. Here, he describes his
  plan to set out again from Ithaca after his

safe return from his adventures after the
Trojan war. Tennyson's story is based upon
Dante's *Inferno*, rather than Homer's
account
Hyades seven nymphs, daughters of Atlas and
  Pleione, placed among the stars in the
  constellation Taurus: they promise rain when
  they rise with the sun

For always roaming with a hungry heart
Much have I seen and known; cities of men
And manners, climates, councils, governments,
15 Myself not least, but honoured of them all;
And drunk delight of battle with my peers,
Far on the ringing plains of windy Troy.†
I am a part of all that I have met;
Yet all experience is an arch wherethrough
20 Gleams that untravelled world, whose margin fades
For ever and for ever when I move.
How dull it is to pause, to make an end,
To rust unburnished, not to shine in use!
As though to breathe were life. Life piled on life
25 Were all too little, and of one to me
Little remains: but every hour is saved
From that eternal silence, something more,
A bringer of new things; and vile it were
For some three suns to store and hoard myself,
30 And this gray spirit yearning in desire
To follow knowledge like a sinking star,
Beyond the utmost bound of human thought.

This is my son, mine own Telemachus,†
To whom I leave the sceptre and the isle –
35 Well-loved of me, discerning to fulfil
This labour, by slow prudence to make mild
A rugged people, and through soft degrees
Subdue them to the useful and the good.
Most blameless is he, centred in the sphere
40 Of common duties, decent not to fail
In offices of tenderness, and pay
Meet adoration to my household gods,
When I am gone. He works his work, I mine.

There lies the port; the vessel puffs her sail:
45 There gloom the dark broad seas. My mariners,
Souls that have toiled, and wrought, and thought with me –
That ever with a frolic welcome took
The thunder and the sunshine, and opposed
Free hearts, free foreheads – you and I are old;
50 Old age hath yet his honour and his toil;

Troy the fortress city of Homer's *Iliad*; also   *Telemachus* the only son of Ulysses and
the land of Troy which had Ilium as its chief   Penelope
city

Death closes all: but something ere the end,
Some work of noble note, may yet be done,
Not unbecoming men that strove with Gods.
The lights begin to twinkle from the rocks:
55 The long day wanes: the slow moon climbs: the deep
Moans round with many voices. Come, my friends,
'Tis not too late to seek a newer world.
Push off, and sitting well in order smite
The sounding furrows; for my purpose holds
60 To sail beyond the sunset, and the baths
Of all the western stars, until I die.
It may be that the gulfs will wash us down:
It may be we shall touch the Happy Isles,[†]
And see the great Achilles,[†] whom we knew.
65 Though much is taken, much abides; and though
We are not now that strength which in old days
Moved earth and heaven; that which we are, we are;
One equal temper of heroic hearts,
Made weak by time and fate, but strong in will
70 To strive, to seek, to find, and not to yield.

1833   1842

From IN MEMORIAM A.H.H.[†]

L

Be near me when my light is low,
    When the blood creeps, and the nerves prick
    And tingle; and the heart is sick,
And all the wheels of Being slow.

5 Be near me when the sensuous[†] frame
    Is racked with pangs that conquer trust;
    And Time, a maniac scattering dust,
And Life, a Fury slinging flame.

---

the Happy Isles the Isles of the Blest lay
    beyond the pillars of Hercules (Gibraltar)
Achilles Greek hero: in the *Iliad*, son of Peleus,
    King of the Myrmidons in Thessaly. During
    the Trojan war, after withdrawing from
    battle, he returns to kill Hector and rout the
    Trojans

In Memoriam A.H.H. an elegiac poem written
    in memory of Tennyson's friend A. H.
    Hallam who died at Vienna aged 22 in 1833.
    It is written in four octosyllabic lines rhyming
    abba, and has 132 sections of varying length
sensuous whose senses can be affected

Be near me when my faith is dry,
10   And men the flies of latter spring,
That lay their eggs, and sting and sing
And weave their petty cells and die.

Be near me when I fade away,
To point the term of human strife,
15   And on the low dark verge of life
The twilight of eternal day.

CXV

Now fades the last long streak of snow,
Now burgeons† every maze of quick.†
About the flowering squares, and thick
By ashen roots the violets blow.

5   Now rings the woodland loud and long,
The distance takes a lovelier hue,
And drowned in yonder living blue
The lark becomes a sightless song.

Now dance the lights on lawn and lea,
10   The flocks are whiter down the vale,
And milkier every milky sail
On winding stream or distant sea;

Where now the seamew† pipes, or dives
In yonder greening gleam, and fly
15   The happy birds, that change their sky
To build and brood; that live their lives

From land to land; and in my breast
Spring wakens too; and my regret
Becomes an April violet,
20   And buds and blossoms like the rest.

1833–50   1850

---

burgeons sends forth new shoots   *seamew* seagull
quick quickset thorn

THE CHARGE OF THE LIGHT BRIGADE†

I

Half a league, half a league,
  Half a league onward,
All in the valley of Death
  Rode the six hundred.
5 'Forward, the Light Brigade!
Charge for the guns!' he said:
Into the valley of Death
  Rode the six hundred.

II

'Forward, the Light Brigade!'
10 Was there a man dismayed?
Not though the soldier knew
  Some one had blundered:
Their's not to make reply,
Their's not to reason why,
15 Their's but to do and die:
Into the valley of Death
  Rode the six hundred.

III

Cannon to right of them,
Cannon to left of them,
20 Cannon in front of them
  Volleyed and thundered;
Stormed at with shot and shell,
Boldly they rode and well,
Into the jaws of Death,
25 Into the mouth of Hell
  Rode the six hundred.

IV

Flashed all their sabres bare,
Flashed as they turned in air
Sabring the gunners there,
30 Charging an army, while
  All the world wondered:

The Charge of the Light Brigade written a
  few weeks after the charge of the light cavalry
  brigade at Balaclava near Sevastopol, during
the Crimean War, where 247 officers and
men out of 637 were killed or wounded as a
result of a misunderstood order

Plunged in the battery-smoke
Right through the line they broke;
Cossack and Russian
35   Reeled from the sabre-stroke
Shattered and sundered.
Then they rode back, but not
Not the six hundred.

V

Cannon to right of them,
40   Cannon to left of them,
Cannon behind them
Volleyed and thundered;
Stormed at with shot and shell,
While horse and hero fell,
45   They that had fought so well
Came through the jaws of Death,
Back from the mouth of Hell,
All that was left of them,
Left of six hundred.

VI

50   When can their glory fade?
O the wild charge they made!
All the world wondered.
Honour the charge they made!
Honour the Light Brigade,
55   Noble six hundred!

1854   1854

Elizabeth Cleghorn Gaskell
1810–65

Elizabeth Gaskell's father was William Stevenson, a Unitarian minister, and Elizabeth was brought up by an aunt in Knutsford, Cheshire. Later several of her novels were to be referred to as the 'Knutsford novels'.

In 1832 she married William Gaskell, and they settled in Manchester, where she gave birth to four daughters, and a son who died in infancy. Her first novel was *Mary Barton* (1848) and it proved immediately successful. Dickens invited her to write for his periodical *Household Words*, to which she contributed some short stories: these were followed by *Cranford* (1851) and then *Ruth* (1853), *North and South* (1855; serialised in *Household Words*), *Sylvia's Lovers* (1863) and *Wives and Daughters* (1866). The last was unfinished: she died suddenly before writing the last chapter.

Mrs Gaskell was friendly with other literary figures of her time, including Charlotte Brontë, whose biography she was asked to write and which was published in 1857, Ruskin, the Carlyles and Kingsley among others. The Brontë biography caused a great upset on publication and parts of it had to be withdrawn and rewritten because of their allegedly libellous content.

Elizabeth Gaskell also wrote novelettes: *Phyllis*, her most famous, was serialised in the *Cornhill Magazine* in 1863–4. She was a novelist who dealt with social problems and was keenly aware of the misery of the oppressed working classes whose lives she described with sensitivity, accuracy for detail and compassion. The contrast between workers and employers and between the wives of those living in industrial areas and those in the more pleasant rural south she described in her most celebrated work, *North and South*.

From NORTH AND SOUTH,[†] Chapter 37
Looking South

'A spade! a rake! a hoe!
A pickaxe or a bill!
A hook to reap, or a scythe to mow,
A flail, or what ye will –
And here's a ready hand
To ply the needful tool,
And skill'd enough, by lessons rough,
In Labour's rugged school.'
– Hood.

Higgins's door was locked the next day, when they went to pay their call on the widow Boucher; but they learnt this time from an officious neighbour that he was really from home. He had, however, been in to see Mrs Boucher, before starting on his day's business, whatever that
5   was. It was but an unsatisfactory visit to Mrs Boucher; she considered herself as an ill-used woman by her poor husband's suicide; and there was quite germ of truth enough in this idea to make it a very difficult one to refute. Still, it was unsatisfactory to see how completely her thoughts were turned upon herself and her own position, and this
10 selfishness extended even to her relations with her children, whom she considered as incumbrances,[†] even in the very midst of her somewhat animal affection for them. Margaret tried to make acquaintances with one or two of them, while her father strove to raise the widow's thoughts into some higher channel than that of mere helpless querulousness.[†] She
15 found that the children were truer and simpler mourners than the widow. Daddy had been a kind daddy to them; each could tell, in their eager stammering way, of some tenderness shown, some indulgence granted by the lost father.
'Is yon thing upstairs really him? it doesna look like him. I'm feared
20 on it, and I never was feared o' daddy.'
Margaret's heart bled to hear that the mother, in her selfish requirement of sympathy, had taken her children upstairs to see their disfigured father. It was intermingling the coarseness of horror with the profoundness of natural grief. She tried to turn their thoughts in some other

---

North and South   the novel contrasts the way of life in southern England with that of the industrial north. Margaret Hale is the daughter of a clergyman who, because of religious doubts, has moved with his family to a northern town which resembles

Manchester. She becomes involved in the industrial/worker relations of a manufacturer, Mr Thornton
incumbrances   hindrances
querulousness   peevishness, complaining

25   direction; on what they could do for mother; on what – for this was a
more efficacious[†] way of putting it – what father would have wished
them to do. Margaret was more successful than Mr Hale in her efforts.
The children, seeing their little duties lie in action close around them,
began to try each one to do something that she suggested towards
30   redding[†] up the slatternly[†] room. But her father set too high a standard,
and too abstract a view, before the indolent invalid. She could not rouse
her torpid[†] mind into any vivid imagination of what her husband's
misery might have been, before he had resorted to the last terrible step;
she could only look upon it as it affected herself; she could not enter
35   into the enduring mercy of the God who had not specially interposed
to prevent the water from drowning her prostrate husband; and
although she was secretly blaming her husband for having fallen into
such drear despair, and denying that he had any excuse for his last rash
act, she was inveterate[†] in her abuse of all who could by any possibility
40   be supposed to have driven him to such desperation. The masters – Mr
Thornton in particular, whose mill had been attacked by Boucher, and
who, after the warrant had been issued for his apprehension on the
charge of rioting, had caused it to be withdrawn – the Union, of which
Higgins was the representative to the poor woman – the children, so
45   numerous, so hungry, and so noisy – all made up one great army of
personal enemies, whose fault it was that she was now a helpless widow.
Margaret heard enough of this unreasonableness to dishearten her;
and when they came away she found it impossible to cheer her father.
'It is the town life,' said she. 'Their nerves are quickened by the haste
50   and bustle and speed of everything around them, to say nothing of the
confinement in these pent-up houses, which of itself is enough to induce
depression and worry of spirits. Now in the country, people live so
much more out of doors, even children, and even in the winter.'
'But people must live in towns. And in the country some get such
55   stagnant habits of mind that they are almost fatalists.'
'Yes; I acknowledge that. I suppose each mode of life produces its
own trials and its own temptations. The dweller in towns must find it
as difficult to be patient and calm, as the country-bred man must find
it to be active, and equal to unwonted[†] emergencies. Both must find it
60   hard to realize a future of any kind; the one because the present is so
living and hurrying and close around him; the other because his life
tempts him to revel in the mere sense of animal existence, not knowing
of, and consequently not caring for any pungency[†] of pleasure, for the
attainment of which he can plan, and deny himself and look foward.'

---

efficacious   producing desired effect
redding   clearing up, tidying
slatternly   sluttish
torpid   dull, apathetic

inveterate   deep-rooted
unwonted   unaccustomed
pungency   sharpness

65   'And thus both the necessity for engrossment, and the stupid content
in the present, produce the same effects. But this poor Mrs Boucher!
how little we can do for her.'
'And yet we dare not leave her without our efforts, although they
may seem so useless. Oh papa! it's a hard world to live in!'
70   'So it is, my child. We feel it so just now, at any rate; but we have
been very happy, even in the midst of our sorrow. What a pleasure
Frederick's visit was!'
'Yes, that it was,' said Margaret brightly. 'It was such a charming,
snatched, forbidden thing.'
75   But she suddenly stopped speaking. She had spoiled the remembrance
of Frederick's visit to herself by her own cowardice. Of all faults, the
one she most despised in others was the want of bravery; the meanness
of heart which leads to untruth. And here had she been guilty of it!
Then came the thought of Mr Thornton's cognizance† of her falsehood.
80   She wondered if she should have minded detection half so much from
anyone else. She tried herself in imagination with her Aunt Shaw and
Edith; with her father; with Captain and Mr Lennox; with Frederick.
The thought of the last knowing what she had done, even in his own
behalf, was the most painful, for the brother and sister were in the first
85   flush of their mutual regard and love; but even any fall in Frederick's
opinion was as nothing to the shame, the shrinking shame she felt at
the thought of meeting Mr Thornton again. And yet she longed to see
him, to get it over; to understand where she stood in his opinion. Her
cheeks burnt as she recollected how proudly she had implied an
90   objection to trade (in the early days of their acquaintance), because it
too often led to the deceit of passing off inferior for superior goods, in
the one branch; of assuming credit for wealth and resources not
possessed, in the other. She remembered Mr Thornton's look of calm
disdain, as in few words he gave her to understand that, in the great
95   scheme of commerce, all dishonourable ways of acting were sure to
prove injurious in the long run, and that, testing such actions simply
according to the poor standard of success, there was folly and not
wisdom in all such, and every kind of deceit in trade, as well as in other
things. She remembered – she, then strong in her own untempted truth –
100   asking him, if he did not think that buying in the cheapest and selling
in the dearest market proved some want of the transparent justice which
is so intimately connected with the idea of truth; and she had used the
word chivalric† – and her father had corrected her with the higher
word, Christian; and so drawn the argument upon himself, while she
105   sat silent by with a slight feeling of contempt.

cognizance   knowledge
chivalric   knightly; considerate of the need to serve others

No more contempt for her! – no more talk about the chivalric!
Henceforward she must feel humiliated and disgraced in his sight. But
when should she see him? Her heart leaped up in apprehension at every
ring of the door-bell; and yet, when it fell down to calmness, she felt
110 strangely saddened and sick at heart at each disappointment. It was
very evident that her father expected to see him, and was surprised that
he did not come. The truth was, that there were points in their
conversation the other night on which they had no time then to enlarge;
but it had been understood that if possible on the succeeding evening –
115 if not then, at least the very first evening that Mr Thornton could
command – they should meet for further discussion. Mr Hale had
looked forward to this meeting ever since they had parted. He had not
yet resumed the instruction to his pupils, which he had relinquished at
the commencement of his wife's more serious illness, so he had fewer
120 occupations than usual; and the great interest of the last day or so
(Boucher's suicide) had driven him back with more eagerness than ever
upon his speculations. He was restless all the evening. He kept saying,
'I quite expected to have seen Mr Thornton. I think the messenger who
brought the book last night must have had some note, and forgot to
125 deliver it. Do you think there has been any message left to-day?'
'I will go and inquire, papa,' said Margaret, after the changes on
these sentences had been rung once or twice. 'Stay, there's a ring!' She
sat down instantly, and bent her head attentively over her work. She
heard a step on the stairs, but it was only one, and she knew it was
130 Dixon's. She lifted up her head and sighed, and believed she felt glad.
'It's that Higgins, sir. He wants to see you, or else Miss Hale. Or it
might be Miss Hale first, and then you, sir; for he's in a strange kind
of way.'
'He had better come up here, Dixon; and then he can see us both,
135 and choose which he likes for his listener.'
'Oh! very well, sir. I've no wish to hear what he's got to say, I'm
sure; only, if you could see his shoes, I'm sure you'd say the kitchen
was the fitter place.'
'He can wipe them, I suppose,' said Mr Hale. So Dixon flung off, to
140 bid him walk upstairs. She was a little mollified,[†] however, when he
looked at his feet with a hesitating air; and then, sitting down on the
bottom stair, he took off the offending shoes, and without a word
walked upstairs.
'Sarvant, sir!' said he, slicking his hair down when he came into the
145 room: 'if hoo'll excuse me (looking at Margaret) for being i' my
stockings; I'se been tramping a' day, and streets is none o' th' cleanest.'
Margaret thought that fatigue might account for the change in his

---

mollified softened

manner, for he was unusually quiet and subdued; and he had evidently
some difficulty in saying what he came to say.
150   Mr Hale's ever-ready sympathy with anything of shyness or hesitation,
or want of self-possession, made him come to his aid.
'We shall have tea up directly, and then you'll take a cup with us,
Mr Higgins. I am sure you are tired, if you've been out much this wet
relaxing day. Margaret, my dear, can't you hasten tea?'
155   Margaret could only hasten tea by taking the preparation of it into
her own hands, and so offending Dixon, who was emerging out of her
sorrow for her late mistress into a very touchy, irritable state. But
Martha, like all whom came in contact with Margaret – even Dixon
herself, in the long run – felt it a pleasure and an honour to forward
160   any of her wishes; and her readiness, and Margaret's sweet forbearance,
soon made Dixon ashamed of herself.
'Why master and you must always be asking the lower classes
upstairs, since we came to Milton, I cannot understand. Folk at Helstone
were never brought higher than the kitchen; and I've let one or two of
165   them know before now that they might think it an honour to be even
there.'
Higgins found it easier to unburden himself to one than to two. After
Margaret left the room, he went to the door and assured himself that it
was shut. Then he came and stood close to Mr Hale.
170   'Master,' said he, 'yo'd not guess easy what I've been tramping after
to-day. Special if yo'd remember my manner o' talk yesterday. I've been
a seeking work. I have,' said he. 'I said to mysel', I'd keep a civil tongue
in my head, let who would say what 'em would. I'd set my teeth into
my tongue sooner nor speak i' haste. For that man's sake – yo'
175   understand,' jerking his thumb back in some unknown direction.
'No, I don't,' said Mr Hale, seeing he waited for some kind of assent,
and completely bewildered as to who 'that man' could be.
'That chap as lies theer,' said he, with another jerk. 'Him as went
and drowned himself, poor chap! I did na think he'd got it in him to
180   lie still and let the water creep o'er him till he died. Boucher, yo' know.'
'Yes, I know now,' said Mr Hale. 'Go back to what you were saying:
you'd not speak in haste –'
'For his sake. Yet not for his sake; for where'er he is, and whate'er,
he'll ne'er know other clemming† or cold again; but for the wife's sake,
185   and the bits o' childer.'†
'God bless you!' said Mr Hale, starting up; then, calming down, he
said breathlessly, 'What do you mean? Tell me out.'
'I have tell yo',' said Higgins, a little surprised at Mr Hale's agitation.
'I would na ask for work for mysel'; but them's left as a charge on me.'

---

clemming starving   *childer* children

190   I reckon, I would ha' guided Boucher to a better end; but I set him off
o' th' road, and so I mun answer for him.'
    Mr Hale got hold of Higgins's hand and shook it heartily, without
speaking. Higgins looked awkward and ashamed.
    'Theer, theer, master! Theer's ne'er a man, to call a man, amongst
195   us, but what would do th' same; ay, and better too; for, belie' me, I'se
ne'er got a stroke o' work, nor yet a sight of any. For all I told Hamper
that, let along his pledge – which I would not sign – no, I could na, not
e'en for this – he'd ne'er ha' such a worker on his mill as I would be –
he'd ha' none o' me – no more would none o' the' others. I'm a poor,
200   black, feckless sheep – childer may clem for ought I can do, unless,
parson, yo'd help me?'
    'Help you! How? I would do anything – but what can I do?'
    'Miss there' – for Margaret had re-entered the room, and stood silent,
listening – 'has often talked grand o' the South, and the ways down
205   there. Now I dunnot know how far off it is, but I've been thinking if I
could get 'em down theer, where food is cheap and wages good, and
all the folk, rich and poor, master and man, friendly like; yo' could,
may be, help me to work. I'm not forty-five, and I've a deal o' strength
in me, measter.'
210   'But what kind of work could you do, my man?'
    'Well, I reckon I could spade a bit –'
    'And for that,' said Margaret, stepping forwards, 'for anything you
could do, Higgins, with the best will in the world, you would, maybe,
get nine shillings a week; maybe ten, at the outside. Food is much the
215   same as here, except that you might have a little garden –'
    'The childer could work at that,' said he, 'I'm sick o' Milton anyways,
and Milton is sick o' me.'
    'You must not go to the South,' said Margaret, 'for all that. You
could not stand it. You would have to be out all weathers. It would
220   kill you with rheumatism. The mere bodily work at your time of life
would break you down. The fare is far different to what you have been
accustomed to.'
    'I'se nought particular about my meat,' said he, as if offended.
    'But you've reckoned on having butcher's meat once a day, if you're
225   in work; pay for that out of your ten shillings, and keep those poor
children if you can. I owe it to you – since it's my way of talking that
has set you off on this idea – to put it all clear before you. You would
not bear the dulness of the life; you don't know what it is; it would
eat you away like rust. Those that have lived there all their lives, are
230   used to soaking in the stagnant waters. They labour on from day to
day, in the great solitude of steaming fields – never speaking or lifting
up their poor, bent, downcast heads. The hard spadework robs their
brain of life; the sameness of their toil deadens their imagination; they

don't care to meet to talk over thoughts and speculations, even of the
235 weakest, wildest kind, after their work is done; they go home brutishly
tired, poor creatures! caring for nothing but food and rest. You could
not stir them up into any companionship, which you get in a town as
plentiful as the air you breathe, whether it be good or bad – and that I
don't know; but I do know, that you of all men are not one to bear a
240 life among such labourers. What would be peace to them, would be
eternal fretting to you. Think no more of it, Nicholas, I beg. Besides,
you could never pay to get mother and children all there – that's one
good thing.'

'I've reckoned for that. One house mun do for us a', and the furniture
245 o' t'other would go a good way. And men theer mun have their families
to keep – m'appen six or seven childer. God help 'em!' said he, more
convinced by his own presentation of the facts than by all Margaret
had said, and suddenly renouncing the idea, which had but recently
formed itself in a brain worn out by the day's fatigue and anxiety. 'God
250 help 'em! North an' South have each getten their own troubles. If
work's sure and steady theer, labour's paid at starvation prices; while
here we'n rucks† o' money coming in one quarter, and ne'er a farthing
th' next. For sure, th' world is in a confusion that passes me or any
other man to understand; it needs fettling, and who's to fettle† it, if it's
255 as yon folks say, and there's naught but what we see?'

Mr Hale was busy cutting bread and butter; Margaret was glad of
this, for she saw that Higgins was better left to himself: that if her
father began to speak ever so mildly on the subject of Higgins's thoughts,
the latter would consider himself challenged to an argument, and would
260 feel himself bound to maintain his own ground. She and her father kept
up an indifferent conversation until Higgins, scarcely aware whether he
ate or not, had made a very substantial meal. Then he pushed his chair
away from the table, and tried to take an interest in what they were
saying; but it was of no use; and he fell back into dreamy gloom.
265 Suddenly, Margaret said (she had been thinking of it for some time,
but the words had stuck in her throat), 'Higgins, have you been to
Marlborough Mills to seek for work?'

'Thornton's?' asked he. 'Ay, I've been at Thornton's.'

'And what did he say?'
270 'Such a chap as me is not like to see the measter.† Th' o'erlooker†
bid me go and be d—d.'

'I wish you had seen Mr Thornton,' said Mr Hale. 'He might not
have given you work, but he would not have used such language.'

'As to th' language, I'm welly used to it; it dunnot matter to me. I'm

---

rucks huge quantities   *measter* master
fettle put right   *o'erlooker* superintendent

275 not nesh mysel' when I'm put out. It were th' fact that I werena wanted
theer, no more nor ony other place, as I minded.'

'But I wish you had seen Mr Thornton,' repeated Margaret. 'Would
you go again – it's a good deal to ask, I know – but would you go to-
morrow and try him? I should be so glad if you would.'

280 'I'm afraid it would be of no use,' said Mr Hale, in a low voice. 'It
would be better to let me speak to him.' Margaret still looked at Higgins
for his answer. Those grave soft eyes of hers were difficult to resist. He
gave a great sigh.

'It would tax my pride above a bit; if it were for mysel', I could stand
285 a deal o' clemming first; I'd sooner knock him down than ask a favour
from him. I'd a deal sooner be flogged mysel'; but yo're not a common
wench, axing yo'r pardon, nor yet have yo' common ways about yo'.
I'll e'en make a wry face, and go at it to-morrow. Dunna yo' think that
he'll do it. That man has it in him to be burnt at the stake afore he'll
290 give in. I do it for yo'r sake, Miss Hale, and it's first time in my life as
e'er I give way to a woman. Neither my wife nor Bess could e'er say
that much again me.'

'All the more do I thank you,' said Margaret, smiling. 'Though I
don't believe you: I believe you have just given way to wife and daughter
295 as much as most men.'

'And as to Mr Thornton,' said Mr Hale, 'I'll give you a note to him,
which, I think I may venture to say, will ensure you a hearing.'

'I thank yo' kindly, sir, but I'd as lief† stand on my own bottom. I
dunnot stomach the notion of having favour curried for me, by one as
300 doesn't knows the ins and outs of the quarrel. Meddling 'twixt master
and man is liker meddling 'twixt husband and wife then aught else: it
takes a deal o' wisdom for to do ony good. I'll stand guard at the lodge
door. I'll stand there fro' six in the morning till I get speech on him.
But I'd liefer† sweep th' streets, if paupers had na got hold on that
305 work. Dunna yo' hope, miss. There'll be more chance o' getting milk
out of a flint. I wish yo' a very good night, and many thanks to yo'.'

'You'll find your shoes by the kitchen fire; I took them there to dry,'
said Margaret.

He turned round and looked at her steadily, and then he brushed his
310 lean hand across his eyes and went his way.

'How proud that man is!' said her father, who was a little annoyed
at the manner in which Higgins had declined his intercession with Mr
Thornton.

'He is,' said Margaret; 'but what grand makings of a man there are
315 in him, pride and all.'

---

lief willingly, gladly   *liefer* more gladly

'It's amusing to see how he evidently respects the part in Mr Thornton's character which is like his own.'

'There's granite in all these northern people, papa, is there not?'

'There was none in poor Boucher, I am afraid; none in his wife 320 either.'

'I should guess from their tones that they had Irish blood in them. I wonder what success he'll have to-morrow. If he and Mr Thornton would speak out together as man to man – if Higgins would forget that Mr Thornton was a master, and speak to him as he does to us – and if 325 Mr Thornton would be patient enough to listen to him with his human heart, not with his master's ears –'

'You are getting to do Mr Thornton justice at last, Margaret,' said her father, pinching her ear.

Margaret had a strange choking at her heart, which made her unable 330 to answer. 'Oh!' thought she, 'I wish I were a man, that I could go and force him to express his disapprobation,† and tell him honestly that I knew I deserved it. It seems hard to lose him as a friend just when I had begun to feel his value. How tender he was with dear mamma! If it were only for her sake, I wish he would come, and then at least I 335 should know how much I was abased in his eyes.'

1854–5   1854–5

---

disapprobation disapproval

William Makepeace Thackeray
1811–63

While at Cambridge University, Thackeray dissipated part of his inheritance, and the rest he lost when the Indian Agency houses in which it was invested collapsed. Born in India of a Collector in the East India Company, he came to England in 1817 and went to school at Charterhouse. At Cambridge he established long-term friendships with Edward Fitzgerald, Tennyson and Richard Monckton Milnes. He left without taking a degree.

He proceeded to travel in Europe, visited Paris and Weimar, met Goethe, returned to England and joined the Middle Temple. He never practised as a barrister, but in 1833 became the owner of the *National Standard*, which failed a year later. By that time, all his inherited wealth had vanished and he had to make his living as a writer. From 1834–7, he was the Paris correspondent for the *Constitutional*, and he contributed to *Fraser's Magazine*, the *Morning Chronicle*, the *New Monthly Magazine* and *The Times*. His writing was astute, witty and often bitter: he had much in common with eighteenth-century satirists.

He married Isabella Shawe in 1836 but she suffered a mental breakdown in 1840: their children were sent to live with Thackeray's mother in Paris. They were not to return to him until six years later.

During the 1840s he established his reputation as a writer. He began writing for *Punch* in 1842, an association he maintained until 1854. His first major novel was *Vanity Fair* (1847). There quickly followed *Pendennis* (1848–50), *The History of Henry Esmond* (1852) and *The Newcomes* (1853–5). His obsession with the hierarchical nature of society, his own idea of the necessity of being a gentleman, the lengths people will go to in order to keep up appearances, make-believe and imposture, all account for major themes in his novels.

He travelled abroad lecturing in the USA and in 1860 became the first editor of the *Cornhill Magazine*. He died at the early age of 52, on Christmas Eve 1863.

From VANITY FAIR,[†] Chapter 9

Family Portraits

Sir Pitt Crawley was a philosopher with a taste for what is called low life. His first marriage with the daughter of the noble Binkie had been made under the auspices of his parents; and as he often told Lady Crawley in her lifetime she was such a confounded quarrelsome high-
5   bred jade[†] that when she died he was hanged if he would ever take another of her sort, at her ladyship's demise he kept his promise, and selected for a second wife Miss Rose Dawson, daughter of Mr. John Thomas Dawson, ironmonger, of Mudbury. What a happy woman was Rose to be my Lady Crawley!
10   Let us set down the items of her happiness. In the first place, she gave up Peter Butt, a young man who kept company with her, and in consequence of his disappointment in love, took to smuggling, poaching, and a thousand other bad courses. Then she quarrelled, as in duty bound, with all the friends and intimates of her youth, who, of course,
15   could not be received by my Lady at Queen's Crawley – nor did she find in her new rank and abode any persons who were willing to welcome her. Who ever did? Sir Huddleston Fuddleston had three daughters who all hoped to be Lady Crawley. Sir Giles Wapshot's family were insulted that one of the Wapshot girls had not the preference
20   in the marriage, and the remaining baronets[†] of the county were indignant at their comrade's misalliance. Never mind the commoners, whom we will leave to grumble anonymously.
Sir Pitt did not care, as he said, a brass farden[†] for any one of them. He had his pretty Rose, and what more need a man require than to
25   please himself? So he used to get drunk every night; to beat his pretty Rose sometimes: to leave her in Hampshire when he went to London for the parliamentary session, without a single friend in the wide world. Even Mrs. Bute Crawley, the Rector's wife, refused to visit her, as she said she would never give the pas[†] to a tradesman's daughter.
30   As the only endowments with which Nature had gifted Lady Crawley were those of pink cheeks and a white skin, and as she had no sort of character, nor talents, nor opinions, nor occupations, nor amusements, nor that vigour of soul and ferocity of temper which often falls to the lot of entirely foolish women, her hold upon Sir Pitt's affections was
35   not very great. Her roses faded out of her cheeks, and the pretty

---

Vanity Fair   Sir Pitt Crawley is a coarse, rough old man who treats his second wife badly. Becky Sharpe, the heroine of the novel, which is a satire of fashionable, worldly society, becomes governess of his children

jade   an inferior, worn-out horse
baronets   knights of the lowest hereditary titled order
farden   farthing: coin of lowest value
pas   precedence

freshness left her figure after the birth of a couple of children, and she
became a mere machine in her husband's house, of no more use than
the late Lady Crawley's grand piano. Being a light-complexioned
woman, she wore light clothes, as most blondes will, and appeared, in
40   preference, in draggled sea-green, or slatternly sky-blue. She worked
that worsted[t] day and night, or other pieces like it. She had counterpanes
in the course of a few years to all the beds in Crawley. She had a small
flower garden, for which she had rather an affection; but beyond this
no other like or disliking. When her husband was rude to her she was
45   apathetic:[t] whenever he struck her she cried. She had not character
enough to take to drinking, and moaned about, slipshod and in curl-
papers, all day. O Vanity Fair – Vanity Fair! This might have been, but
for you, a cheery lass: – Peter Butt and Rose a happy man and wife, in
a snug farm, with a hearty family; and an honest portion of pleasures,
50   cares, hopes, and struggles: – but a title and a coach and four are toys
more precious than happiness in Vanity Fair: and if Harry the Eighth
or Bluebeard[t] were alive now, and wanted a tenth wife, do you suppose
he could not get the prettiest girl that shall be presented this season.

The languid dulness of their mamma did not, as it may be supposed,
55   awaken much affection in her little daughters, but they were very happy
in the servants' hall and in the stables; and the Scotch gardener having
luckily a good wife and some good children, they got a little wholesome
society and instruction in his lodge, which was the only education
bestowed upon them until Miss Sharp came.

60   Her engagement was owing to the remonstrances of Mr. Pitt Crawley,
the only friend or protector Lady Crawley ever had, and the only
person, besides her children, for whom she entertained a little feeble
attachment. Mr. Pitt took after the noble Binkies, from whom he was
descended, and was a very polite and proper gentleman. When he grew
65   to man's estate, and came back from Christchurch, he began to reform
the slackened discipline of the hall, in spite of his father, who stood in
awe of him. He was a man of such rigid refinement, that he would have
starved rather than have dined without a white neckcloth. Once, when
just from college, and when Horrocks the butler brought him a letter
70   without placing it previously on a tray, he gave that domestic a look,
and administered to him a speech so cutting, that Horrocks ever after
trembled before him; the whole household bowed to him: Lady
Crawley's curl-papers came off earlier when he was at home: Sir Pitt's
muddy gaiters disappeared; and if that incorrigible old man still adhered
75   to other old habits, he never fuddled himself with rum-and-water in his
son's presence, and only talked to his servants in a very reserved and

---

worsted   woollen yarn   *Bluebeard*   a many times married, murderous
apathetic   indifferent   tyrant in Charles Perrault's *Contes du Temps*
(1697)

polite manner; and those persons remarked that Sir Pitt never swore at Lady Crawley while his own son was in the room.

It was he who taught the butler to say, 'My lady is served,' and who
80 insisted on handing her ladyship in to dinner. He seldom spoke to her, but when he did it was with the most powerful respect; and he never let her quit the apartment without rising in the most stately manner to open the door, and making an elegant bow at her egress.†

At Eton he was called Miss Crawley; and there, I am sorry to say,
85 his younger brother Rawdon used to lick† him violently. But though his parts were not brilliant, he made up for his lack of talent by meritorious industry, and was never known, during eight years at school, to be subject to that punishment which it is generally thought none but a cherub can escape.

90 At college his career was of course highly creditable. And here he prepared himself for public life, into which he was to be introduced by the patronage of his grandfather, Lord Binkie, by studying the ancient and modern orators with great assiduity,† and by speaking unceasingly at the debating societies. But though he had a fine flux of words, and
95 delivered his little voice with great pomposity and pleasure to himself, and never advanced any sentiment or opinion which was not perfectly trite and stale, and supported by a Latin quotation; yet he failed somehow, in spite of a mediocrity which ought to have insured any man a success. He did not even get the prize poem, which all his friends
100 said he was sure of.

After leaving college he became Private Secretary to Lord Binkie, and was then appointed Attaché† to the Legation at Pumpernickel, which post he filled with perfect honour, and brought home despatches, consisting of Strasburg pie, to the Foreign Minister of the day. After
105 remaining ten years Attaché (several years after the lamented Lord Binkie's demise), and finding the advancement slow, he at length gave up the diplomatic service in some disgust, and began to turn country gentleman.

He wrote a pamphlet on Malt on returning to England (for he was
110 an ambitious man, and always liked to be before the public), and took a strong part in the Negro Emancipation question. Then he became a friend of Mr. Wilberforce's,† whose politics he admired, and had that famous correspondence with the Reverend Silas Hornblower, on the Ashantee Mission. He was in London, if not for the Parliament session,
115 at least in May, for the religious meetings. In the country he was a

---

egress going out
lick beat
assiduity perseverance
Attaché someone attached to an ambassador's staff

Wilberforce William Wilberforce (1759–1833), MP for Yorkshire, philanthropist and slave-trade abolitionist

magistrate, and an active visitor and speaker among those destitute of religious instruction. He was said to be paying his addresses to Lady Jane Sheepshanks, Lord Southdown's third daughter, and whose sister, Lady Emily, wrote those sweet tracts, 'The Sailor's True Binnacle,' and
120 'The Applewoman of Finchley Common.'

Miss Sharp's[†] accounts of his employment at Queen's Crawley were not caricatures. He subjected the servants there to the devotional exercises before mentioned, in which (and so much the better) he brought his father to join. He patronised an Independent[†] meeting-
125 house in Crawley parish, much to the indignation of his uncle the Rector, and to the consequent delight of Sir Pitt, who was induced to go himself once or twice, which occasioned some violent sermons at Crawley parish church, directed point-blank at the Baronet's old Gothic pew there. Honest Sir Pitt, however, did not feel the force of these
130 discourses, as he always took his nap during sermon-time.

Mr. Crawley was very earnest, for the good of the nation and of the Christian world, that the old gentleman should yield him up his place in Parliament; but this the elder constantly refused to do. Both were of course too prudent to give up the fifteen hundred a year which was
135 brought in by the second seat (at this period filled by Mr. Quadroon, with carte-blanche[†] on the Slave question); indeed the family estate was much embarrassed, and the income drawn from the borough was of great use to the house of Queen's Crawley.

It had never recovered the heavy fine imposed upon Walpole Crawley,
140 first baronet, for peculation[†] in the Tape and Sealing-Wax Office. Sir Walpole was a jolly fellow, eager to seize and to spend money ('alieni appetens, sui profusus,' as Mr. Crawley would remark with a sigh), and in his day beloved by all the county for the constant drunkenness and hospitality which was maintained at Queen's Crawley. The cellars
145 were filled with Burgundy then, the kennels with hounds, and the stables with gallant hunters; now, such horses as Queen's Crawley possessed went to plough, or ran in the Trafalgar Coach; and it was with a team of these very horses, on an off-day, that Miss Sharp was brought to the Hall; for boor as he was, Sir Pitt was a stickler for his dignity while at
150 home, and seldom drove out but with four horses, and though he dined off boiled mutton, had always three footmen to serve it.

If mere parsimony[†] could have made a man rich, Sir Pitt Crawley might have become very wealthy – if he had been an attorney in a country town, with no capital but his brains, it is very possible that he
155 would have turned them to good account, and might have achieved for

---

Miss Sharp Rebecca Sharp (Becky), a leading character in this novel
Independent Congregationalist religious sect

carte-blanche blank paper on which to write own terms: discretionary power
peculation embezzlement
parsimony stinginess

himself a very considerable influence and competency. But he was
unluckily endowed with a good name and a large though encumbered[†]
estate, both of which went rather to injure than to advance him. He
had a taste for law, which cost him many thousands yearly; and being
160　a great deal too clever to be robbed, as he said, by any single agent,
allowed his affairs to be mismanaged by a dozen, whom he all equally
mistrusted. He was such a sharp landlord, that he could hardly find
any but bankrupt tenants; and such a close farmer, as to grudge almost
the seed to the ground, whereupon revengeful Nature grudged him the
165　crops which she granted to more liberal husbandmen. He speculated in
every possible way; he worked mines; bought canal-shares; horsed
coaches; took government contracts, and was the busiest man and
magistrate of his county. As he would not pay honest agents at his
granite quarry, he had the satisfaction of finding that four overseers
170　ran away, and took fortunes with them to America. For want of proper
precautions, his coal-mines filled with water: the government flung his
contract of damaged beef upon his hands: and for his coach-horses,
every mail proprietor in the kingdom knew that he lost more horses
than any man in the country, from underfeeding and buying cheap. In
175　disposition he was sociable, and far from being proud; nay, he rather
preferred the society of a farmer or a horse-dealer to that of a gentleman,
like my lord, his son: he was fond of drink, of swearing, of joking with
the farmers' daughters: he was never known to give away a shilling or
to do a good action, but was of a pleasant, sly, laughing mood, and
180　would cut his joke and drink his glass with a tenant and sell him up
the next day; or have his laugh with the poacher he was transporting
with equal good humour. His politeness for the fair sex has already
been hinted at by Miss Rebecca Sharp – in a word, the whole baronetage,
peerage, commonage of England, did not contain a more cunning,
185　mean, selfish, foolish, disreputable old man. That blood-red hand of Sir
Pitt Crawley's would be in anybody's pocket except his own; and it is
with grief and pain, that, as admirers of the British aristocracy, we find
ourselves obliged to admit the existence of so many ill qualities in a
person whose name is in Debrett.[†]
190　　One great cause why Mr. Crawley had such a hold over the affections
of his father, resulted from money arrangements. The Baronet owed
his son a sum of money out of the jointure[†] of his mother, which he
did not find it convenient to pay; indeed he had an almost invincible
repugnance to paying anybody, and could only be brought by force to
195　discharge his debts. Miss Sharp calculated (for she became, as we shall

---

encumbered　burdened (with debts)
Debrett　published book which lists the
peerage, so named after its first compiler,
John Debrett

jointure　estate settled on a wife, to be enjoyed
by her after her husband's death

hear speedily, inducted into most of the secrets of the family) that the mere payment of his creditors cost the honourable Baronet several hundreds yearly; but this was a delight he could not forego; he had a savage pleasure in making the poor wretches wait, and in shifting from
200 court to court and from term to term the period of satisfaction. What's the good of being in Parliament, he said, if you must pay your debts? Hence, indeed, his position as a senator was not a little useful to him.

Vanity Fair – Vanity Fair! Here was a man, who could not spell, and did not care to read – who had the habits and the cunning of a boor:
205 whose aim in life was pettifogging: who never had a taste, or emotion, or enjoyment, but what was sordid and foul; and yet he had rank, and honours, and power, somehow: and was a dignitary of the land, and a pillar of the state. He was high sheriff, and rode in a golden coach. Great ministers and statesmen courted him; and in Vanity Fair he had
210 a higher place then the most brilliant genius or spotless virtue.

Sir Pitt had an unmarried half sister who inherited her mother's large fortune, and though the Baronet proposed to borrow this money of her on mortgage,† Miss Crawley declined the offer, and preferred the security of the funds. She had signified, however, her intention of leaving
215 her inheritance between Sir Pitt's second son and the family at the Rectory and had once or twice paid the debts of Rawdon Crawley in his career at college and in the army. Miss Crawley was, in consequence, an object of great respect when she came to Queen's Crawley, for she had a balance at her banker's which would have made her beloved
220 anywhere.

What a dignity it gives an old lady, that balance at the banker's! How tenderly we look at her faults if she is a relative (and may every reader have a score of such), what a kind good-natured old creature we find her! How the junior partner of Hobbs and Dobbs leads her smiling
225 to the carriage with the lozenge† upon it, and the fat wheezy coachman! How, when she comes to pay us a visit, we generally find an opportunity to let our friends know her station in the world! We say (and with perfect truth) I wish I had Miss MacWhirter's signature to a cheque for five thousand pounds. She wouldn't miss it, says your wife. She is my
230 aunt, say you, in an easy careless way, when your friend asks if Miss MacWhirter is any relative. Your wife is perpetually sending her little testimonies of affection, your little girls work endless worsted-baskets, cushions, and footstools for her. What a good fire there is in her room when she comes to pay you a visit, although your wife laces her stays
235 without one! The house during her stay assumes a festive, neat, warm,

---

mortgage property conveyed by debtor to creditor as security for debt with proviso that it shall be recovered on payment of debt

within a prescribed time
› *lozenge* diamond-shaped heraldic shield bearing the arms of a spinster or widow

jovial, snug appearance not visible at other seasons. You yourself, dear sir, forget to go to sleep after dinner, and find yourself all of a sudden (though you invariably lose) very fond of a rubber.[†] What good dinners you have – game every day, Malmsey-Madeira, and no end of fish from London. Even the servants in the kitchen share in the general prosperity; and, somehow, during the stay of Miss MacWhirter's fat coachman, the beer is grown much stronger, and the consumption of tea and sugar in the nursery (where her maid takes her meals) is not regarded in the least. Is it so, or it is not so? I appeal to the middle classes. Ah, gracious powers! I wish you would send me an old aunt – a maiden aunt – an aunt with a lozenge on her carriage, and a front of light coffee-coloured hair – how my children should work workbags for her, and my Julia and I would make her comfortable! Sweet – sweet vision! Foolish – foolish dream!

240

245

1845–7   1847–8

---

rubber   three successive games between same
sides or persons at whist, bridge, etc.

Charles John Huffman Dickens
1812–70

The greatest of all English novelists is Charles Dickens. His range of imagination, his characterisation, his descriptive powers, his commentary on life and society, his humour and satire, and his narrative skill, set him among the best story-tellers in the world.

He was born the son of a clerk in the Royal Navy's pay office in Portsmouth, and his early years were spent there and at Chatham. During his boyhood, Dickens's father was imprisoned for debt in the Marshalsea prison and in order to help the family's fortunes, Charles, at the age of twelve, had to work in a boot-blacking warehouse: these years of hardship inspired much of the content of his novels, and seriously influenced his thinking about social conditions. A most notable example is *Little Dorrit*, 1855–7.

He soon realised that he possessed an ability to write well, became an office boy, learned shorthand, and secured the job of reporting parliamentary debates for the *Morning Chronicle*. He was soon writing a variety of articles for magazines and journals which were eventually collected and published as *Sketches by 'Boz', Illustrative of Every-Day Life and Every-Day People* (1836–7). The publishers, Chapman and Hall, then engaged him to write twenty monthly episodes in the life of Mr Pickwick. These were published in 1837, when Dickens was twenty-five, as *The Posthumous Papers of the Pickwick Club*, which sold extremely well.

Dickens married Catherine Hogarth, and on Christmas Day, 1836, he met John Forster who was to remain lifelong his closest friend and eventual biographer. In 1837 he became editor of Bentley's *Miscellany* in which he published in instalments both *Oliver Twist* and *Nicholas Nickleby*. 1840 and 1841 were two productive years in which appeared *Master Humphrey's Clock*, *The Old Curiosity Shop* and *Barnaby Rudge*. In 1842 he visited America which inspired *American Notes* and *Martin Chuzzlewit* (1843–4): he returned as an adherent to the cause of slavery-abolition. He published one of his most celebrated shorter works in 1843, *A Christmas Carol*. A year later he founded the *Daily News*.

During a visit to Switzerland in 1846 he wrote *Dombey and Son* (1848), and in 1850 founded the popular and influential magazine,

Household Words: in it he was to publish such other famous novelists as Elizabeth Gaskell. The weekly magazine was incorporated into *All the Year Round* in 1859 and the busy Dickens remained editor until his death. *David Copperfield* was published in instalments (1849–50).

In addition to *A Child's History of England*, the next fifteen years produced some of his most important novels: *Bleak House* (1852–3), *Hard Times* (1854), *Little Dorrit* (1855–7), *A Tale of Two Cities* (1859), *Great Expectations* (1860–1), *Our Mutual Friend* (1864–5).

Although he had a large family, he and his wife grew apart, and in 1858 they separated. He enjoyed an enormous circle of friends and formed a close relationship with the actress Ellen Ternan. He devoted much of his time and energy to public tours and readings from his novels. In 1867–8 he was on tour in the USA. He died suddenly in 1870, leaving *The Mystery of Edwin Drood* unfinished.

He was held in the highest regard by his contemporaries, and his critical acclaim has for the most part remained constant. He has been compared to Tolstoy, and was admired by Dostoevsky. Queen Victoria approved mightily of him.

From THE OLD CURIOSITY SHOP

The Death of Little Nell†

The dull, red glow of a wood fire – for no lamp or candle burnt within the room – showed him a figure, seated on the hearth with its back towards him, bending over the fitful light. The attitude was that of one who sought the heat. It was, and yet was not. The stooping posture
5   and the cowering form were there, but no hands were stretched out to meet the grateful warmth, no shrug or shiver compared its luxury with the piercing cold outside. With limbs huddled together, head bowed down, arms crossed upon the breast, and fingers tightly clenched, it rocked to and fro upon its seat without a moment's pause, accompanying
10   the action with the mournful sound he had heard.

The heavy door had closed behind him on his entrance, with a crash that made him start. The figure neither spoke nor turned to look, nor gave in any other way the faintest sign of having heard the noise. The

The death . . . Nell   this scene was, in its time, one of the most celebrated extracts from Dickens's novels. It later became a notorious   example of Dickens's use of sentiment and pathos

form was that of an old man, his white head akin in colour to the
mouldering embers upon which he gazed. He, and the failing light and
dying fire, the time-worn room, the solitude, the wasted life, and gloom,
were all in fellowship. Ashes, and dust, and ruin!

Kit tried to speak, and did pronounce some words, though what they
were he scarcely knew. Still the same terrible low cry went on – still
the same rocking in the chair – the same stricken figure was there,
unchanged and heedless of his presence.

He had his hand upon the latch, when something in the form –
distinctly seen as one log broke and fell, and, as it fell, blazed up –
arrested it. He returned to where he had stood before – advanced a
pace – another – another still. Another, and he saw the face. Yes!
Changed as it was, he knew it well.

'Master!' he cried, stooping on one knee and catching at his hand.
'Dear master. Speak to me!'

The old man turned slowly towards him; and muttered, in a hollow
voice.

'This is another! – How many of these spirits there have been to-
night!'

'No spirit, master. No one but your old servant. You know me now,
I am sure? Miss Nell – where is she – where is she?'

'They all say that!' cried the old man. 'They all ask the same question.
A spirit!'

'Where is she?' demanded Kit. 'Oh tell me but that – but that, dear
master!'

'She is asleep – yonder – in there.'

'Thank God!'

'Ay! Thank God!' returned the old man. 'I have prayed to Him,
many, and many, and many a livelong night, when she has been asleep,
He knows. Hark! Did she call?'

'I heard no voice.'

'You did. You hear her now. Do you tell me that you don't hear
that?'

He started up, and listened again.

'Nor that?' he cried, with a triumphant smile. 'Can anybody know
that voice so well as I! Hush! hush!'

Motioning to him to be silent, he stole away into another chamber.
After a short absence (during which he could be heard to speak in a
softened soothing tone) he returned, bearing in his hand a lamp.

'She is still asleep,' he whispered. 'You were right. She did not call –
unless she did so in her slumber. She has called to me in her sleep before
now, sir; as I sat by, watching, I have seen her lips move, and have known,
though no sound came from them, that she spoke of me. I feared the light
might dazzle her eyes and wake her, so I brought it here.'

He spoke rather to himself than to the visitor, but when he had put the lamp upon the table, he took it up, as if impelled by some momentary
60   recollection or curiosity, and held it near his face. Then, as if forgetting his motive in the very action, he turned away and put it down again.
'She is sleeping soundly,' he said; 'but no wonder. Angel hands have strewn the ground deep with snow, that the lightest footstep may be lighter yet; and the very birds are dead, that they may not wake her.
65   She used to feed them, sir. Though never so cold and hungry, the timid things would fly from us. They never flew from her!'

Again he stopped to listen, and scarcely drawing breath, listened for a long, long time. That fancy past, he opened an old chest, took out some clothes as fondly as if they had been living things, and began to
70   smooth and brush them with his hand.

'Why dost thou lie so idle there, dear Nell,' he murmured, 'when there are bright red berries out of doors waiting for thee to pluck them! Why dost thou lie so idle there, when thy little friends come creeping to the door, crying "where is Nell – sweet Nell?" – and sob, and weep,
75   because they do not see thee. She was always gentle with children. The wildest would do her bidding – she had a tender way with them, indeed she had!'

Kit had no power to speak. His eyes were filled with tears.

'Her little homely dress – her favourite!' cried the old man, pressing
80   it to his breast, and patting it with his shrivelled hand. 'She will miss it when she wakes. They have hid it there in sport, but she shall have it – she shall have it. I would not vex my darling, for the wide world's riches. See here – these shoes – how worn they are – she kept them to remind her of our last long journey. You see where the little feet were
85   bare upon the ground. They told me, afterwards, that the stones had cut and bruised them. *She* never told me that. No, no, God bless her! and, I have remembered since, she walked behind me, sir, that I might not see how lame she was – but yet she had my hand in hers, and seemed to lead me still.'
90   He pressed them to his lips, and having carefully put them back again, went on communing with himself – looking wistfully from time to time towards the chamber he had lately visited.

'She was not wont† to be a lie-abed; but she was well then. We must have patience. When she is well again, she will rise early, as she used
95   to do, and ramble abroad in the healthy morning time. I often tried to track the way she had gone, but her small fairy footstep left no print upon the dewy ground, to guide me. Who is that? Shut the door. Quick! – Have we not enough to do to drive away that marble cold, and keep her warm!'

---

†*nt*   accustomed

100   The door was indeed opened, for the entrance of Mr. Garland
and his friend, accompanied by two other persons. These were the
schoolmaster, and the bachelor. The former held a light in his hand.
He had, it seemed, but gone to his own cottage to replenish the
exhausted lamp, at the moment when Kit came up and found the old
105   man alone.

He softened again at sight of these two friends, and, laying aside the
angry manner — if to anything so feeble and so sad the term can be
applied — in which he had spoken when the door opened, resumed his
former seat, and subsided, by little and little, into the old action, and
110   the old, dull, wandering sound.

Of the strangers he took no heed whatever. He had seen them, but
appeared quite incapable of interest or curiosity. The younger brother
stood apart. The bachelor drew a chair towards the old man, and sat
down close beside him. After a long silence, he ventured to speak.

115   'Another night, and not in bed!' he said softly; 'I hoped you would
be more mindful of your promise to me. Why do you not take some
rest?'

'Sleep has left me,' returned the old man. 'It is all with her!'

'It would pain her very much to know that you were watching thus,'
120   said the bachelor. 'You would not give her pain?'

'I am not so sure of that, if it would only rouse her. She has slept so
very long. And yet I am rash to say so. It is a good and happy sleep —
eh?'

'Indeed it is,' returned the bachelor. 'Indeed, indeed, it is!'

125   'That's well! — and the waking,' — faltered the old man.

'Happy too. Happier than tongue can tell, or heart of man conceive.'

They watched him as he rose and stole on tiptoe to the other chamber
where the lamp had been replaced. They listened as he spoke again
within its silent walls. They looked into the faces of each other, and no
130   man's cheek was free from tears. He came back, whispering that she
was still asleep, but that he thought she had moved. It was her hand,
he said — a little — a very, very little — but he was pretty sure she had
moved it — perhaps in seeking his. He had known her do that before
now, though in the deepest sleep the while. And when he had said this,
135   he dropped into his chair again, and clasping his hands above his head,
uttered a cry never to be forgotten.

The poor schoolmaster motioned to the bachelor that he would come
upon the other side, and speak to him. They gently unlocked his fingers,
which he had twisted in his grey hair, and pressed them in their own.

140   'He will hear me,' said the schoolmaster, 'I am sure. He will hear
either me or you if we beseech him. She would, at all times.'

'I will hear any voice she liked to hear,' said the old man. 'I love all
she loved!'

230   was stirring nimbly in its cage; and the strong heart of its child-mistress
was mute and motionless for ever.

Where were the traces of her early cares, her sufferings, and fatigues?
All gone. Sorrow was dead indeed in her, but peace and perfect
happiness were born; imaged in her tranquil beauty and profound
235   repose.

And still her former self lay there, unaltered in this change. Yes. The
old fireside had smiled upon that same sweet face; it had passed like a
dream through haunts of misery and care; at the door of the poor
schoolmaster on the summer evening, before the furnace fire upon the
240   cold wet night, at the still bedside of the dying boy, there had been the
same mild lovely look. So shall we know the angels in their majesty,
after death.

The old man held one languid arm in his, and had the small hand
tight folded to his breast, for warmth. It was the hand she had stretched
245   out to him with her last smile – the hand that had led him on through
all their wanderings. Ever and anon he pressed it to his lips; then
hugged it to his breast again, murmuring that it was warmer now; and
as he said it he looked, in agony, to those who stood around, as if
imploring them to help her.

250   She was dead, and past all help, or need of it. The ancient rooms she
had seemed to fill with life, even while her own was waning fast – the
garden she had tended – the eyes she had gladdened – the noiseless
haunts of many a thoughtful hour – the paths she had trodden as it
were but yesterday – could know her no more.

255   'It is not,' said the schoolmaster, as he bent down to kiss her on the
cheek, and gave his tears free vent, 'it is not on earth that Heaven's
justice ends. Think what it is, compared with the World to which her
young spirit has winged its early flight, and say, if one deliberate wish
expressed in solemn terms above this bed could call her back to life,
260   which of us would utter it!'

1840   1841